Dialectical Practice in Tibetan Philosophical Culture

For a set of Interactive Debate Tutorials, including photographs of debates; a guide to the participants; a grammar of Tibetan debating; the ethnomethods employed by debaters; videos of illustrative debates; and an appendix comprising an interactive debate, glossary, manual, and illustrations, please see the accompanying website.
http://www.thdl.org/DebateTutorials/

Dialectical Practice in Tibetan Philosophical Culture

An Ethnomethodological Inquiry into Formal Reasoning

KENNETH LIBERMAN

ROWMAN & LITTLEFIELD PUBLISHERS, INC.
LANHAM • BOULDER • NEW YORK • TORONTO • PLYMOUTH, UK

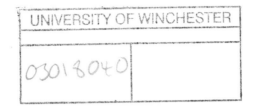
ROWMAN & LITTLEFIELD PUBLISHERS, INC.

Published in the United States of America
by Rowman & Littlefield Publishers, Inc.
A wholly owned subsidary of The Rowman & Littlefield Publishing Group, Inc.
4501 Forbes Boulevard, Suite 200, Lanham, Maryland 20706
www.rowmanlittlefield.com

Estover Road, Plymouth PL6 7PY, United Kingdom

British Library Cataloguing in Publication Information Available

**The hardback edition of this book was previously cataloged by the Library of
Congress as follows:**

Liberman, Kenneth, 1948—
  Dialectical practice in Tibetan philosophical culture : an ethnomethodological inquiry
into formal reasoning / Kenneth Liberman.
      p.   cm.
  Includes bibliographical references and index.
      1. Philosophy, Tibetan. 2. Philosophy, Buddhist. I. Title.

B5233.T53L53   2004
184'.1–dc22

2004042703

ISBN-13 : 978-0-7425-2744-7 (cloth : alk. paper)
ISBN-10 : 0-7425-2744-1 (cloth : alk. paper)
ISBN-13 : 978-0-7425-5612-6 (cloth : alk. paper)
ISBN-10 : 0-7425-5612-6 (cloth : alk. paper)

Printed in the United States of America

♾™ The paper used in this publication meets the minimum requirements of American
National Standard for Information Sciences—Permanence of Paper for Printed Library
Materials, ANSI/NISO Z39.48-1992.

Contents

Acknowledgments

I acknowledge with lifelong gratitude the contributions of these fine teachers who taught me the ways of the world. In chronological order, Eleanor Paola Liberman, Dolores Martin Bielenson, Herbert Dodge, Prof. W. T. Jones, Prof. Lee McDonald, Prof. W. Russell Ellis, Rabbi Shlomo Carlebach, Prof. Peter Berger, Prof. Harold Garfinkel, Prof. Herbert Marcuse, Prof. Frederick Olafson, Lama Thubten Yeshe, H. H. XIVth Dalai Lama, H. H. XVIth Gyalwa Karmapa, Geshe Sonam Rinchen, Khenpo Aped, Swami Gitananda Giri, Sri Pattabi Jois, Prof. Satyanarayana Shastry, Kensur Lobsang Tenzin, Geshe Lhundrup Sopa, Khenpo Jhado Rinpoche, and my three best friends (two of whom are deceased) Mark Casady, John Raser, and Jon Ewing.

It is one more sign of our degenerate age that I am incapable of replacing any of my teachers who are listed here, whose brilliant insight and compassionate energy will always exceed my own.

A project of this length requires not merely some financial assistance; the occasional external expression of confidence of its worth was vital for sustaining the researcher's own confidence and self-discipline. Such encouragement and financial support for field research undertaken during the period 1984-1999 was provided by the University of Oregon's Office of Research (1984 and 1988), the Oregon Humanities Center (1995), the American Institute of Indian Studies (1985 and 1995), the American Philosophical Society (1991 and 1997), and the American Council of Learned Societies (1992). It is my hope that this study will provide an enduring documentation of a most remarkable and ancient philosophical practice that is part of humanity's legacy. If this record of that practice endures for a time, then the confidence expressed by the aforementioned institutes and offices will have been justified.

Foreword

Harold Garfinkel

University of California, Los Angeles

What is so edifyingly sociological about Ken Liberman's description of debates by Tibetan monks?

Although his book's central subject—the dialectical practice of formal analysis in philosophical culture—is highly technical, background features of this exceptional ethnography are relevantly distinctive in their own right. The debates are exhibits of embodied work by Tibetan monks in immediately observed choreographed details of correctly argued displays of reason. These displays are the local conversations of six hundred or more students and faculty, who are gathered in the monastic university's courtyard, some as performers in the philosophical debating and others (by turns) as the audience.

Needless to say, it is a noisy affair. The observers of each conversation are noisily watching, against a background of others noisily watching other local conversations, a succession of single pairs of debaters. Audience and judges are examining each pair of debaters in its turn as a properly charitable but cutthroat display of congregationally witnessed and judged technical issues of truth, reason, rationality, errors, mistakes, confusion, hoax, fraud, imitation, reification, theater effects, order, and methods made expertly arguable by each debating pair. These issues, extracted from medieval texts in ancient words of Buddhist philosophy, are made witnessable here-and-now as correctly disputed phenomena of order in synesthesias of said/shown, listened to, listened for, heard, paced, rhyming, rhythmic, enacted real-world details. Venerated Buddhist texts are the sources of these debates, but not as texts from contemporary Western academic studies in Tibetology or Orientalism. These are the texts as Tibetans themselves have them.

On one occasion, I was telling one of the first Ph.D.'s in ethnomethodology, who was also an early author of ethnomethological studies, about Ken Liberman's study of debates by Tibetan monks of witnessed reason in its lived, embodied, choreographed exhibits of organizational Things in their details. I praised Liberman's academic virtues. To even begin his studies, let alone to develop them over a professional academic career, he had to learn to speak Tibetan and to correctly and fluently read and translate medieval Buddhist texts. He had to raise his own funds. To acquire a recognized competence with their debates, he lived in the monastery with the monks. He earned his right to take notes and make video recordings by engaging them in serious debates with texts on their own terms. He accorded their texts priority of relevance, with his performances being closely watched by the Tibetan scholars for their culturally accurate, adequate, unmistakable respectfulness.

I had hardly begun to praise Liberman before this author had as much of it as he could take, whereupon he out-shouted me: "SO WHAT! A debate is a debate. Why go to Tibet to study debates?"

My task in these introductory remarks is to answer that demand, singling out this occasion by sketching reasons to celebrate the publication of Ken Liberman's book. *Dialectical Practice in Tibetan Philosophical Culture* is an ethnomethodological study of work in Tibetan debate-specific, work-place and site-specific particulars that answer the demand: Why indeed go to Tibet to study debates? What is notable about this study of the lived details of the philosophical work of Tibetan monks? Particularly, what is notable about this study of their work sociologically? What is notable in work-place details of debating issues of formal analytic reason, just that, described sociologically?

Liberman contributes one more detailed ethnomethodological description of a work-site. On the occasion of a different work-site, the parties could be occupied, for example, with making music together. They are not making music together; not actually, not symbolically, not conceptually, not representationally with models or with metaphors. Or the parties studied ethnomethodologically could be those who are charged with convincing the U.S. Department of Defense that the 180 C-47 cargo planes to be built by McDonnell Douglas over twenty years at a cost of one-half billion dollars each, free of causes for customer complaints, will be delivered according to contract (just as is claimed by the McDonnell Douglas front office protocol accounts of production costs, protocols that have lost sight of the "shop floor" work of those who will build the airplanes).

Instead, Ken Liberman's study of the "shop floor problems" of Tibetan dialecticians makes it possible to ask perspicuous, sociological questions about the local organizational work of formal reasoning. Liberman's study of reason as a public activity contributes to the redescription of the magesterial subjects of technical reason, rationality, method, and order in, about, as, as of, and inside with the local production and local accountability of sociology's organizational Things in their details of ordinary society.

And what about Ken Liberman's ethnomethodological studies of the work of Tibetan monks in their actual debating practices arguing the exhibited adequacy and exhibited evidence in locally produced, locally accountable, coherent congregationally witnessed details of reason and order, in ancient texts of Buddhist philosophy, contributes to the edification of social order as professional sociology's subject—its singular, distinctive, and unique subject—by renewing that subject in its unavoidable properties of the Shop Floor Problem, that is, in its immediate and unmediated, observed, coherent work-place details?

Sociology's distinctive subject is epitomized in his title: *Dialectical Practice in Tibetan Philosophical Culture: An Ethnomethodological Inquiry into Formal Reasoning.* By specifying the Shop Floor Problem in the local production and local accountability of formal reasoning, the book marks a special occasion in the literatures of the social sciences, natural sciences, arts, and humanities. By identifying the Shop Floor Problem in the local production of formal reasoning, Liberman's said/shown, textually described, audiovisually exhibited, digital recordings have composed accompanying studies of work in detailed exhibits. Over the nine chapters of his book, the work in audiovisual details of debating the adequate truth of ancient Buddhist texts is displayed and specified with properties of the Shop Floor Problem.

These properties of debaters' work are collected and exhibited in the CD-ROM that accompanies Liberman's book as the alternately read and readable, instructable, congregationally done, and witnessable details of the Shop Floor Problem. His book and its affiliated disc are one unified document. Liberman's account is contrary to those descriptions of Tibetan debating whose intelligibility is guaranteed with generically theorized expertise, and Liberman requires for the observed intelligibility of Tibetan debaters' work a reading of combined text and graphics in his book and CD-ROM.

In their details, the properties of each debating pair's Shop Floor Problem consists of the following: (1) originality; (2) probativeness; (3) the Missing What of organization in the details of Things in their generality; (4) a specification of what fills the lacuna left by previous research into Tibetan Buddhist debating, a lacuna that in Liberman's ethnomethodological research policy is termed "There's a Gap in the peer-reviewed Literature"; (5) the identifying orderliness of work-place particulars; and, (6) sine qua non in their priority-of-relevance-to-the-parties, Tibetan debating's congregational solution to the characterization problem.

Limits of space permit me to discuss only three properties of the debaters' Shop Floor Problem: (1) In their exhibited details, their originality; i.e., what does their originality consist of? (2) In their exhibited details, their probativeness; what does their probativeness consist of? (3) In their exhibited details, what does their solution to the characterization problem consist of?

(1) The originality of Liberman's description of the actual work of carrying out proof accounts as visible/displayable matters in the Tibetans' philosophical debating consists of their notable absence in peer-reviewed literatures. Throughout Liberman's nine chapters the debater's Shop Floor Problem is detailed and emphasized as debating's central property and its identifying orderliness. These same properties are specifically and demonstrably absent in all peer-reviewed literatures, shelved as they are as major holdings of treatises in all the libraries of the arts and sciences. And the real world details are absent as well in the libraries of the Tibetologists. The same details that are emphasized in Liberman's

study as debating's central properties, exhibited over the course of the account-able coherent details of any just this particular debate, are carefully ignored and therein are absent in all peer-reviewed literatures of the endless arts and sciences of practical action and practical reason, immersed as they are in their own disci-plinary expertise and academic, departmentally privileged, universal jurisdic-tion. I submit that this absence in the literature and emphasis in Liberman's ex-positions of their details be called the originality of their details.

(2) In their detail, the probativeness of the debates is not imagined, con-structed, modeled, or "hidden in heads" with either intentionalities of formal analytic consciousness or brains. Rather, their probativeness is seen. It is seen in the coherence of their public details, in what Eric Livingston in his studies of the lived work by mathematicians of mathematical theorem-proving describes as "specific domain steps of their accountable production." Namely, that these ob-served steps of their accountable production by reason of their accountable ob-servation, settle the issues they describe. In their specific domain descriptions of the issues they describe, their domain specificity makes the issue pointless to dispute.

The work of competent participant/members is to produce a seen, stepwise domain of proving with congregationally witnessable adequacy and evidence. In light of the unavoidable temporal properties of empirical contingencies of ac-countably produced phenomena of order, meeting their stepwise empirical con-tingencies makes the particular phenomenon that calls for further description pointless to dispute. Call this property of debating pair's work in witnessed par-ticulars their work's probativeness. The CD-ROM that accompanies Liberman's book makes that probativeness available to the reader's critical inspection.

(3) The characterization problem: What over the course of its local endoge-nous production, in and as of its coherence of observed details, makes the phe-nomenon of order what it accountably is? And in this case, what are *logic's* lo-cal, lived, in their course congregational Durkheim's Things-in-their-details?

The relevance of Liberman's studies of Tibetan debates for the renewal of sociology's distinctive study of social order begins with these three properties of the Shop Floor Problem in Tibetan debates—their originality, their probative-ness, and their solution to the just-this-instant debate's characterization problem. By renewing that subject, these properties contribute without precedent to the study of social order by sociology as sociology's distinctive and unique subject.

Through the course of his extraordinary book with its accompanying CD-ROM, Liberman specifies a description that is readable as an account or, alter-nately, as a watchable, instructed action. These details specify as a first case a reading that starts with the properties of originality, probitiveness, and debat-ing's solution to the characterization problem.

By considering his chapters both as descriptions and alternately as in-structed actions (and that means reading his texts while examining the accompa-nying CD-ROM), readers will see that Liberman's descriptions are marked by having the property that the reader can further edify them and/or develop autonomous criticism of their originality, their probativeness, and debating's solution to the characterization problem. Liberman's ethnomethodological accounts specify the phenomenon of the Shop Floor Problem in real-world debates by Buddhist monks.

That alternate reading of text and disc, textual description, and said/shown instructed actions also exhibits further properties such as the Missing What of organization in the details of debating's classically described Things; debating's strategies; debating's standing response to ethnomethodology's research policy, "There's a Gap in the Literature"; that ethnomethodology's corpus of alternate studies of work and science are provided as subjects in proofs of adequate and evident description in peer-reviewed literatures.

Consider Jeff Coulter's question to me when he learned that I was preparing to talk to a Nottingham conference: "Do you plan to give over to sociology ethnomethodology's achievements?" I replied: "Of course not. I am talking sociology." As Ken Liberman shows, talking sociology consists of describing the identifying orderlinesses of ordinary society that are particular Things of the Shop Floor Problem. These are unfamiliar and strange to peer-reviewed literatures. They are also true. Ken Liberman's study is the most recent in a bibliography of distinguished studies of work and science by ethnomethodology's authors.

Part I

A Postcolonial Inquiry into Tibetan Dialectics

Chapter 1

Orientalism and Tibetological Praxis

Academic training was (and still is) more concerned with perpetuating the mistaken notions of a bygone era, and with imposing them on the original textual
material, than with finding out what the texts themselves had to say. . . . It
seemed that *understanding* fell outside the scope of this training.

—Herbert Guenther (1989a: 60)

That the world does not exist in itself just in the way that it appears for a perceiver is an epistemological observation shared by European and Tibetan philosophical cultures. Both of these scholarly traditions consider it naive to accept
straightforwardly a reality that is presumed to exist unmediated by the system of
interpretation used to organize its sensibility. For some philosophers of each
tradition, the interpretation *is* the experience; and for others this latter notion is
considered flirtation with a paralyzing nihilism. It has been the hallmark of most
Mahayana Buddhist scholarship to find "a middle way" between these two ori-
entations.

European researchers who investigated Buddhism's own scholarship have
buried the indigenous philosophical practices of those they studied beneath an
avalanche of naively ethnocentric interpretations, straightforwardly presuming
that the Tibetan Buddhism produced by their expository schema exists in itself
without any need for interpretation. The long monologue of Orientalist studies
concentrated its genius upon its own methods of philological analysis, ignored
almost entirely the life-world of Tibetan scholars, and lost sight of the mediation
that their disciplinary interpretation performed. Researchers who have treated
the lived practices of Tibetan philosophical scholarship with the empirical attention it deserves have been condemned by the discipline of Indology for being
biased and unprofessional. Curiously, cultural imperialism became a professional creed of ethical dimensions for Indological and Tibetological scholars
who for the most part confined themselves within interpretive regimes that
emerged from nineteenth-century Eurocentrism, and those disciplines *remain
incapable* of comprehending, with anything like a basic sociological adequacy,
South Asian or Tibetan philosophical practice as lived traditions.

Orientalism in South Asian Studies

Indology and Tibetology (by which I mean to include here South Asian Studies, Sanskrit Studies, Buddhist Studies, Tibetan Studies, Comparative Philosophy, etc.) are "fields of learned study" (Said 1978, 49). As disciplines within the Western university, students receive their introduction to Indian or Tibetan thought by means of the discipline's institutions and discourse. The students' initial expertise is the mastery of a Western secondary literature, a responsibility that will remain preeminent throughout a student's professional career. Only after the discipline's interpretative schema are secured is the student introduced to "the texts" themselves, which compose a highly selective canon reflecting two centuries of domination by the parochial interests of the Royal Asiatic Society, La Société Asiatique, the American Oriental Society, and their relatives and descendents. Only after the field has been "written" for the student, is he or she permitted a brief sojourn to the subcontinent that will adorn her myopia with the appearance of cultural adequacy. Even this fieldwork is not mandatory, as library reviews of texts alone provide the core of the discipline's work. This bears out the contention of Edward Said, who has argued that Western Orientalists have *first* recourse to Orientalist works and discourse, with Oriental sources available only in interpreted versions. Said (1978, 7-8) describes this epistemic enterprise:

> Under the general heading of knowledge of the Orient, and within the umbrella of Western hegemony over the Orient during the period from the end of the eighteenth century, there emerged a complex Orient suitable for study in the academy, for display in the museum, for reconstruction in the colonial office, for theoretical illustration in anthropological, biological, linguistic, racial, and historical theses about mankind and the universe, for instances of economic and sociological theories of development, revolution, cultural personality, national or religious character.

Orientalist research commences with texts and not with people. Isolated manuscripts shipped back to European museums by colonial officials or textual studies performed by colonial administrators (occasionally laid up with illness and finding themselves with time on their hands) formed the germ of Indology. The Boden Chair in Sanskrit was established at Oxford in the latter part of the nineteenth century with the assigned task of translating the Bible into Sanskrit so as "to enable his countrymen to proceed in the conversion of India to the Christian religion" (cited in Dallmayr 1987, 100).

At the end of the nineteenth century, there were two sorts of Oriental scholars—philologists and historiographers. The philologists were motivated by a fascination for retracing the origins of European culture in what some of them considered the primordial common origin of Vedic-believing Aryans and Europeans, which made it an orientation that was not well suited to discovering what might be the truth of a non-European. They studied the lexical and grammatical parallels between Sanskrit and European languages with the principal aim of developing insights regarding Europe. Although India has its own sophisticated traditions of grammatical and linguistic analyses, these were largely ignored since Indologists and Tibetologists were compelled mainly by their "comparative" agenda, by which they meant locating only features that could be related to European interests. The central topics of the texts they studied were hardly engaged, and still less were the Indian pandits or Tibetan lamas who used the texts in a lived cultural form.

The critical issues regarding the Indian and the Tibetan canons were thought to be primarily philological matters and not philosophical ones. Since most Western scholars believed that philosophy was exclusively a Greek phenomenon, it was natural for them not to be impressed by Hindu and Buddhist philosophical matters. Since most Indologists and Tibetologists did not even consider the people they studied to be capable of philosophical reflection, the notion that philosophical interests (of their own, let aside those they study) could set their research agendas rarely occurred to them. Of course the story of philosophy as a product of Greece, and hence of Europe, blatantly overlooks the fact that at the time of Plato Greece was predominantly an African and Asian civilization, and Oriental scholarship fails to address adequately what Greek thinkers owed to other peoples. When many cultural and linguistic features moved from the east to the west, why must philosophical praxis have moved only from the "West" to the "East"? As the philosopher Robert Bernasconi (1995, 333) has argued, "The unquestioned insistence on identifying philosophy as Greek is both artificial and oppressive."

Philologists founded a brilliant text-critical method that was capable of producing accurate, "authoritative" translations—though not necessarily according to the Asian traditions themselves, which insist that an authoritative understanding of a text is unlikely to emerge when working independently of a teacher. With a bout of superciliousness, these scholars censure Occidental scholars who do study in the context of an indigenous setting, especially when they are unobjective enough to want to seek wisdom while doing so. Since every means that philosophy could provide is considered to be extant within the European tradition, anything short of sustained Eurocentric monomania is dismissed as "escapist." Contemporary Tibetologists who attempt to think beyond the limitations of this Orientalist scholarship are considered merely to be overly susceptible to what has become "fashionable." Andrew Tuck (1990, 13) has commented about Buddhology, "This type of textualist positivism has been reinforced by the view that the interpretation of another culture's texts is primarily a philological matter and that the production of a good translation is tantamount to solving most important interpretive questions." Trained as linguists and historians and *not* as sociologists or philosophers (although they may have had some training in religion), these scholars set the standards that the Orientalist disciplines still enforce today via their entrenched positions on editorial boards and grant review committees. And scholars from other disciplines who take up studies of India and Tibet are generally required to conform to these essentially nineteenth century standards.

Their insistence upon "objectivity" belies the fact that Orientalist representation obscures the empirical social practices of Hindus and Buddhists. The very thing that would provide them access to the indigenous experience, interaction with a teacher and participation in the practices of an indigenous discipline, is ruled out from the start. Max Mueller, one of the founders of Indology, forbid his students from even going to India to do their research; they were consigned to the texts alone (Nandy 1983, 17). The canon of Indology—"the corpus status of its bibliographies," which for Garfinkel (2002, 122) includes the problems that are provided as relevant for researchers, along with a professional history of those problems as bona fide concerns—sustained the precedence of the professional interests of European academicians over the interests of the practitioners themselves, whose life-world remained untouched. Mueller himself never visited India (Inden 1990, 105). Any competent social scientist would have been able to observe that one cannot define yoga, for example, exclusively by studying its texts. Yoga is a practice that leads to an experience; it cannot be reduced to its literary representation without inflicting some epistemic damage.

The discourse of Orientalist studies was an exercise in labeling peoples, and the objects of study produced by means of these labeling practices were for the most part European artifacts bearing scant resemblance to an actual state of affairs. Given the myopia and racism of these primarily colonial enterprises, enduring notions were established that made social scientific inquiry difficult, although not impossible. Richard King (1999, 144) remarks, "It is not clear that the Tibetans, Sinhalese . . . conceived of themselves as 'Buddhists' before they were so labeled by Westerners." The notion "Hindu," which is the principal object of Indological research, is a recent idea that emerged from India's encounter with foreigners. The word "Hindu" never appears in a purely intracommunal Indian context (Halbfass 1988, 192). Romila Thapar (1991) has observed that there was no reference to the term "Hindu" until the fifteenth century, well after the principal texts had been composed. Inden (1990, 88) remarks, "The Hinduism we shall examine is the outcome of differing European commercial and political projects of the nineteenth century and involved the placing of Hinduism in relationship to European systems of thought and religious practice."

Hindu religious practice is highly variegated and decentralized, and "Hinduism" does not present the picture of an organized religion in the Western (Judaic, Christian, or Islamic) mode. There are many localized religious practices in "India," but there is no monolithic "Hinduism." More importantly, these practices can never be encountered by philologists for whom they are a distraction, if not a threat to the objectivity of their discipline (or to Western rationality as a whole). The philosophies and religions of South Asia were engaged not objectively but in a defensive and competitive pose. The earliest missionary-ethnographer of Tibetan philosophical culture, Ippolito Desideri (1931, eighteenth century) set for his principal intellectual project the refutation of the errors of Buddhist doctrine, a text he planned to write in the Tibetan language. And Inden (1990, 53) contends that Hinduism was defined by what it lacked, understood only in so far as it was an "irrational and defective version of its Western equivalents."

What do the Indologists study? In place of actual religious or philosophical practices, a highly selective and idealized "Hindu" canon was composed by Indologists, comprised mainly of some *upanishad*, the *Bhagavad Gita*, and a few vedic hymns. As one Indian reviewer (Rao 1992) observes, "The Hindu religion as it is practiced by millions in this country is far removed from the deeply philosophical and esoteric doctrines set out in the *upanishad*. Believing Hindus today use a different set of texts and forms of rituals, and they have only the vaguest notion of what the *vedas* and the *upanishads* are all about." One of Indology's founders, Monier Monier-Williams and other scholars emphasized the vedic literature because they believed they had a common origin with European religious sentiments. Buddhist texts were incorrectly treated as exercises in nihilism, since their philosophical precepts were at variance with the essentialist European philosophical biases and their atheism was a threat to Western religious predelictions.

At the forefront of the agenda of Indologists was their interest to link South Asian notions and practices to European ones. Monier-Williams writes (cited in Inden 1990, 99), "These were probably the very deities worshipped under similar names by our Aryan progenitors in their primordial home somewhere in the table-land of Central Asia." What the Hindu religious practices were *for Indians* was of secondary interest. Halbfass (1988, 111) explains that some Indologists found too much unnecessary mythological fiction in Hindu concepts of reunion of the soul with *Brahman*, *paramatman*, etc., and so de-emphasized these aspects, stressing instead those beliefs that resonated more closely with the ancient Greek and Roman traditions.

Indological interpreters of Indian society developed a racist interpretation that favored brahminical and Aryan elements, which were believed to share prehistorical origins with Europe, while they condemned non-Aryan elements, including Dravidian influence, as responsible for Indians' irrationality and the absence of individualism. The definitive Indologist Max Mueller argued that the "noble stamp of the Caucasian race" could be seen in the brahmins (cited in Trautmann 1997, 175). Herbert Risley (1891, I, xxxviii) wrote, "The motive principle of Indian caste is to be sought in the antipathy of the higher race for the lower, of the fair-skinned Aryan for the black Dravidian." Much of what was believed to go wrong with the proto-European Aryans who migrated to South Asia was blamed upon the black Dravidians. According to Inden (1990, 113), "The Sanskritist constitutes Hinduism as the product of the Aryan mind gone astray because it is in a tropical setting." The racist and colonial notion operative in Indology was that aboriginal India was backwards and primarily Dravidian, and it became civilized only when Aryans, who were the racial and linguistic cousins of Europeans, invaded and conquered India (Inden 1990, 178). Tibetans were viewed as an uncivilized mountain people, and having no connection with Aryans, they were judged (both by elitist Europeans and by elitist brahmins) to be primitives and semibarbarians, unworthy of sustaining anything but derivative philosophical notions.

Further, the West's image of itself as the epitome of the modern has partly depended, for two hundred years, on a portrayal of India as the archetypal ancient (Inden 1990, 6). A false essentialist dichotomy has been drawn between "ancient" and "modern" and "East" and "West," in which European civilization derives its superior value by its relation to a politically and culturally "backward" India. The free will of the modern European is contrasted favorably with the social determinism of the caste system, although the caste system has yet to be described as the developing and ongoing social praxis of living human agents that it is (cf. Gail Omvedt 1995). The term "caste" itself is *not* an indigenous term but was imported from the Portuguese "*casta*." For a variety of actual social practices of Hindus, Indologists have substituted Eurocentric caricatures.

Those scholars taking up studies of Buddhist texts (one cannot claim, and frequently they did not wish to claim, that they were studying Buddhism) were not much better off. As the colonial occupation of the subcontinent expanded and the variety of India's religious and philosophical traditions was appreciated, the texts of Tibetans were studied. What interested scholars about Tibetans was not their religious or philosophical practices but their translations of Sanskrit texts that were lost in India but were preserved in Tibet (Lopez 1998, 4). The pioneering work was often performed by missionaries (e.g., Jaschke). Since the Indologist's primary interest was Sanskrit, the study of Tibetan was considered to be of secondary importance, a pursuit necessary only when important Sanskrit texts were no longer extant except in their Tibetan translations. Few Indologists of the nineteenth century entertained the notion that the Tibetans might bear a philosophical culture that merited study as a social phenomenon in its own right. Its Buddhism was merely derivative. Yet *every* society is necessarily derivative—what is accepted as "original" is little more than social construction and cultural prejudice.

Even today grants in Tibetology are for the most part reserved for scholars who have trained in Sanskrit, under the argument that one cannot appreciate Buddhist ideas without knowing the language in which the notions were first formulated, and so the Orientalism of the discipline is perpetuated. While knowing Sanskrit is surely a boon to Buddhist studies, if one applied this criteria universally the Tibetans' own scholars and lamas would be excluded from Buddhist studies. What is worse, many Indologists and Tibetologists posit just such an exclusion, and on those grounds. An *understanding* of what the texts describe is not sought, while a solid grounding in the biases of nineteenth-century philology is considered indispensable.

The other strain of South Asian Orientalism, historiography, offers only slight improvements. These are scholars concerned to establish the facts, dates, and historical details surrounding texts and schools of thought. Martin Heidegger (1962, 430-31) has made an important distinction between history properly conceived and historiology. History is the concern to identify the cultural vision and aspiration of a people of any given period. Historiology, or historiography, disdains such existential concerns in favor of a focus upon the brute "facts" and figures of a period. The live practices of social being and its accompanying temporality are missed and replaced with docile objects amenable to manipulation within European calculative schema. Heidegger (1962, 344) argues that in historiography, "history is accessible in this line of questioning only as the *object* of a science. The basic phenomenon of history, which is prior to the possibility of making something thematic by historiography and underlies it, is thus irrevocably set aside." Historiographers look for the recurrent structures that are comparable and ignore everything else. It is external and structural, and its analyses proceed according to well-defined and thoroughly Europeanized categories.

Even in his time, Hegel derided these facile comparative studies (Halbfass 1988, 425) as utterly abstract, mechanical, and extrinsic activities of thought, which never reach the inner essence of what they deal with. Tuck (1990, 7) observes, "Throughout the 19th century European scholars consistently grafted their own intellectual concerns and discursive practices onto an India that was virtually of their own creation and read Indian texts as exotic expressions of their own presuppositions and philosophies." Trained for a time as an Orientalist, I once browbeat an Indian Sanskrit scholar who had translated Patanjali's *Yoga Sutra*, in an attempt to elicit his view of the actual date of Patanjali's composition. This scholar, who was also a swami (Venkatesananda, now deceased) and who trained under the direction of Swami Sivananda of Rishikesh, refused to answer my question. Instead, he advised, "It does not matter whether it was written five thousand years ago or yesterday. What matters is whether it has something useful to offer you. And if it is of no benefit, then why concern yourself about its date of composition? Concern with the date will only distract you from the experience." No advice could be more remote from the culture of Orientalist scholarship.

Radakrishnan (Halbfass 1988, 382) contrasted what he calls the Indian "religions of experience" with the "dogmatic religions" of the West, in which objective truth and objectified theoretical and institutional structures have priority over lived experience. When questions concerning truth and meaning are evaded in the face of a disciplinary praxis that transforms experience into data accessible to "objective" research, then the problem of adequacy of methods must be raised. Historiographic practice is not to be derided, but the question to be considered is whether it has the capacity to comprehend Indian or Tibetan thought and tradition, the primary task here. As Halbfass (1988, 170) dares to suggest,

Indian traditions "may, in fact, reach far beyond our current *capacity* of comprehension. They may not be accessible to the very ideas of 'research' and 'theoretical mastery.'" It is a real possibility, and so at least must be entertained by any sociological effort that wishes to move into a postcolonial mode of scholarship. Although the term "postcolonial" is a red flag to many Orientalist scholars, and they may add it to their list of what is too fashionable, its scholarship is to be preferred to any colonialist episteme.

Colonialism and Racism in Indology and Tibetology

The colonial expansion of Europe was an exercise in domination, and while military and economic control was paramount, epistemic control was a full partner in keeping the colonial subjects docile and subservient. Trautmann observes (1997, 21), "The government formed by Warren Hastings after the conquest of Bengal was committed . . . to developing and controlling knowledge of them through knowledge of Indian languages." From the start, each of the Orientalist disciplines had a colonial interest: "Area studies pursued a somewhat predatory aim, that of incorporating or assimilating non-Western life-forms into preestablished frames of reference" (Dallmayr 1996, 115). Used to conceiving the enterprise of colonialism as the benevolent struggle between "Civilisation" and primitives, one can imagine the bewilderment of the European explorers who discovered the elaborate philosophical practices of Indians and Tibetans. According to Trautmann (1997, 3), Victorian anthropology was challenged by the problem of encountering a dark-skinned people who were civilized and possessed a fully developed philosophy. It became part of the colonizing enterprise to gain some control over that philosophical practice and to neutralize it. Historiography and ethnology were charged with controlling the definitions of what "Buddhism" and "Hinduism" were (the terms themselves were European inventions) and of what were the racial origins of the people of the subcontinent (though "race" has been proven to be a concept without scientific validity). The German historiographer J. J. Brucker (1696-1770) represented Indian philosophy as having borrowed from the Persian; Persian philosophy in turn was borrowed from the Chaldean, and the Chaldean from the Hebrew. In this way Indian philosophy was denied any originality and viewed as only derivative (Viyagappa 1983, 12).

That culture, language, religion, racial appearance, etc., are all evolving and variable phenomena did not deter Europeans from defining authoritatively what could rightfully constitute authoritative Buddhism. When there were Himalayan valleys whose people practiced Buddhist rituals but called themselves Hindu and other valleys whose people practiced Hindu rituals but called themselves Buddhist, such variance from the disciplinarily established norm was only grounds for dismissing their experience altogether.[1] The decentered character of Hinduism itself was dizzying, entirely foreign to European religious culture, and colonial scholarship sought to provide some epistemic order; but nowhere were indigenous people permitted their own agency. Only Europeans were permitted agency, yet trapped deep within their own imaginary constructs which they straightforwardly mistook for reality, they could witness little with any real clarity.

Hegel has written that the struggle between the master and the slave is at base a struggle for agency—one seeks to control the Other by defining him/her, objectifying him as it were, while retaining the freedom of subjectivity only for oneself. Hegel (1967, 231) writes, "One is merely recognized, while the other only recognizes," and (Hegel 1977, 111) "One does not see the other as an essential being but in the other sees only one's own self." But one's own status as "master" is necessarily tied to having the other recognize one's mastery—"Our own self-consciousness attains to the truth of its self-consciousness only through achieving its recognition by the other person" (Gadamer 1975, 308). According to Hegel, we resent this dependence upon others for establishing the meaning of who we are, and we experience this dependence as alienation. This resentment and alienation cause us to initiate a struggle with the Other over the power to control these social definitions. No self-consciousness exists alone, but each exists for the other. "Each is the mediating term to the other, through which each mediates and unites itself with itself" (Gadamer 1975, 231). There is no such thing as a "Westerner"; rather, it is a concept that is dialectically entangled with how it engages *and is engaged by* an "Asian." A struggle for control of each party's own self-definition ensues, but there can be no final resolution since there is no epistemic hegemony so absolute that it could control forever the meaning of one's self-consciousness; and that is because the truth of the Other is that as well as being an object that we have objectified, the Other is a subject who *also* defines us. We objectify the identity of the Other, while the Other is engaged in a task of objectifying us; that is, each subject produces a corresponding object. Following such objectification a competition takes place over the enforcement of these recognitions. One is frequently indifferent to the damage inflicted by our objectification of the Other while highly sensitive to others' objectifications of us because they rob us of our control over our being.

The Indian psychologist Ashis Nandy (1983) and Indian social critic Gayatri Chakravorty Spivak (1990) have applied Hegel's dialectics of the master and the slave to colonialism in India, including the contemporary postcolonial period of cultural politics. They describe the instability of these objectifications, and in their account of "the mechanics of the constitution of the Other" (Spivak 1988, 294) describe the unhealthy compulsion, on the part of the colonized as

---

1. The Tibetan scholar Gendun Chophel (*dge 'dun chos 'phel*) has commented that there exists a different reality on the other side of every Himalayan pass.

well as the colonizers, to stabilize them. Our self-knowledge cannot be stabilized until the Other her/himself is stabilized. It is as if we are unable to rest secure until we have made the Other into a thing. Hegel (1967, 234) writes, "They let one another go quite indifferently, like things . . . The one is independent, and its essential nature is to be for itself, the other is dependent, and its essence is life or existence for another. The former is the Master, or Lord, the latter the Bondsman."

While there is no conclusion to this struggle for epistemic control, it is possible to respect others by witnessing their subjectivity, including their own free, world-constituting processes. So long as we reduce others to objects, we will never witness their truth. To the extent that they are consigned to their objectivity *they* have already witnessed our subjectivity, so in an important respect their understanding is superior to ours. The hermeneutic task for social researchers is to witness their subjectivity. This can hardly be achieved by a naively romantic engagement, for that is just one more variety of objectification (cf. Lopez 1998), and neither is liberal tolerance very effective for the sort of intimate engagement that is required. One sure way to witness the Other's subjectivity is to permit oneself to be objectified by the object, so to speak, or in the words of bell hooks (1992) to place oneself in a situation where the Other *looks back*. Merleau-Ponty (1962, 357) has keenly perceived, "Once the Other's gaze fixed upon me has, by inserting me into his field, stripped me of part of my being, it will readily be understood that I can recover it only by establishing relations with him." Only when one has opened oneself up to being alienated, exposing oneself to the Other's powers to define reality, can one discover the truth of the social relations.[2] So long as Orientalist scholarship has kept the threat of the Other well tamed by these objectifying practices, then a competent social inquiry will be uncompleted, and there will be no opportunity to learn what it is that Tibetological understanding does not yet know.

The study of religion was especially implicated in the distortions of this colonizing process (Haberman 1999, 21). So long as Mahayana Buddhism resided in palm-leaf manuscripts or in archaeological artifacts, the master status of the British in South Asia could be kept secure (King 1999, 144), for in such situations no one could look back at them and objectify the Europeans' stare in turn. Tibetans were nearly always non-participants in the European discourse about them. As Said (1978, 207) observes, "Orientals were seen through, analyzed not as citizens, or even people, but as problems to be solved or confirmed or . . . taken over." On occasion Tibetologists had some competition from Tibetan lamas for whom the manuscripts were still part of a live tradition, and so a rivalry ensued over who controlled the authoritative Buddhism. Whereas most of the Sanskrit and Pali texts were under the control of colonial institutions—not merely the physical texts themselves but also the means of disseminating them,

2. For a more extensive discussion, see Liberman (1999c).

and defining and authorizing their significance—most of the Tibetan texts were not preserved in European libraries and so "not under European control" (Lopez 1998, 37); hence, they constituted an epistemic threat. Tibetological praxis was implicated in the colonial struggle for epistemic hegemony. I have myself observed occasions when Tibetologists have displayed some resentment about Tibetans having a tradition with the same texts that the Tibetologists have used to establish their careers, so this essentially colonial struggle is not yet finished; in fact, as Tibetan scholars gain greater access to international forums, doctoral degrees, conferences, etc., the battle is being waged more fiercely as ever.

By the latter part of the nineteenth century all of the Buddhist traditions of Asia except that of Tibet were under the sway of the West (Lopez 1998, 41), and this posed a challenge to Orientalist praxis. A common response of Tibetologists was, and is, to dismiss the importance of the Tibetans' philosophical activities. Brian Hodgson, largely responsible for establishing the British collection of Sanskrit texts, collected them not because he had an interest in what he considered the "sheer absurdities of Buddhist philosophy" (cited in Tuck 1990, 32) but merely as the fastidious labors of a colonial functionary, an avocation during his lengthy convalescence. Even today, the best respected Tibetologists justify and legitimate their study of Tibetan texts on the basis of their importance to the study of Indian Buddhism (Cabezón 1995, 237), not as a component of a philosophical culture that is worthy of study in its own right. The few academic departments that accept Tibetan texts as primary phenomena, such as the Department of Religious Studies at the University of Virginia, are criticized. That Tibet existed in isolation from European Orientalist practice and entirely without the presence of any academic institutions that were under the sway of colonial influence (at least until the Chinese occupation) only complicated the European interest in controlling Buddhist knowledge.

Racism operates at the core of Indological and Tibetological practice, and even the majority of scholars who are not racist are compelled to employ the methods and speak the discourse developed by colonialists who were racists. A racist view of Tibetans was already prepared for Europeans by Indian brahmins, for whom these unwashed non-Hindu pastoral nomads from the mountainous hinterlands were and continue to be considered uncivilized. It was not difficult for Europeans to view the Buddhism of Tibetans as "most degenerate and inauthentic, not deserving even to be called Buddhism or Tibetan Buddhism but, instead, Lamaism" (Lopez 1995, 7 and 261). Because they appeared to be primitives, any notion of philosophical prowess was discarded. Hodgson expressed surprise that literature "should be so widely diffused as to reach persons covered with filth and possessed of not one of those grand luxuries which, at least in our ideas, go before the great luxury of books" (cited in Lopez 1995, 28). Colonel Younghusband (cited in Lopez 1998, 37), not a Tibetologist but a leader of the military vanguard of the colonialism that gave rise to Tibetology, commented disparagingly of the senior scholar of the Gelug order (the Ganden Tripa): "His

spiritual attainments . . . consisted mainly of a knowledge by rote of vast quanti-
ties of his holy books. The capacity of these Tibetan monks for learning their
sacred books by rote is, indeed, something prodigious; though about the actual
meaning they trouble themselves but little." Nothing could be more preposter-
ous. Although we do not want to conflate the opinion of a colonial official with
that of an Oriental scholar, many Indologists and Tibetologists were colonial
operatives, and Dallmayr (1996, xi) has remarked upon "the complicity of much
traditional scholarship with European colonial expansion."

Buddhist studies was conceived as a literary enterprise, as an offshoot of
philology (Lopez 1998, 158). Accordingly, just as the actual Hindu practices of
Indian villagers were, according to the Indian sociologist Veena Das (1982, 5),
dismissed as "superstitions," a bastardization of the "true" Hinduism that was a
colonial invention and to be found only in Sanskrit texts controlled and interpreted by Indologists, the Buddhism of the Tibetans was a derivative and inferior version of the "real" Buddhism over which Buddhologists had control. In
establishing disciplinary hegemony, Orientalist scholars invoked one epistemological structure in particular that was derived from the premier location of
Greek or Latin within European studies—in a similar way, Sanskrit was respected as the proper repository of Buddhist knowledge, and Tibetan was not to
be taken as legitimate on its own. The religion itself was defined authoritatively
as abiding within an established corpus of seminal Sanskrit texts. King (1999,
145-46) describes

> the tendency for Orientalists to reify the object of their discourses and to locate
> that reified "essence" (now labeled "Buddhism") firmly within a clearly de-
> fined body of classical texts. . . . Locating the essence of "Buddhism" in certain
> "canonical" texts, of course, allows the Orientalist to maintain the authority to
> speak about the "true" nature of Buddhism, abstractly conceived.

Once Buddhism was tamed by such epistemic strategies, Orientalist research was safe from contestation. Robbed of any agency, Tibetans had nothing
to contribute except some translations of texts whose Sanskrit versions were
lost. Only "biased" scholars accepted Tibetan philosophical practices as worthy
of study in their own right. Blinded by their own Eurocentrism, Indologists and
Tibetologists were incapable of investigating one of the world's most remarkable philosophical cultures. The father of Indian sociology M. N. Srinivas
(1962) has commented upon the limitations of such a methodology with respect
to Indian society, and his comment may be applied to Tibetan studies: "The
book-view of Indian society is only a 'sectional' view of social reality, and it
vitiates actual observation of social behavior."

Among other things, the "book view" is a strategy for epistemic control,
one that minimizes direct social contacts that could increase the instability of
how the knowledge has settled into a colonial acquisition. But the control of
Tibetology over the meaning of Tibetan Buddhism is already unstable—first

because of the Hegelian struggle that we have described; second, by the success Tibetans had in escaping colonization; and third, by the fact that most Tibetologists are dependent upon Tibetans to explain the most difficult portions of their philosophical and religious texts. Writes Lopez (1995, 4), " [The Tibetologist] is reluctant to place his trust in the authority of the native scholar, yet he cannot read the text without him. The native is thus portrayed as merely a supplement to the text whose answers must be checked against the original, access to which is provided initially by the native."

Hegel (1977) observes that one cannot afford to dominate the Other entirely because it would devalue the recognition that the Other provides. Just as the slave is dependent upon the master, the master is dependent upon the slave. The whole system driving colonial oppression is unstable. In the master's addiction to his self that the slave provides for him, he seeks to wrench this self away from the slave and make himself the basis for it. Despite the impossibility of this project, he is obsessed by the effort to become his own foundation, and it is an obsession that motivates him to further domination. Lopez (1995, 262) comments upon this irony which operates at the heart of Tibetology, "We see here the playing out of the relationship between the top and the bottom, in which the dominant member of a hierarchy (in this case Britain) attempts to eliminate the subordinate member, the other (in this case Tibet), for reasons of prestige or status but cannot because it is ultimately dependent on the other for that status."

Richard King (1999, 150) elaborates further:

> The involvement of native informants was usually subordinated to the insights to be gained from a careful reading of the "canonical" works of ancient Buddhists. This was seen as the most effective way to discern the true essence of Buddhism. The consequence of this trend was that "pure" or "authentic" Buddhism became located *not in the experiences, lives or actions of living Buddhists* in Asia but rather in the university libraries and archives of Europe— specifically in the edited manuscripts and translations carried out under the aegis of Western Orientalists. The authorial presence of Western Orientalists in the construction of this textualized "Buddhism" was safely hidden from view by a *philological positivism* which claimed to be revealing, through the medium of translation, nothing more than the meaning embodied in the original text itself.[3]

It has been my observation that translators who work without the guidance of any Tibetan teacher produce inferior translations. If this is the case, then the Orientalist prejudice against relying on teachers or on the system of Tibetan dialectics in which the texts are lodged is a flawed methodological policy. First, it presumes that when one "reads" a text in a European way, one is engaging that text in a manner that approximates the being of the text for the people who use the text as part of their religious or philosophical activities, the implication being

---

3. The emphases are mine.

that the book bears its essence within itself in a positive way. Ultimately, the essence of the book is not believed to be relevant to the meanings that emerge from how it is used. Here once again is the positivist's naivete, as ignorant as it is straightforward. To read a text in a Tibetan way is a necessary requirement for understanding Tibetan philosophical practice; "reading" in a Tibetan monastic university differs greatly from "reading" in a European university, and the latter is a much more individualized experience. A sound cultural hermeneutics would seek to fathom the context in which indigenous readings are made. This does not mean that the products of those Tibetan readings could not be contested, but the proper order of inquiry is to understand their "readings" *first* and only afterwards contest them.

But there is an even greater methodological lacuna in customary philological practice, and that is that most Tibetan "reading" is performed in the midst of the activity of debating the topics of the text publicly, section by section. It is not just that a text's topics are exposed to formal dialectical examination, the texts are *read* with an eye kept open *for* how they can become part of that dialectical engagement. In Gelug monastic universities especially, the dialectics come first, and the texts feed into them. For example, at Sera Monastic University a student might read a new portion of the text with a concern for finding a philosophical point about which he could gain sufficient expertise to use effectively in the debating courtyards that evening. During his professor's explanation of the text during class he may receive additional advice about what effective debates could be drawn from the reading. Then, having settled upon a topic or two, he might try out his notions upon a few close colleagues whose perspectives on matters he finds to be of value. After some practice with engaging his ideas dialectically, he might try some of them out on scholars he doesn't know quite so well, or upon a rival from the previous evening. These debates could go on for many hours, even late into the night; then he might bring questions raised during these debates, sharpened by his reflection upon how they fared in the debating, back to his reading of the next day's passage; and he could request further clarification from professor the next day, which can lead to further refinement, and further use, and further reading. By comparison, a European reading is performed in isolation or with some textually based dialectics, an experience that no way approximates the experience of the Tibetan scholar.

It may be that Tibetans are not "philosophers," but their training in the formal analysis of philosophical notions is such that it is relatively an easy matter for Tibetans to set the heads of Tibetologists spinning, unless the Tibetologists can avoid them. The complaint has been that those are just sophistic strategies, and lawyers are not philosophers, etc. One of my colleagues at Sera, Kube Rinpoche, a very humble man, made the observation to me that his training prepared him well for any questions that European scholars had posed to him during their visits to Sera. He had not studied the colonial and racist practices of Tibetology and so had not learned that Tibetan scholars were not competent enough to be philosophers. Since he had not internalized the objectification of Tibetan scholars that is common among Tibetological practitioners,[4] he was fully capable of effectively using his own disciplinary practices against them.

Some Practices of Philological Positivism

The privileging of the isolated written text over the text-in-use may be viewed as the victory of European academic practice over Tibetan academic practice, and it has made it possible for Tibetologists to exercise hegemony over the definition of Buddhism in the West. Seyfort Ruegg (1962, 320) is careful not to claim to be studying Tibetan Buddhism but to be studying Buddhism "guided by principles derived from the study of Tibetan sources." The people responsible for those "sources" are left without agency. C. W. Huntington, Jr. (1989, 6) offers this summary of philological praxis:

> The philological component is realized in the establishment of authoritative texts through the production of meticulous critical editions, heavily annotated translations, detailed indexes, and other reference tools . . . The historical aspect of text-critical scholarship consists in the contextualization of these editions and translations, relating them to each other and to known historical events. The aim of this approach is to define a coherent tradition for the continuum of texts which provide the raw material for research activities.

Another Tibetologist, José Cabezón (1995, 245-46) provides this concise account of the practices of philological positivism:

> Positivists conceive of texts—whether linguistic (written or oral), or cultural (behavioral, artistic, etc.)—as the beginning and end of the scholarly enterprise. In its philological variety, positivism sees a written text as complete and whole. It maintains that the purpose of scholarly textual investigation—and the use of science as a model for humanistic research here is always implied—is to reconstruct the original text (there is *only one* best reconstruction): to restore it and to contextualize it historically[5] to the point where the author's original intention can be gleaned. The principles of textual criticism represent an established, fixed and finely tuned scientific method; hence, there is no need for further methodological reflection. To reconstitute the text in this way is to make it available in a neutral, untampered-with and pristine fashion. This is not only sufficient and worthwhile, it is in any case all that is achievable, even in principle. Once the text has been reconstituted in this way, its meaning unfolds from within itself, without any need for interpretation. The goal of scholarship is to allow texts to speak for themselves. Scholars are not multifaceted prisms through which texts pass and refract. They are mirrors on which texts reflect and congeal into wholes.

---

4. Even in exile, Tibetan cultural institutions still provide them considerable isolation from European colonialism.

5. More precisely, the preoccupation of philologists is historiography.

Contemporary hermeneutic scholarship questions whether such an authoritative version of a text is at all possible, even for the text's author, who is necessarily engaged with multiple and indeterminate horizons of meaning. Mark Lilla (1998) challenges the naive notion of language as a transparent medium, which he believes stands at the root of the European metaphysical tradition. Similarly, Huntington (1989, 6) criticizes philological positivism: "Questions of a text's meaning are generally subordinated or dismissed altogether as irrelevant." The task faced by philology is a technical one that does not involve hermeneutic inquiry. Alternative methods are rejected by "a paternalism that simply refuses, through the sheer force of will or the exercise of power, to acknowledge the existence of viable methodological perspectives and styles of scholarship" (Cabezón 1995, 242), and their rejection is enforced by the disciplinary control that philologists retain over the awarding of research grants, scholarly appointments, approval of submissions for publication, etc. This textual empiricism is nothing less than an ethnocentrism that originated with the writing-centered practices of European scholarship developed in the seventeenth and eighteenth centuries (Gayatri Spivak 1990, 294). It is difficult to imagine an academic culture that would be less likely to appreciate the intellectual resources of indigenous dialectics.

But just how do philologists build up such a definitive reading? In their application of meticulous and often brilliant textual research, they have to make many decisions that are dependent upon the immediate lexical choices they face there, on any given page of indigenous text. Although they may not conceive of their discipline as involving interpretation, the contingencies of those choices regarding terms and meanings determine the final product. If they believe that this final product stands alone unmediated by any system of interpretation, it would be fair to conclude that *they* are the unphilosophical culture.[6] There is a tendency toward conservatism in their translations, whereby a well-worn phrase will be employed even when its meaning conveys little about a passage's significance, and even when the translator herself has little or no understanding of what a term implies—is this a species of the same knowing "by rote" as some Tibetologists have described Tibetan scholars?

Trained first as Sanskrit scholars, Tibetological philologists tend to read the principles of Sanskrit's highly rule-governed grammar into the more context-dependent, even opportunistic grammar of Tibetan. For example, Alex Wayman (1979, 305) translates "*mi bden bzhin du'ang rang gi byad bzhin mdzes par bsgrub bya'i phyir*" (Tsong Khapa 1997, 628) as "Because one may beautifully prove that it (the unreflected image) is like a lie in the manner of (taking resource to) one's own face (a looker upon the mirror while one washes one's face)," that is, treating the "beautiful" (*mdzes par*) to be an adverbial modifier of the act of proving, when in fact "beautiful" (*mdzes pa*) is intended to modify the

---

6. See page three.

noun "face" and the "-*r*" merely connects the nominal phrase involving "face" with the act of proving. Though it is child's play to find faults with translation,[7] what is significant here is that this particular sort of mistake involves constraining Tibetan grammar in ways that Sanskrit grammar may be constrained. But Tibetan is a different and unrelated language and requires its own skills, especially since the connective resources of Tibetan grammar are relatively more labile. I would argue that there may be more scope for interpretative work by the reader in Tibetan than in the case of Sanskrit.[8] And, equally important, the work of piecing together a contingent and sometimes idiosyncratic translation of a passage by fashioning some "mechanical transposition of words from one language into another, desperately trying to suppress any traces of experience and understanding" (Guenther 1992, xii), and entirely independently of any endogenous readings or guidance to the passage involves a degree of cultural arrogance that is methodologically unsound. The vanity of the empiricism that such philologists believe they practice reveals itself in their ubiquitous use of parenthetic passages, as if all of the interpretation is confined to the parentheses and is never introduced into the authoritative text proper. A real empiricism would involve studying Tibetans using the texts.

In any event, Wayman's Sanskrit-influenced myopia inhibits his ability to render an accurate translation of the Tibetan. He and other highly regarded Tibetologists routinely provide in parentheses the Sanskrit words for English terms, *even when the text, and context, are strictly Tibetan.* In his "Introduction" to his translation of Tsong Khapa's *Calming the Mind and Discerning the Real*, Wayman frequently *excludes* the Tibetan term that he has translated into English, offering in its stead an equivalent Sanskrit term, although it is an *original* Tibetan philosophical treatise that he is translating. While a scholar studying Tibetan philosophical thinking can be informed by investigating the meaning of equivalent Sanskrit terms, that does not mean that the thinking of the Tibetans must be strictly derivative in every respect. Contemporary semiotics has learned that the function of a term relates to the sign system in which it plays a part and not to any absolute meaning that may be guaranteed by dictionaries (Liberman 1999a). The Tibetans have their own interpretations of some key Sanskrit terms they have adopted; for example, in Sanskrit both *jnana* (*ye she* in Tibetan) and *prajna* (*she rab* in Tibetan) can mean "wisdom" in English, but the more penetrating spiritual term for wisdom is *prajna* in Sanskrit but it is *ye she* in Tibetan,

7. Recognizing the impossibility of perfection in translation, I tend toward an ecumenism regarding others' practices of translation, believing that there is something to be learned from most translations. Since the perfect translation is a work-in-progress, I genuinely admire scholars who risk venturing beyond the routine translation regimes (e.g., Batchelor 2000) in the direction of attempting to convey an understanding of a text's meaning.

8. Elsewhere (Liberman 1982), I have argued that languages vary in demanding greater or lesser work on the part of listeners.

with *jnana* and *she rab* having more general worldly applications. This partial reversal of semantic domains instructs us that a routine practice of relying upon Sanskrit equivalents for authoritative interpretations cannot be applied mindlessly, and if it is so applied it becomes merely a logocentrism derived from nineteenth century philological practice. The irony is that the English translation "wisdom" obscures all of these subtleties and especially misses the dynamic, spontaneous character of *ye she* altogether, yet few translators address the matter, which is a problem for cultural hermeneutics What is required is a more empirical method of social inquiry that engages the culture in which Tsong Khapa and his followers are operating.

In a similar mode, Seyfort Ruegg (1989, 85) writes about another original Tibetan treatise, "Nevertheless, in the *Chos 'byung Me tog* there is recorded the King's decree to the effect that Nagarjuna's theory was henceforth to be accepted, and that the practice of the Paramitas and the yoking together in *yuganaddha* of Upaya and Prajna should be observed." Why does Ruegg reduce what is a debate in Tibetan, among Tibetans, that had important historical consequences for Tibetans, to a Sanskrit discourse, while for the most part overlooking the Tibetan terms? It seems to miss the proper object of inquiry in this case and so be less than a strictly empirical practice. If the text was a translation of a Sanskrit work, it might be an acceptable practice, even if the Sanskrit text was no longer extant. But for an original Tibetan text being translated into English, it is as if two imperialisms have ganged up on the Tibetan philosophical community. Guenther has remarked upon such "'Sanskrit-only' glaucoma" (1992, xii): "Reading Tibetan texts through 'Sanskrit eyes' can result in hilarious nonsense" (1994, 67).

The practice derives from an elitism that accompanies Tibetological practice, and this elitism can display itself in unexpected circumstances. I once participated on a panel with Alex Wayman at a conference on Buddhist Tantra in India that involved both Western and Tibetan scholars. When some Tibetans questioned Wayman about his interpretation of "tantra," he referred them to the meanings one can find in Monier-Williams's Sanskrit-English dictionary, a definitive text in philological practice. Wayman unapologetically challenged the Tibetan scholar-monks, most of whom had been practicing tantra for most of their lives, "You don't find that meaning of 'tantra' in Monier-Williams, do you?" The implication was that he knew better the meaning of tantra than the Tibetans did since he was well grounded in Sanskrit and they were not. Monier Monier-Williams was himself an Indologist whose work had more to do with Christian missionary aims than with cultural hermeneutics (Halbfass 1988, 49, 51, and 469). Such absurdities can arise only when the scholarly praxis operates at a great remove from real people. At the end of the aforementioned panel, Wayman graciously thanked the participants in the audience, telling them, "I've never seen so many Tibetans in my life!" I am sure that it was the case, for his pronunciation of Tibetan was unintelligible to any one not a Tibetologist.[9]

This is not to deny the competency that philologists do have, which is quite significant. But their competency is a European practice far removed from the life-world that Western scholarship does not yet know. And it is neither necessary nor customary for Tibetologists to have a genuine interest in what they investigate. Cabezón (1995, 253) dares to ask an impertinent question, "What social processes are involved in becoming employed as a Buddhologist, in the granting of tenure and in the making of reputations?" A frank reply, without either romanticism or defensiveness, would certainly include a recognition that as Western academics much of their motivation is driven by careerism. In some cases the study of Tibetan language has been motivated by an ego-centered interest in getting "a leg up" on Sanskrit scholars who did not know any Tibetan, and was not motivated by any interest in learning about Tibetan philosophical culture. A vital part of Tibetological disciplinary practice involves making one's scholarship available to the critical reception of other Orientalist scholars, though the subjected people are left without a voice in this (until quite recently). Accordingly, the work of the Tibetologist includes reading other Tibetologists' texts, and it is not always read with an ear for learning something new but instead with an eye for finding the flaws they contain. While this practice is certainly necessary for improving scholarly reflection, when a "flaws first" reading is made, the competitive energies involved can eclipse the more creative possibilities that lie in hearing what an author does have to say. A professor of sociology, who for a time served as Director of the American Institute of Indian Studies, once asked me during a private meeting, "Since Buddhism makes so much out of selflessness and kindness towards others, why are Tibetologists so hypercompetitive and conflict-ridden in their relations with each other?" At the risk of appearing overly romantic myself, let me suggest that they did not learn it from a period of fieldwork with Tibetan scholar-monks.[10]

The Representation of Indian Philosophies

Heidegger (1957, 80) has written, "Knowledge as research calls reality to ac-

---

9. For example, he pronounced all of the silent letters in Tibetan words (e.g. "Kahsgrup" for Khedroop (*mKhas grub*) and "Red-da-ba" for Rendawa (*Red mda' ba*). I am reminded of another philologist, responsible for the principal Mongolian-English dictionary, who discovered upon arriving in Ulan Bator that he could not order in Mongolian a yard of cloth from a shopkeeper, and he required a translator.

10. It has been reported to me that in Tibet a scholar's first manuscript would be dragged through the dirt and mud of the street at the end of a rope which was tied to a horse. The explanation given to me was that it was done for the sake of reducing the author's pride. It is no mere supposition to observe that criticism by Tibetologists is not done to reduce the pride of one's colleagues (and I have never heard of anyone making this claim); it is more likely that it is motivated by pride in oneself.

count how and to what extent it can be made available to representational think-ing," and he acknowledged that the very act of reducing phenomena to objectiv-ities and representedness (Heidegger 1967) already introduces an ontological interpretation of the reality that is under investigation. The representation of Indian philosophical culture that emerged within Western research had some-thing of an inglorious beginning. The first book on Indian thought was a study of a brahmanical text and was entitled, *Open Door to Hidden Heathendom.* In-deed, Christianity was the principal lens through which Hindu and Buddhist concepts were understood and evaluated, whether the evaluation was negative or positive.

The negative mode was in force throughout the seventeenth and eighteenth centuries. Commentators decried the lack of morality (read: "lack of moral indi-vidualism") in Hinduism, and Buddhism was derided as a form of diabolical nihilism. Such fundamental terms and practices as "wisdom," "meditation," "*nirvana,*" and even "Buddha" (conceived as an absolute, when it is a verb; Guenther 1992, 174) were obscured and misinterpreted. These distortions are alive in contemporary Tibetological scholarship, which has "entombed Bud-dhism in concepts appropriate for another era" (Guenther 1989b, ix). Even so universally praised a humanist as Albert Schweitzer "never tired of drawing a dichotomy between an ethical life-affirming Christianity and a Hindu mysticism indifferent to ethics and life-negating" (Inden 1990, 105).

During the nineteenth century a more favorable Christian interpretation be-gan to emerge. Schopenhauer saw in Hinduism a "truly Christian philosophy" and declared that Christianity had "Indian blood in its veins" (Halbfass 1988, 112). Kantians (e.g., Stcherbatsky) represented Buddhist philosophy as a Kant-ian enterprise; moreover, yoga was dismissed altogether as a nonphilosophy because it did not deal explicitly with Kantian issues. Indian theoretical tradi-tions were judged according to how consistent were their positions with Euro-pean issues (e.g., materialism versus. rationalism and the subject-object dual-ism). The Indians' and Tibetans' own agendas, which ought to be the main ob-ject of interest for any objective social inquiry, were *missed* entirely, including their noteworthy efforts to overcome reification in thinking. European ideas were simply imposed upon Asian thought, and if something did not reflect European interests it was dismissed as superstition; when Asian thought did re-late, or was made to relate, its shortcomings were defined in terms of European measures. Such misrepresentations were so influential that they became the standard view for European scholars (Tuck 1990, 53). Comparative philosophy was a monologue.

German theorists were slightly more inclined to find philosophical merit in Indian thought than the English, French, and Italians. Deussen (cited in Inden 1990, 103) contended that "the deep fundamental concept of Plato and Kant was precisely that which already formed the basis of *upanishad* teaching." Nietzsche, always a keen critic of European reductionism, viewed the Indologists as "animals to the lyre" (Halbfass 1988, 88), but his outlook was otherwise flawed. The English, on the other hand, discounted Indian philosophy. In 1879, A. B. Keith (1923) wrote, "Regarded as serious contributions to the solution of the fundamental problems of philosophy, the value of the *Upanishads* must be considered comparatively small."

Hegel asserted that all the Orient is static and that only Europe was historical and so truly philosophical. Hegel's view cannot be dismissed summarily; however, before one can promote the West as the supersession of the East, one should at least comprehend the basic elements of Eastern thought. To argue, as Hegel does, that the lack of any self-affirmation of the free and unique individual is a limitation of Indian philosophy once again merely promotes a Eurocentric value as a "universal" standard. For the Indian practitioner, there is little to be valued in individualism, and the person in its ultimate nature is *not* unique. On the contrary, it is the task of Hindus and Buddhists alike to disaffirm the ego and to subdue the self. For them true freedom involves something more than giving free reign to individualistic prejudice, and they see nothing at all universal about egoistic individuality.

In the twentieth century more contemporary representations of Indian thought have arisen. The editor of the multivolumed *Encyclopedia of Indian Philosophy* (a masterpiece of twentieth century Indology), Karl Potter, has inscribed Indian thought into a behavioristic representation. Tuck (1990, 64-65) writes of Potter:

> Like a Skinnerian therapist intent on expunging all mention of emotions, hidden motivations, and unconscious from psychological discussion, Potter redescribes the Indian philosophical endeavor as a purely rational game with fixed rules—a test of skill and control based entirely around mechanical laws of causation. Replete with schematic charts, fifteen pages of Venn diagrams . . . Potter's obsession is with causal chains and final results. Consequently, he sees Indian philosophers as participating in this same obsession.

The European intellect is committed to the world as representation. Its truth does not lie in experience but in words, in the *logos*, and in a formally validated logic. Even its political forms are logocentric—the theory is that governments are not of men, but of laws. India's scholars were not without admiration for this European praxis: as early as the sixth century a brahmanical scholar praised the Greeks' scientific capabilities (Halbfass 1988, 186). But throughout Indian philosophical reflection there is a vigilance against permitting intellectual cleverness to lead to what in Heideggerian terms may be described as a forgetfulness of being. Whereas the West placed its faith wholeheartedly in the powers of rationality, in the control and planning exercised by means of objectified representations, in India the rational project was made the servant of personal development. This has been interpreted to be merely irrational and subjectivist, instead of a sibling effort to do battle with the same demons of humanity's rational capacities that European humanity faces.

One of Europe's great historical achievements was its separation of rationality from religion. This led to a value-free study of knowledge for its own sake. The pursuit of philosophy free from practical interests, a concern with "pure theory," was the ideal. But is it the reality? Is not theory in the West always placed at the service of the technological mastery over nature and the pursuant commercialization? Is not rationality in the West *always* instrumental rationality, that is, obligated from the outset to serve the capitalists' interests? Habermas has concluded that the value-free theory of European rationality is only a myth. And is Asian reflection really so mired in subjective bias? The development of wisdom (*jnana*) in any Indian tradition involves a disattachment from worldly concerns and "abandons all claims to causal and conceptual mastery" (Halbfass 1988, 273). Is this detachment not something that is value free in a different sense?

The gap may not be bridgeable. But it would be facile to merely rule out Buddhist reflection as nonphilosophical, when it brilliantly problematizes representational thinking. It is not heresy to propose that Indian and Tibetan thought pose to the West a philosophical challenge at least as serious as the one which the West poses to it. The thirtieth vow of a *bodhisattva* in Mahayana Buddhism cautions against purposeless study, a vow most Tibetologists violate as a cardinal rule. At an academic conference I once queried an Indian-born Tibetologist about what he thought of Europeans who insist that there was never any philosophy in South Asia in the true sense of a value-free, objective pursuit of knowledge. He replied that he agreed completely, and that Indians and Tibetans have no interest in a discipline that by statute renders itself irrelevant to any spiritual or personal concerns. Knowledge, he proposed, should always be tethered to the evolution of the human spirit, for without that concern it will be left sterile and undisciplined. One does not need to adopt the perspective of Asian thinkers in order to study them—but one does need to study them. Lost within a caricature of Tibetan scholar-monks and constitutionally incapable of *understanding* their philosophy, Tibetologists have been inclined to become lost within the fetishization of their own disciplinary ideas; instead of a penetrating view of a non-European philosophical culture, they are merely left with careers.

Chapter 2

Ethnomethodology and the Retrieval
of Ordinary Society

It is not that the established literature is wrong. It is that it is absurd.

—Harold Garfinkel

Tibetans have been the object of European curiosity for three centuries. Despite countless travelogues, diaries, professional research, novels, and commercial films, in which Tibet has been a vestibule for the imagination of non-Tibetans, the actual lived world of the Tibetan people has not shown through clearly. Some of this may be the result of the Tibetans' own preferences. For most of this time its government deliberately elected to avoid contacts with the wider world, perhaps not wishing to pollute their mental environment with the more worldly concerns of non-Buddhist foreigners. They passed up an opportunity to be admitted to the League of Nations because they did not want to open their country to outsiders (Shakya 1999, 53), a move that could later have spared them from wholesale takeover by the Chinese. In Dharamsala, the Tibetan capital-in-exile where I lived for eighteen months, I once overheard Tibetans referring to Americans as the *nga dang po* ("me-first") people, and Tibetans there cultivate a degree of insularity that can manifest as a reluctance to open themselves up to Westerners. It has been far easier, and less risky for both sides, for Westerners to study their texts.

    I went to the one of the more remote settlements in the south of India where few Tibetans had English language skills in order to increase my opportunities for conversing in Tibetan and to find more intimacy in my relations with Tibetans. Scholar-monks of the remote monastic universities were more generous with their ideas. At some sacrifice of their own limited resources, they introduced me to their daily scholarly lives. The Tibetan professors and their students devoted many hundreds of hours to instructing me and never asked for compensation.[1] In the end, only this generosity enabled me to study the lived work of Tibetan philosophical reasoning.

The European fascination with the phenomenon of philosophical debate is almost as longstanding as their enchantment with Tibet proper. The first detailed account of Tibetans philosophical debating was published in the early eighteenth century by a Catholic priest and scholar, Ippolito Desideri (1931), who traveled in Tibet from 1712-1727 and spent several years in the very same monastic university in which I lived for two years some 280 years later, Sera Monastery. Of course, Desideri's aim was not to learn from Tibetans or even to study them, but to prove to them that their Buddhism was ill-conceived and to refute their doctrines. Oddly, this aim fit in well with the Tibetans' practice of theological and philosophical disputations, and Desideri appeared to have cultivated some successful scholarly relationships. He describes the regular visits of Tibetan professors to his room to take up inquiries and disputes with him. Desideri (103-4) also describes the Tibetans' own "frequent disputations," but his account fails to provide very much specific detail about the *in vivo* skills that their practices of reasoning involved:

> It must be known that the Thibetans have their dialectics, definitions, divisions and arguments, all in the form of simple enthymemes; and a way of starting arguments, of denying and of admitting, of denying the supposition, distorting an argument, and convincing by implication, and so on. They have also a talent for propounding, discussing, and analyzing problems in the same manner as we do; their formula being to propose the distinctive trait of the subject, to state the opinion of others, to conflate those opinions, to place their own views beyond dispute by demonstrating facts, and finally to reject all objections made by the adversary. Those artifices are found not only in their books, but are in constant use in this [part of] Thibet, where the practice is taught in several large universities, frequented by such a vast number of students as to be incredible to anyone who has not been among the monks.

European travelers and scholars who succeeded Desideri have never failed to be captivated by the sight of so much enthusiastic scholarship and by the intensity with which epistemological matters are taken up almost as if lives depended upon it. Unfortunately, detailed description that is full of specifics, and most especially, infused with *the looks of the world* for these philosopher-monks, eluded most of the Tibetologists who succeeded Desideri. It has not been until recently, when researchers influenced by modern social scientific methods arrived to have their curiosity similarly aroused, that detailed systematic descriptions of the social interaction of Tibetan debaters have been attempted for the

---

1. It should be acknowledged that an hour spent tutoring a Westerner must be deducted from instructing young Tibetan scholars, whose classes could involve ten to twenty students. Hence, it was a major act of generosity and one that was in some ways counter-productive to the long-term survival of their philosophical tradition.

first time.[2] Fortunately, these practices have survived to the present day. With the invasion of Tibet by Maoist Chinese and the subsequent Tibetan exodus, these features of Tibetan Buddhist scholasticism are more available to European scholarship than ever before. The present study is an attempt to provide an exhaustive microsociological account of what Desideri so enthusiastically related to his European readers 275 years ago. It is an extraordinary coincidence that these investigations were mostly pursued at the same monastic university (reconstructed in exile) where Desideri commenced his own examination of Tibetan philosophical culture.

Textual Inquiry

Tibetological practice has reduced the live philosophical praxis of Tibetan scholar-monks to docile texts. These texts, removed from its natural setting in live debates, are then colonized for their own purposes, which may relate to various European religious concerns, issues in European philosophy (from Kantian to postmodern), enduring philological issues in Sanskrit studies, or merely the career interests of the Tibetologist. At best, indigenous Tibetan philosophy is engaged at the level of ideas, but never recognized as the actual *in vivo* social practices that compose real debating in the courtyard. It is not that some Tibetan notions do not lead Tibetologists to vital insights, it is only that these insights have made minimal contact with naturally endogenous experience; indeed, *the very methodology* of Tibetology rules out such contact since it is essentially a literary engagement with texts and nothing like a Tibetan engagement with those same notions. Until those notions are captured *in just the way* that Tibetan scholar-monks come to them, little of sociological interest can be learned. It is not that Tibetologists have not come upon anything profound; it is that the profundities they have come upon are neither Tibetan nor Buddhist.

Tibetologists operate from a secure vantage point that is seldom placed at risk by indigenous Tibetan practices. Speaking in the voice of a Master Narrator, inherited from the colonial era of social studies, much of their analysis relies mostly upon taxidermal approaches as if all the live subjects had expired long ago and those who remain have no relevant competence. Inden (1990, 1) has complained that Indological scholars have kept India eternally ancient and has criticized "the essentialism that lies behind the dichotomy of traditional and modern" (159), as if contemporary "traditional" practices lack sufficient standing to be taken as serious phenomena in their own right. Rather, in a fetishization of the esoteric, the Tibetologist speaks authoritatively on behalf of the long-ago whose protagonists have been silenced or speak only rarely. The Tibetologists' authority proceeds from considerable philological competence, but it also

---

2. Cf. especially Dreyfus (2002), Goldberg (1985), and Sierksma (1964).

proceeds from the careful cultivation of the standpoint of the universal observer whose transcendental status is insured by means of literary devices. The observation of actual people engaged in live situations occurring naturally as part of their ordinary lives, made not from a purportedly "universal" vantage point but from the vantage point of the actors themselves, is not a method used, or approved of, by most Tibetological researchers.[3]

Much of the education in Tibetan philosophical culture takes place on the debate grounds of the monastic university, where Tibetans engage each other in a dialectical pursuit of philosophical understanding;[4] hence, any methodology that is so exclusively concentrated upon textual analysis that it misses that vital social practice will *necessarily* fail to capture what most identifies this philosophical culture, which has its roots in ancient South Asian society. Even contemporary Tibetologists who today do travel to and live in the monasteries spend most of their time there in their rooms translating texts instead of studying and participating in the actual philosophical practices of Tibetan scholars.

For anyone studying Tibetan philosophy, the important question to ask is, *what is it that Tibetans do* that preserves for them the productive life of their thought? Such a question can only be pursued by capturing "the role of rationality within the interstices of its dynamics" (Schrag 1992, 8-9), that is, by an "extended preoccupation with rationality as a *praxis*." There is in the philosophical practice that Tibetologists study what Harold Garfinkel calls "a missed orderliness," an orderliness which the debating Tibetan scholars themselves produce, maintain, and exploit for investigating the nature of reality and for placing into formal statements their own ideas of "universal" truth. This orderliness is an incredibly rich phenomenon, and its detailed description is the focus of the present study.

Although I have consulted the Tibetans' own authoritative texts about debating and about epistemological inquiry, it would be to mistake the topic of inquiry for the actual resources for making that inquiry to adopt a strategy of research that would limit one's study to what the Tibetans' authoritative texts say about debate. Tibetological studies that are exclusively textually based,[5]

---

3. One of my early Tibetan teachers, Professor Thubten Jigme Norbu, the elder brother of the present Dalai Lama, would deliberately mispronounce "Tibetology" as "Tibeto-ology," in order to satirize its self-importance.

4. Some Tibetologists will object to this characterization of Tibetan scholastic life as "philosophical," Eurocentrically reserving the term "philosophy" only for traditions that were derived from the Greeks. Just as for a time British colonials objected to any reference to Australian Aboriginal social life as a "civilization," Indologists scrutinize the shortcomings of Tibetan philosophical investigations and find them wanting, measuring them always by the standards of European practice. This is an important theoretical topic; however, further discussion is beyond the scope of the present work and is taken up in detail in the sequel to this study, *Reason and Wisdom*.

5. Take for instance the excellent textual studies by Perdue (1976 and 1992).

which is their normal *modus operandi*, miss, by their disciplinary practice, the indigenous social activities that should be the primary object of investigation. The Tibetans' texts themselves are idealizations of debates and discussions about debates; what occurs in actual debates is much more dynamic, multiply determined, and even messy. This messiness is not only offensive to Tibetologists, who have a modernist European preference for definitive and static accounts, they can be offensive to Tibetan philosophers as well. That is because in Tibetan society, as in every society, the local orderliness is easily missed and idealized accounts of that orderliness are substituted. When I first began videorecording Tibetan debates, I found it very difficult to locate a "clean" debate. On several occasions when I thought I had found a lively and interesting debate, I would show it to the abbot of the Tibetan School of Dialectical Studies, the Ven. Gen Lobsang Gyatso, and he would point out the many flaws in it and reject its use as a paradigmatic case. After several such failed attempts, Gen Gyatso volunteered to organize a "proper" debate for me. He collected two of his finest debaters and worked with them about just how the debate should proceed. After this instruction and some practice, they informed me that they were ready for filming. What I recorded, however, was not the spirited struggle of a live Tibetan debate but a lifeless dialogue that played as if each party was dryly reading a script for an audition. Gen Gyatso observed the filming, and when it was finished he informed me that I had indeed recorded a "proper" debate and should proceed with analyzing it. The problem was that it in no way displayed any of the characteristics of the hundreds of debates I had witnessed at the Dialectical School. It was not possible for me to explain to him about the "missed orderliness" of ethnomethodological investigation that was lacking, for that orderliness was missing for the abbot as well as the Tibetologists, although the abbot knew fully well how to perform those interactional practices which Tibetan debaters use to produce philosophical understanding. *In vivo* practices are hidden in the looks of the ordinary world, and one does not see them readily, for according to a metaphor suggested by Harold Garfinkel they are the water in which the fish are swimming.

Later, when I showed my Tibetan colleagues some of the better debates (including debates whose debaters had received high marks in their evaluations), they would always apologize for the sloppy quality of the debating, informing me that that was not how debate was "really" supposed to de done, that I should not take such mistakes for the standard, etc. In the end I could only conclude that life, real life—the object of sociological research and not Tibetological scrutiny—always includes flaws and that no debate could be an "ideal" debate, for such an ideal existed only in the imagination. Similarly, when I turned to Tibetans accomplished at spelling for assistance in preparing my Tibetan transcriptions of the debates,[6] the inclination of these scholars was to clean up the debate. Even after I gave them long lectures about how I wanted to record only what was hearable on the tape, in just the way it appeared on the tape, complete with blemishes, they still would try edit obvious mistakes, informing me, "But that is not the right way to debate this one." I told them that the only right way I wanted to know was the way that the debaters actually, not imaginably, accomplished it.

The founding siblings of Orientalism, philology and historiography, have had a two-hundred-year monopoly on Tibetan studies. In recent decades social scientific disciplines have intruded into the Tibetological establishment with fieldwork based methodologies, but they have not been very welcomed by Tibetologists. Tibetological reviewers of applications for research funding can be dismissive of studies that nominate features of Tibetan life that are most identifying of the actual work that Tibetans perform as their daily concern. Onoda (1992, 6) is typical of Tibetologists in his speaking dismissively of sociological approaches: "A description of Tibetan monastic debate was reported by Sierksma, though primarily from the point of view of sociology, rather than Buddhist Studies or logic." It is odd that Onoda's own study relies almost exclusively on textual sources, since its very title, *Monastic Debate in Tibet* clearly suggests a live social activity. He reviews with some brilliance the record of Sanskrit, Tibetan, and Mongolian sources from various historical periods regarding the thinking of scholars about the principles of consequence logic and making correct formulations, but the actual dialectics is never captured in its natural setting. Venturino (1998) observes that Western social scientific methodologies are beginning to challenge the supremacy of textual analysis in Tibetan studies, and he cites the additional influence of a "growing trans-nationalism and democratization" that has brought Western-trained Tibetans to the meetings of Tibetological societies, thereby exposing the formerly secure vantage point of Tibetologists to indigenous challenge.

Is Tibetological practice empirical even in its reading of Tibetan texts? Anne Klein (1994, 2) throws considerable light on this problem:

> What does it mean to *read* a text such as Tsong-kha-pa's in a Tibetan context? Do contemporary Western concepts of *reading*, especially as practiced in Western academies or seminaries, which are modern Western culture's closest

---

6. Spelling in Tibetan is extremely difficult, since many letters are silent or affect the tone in only minor ways (which are frequently ignored by speakers of some Tibetan dialects), yet spelling is important for distinguishing among homonyms, and so can drastically alter the meaning of a word. Most Tibetan scholars themselves cannot spell well. This does not mean that they are ignorant, only that spelling was not emphasized during their education to the extent that it is for Western students, just as memorization no longer plays a significant role in the education of Westerners, making them very poor at reciting passages (and Tibetans judge Westerners poorly for this inability).

analogues to Tibetan monastic universities, suffice to explore the variety of activities encompassed by textual engagement in a traditional Tibetan setting?

Klein describes the role of reading, including memorization, alongside the more experimental style of oral commentary in the *dped khrid* classes and debate. The texts are not simply read, as in a library; rather, they are read with an eye to the coming debate. A European who was studying at Sera as a monk reported to me, "I don't feel I really understand a portion of a text until I've debated it thoroughly. After I learned how to debate, I began to read the texts differently, and more carefully." Professor Emeritus Geshe Lhudrup Sopa, a scholar with the imprimatur of both the American and Tibetan academies, warns that the correct way to read a Tibetan text is with the context of the debates that the text fosters in the monastic courtyards. When Geshe Sopa teaches to Westerners, he always annotates key passages by engaging his students in some of the dialectical disputations that are meant to accompany the passages. Reading the text without this praxis is to not have read the text in a Tibetan way.

Tibetan scholar-monks are dismissive of Europeans who wish to "translate" texts by just sitting at their desks without intimate engagement with Tibetans. I was once scolded by the Kargyud Geshe Thrangu Rinpoche, living at Rumtek at the time, for suggesting that I could translate adequately a subtle philosophical text without having undergone years of Tibetan-style training, including debate and extensive oral commentary. Yet, oddly enough, some Tibetologists who translate texts disguise the contribution of their Tibetan collaborators ("teachers" is closer to the real truth, but this cannot be admitted given the arrogance of European academic culture). In a typical instance a seminal text by a great Indian yogi was translated by a European under the following protocol—the Tibetan geshe explained the text in Tibetan, a Tibetan translator translated his explanation into English, and the Tibetologist operated the controls on the tape recorder. The tapes produced in this way became the principal source for the translation. Neither the name of the geshe nor his translator figured as prominently in the "author" line of the book as did the name of the Tibetologist, much as a puppet might claim credit for the words of the ventriloquist. Here again, live Tibetans are silenced.

The Intimate Methods of Microsociology

What are the actual experiences through which the Tibetans' philosophical insights are registered? Social phenomenological studies, including ethnomethodological investigations, proceed not from a review of treatises but from an examination of the lived experience of persons. That does not mean, of course, that the philosophical interests of these scholars have no relevance for such research. Rather, it means that the idea of rigor for microsociological researchers differs considerably from that of Tibetologists. The sociologist Randall Collins (1998, 25-27) has undertaken an exhaustive (1098 pp.) sociological examination of the history of intellectual networks, and he has concluded that it is the face-to-face interaction that is responsible for breathing vitality into every important philosophical event:

> Although lectures, discussions, conferences, and other real-time gatherings would seem to be superfluous in a world of texts, it is exactly these face-to-face structures which are constant across the entire history of intellectual life . . . . Without face-to-face rituals, writings and ideas would never be charged up with emotional energy.

Collins (1998, 53) laments the fact that "intimate materials on the micro-level of the sociology of thinking are not available" for most of the philosophical networks he is examining. The incredible fortune of the present study is that the social life of Tibetan scholastic practices is fully available to this investigation because these medieval philosophical practices—in large part inherited from the classical period of South Asian culture—are also contemporary practices. Ed Rose, who has studied European medieval scholastic debate and who wrote that cultural scientists should devote more of their energies to investigating "ethno-ontologies" and the practices that constitute them, was overjoyed when he discovered the present studies. He advised me, "You have the opportunity that students of medieval scholarship have always lacked—you can perform the ethno-investigations!" There is every reason not to reduce such studies to a philological examination of the Tibetans' texts.

The objective of this study, then, is to gain intimate access to the local interactional practices that Tibetan philosophers use to provide for the orderliness of their dialectical inquiries. Without gaining some expertise in the ethno-methods of Tibetans, some European expertise will, by default, substitute for the Tibetan expertise. However, local expertise is always a very detailed, complicated affair, enriched with particularities. One of the first social scientists to study the "ethno-ontologies" of Tibetan scholars, the anthropologist Margaret Goldberg (1985, 910), comments,

> Much of the kind of information needed to understand the process of individuality and improvisation occur in the multiple minute decisions, acts, feelings, and thoughts of each moment. The complexity of moment-to-moment individual experience has sent social scientists to seek shortcuts—social principles or natural laws which operate above the level of the individual and which usually avoid describing the subjective components of experience.

Harold Garfinkel (2001) has observed that the very concreteness of these local affairs can defeat any effort to come upon them. But Garfinkel strongly encourages fighting the urge to take any of the shortcuts of "principled versions" of actual social interactions. Merleau-Ponty (1964a, 50) spoke of the inexhaustible further explanation that any phenomenology of local experience requires, for there is indeed no end to what local affairs can look like. Garfinkel suggests that it is all right to try to settle the matters of just what, and just how, a local cohort of social actors do what they are doing, so long as one recognizes that any time such a matter gets settled "it only gets settled for the time being. If you cannot take the two[7] together, then ethnomethodology is not for you." This is a very severe form of discipline under which to undertake microsociological studies, but it is one that always keeps oneself open for *what one does not yet know.* At the very least, the aim in micro-level studies of Tibetan philosophical practices should be to preserve and sustain the site of the Tibetans' own philosophical efforts. Above all, that site should not be lost, as it is for most Tibetological inquiry, for only within those intimacies can any real life phenomena be observed.

The Missing Interactional "What"

Garfinkel offers the keen insight that not only do most theoretically constructivist, ("principled") strategies of disciplinary analysis miss the identifying social praxis, they missed it *necessarily* by virtue of the principled methodologies that such researchers assiduously employ. Garfinkel (1977a, 10) criticizes authoritative textual studies that operate by "formulating some body of professional work as a mystery, and then, after settling upon authoritative writings, and entirely by reading and writing texts, solving the mystery." Such mysteries are essentially mysteries for only a small cohort of researchers, and they have little to do with the actual interests of the people being studied. The studies are essentially literary enterprises that work by fitting concepts together. The life-world of a people is engaged—"colonized" is a more accurate term—only to the extent that they can provide a canvas for the sketching of some of these disciplinary notions. Instead of concept-fitting, Garfinkel recommends working more empirically by studying "the locally produced real worldliness of ordinary activities."

The real discipline for Garfinkel and ethnomethodology is to recover what Garfinkel and Wieder (1992, 203) call "the missing interactional What," that is, to investigate *what* people are actually doing. This "What" is the topic that should be of principal interest to any social scientist, yet this "What" has gone missing in much social research, in large part because the "What" is an *activity* and not a thing. Accordingly, the disciplinary task now becomes capturing what methods the people themselves use in their local setting, as a matter of their routine lives, to do the work that is the heart of their life-world. The ethnomethods used by the people who staff the culture being studied must be located, identified, and described in that work's own identifying details, and these ethnomethods cannot be invented in advance, even during one's composition of applications for research grants, because they are *only* to be *discovered.* That is be-

---

7. That is, "the matter is settled" and the "for the time being."

cause they are the proprietary activities of the people one is studying. Oddly, the very mundaneity of such affairs makes their investigation uninteresting to most positivist researchers, whose imagination is sparked principally by their own disciplinary interests. Again, the local work of naturally producing a setting's orderliness is difficult to notice because it is like the water in which fish are swimming, yet once it is noticed it seems that it is everywhere one turns, and its intricate detail can exceed the capacity of any method for investigating it.

Tibetological scholarship has failed to capture the identifying details of the Tibetans' own worksite practices of reasoning. Instead, the emphasis has been upon certain philosophical ideas themselves. Some of this was motivated, as in the case of Desideri, to prove that the Tibetans' fundamental philosophical and religious tenets were flawed, and an empirical engagement with local social practices was not even an interest. Early Tibetological scholars were concerned to do battle with heathenism or "Lamaism," a term popularized by L. Austin Waddell, the son of a Scottish Presbyterian minister who served as a colonial functionary in Darjeeling, an imagined nihilism[8] (again the product of European misinterpretation), and the atheism that is a component of Buddhist practice. In contrast to this, we propose that studies of Tibetan philosophical culture study the actual praxis of Tibetan scholars by treating reason as the haecceity of ordinary Tibetan scholastic society. Tibetan scholasticism may be a literary and theoretical society, but we do not want to begin and end with "generically theoretical representations," as Garfinkel calls it, but with logic as the endogenous work of their philosophizing. As Dreyfus (2002) has discerned, "The mark of [Tibetan] scholarly competence is not the possession of the literary skills usual in Tibetan culture but the ability to engage in intricate oral debates." It is the aim of this study to make some of that intricacy available to the readers.

If the gloss, "the missing interactional What," offers a coarse definition of our research objective, the target of ethnomethodological inquiry is more formally presented by Garfinkel (1998, 108):

> how members concert their activities to produce and exhibit the coherence, cogency, analysis, consistency, order, meaning, reason, and methods—which are locally, reflexively accountable orderlinesses—in and as of their ordinary lives together in detail.

Gisela Hinckle (Korenbaum 1977, 35) has abbreviated this description by stating that the task is "to communicate the sense of order that is reflexively maintained." "Reflexive" here does not refer simply to thinking, but to the parties' continual monitoring of their *in vivo* social productions; by a sort of feedback, members of a social enterprise adjust their behavior to produce the necessary social alignments and to develop and achieve the practical interests at hand. That is, *social life is dynamic*, and any scientific social research will capture it as

---

8. Waddell's (1972, 10) term was "sophistic nihilism."

such, spurning any opportunity to reduce it to a more easily tamable but static literary reduction.

Theodor Adorno (2000, 72) has advised, "Method cannot be posited as absolute in opposition to its subject matter; rather, the method of sociology must stand in a living relationship to this subject matter and must, as far as possible, be developed from it." In Tibetan studies, the notion of developing one's methods *from* the living subject matter is considered to be a dangerous, romantic, and practically treasonous abandonment of one's professional responsibility to the civilizing project of the Enlightenment. Nevertheless, for ethnomethodological research the only methods that are of interest are the ethnomethods employed by the people themselves, and the methods that ethnomethodologists employ are uniquely adequate to the particular ethnomethods that have been located. They are unique because they are identical with "What" the people are doing only there. Accordingly, ethnomethodologists cannot speak on behalf of "all Tibetans," as might have been done in the halcyon days of Promethean anthropology, but only on behalf of the actual people whose lives one has engaged and whose ethnomethods are documented in one's research materials. The very methods that these people use to signal their activities to each other, and to make observable their collaborative work in producing the orderliness of their ordinary society, are—because they are designed for their observability—available to the ethnomethodological researcher. And those methods are uniquely adequate for those occasions. They can only be discovered. It would be a caricature of cultural imperialism to presume that they could be anticipated in advance of the field research.

In one ethnomethodological inquiry after another there seems to be two alternative projects at hand. First, there exists an established version of a given social world, and that version is usually presented in a formal literature. According to Garfinkel (2002), "It is not that the established literature is wrong. It is that it is absurd." Its absurdity arises from its irrelevance to what the people, on behalf of whom the literature speaks, are actually doing. The second project is an ethnomethodological investigation that respecifies the topics in terms of the actual looks of the world from the perspective of the actors themselves, capturing their horizon of meaning and their practical activities in as much of its particular details as possible. Garfinkel advises caution: "Fascination for what the people are really doing will get you into a lot of trouble because the authors of the established literature will become antagonistic." In the present case, there exists a huge corpus of established Tibetological research that has topicalized Tibetan philosophical practices but has missed the in-the-course character of what Tibetan scholars are actually doing. Our own inquiries are not investigating the transcendentalized logician or the philosophy as a recitation of its principles; instead, our objective is a description of the work of the actual, endogenous philosophers inscribed in their world, and what that world looks like to them.

An Ethnomethodological Respecification of Reason

Philosophy is more than knowledge. Robert Williams (1992, 103) has argued, "Knowledge can never be simply a matter of immediate assertion or *a priori* determinations, but requires the overcoming of one-sidedness, partial insight and error. Truth cannot be simply immediate, although immediacy is a 'moment' of truth." In other words, "philosophy" is a practice. Kant was fond of saying that one cannot learn philosophy, but only how to philosophize; that is, philosophy is not a matter of theories but consists of particular practices, ways of thinking, dialectics, etc., that must continually be attended to: philosophy is an activity. It is dynamic, it moves; and if it is to be captured by social researchers, it must be caught as it moves, on-the-wing as it were, or its essence will be missed. The real activity of a philosophical culture is visible only as a course of affairs. Ethnomethodology can carry us, in a rigorous way, to an identification and appreciation of the very practices that constitute logic and reason. But the object of such inquiries is not philosophy construed as a body of docile texts but as the locally produced orderliness of ordinary philosophical activities.

The production of a local orderliness consists of the very practices with which indigenous philosophers make the work of their reasoning observable to each other. And all of the well-known work of formal reasoning—providing coherent argumentation, offering evidence, giving grounds, being rational, identifying inconsistencies, etc.—are not to be described merely in their theoretic versions but can be respecified as the *in situ*, local, and concrete social accomplishments of the philosophers. Because scholars, in their philosophizing, give and receive warrant for the products of their collaborative reflections, they are continuously making this work *of theirs* observable for each other. In their philosophical discourse they do not merely formulate assertions, they exhibit a course of reasoning for each other so that all of the parties can share, amend, validate, reject, develop, etc., that course of reasoning. And because this work is exhibited in public it is available *also* to the scrutiny of researchers, should they care to notice; in this way the methods that these scholars use to carry out their ordinary work are identifiable by ethnomethodological investigators. Instead of imposing an alien order of inquiry to organize the indigenous philosophical activities, the methods of the indigenous practitioners themselves direct the researcher about what to study. Such a project of research is much more difficult to accomplish than reading a collection of texts in one's study at home, or in a room in a Tibetan monastic university.

A course of philosophical argument is a real world activity, although the results that appear in docile texts may seem to be disengaged and universal in their character. These arguments do not appear in the natural world unless their way has been prepared by the elaborate work of scholars who are engaged in organizing their discourse to provide for an orderliness that can permit anything like philosophical reflection to occur. For example, the cogency of any argument is only demonstrably cogent, and any such demonstrations are performed on the scene by philosophers for philosophers, within the philosophers' collective talk. Philosophy first finds itself already embodied in the organizational work that is involved. If a disengaged version of philosophy is encountered, it is certain that in addition to the work of organizing the philosophizing, the disengagement of the products of the philosophizing from that philosophizing has been organized as well.

In formal reasoning much of the exhibition of the local organization of philosophizing is achieved by means of "legitimate" argument and philosophical formulations. Ethnomethodological researchers pay attention to "how formalizations are developed and used in and as local courses of practical actions" (Lynch 1993, 25). The formal character of Tibetan debate demands that participants communicate clearly with each other about the developing rigor of a course of argumentation, and this communication takes place mostly by means of logical formulations that are made to occupy places within a formal dialectics. A logical superstructure, so to speak, is erected along with (sometimes afterwards, sometimes before) some philosophical insight. This formal apparatus is the means with which Tibetan scholars pursue their inquiries, and on occasion it variously assists, directs, impedes, or distorts the development of philosophical insight. It *is* the philosophizing.

Because the philosophizing of Tibetans depends heavily upon the formal presentation and development of logical formulations, Tibetan philosophical debate provides a setting that makes the work of formal analytic reasoning perspicuous; accordingly, one can learn a good deal about philosophical practice by making a careful study of it. However, because the philosophical work is embedded within such a rich, and unfamiliar, collection of local particular details it is often impenetrable to shallow social inquiries. In Garfinkel's (2001, 19) terms, such local work consists of "the holy hellish *concreteness* of things." Once one has located the actual worksite of indigenous practitioners one becomes swamped by the details. Further, when one begins to speak about those details, there may be no end to their telling. A serious risk is whether any audience will have the interest or the patience to learn such a level of detail. But there is no alternative but to try to make one's way through what Bar-Hillel (1964) calls "the jungle of daily discourse":

> The deeper we go into the jungle, the more difficult it is to advance. More than once, the pathways we uncover re-grow with savage vegetation that threatens to return us to our former condition. Scholars are attracted in droves to the few areas where the sun has arisen, instead of continuing to open up the jungle.

At this point there is every incentive for the sociologist to summarize, to theorize one's way through the data, and to seek shortcuts that abbreviate the particular details of the local work of philosophizing, instead of seeking out the ethnomethods that the parties themselves use to make their way through that "holy hellish" complex of affairs of theirs. In brief, the temptation is to talk "about" the work of the parties instead of describing the *in vivo* looks of the world for its inhabitants. William James (1890, 221-22) offered an important distinction between the intimate "knowledge of acquaintance" and a "knowledge about" that operates at a distance from the former knowledge. Elaborating upon this distinction, Alfred Schutz (1971, Vol I: 93) contrasted vague knowledge "about" a phenomenon's general style and structure with the explicit knowledge "of" its elements. Following Schutz, Garfinkel has insisted that ethnomethodological researchers address themselves to the intimate study *of* the ethnomethods practiced by social actors and eschew mere talk *about* what the actors may be doing in their work.

To talk merely *about* the philosophical practices of Tibetan debaters, one can assume the standpoint of the universal observer. In classical social anthropology, this researcher was nowhere visible in the ethnographic account. In the case of Tibetan philosophical debate, a study might be carried out by observing debating carefully from a distance, and judgments might be made *about* the methods of debaters, their adequacy, originality, etc. But that would be like studying a rat being cornered by a cat while doing one's investigation while gazing in from outside the kitchen window. One can record all the events of the encounter, produce exhaustive lists of the strategies a rat uses to survive, including critical assessments of those strategies, etc.; however, until one surveys the horizon of the event (the looks of the world) from the perspective of the rat in the corner who is looking for her way out, one will not know the phenomena very intimately nor be capable of judging fairly what originality may be involved in the rat's efforts to escape. Until one has had one's thinking cornered by a clever dialectician, or at least come to witness the looks of the world from the perspective of one so dialectically cornered, one is in no position to sit in pronouncement of the originality of Tibetan scholarship, as Tibetologists have done. To cite here just three additional Tibetological diminutions of Tibetan philosophical practice, Tucci (1987, 33) has commented, "Hardening of the arteries set in with the threat of formulas replacing the mind's independent striving after truth . . . . A tendency to formalism and worship of the letter gained ground on spiritual research." Ruegg (1989, 8) has complained about an overdone "intellection of apophaticism." And Smith (1969, 10) has denigrated Tibetan dialectics as the mere "parroting" of memorized sequences without really probing the underlying meanings.

Here ethnomethodological research can repair some of the damage done to Tibetans by colonialist research by retrieving the Tibetans' actual social practices. By following the philosophical dialectics of Tibetan scholars as a course of their developing reflections, rather than as a body of static ideas whose legitimacy is authorized by a study of docile texts undertaken without ever leaving one's library or with only the most casual observation made at some considerable distance from any live dialectics. Everything that philosophizing is—logic, reason, formal argumentation, etc., including all of the topics vital to Buddhist philosophical reflection—can be respecified as the worldly work of live, interacting professional Tibetan scholars; and it can be identified, captured, described, and analyzed in its material particular details just in the way those details are witnessed and used by the Tibetan scholars themselves. Here we have another instance of a procedurally accountable technical formal analytic tradition—Tibetology—that misses the *actual* orderliness of a social phenomenon that is their subject matter (see Garfinkel 2002, 104), and we have an alternative ethnomethodological investigation paired with it that recovers the endogenous, *in vivo* world as it is experienced *in its course* by the debating Tibetan scholar-monks themselves.

The Ethics of Ethnomethodological Inquiries

Up to this point we have been discussing the methodological benefits of taking seriously the actual practices of reasoning of Tibetan scholars and investigating them as phenomena in their own right. But there is another reason for recommending the strategies of ethnomethodological research: taking people seriously, and studying them in their own life-world, is an ethical way to treat research subjects.[9] Much of the ethical damage inflicted by Tibetological methods can be repaired by adopting ethnomethodological analyses that take their direction from the real things that research subjects are doing as their day's work. We have observed that the methods of ethnomethodology are uniquely adequate to the ethnomethods employed by the people being studied and that these methods "are only to be discovered." In restraining the imposition of methods and ontological interests that are external to the life-world of a people and in seeking to discover what is most identifying about their social life, the sociological skill rests as much in what the researcher refrains from doing as it does in what active things the researcher does. When one *discovers* a people's world only after, and by means of, meeting with them, one is treating people in a just manner. In order to *see* what the Other is doing, one cannot presume that one already knows what they are doing better than the people themselves do. A fundamental respect for the life of a given people may be implicit in ethnomethodology's relative *inactivity*, by its willingness to suspend its theorizing until endogenous social practices display themselves from themselves. In fact, some humility can improve the quality of sociological scholarship.

Edward Said (1978, 3) alleged that Orientalism is "a Western style for dominating, restructuring, and having an authority over" the people it investigates. Ethnomethodology does not seek "an authority over" its research subjects. Such a demurral from methodological arrogance contributes to ethics in socio-

---

9. Cf. also Liberman (1999b).

logical scholarship. A discipline that respects the ethnomethods of a people treats people with more dignity than do methods that reduce research "subjects" to *objects*, thereby robbing them of their epistemological freedom and any real subjectivity. By asking, "What is it in the praxis of Tibetan scholars that preserves for them the productive life of their thought?" and by retrieving from Tibetological obfuscation the ordinary society of Tibetan philosophical culture, ethnomethodologists are respecting the authority of the Tibetans. There is an important ethical dimension to this.

Certainly such an ethical position cannot be assured by statute, however, and ethnomethodology is not immune from methodological arrogance. On the contrary, as ethnomethodology has developed it too has generated its own orthodoxies of method that have from time to time lost sight of the difficult reflexive work necessary to preserve the authority of the subjects under study. In any microsociological research there is a danger of simply applying mindlessly one or another routine of analysis, and this can even be done with a professional swagger. Garfinkel has called one such research routine "an ethnography of sentences." Although one may begin by following the lead of one's subjects, once one's interests are established it becomes a facile matter to poke around and collect whatever and only what matches with those interests. The "sentences" one identifies may be collected empirically and gathered verbatim on video or audio, but instead of identifying the complex, autochthonous ethnomethods being exercised, the transcripts of the tape are simply colonized for one's own proprietary interests. There are no ready and routine methods, ethnomethodological or otherwise, that are capable of guaranteeing that the authority of the ethnomethods is respected. One can only retain a reflexive attitude to one's methodology and try to keep observing how one's formulations of the local practices may be distorting one's vision.[10]

In these investigations, our principal interest is not to review the formal insufficiencies of Reason (Husserl), nor the social or political hegemonies that influence reasoning (Foucault), nor its place in the history of Buddhist ideas or even Buddhist practice, etc., but to investigate empirically and in its identifying details—that is, in the very way in which reasoning works—how the Tibetans' formal reasoning, *by* its very own practices and *as* its very own practices, accomplishes, enhances, and constrains their philosophical reflection. By claiming to be investigating "dialectics" we are not even taking that term as a sign for a European practice; rather, along with Gadamer we are recovering the more basic meaning of that term as the fundamental dialogical character of language and thinking. Gadamer writes (cited in Dallmayr 1987, 134), "It was my intention to grasp dialogue as the original phenomenon of language. This meant simultane-

---

10. This practice is related to the sort of self-purification recommended originally by Husserl. But Husserl himself tried to routinize such "purification." There are no safe and secure methods — only a self-critical vigil, and nothing routine, is adequate to the task.

ously a hermeneutical reconstruction of 'dialectics,' that is, an attempt to trace dialectics—construed by German idealism as a speculative methodology—back to the art of living dialogue." It is also not to even privilege individual subjectivity (also a component of European idealism) or any European doctrine such as phenomenology that systematically invokes it. Rather, as a social practice the agency of reason is discoverable as the concerted participation of philosophical colleagues. While surely cultural prejudice of some sort is unavoidable (as Gadamer has also taught us), the ontological and epistemological values we bring to the research can be critically and reflexively examined. Such reflexive criticism also has ethical consequences. Phil Agre (1998) has commented, "Ethnomethodology is at bottom an ethical project—a resistance to the reduction of the world to its formal aspects."

Critics of ethnomethodology have complained that its practice of recording, in all of its minutae, the looks of the world for actors and describing the particular details of *just what* they are doing is too esoteric a method, but that is a distortion of the facts. Ethnomethodology is specifically exoteric, directed as it is to the mundane specifics of the everyday world. Rather, formal analytic social science, whose interests operate at such a great remove from the interests of the people they study, is the discipline whose practices are esoteric. It is only because those interests are the familiar and time-honored but parochial interests of established disciplines that their esoteric character is unrecognized.

Unfortunately, as ethnomethodology has matured, it has come to develop its own disciplinary interests which themselves threaten to eclipse the life-world of the subjects; however, those parochial interests can be kept in check by the reflexive discipline of the methodology. Without relief, Garfinkel always asks of himself, and of his students, the question, *"How is it that I can lose the phenomenon?"* This question interrogates the methods that one has developed and challenges any reductions of the indigenous phenomenon that may be in force, including the diabolic ways in which the sociologist's own practices foster their own delusions. The interests of conversational analysis, for example, have so matured that in some versions they have become routinized to the point that there is a danger of their losing the reflexivity and becoming an off-the-shelf methodology, readily taught and replicated but blind to some of the ethnomethodological phenomena that should be motivating them. In fact it is not only the genius of their madness but also the relative ease of replication that has contributed to the popularity of conversation analysis in academic departments. Some conversational analysts could well analyze Tibetan debate for the properties of their ordering their talk and miss entirely any philosophical interests that Tibetans might display or how those concerns might affect their strategies for organizing the interaction. While analyzing adjacency pairs, for example, is a pertinent analysis to make of Tibetan dialectics, it is hardly necessary to go all the way to Himalayas and spend ten years learning Tibetan in order to restrict one's research to adjacency pairs.[11]

It is not only a few conversation analysts who have at times reduced Garfinkel's method to slogans. With the maturation of ethnomethodology has come the development of standards and conventions that threaten to reduce ethnomethodological practitioners to positivists, devoid of any serious insight into the workings of reflexivity in their own methodological practice. More attention is paid to following rigor in the preparation of transcripts or about how those transcripts should be placed in a monograph than to the life-world practices of the people under investigation. In their effort not to ontologize their research, an increasing number of ethnomethodologists avoid training in phenomenological reflection, despite the fact that the cultivated suspicions that Heidegger, Gadamer, Merleau-Ponty, and Derrida have for routines of method in thinking (especially when they are radicalized by Garfinkel's reading of them) could expand their ethnomethodological sight.

In the present study, we do not need to read "philosophy" into the work of the Tibetans, but we do want to witness what *they* are doing. We hardly need more transcendental arguments, but in the words of Lynch (1993, xvi) we need "thick ethnographic accounts of knowledge-producing activities." In these investigations we pay particular attention to the ordering of the Tibetans' talk-in-debate, and the organizational issues *for the Tibetans* are pivotal to our research; however, we cannot lose the philosophical pursuits that motivate many of the scholars we are studying. For one thing, the transcripts of their debating are unintelligible without some cognizance of their philosophical interests. To lose their philosophical pursuits, and to substitute for them some irrelevant disciplinary interests from discourse analysis, would have ethical problems of its own, for that would be to lose the phenomenon in just the way that Howard Becker lost the jazz music in his famous study "The Dance Musician." Ethnomethodology does not get a free pass from these ethical concerns. There are no free passes, no matter how compelled microsociological researchers may feel to seek security in some orthodoxy of methods. Respecting the phenomenon means respecting the people, and vice versa. And we need to do more than throw a bone in the direction of the interests of the subjects, as Rips et al. (1999, 175) do when they write, "In addition to dialogue structure, the content of individual moves is obviously important." Here our phenomenon, and it is no "additional" matter, is the active work of Tibetan scholars in understanding philosophical matters while maintaining the order in a debate.

---

11. Conversation analysts have expressed some incredulity regarding why I would need to travel so far to undertake ethnomethodological studies. The flaw may be that their imagination has been limited to the extraordinary disciplinary achievements they have secured, obscuring from their sight the relevance that the practices of non-Europeans may have for their interests. In the end, it is an ethnocentrism of another order.

But we are not doing philosophy, we are doing sociology. Our inquiry is not motivated by the topics that the Tibetans are debating; rather our interest is in *how* they debate and *how* they reason. Our first goal is to present an accurate and detailed account of what they do. Then we are interested in analyzing their ordinary work of formalizing their thinking to learn how that work assists them to think or may limit what they think. It may be that such assistance and limitation applies not merely to Tibetans but to thinking in general, and if and when that is so, then there will be philosophical anthropological consequences to our investigations. Some of our findings will be pertinent only to Tibetan philosophical debate; other findings may be relevant for discourse in general; and there will be some elements that will pertain to formal analytic discourse in particular. If that occurs, and the inquiry becomes a philosophical inquiry, it will not be a "philosophical" that started out as philosophy. It will be an inquiry that commenced with the practices and interests of Tibetan philosophical practitioners and took those interests seriously, as a phenomenon worthy of study in its own right, the disciplinary priorities of Tibetology or ethnomethodology notwithstanding. The task is to retrieve the ordinary society of Tibetan scholars who philosophize, and the priority here—which is ethical and well as professional—is to capture the looks of their world, for them.

The Particularity of Interaction's Technical Details

Because people interact with particulars and not generalities, ethnomethodology scrutinizes the specific details of people's ordinary work with an eye for what makes up that work's technical expertise. That ethnomethodology's interest is *always* technical is no solace for the reader who must quickly bring her/himself up to speed on the expertise of some local practices if one is to win any vision into the endogenous looks of the world. While the in-the-course character of the phenomenon can be made available, the costs to the reader are not moderate. One must enter the life-world of others and gain the same sort of expertise that members of that world have, and not a few readers will give up before the expertise is won. Lynch (1993, 285) writes that although the talk of the laboratory scientists he studies can be made sensible, "it is sensibily related to an immediate complex of activities, things, equipment, and horizonal possibilities. But to see how that is so, we must stay in tune with the 'thises and that's.'" Lynch (1993, 104) also remarks,

> "Social" phenomena are inextricably bound to "thick" technical talk and action. To demonstrate these phenomena requires tutoring one's audience in the competence systems in which the actions are embedded. Even then, readers are likely to treat "thick" description as "opaque" description or "tedious reportage."

The last two adjectives (in scare quotes) were lifted from a book review of one of Lynch's earlier ethnomethodological studies of scientific practices. The technical detail of laboratory scientists is certainly a challenging task to set for the reader of an ethnography; however, the technical detail of Tibetan scholars who are practicing an essentially medieval philosophical practice from a non-Western spiritual tradition in a non-European language may present readers with a task that is impossible. Recognizing the difficulty of the problem that ethnomethodology's preoccupation with technical details presents, Garfinkel (2001) has suggested, "Do what you can to ease the frustration to the reader when describing the properties that are only witnessable." But such witnessing can come only at the cost of learning, in its local details, the practices that people develop together for providing the orderliness of their ordinary lives. This requires a considerable investment of intellectual energy. If the reader is to witness the life-world of an Other, and not merely rehearse again the routines and slogans of one's own discipline, s/he must learn *something new*. Garfinkel advises further, "There is no need to introduce any additional frustration into the reader's task by mystifying those properties." But how does one *not* mystify the practices of reasoning of Tibetan Buddhist monks? The heuristic task is immense, and the tedium is almost assured by the requirement to gain adequate technical expertise regarding their activities; nevertheless, everything here rests in the particulars, so we will do what we can.

One of the main difficulties is that the meaning of these debates are both overdetermined and, ultimately, indeterminate *not only* for us the readers, they are indeterminate *for the Tibetan debaters themselves*. The events in a debate move very quickly, and it is impossible for the participants, let alone the audience, to follow up every possible relation. The debaters themselves are not fully aware of what they are doing. Given that, how can I present a tidy account of their work that presumes to be complete? Many times I asked one of the debaters I filmed to review the tape and explain to me what he or his partner meant at a certain point. Very frequently they were not able to say precisely just what was intended. On occasion they would confess to me, "Well, I'm not really sure, maybe. . . ." If for them such indeterminacy is natural to the occasion, then this indeterminacy is not to be emasculated, even by a European analysis that prefers exactitude. It would be a sign of ethnomethodological rigor to sustain any indeterminacy that is really there. In this, ethnomethodology is compatible with Levinas's praise of meaning as infinity. That an indeterminacy or "infinity" is empirically true does not lessen the rigors of the labor that the reader faces.

Some debates are like koans—they are open-ended in their application. They contain interweaving thoughts that are deliberately left with their open horizon of possible sense. They are not always solved pieces but are live reflection, and the loose ends *are always capable of doing something more*. This can become dizzying for a reader, though that, too, is only more of "the looks of the world." But if the debaters remain open to further possibilities, then so must I, and so must the reader. As Garfinkel has advised, "Ethnomethodology is for those who know how to make sense of it. Those who would rather have Truth, in any of its forms, are better off to ignore it." In fact, one of the principal discoveries of this study is that Tibetan debaters themselves use the formal apophantic structure of their reasoning to clarify the indeterminacies that they face, to tie up the loose ends so to speak.

Can I say that because of the hundreds of hours I have spent analyzing each of these debates that I have mastered them? Mastery is too much to claim, and frequently even the debaters are unable to make such a claim. I can say that because of the time I've spent with the videotapes and transcripts, and because of the capabilities of such tools unavailable to previous scholarship, I understand some of the debates better than their participants; however, error-free understanding is unattainable. It may be that in attempting to exhibit the technical details of Tibetan philosophical debating I have presented more about the classical practices of Tibetan Buddhist formal analytic reasoning than any Western reader would care to know. But I have gone into extensive detail about their practices for the reasons that (1) they are interesting in their own right and deserve being carefully recorded while they are still available to scrutiny; (2) they provide a window into practices similar to those exercised during the classical period of South Asian philosophical scholarship, which are otherwise entirely unavailable; and (3) humanity needs to learn more, and in its technical detail, about the uses and abuses of formal analysis, since human beings' ability to think leads them everywhere to formally organize their thinking: for better or worse it is our nature, especially in philosophical cultures, to become *Homo apophantikos*, the species of the genus *Homo* that feels compelled to rely heavily upon formal analyses.

Two sorts of persons will be interested in reading this text closely. The first are students interested in practicing Tibetan dialectics or Tibetologists interested in learning more about debate. The second group are ethnomethodologists who have a technical interest in the *local details of the organization of rational discourse*. Other readers may find that too much work is required to learn the endogenous structures of Tibetan debating. Readers brought to this book by a casual fascination with Tibetan culture should be warned that the rigors of following ethnomethodological arguments may prove too great a price to pay for some increased understanding. Writing much of this book was like herding cats. The presentation could have been made more straightforward by adopting one or another taxidermal strategy, embalming the "cats" in analytic caricatures; but I wanted to keep the cats alive. This meant keeping the analysis open, refraining as best I could from providing "just so" stories about them, and somehow allowing the reader to get access to the actual phenomena instead of being exclusively dependent upon my representations.

I may not have been entirely successful, but I have labored hard at the task. Some of the phrases I used to describe the interaction-in-debate may appear too

profane or colloquial for use in a scholarly study of Tibetan philosophical practice (e.g. "jump start," "put-up or shut-up," "pulling the rug out," etc.); however,
the events I am describing are highly mundane in their own right, and my scholarly aim is to capture them in their everyday mundanity. To mystify these activities by employing the imperiousness of classical Tibetological studies is not
only to miss the phenomenon itself—the looks of the world for Tibetan debaters—but to misrepresent and misconstrue the endogenous practices for an idealized version of what they are. It may well be the case that my use of colloquial
phrasing is only another narrative device, frequently used in ethnomethodological scholarship to emphasize and convey the mundanity of their local affairs.
But the practice can earn its validity when it becomes a fair and objective description of the ordinary orderlinesses of Tibetan debating, and not their idealized representation.

Recognizing the problem of explaining the technical details of these affairs
in ethnographic prose, I began to experiment with referring the reader to video
and audio records of what I was describing. Because these records were in Tibetan this was quite challenging; however, gradually I experimented with a variety of interactive multimedia presentations of the data. This was highly appropriate since these analyses were heavily dependent upon the resources of multimedia software for analyzing microinteraction.[12] To the variety of ethnomethodological research tools—direct observation, interviews, participant observation,
video and audio documentation—must be conjoined a new one, multimedia
analysis. This led directly to an entirely new phenomenon in ethnographic
monographs: multimedia presentation. The demonstration of ethnomethodological arguments by means of multimedia materials promises to transform and in-
vigorate ethnomethodological pedagogy. Here I am not claiming success—this
is only a first attempt to augment the presentation of the technical details of microinteraction by referring readers to the multimedia tools which are available
separately from this textual edition.

Neither I nor the readers (nor even always the debaters) can claim an exhaustive expertise regarding the philosophical discourse with which the debaters
engage themselves. Nevertheless, it is hoped that those aspects that are valuable,
pertinent, and insightful about these Tibetan practices of reasoning and that can
be identified may also be communicated to the reader. At times I have drawn
upon the aid of multimedia materials for assistance in attempting this. Although
in the long run it may lighten the reader's load by rendering more lengthy ethnographic prose unnecessary, since the tape can present the same material in less
time, it also adds an additional burden to the reader's task—in addition to pur-
chasing the CD-ROM, some flipping back and forth between the CD-ROM and
the text will be necessary. Firing up a computer in the midst of some contented,
concentrated reading may prove to be inconvenient (we will learn together from

12. Cf. Liberman (2001).

this attempt). But observing directly the choreography of the Tibetans' debating is vital to an adequate appreciate the technical character of their art. The interactive buttons and video scrolls of the CD-ROM interface should help to facilitate repeated review of the data and serve to keep the temporality of the multimedia exegesis in the hands of the viewer. In much of the digital presentation, the debate proceeds turn by turn at the control of the viewer, and each turn includes the English translation, as well as explanatory notes, on the screen. Although the best strategy for using the CD-ROM is yet to be determined,[13] I would suggest viewing the introductory tutorial first, then reading chapter 3, and then viewing the more advanced tutorials (including "The Grammar of Tibetan Debate" and "Ethnomethods"). The reader can then read chapters 4 and 6, and study the "Illustrative Debates." Attempt the "Interactive Debate" in the Appendix (in which the viewer plays the role of a Defender) only after chapter 7 has been completed. The hope is that at times the multimedia presentation may assist the reader/viewer in winning access to the original phenomena, the actual—not imagined—looks of the world for Tibetan scholar-monks.

The Worksite

I lived for three years in Gelug and Sakya monastic universities. I also have some familiarity, and even had some formal association, with both Kagyu and Nyingma Tibetan orders, though I have not undertaken any detailed philosophical studies with them. I chose to focus my studies within the Gelug order, which is well known for its emphasis upon formal reasoning. Firstly, my original Tibetan teachers were Gelug sect practitioners. Secondly, being an academic myself I felt quite comfortable with the Gelugpa academic approach to philosophical knowledge. Finally, like many Westerners I was fascinated from the beginning with the vociferous and energetic philosophical debating that is emphasized by the Gelug order. The Sakya order also places considerable emphasis upon debating (but it amounts to only one or two hours a day instead of three to six hours), and I spent six months in a Sakya monastic university. The Kagyu and Nyingma practice some debating, but not so extensively as the Gelug or Sakya, and I have heard some Kagyu and Nyingma monks complain about the mistake of committing too much of one's energy to formal analytic exercises; occasionally they have stated a preference for more meditation earlier in a monk's career. Because Western academics feel so comfortable with the Gelug orientation, the philosophical methods of that order are better known than those of the other sects, and a number of Tibetologists have complained about that. It would be foolish here to reproduce these internecine debates, and they are especially unnecessary for Western students of Buddhism; however, it is important to make it

---

13. Yes, keep your cards and letters coming.

clear that the present account of philosophical dialectics cannot claim to be an exhaustive account of all Tibetan Buddhist practitioners.

Sera (*se rwa*) Monastic University, where most of my inquiries were undertaken, was established in 1419 by Jamchen Choje (*'jam chen schos rje*), one of the principal disciples of Lama Tsong Khapa, the founder of the Gelug sect. The Je college of Sera was created in 1481. It has been reestablished in South India following the Tibetan exodus of 1959, and their subsequent exile. Sera Je has twenty-two regional houses, which serve as dormitories and intellectual centers for the monks and serve Tibetans according to the home districts where they were raised; Sera Me has fourteen such regional houses. I lived quite happily for a time in one of those houses, but after six months I learned that a greater variety of Tibetan teachers were available to me if I lived independently of any formal house. In 1959, Sera in Tibet had a population of around 9,000 monks (Cabezòn 1997, 336). There were 1900 monks at Sera in South India during the thirteen months of my initial stay in 1991-1992, and in 2000 there were 3,200 monks, with new young monks arriving each week after making their way to the Nepalese or Indian border on foot.

Since Tibetans themselves read a great many texts in preparation for the public debates, I systematically read through most of the principal texts, at first in private tutorials and then in the Tibetans' ordinary classes (*dped khrid*). These included classical commentaries, but more usually they were college manuals and textbooks that were themselves written with an orientation to public debating. When Tibetans read more soteriological texts (e.g., the *Lam Rim, Gom Rim, Legs bshad snying po, Thong mthun chen mo,* etc.) it is usually as part of public festivals whose centerpiece is a famous lama, such as an Abbot or the Dalai Lama, so it is philosophy via pageant, and I have attended many hundreds of hours of these as well. The original *sutra* of the Buddha are never studied, except for the *Heart Sutra*. Throughout all of their preparations—which includes private reading, formal classes, individual tutorials, public teachings, etc.— philosophical debating remains the centerpiece of Gelug monastic culture, and argument and disputation exceeds lecturing in both the time Gelug scholars devote to their study and in the energies they expend.

As quickly as I was able, I tried to participate in the debates. My new Tibetan colleagues were eager to invite me along for debating, but it seemed that (not being a monk) it was unseemly for me to take the role of a challenger, and I was usually relegated to the role of a defender. Since my language skills were not fully developed it was relatively easy for my friends to twist my words about, and I found that certain dialects from the more remote regions of Tibet were mostly unintelligible to me (actually, Tibetans themselves find it impossible to comprehend the speaking styles of the dialects of all the scholars on the debate grounds). Adding to my frustration was the sheer level of noise in the debating courtyard, where sometimes as many as five hundred voices can be shouting at once. Even in one debate there could be two or three questioners attacking a defender at one time. Audio recording such white noise was impossible, and so I endeavored to record some of the public examinations during which most of the audience remained in silent attendance.

During two years at Sera over four separate visits, I videotaped some twenty hours of formal debate, mostly on Madhyamaka topics. I prepared for those by reading most of the critical texts involved, in classes and in private tutorials. The best recordings were filmed during the annual public examinations when each debater was being ranked by a panel of senior scholars. Because they were being evaluated, the debaters put their best arguments forward. Also, the other young scholars present, who would usually be shoving their way in to pose their own questions, respected the priority of the examinee's arguments. These debates were relatively short, typically ten minutes in duration; such a short period provided me with technical detail limited enough for me to be capable of mastering. Of these debates I selected fifteen for transcription, guided by their rankings (which were posted), my own judgment of the debate, and the recommendation of colleagues. I translated all of these fifteen debates and spent many dozens of hours analyzing each one, and more frequently hundreds of hours when the time for the transcribing and translation, and showing them to the debaters being filmed and to other colleagues, is included. My field work required three years of residence in monastic universities, and it was proceeded by six years of Tibetan language study. The transcription, rechecking the transcription, making the translation, rechecking the translation, analyzing, posing questions about my analyses, etc., occupied an additional three years. Only after these tasks did the writing begin, which itself was interrupted by heart surgery, and by having to reanalyze some debates, and also by the need to spend two additional years learning the multimedia programs necessary for me to analyze my tapes digitally and to prepare the digital record on the CD-ROM.

Even after such a length of time I was faced with the questions, how many debates were enough and how much analysis was sufficient. Many ethnomethodological researchers prefer to analyze a few minutes of microinteraction with terrific care and attention. Feeling responsibile to capture the phenomenon in a way that was ethnographically faithful to the broader phenomenon of philosophical discourse among Gelug scholars, I spread my ethnomethodological analyses over a larger corpus (some 150 minutes or so of debating). I learned that when the phenomena came to be familiar, and even began to be repetitive, I had tape-recorded and analyzed a sufficient number of debates. And when my collection had covered a fair portion of the topics raised in the formal classes I attended, I considered that I had done justice to the Tibetans' enterprise. It was only after a thousand hours of reviewing the debates that I began to get a sense for the spontaneity of the negative dialectics that Tibetans practice.

Key to the Transcription

The reader will quickly observe that the transcripts are verbatim. They contain partial sentences, half-baked syllogisms and a number of "Mm"s and "Uhh"s. When irrelevant exclamations grew to be too much of an obstacle to the readers' understanding of an already difficult philosophical utterance I deleted them, but only occasionally and only during the final stages of preparing the manuscript. There are a number of conventions employed in preparing the transcripts. "T" stands for "the person who clarifies the reasoning" (*rTags gsal gtang mkhan*) in a Tibetan debate, and "L" stands for the "respondent" (*Len pa po*). When there is more than one respondent, L', L", etc. distinguish their replies. A single slash ("/") on two adjacent lines indicates the start of a conversational overlap, and a double slash ("//") indicates the end of an overlap. The precise clock time from the videotape is retained and may be used to synchronize the reading of the transcript with the video or audio record on the CD-ROM. When a time is only approximate, the seconds appear in parentheses in the text. The times include precise times [e.g., 6:03:10] and approximate times [e.g., 6:03:(10)]; the audio times include three digits surrounded by a hyphen [e.g., -145-] when they are precise and surrounded by parentheses [e.g., (044)] when they are estimates. Anything appearing within parentheses is a best guess of what was uttered; when a reasonable guess cannot be attempted the space between the parentheses is left blank. Phrases that appear CAPITALIZED are phrases that are standardized performatives, tokens of the Tibetans' formal analytic argument. Italicized phrases in the transcripts are verbatim textual citations. Finally, the hand-gestures of the clarifier of the reasoning are indicated by a ">~" for a regular hand-clap and a "=v=" for a back-handed hand-clap. Each of the fifteen debates has been assigned a two-part number [e.g., "II.3"].

Chapter 3

The Organization of Reasoning in
Tibetan Philosophical Debates

Debating is like a river. It's not just a class, it flows all of the time.

—A young Tibetan scholar

At Sera Monastic University, from 8-10 AM in the mornings and especially from 5:30-10 PM in the evenings, a large roar slowly commences, gradually gaining in pitch and force, similar to the way mosquitoes begin to stir on summer mornings in Alaska. From where I was lodged, two blocks away, the roar speaks with one voice. It moves in pitch and volume with the shifting wind, and so is akin to a natural element. As one walks in the direction of the tumult, one begins to distinguish individual hand-claps (sounding something like rain on a rooftop) among the hundreds of pairs of hands, and an occasional shout that is distinctly human. The roar waxes and wanes with the wind and with the enthusiasm of the participants, so one recognizes that it is an orderly phenomenon and not a riot, although it is riotous.

Upon approaching the Dharma Court (*chos rwa*), one sees that the sound is coming from several hundred maroon-robed monks, divided in pairs. Half of each pair is seated and the other is standing, posing philosophical quandaries to the seated party and punctuating the conclusion of each formulated quandary with a hand-clap. There is intensive listening as well as intensive speaking. These are Tibetan debaters, monks in training who are practicing philosophical reflection in public, en masse, and with considerable enthusiasm.

Dialectics

Philosophy has its heritage in dialogue. Long before our present era of philosophical soliloquy, ancient philosophers pursued the problems of human reason and experience within living reason and experience within living dialogues in which thinking was a public activity. The term "dialectic" has etymological affinity with the word "dialect," which in Greek means "conversation." Dialectical reason had its origin in the West with the Socratic "dialogue," in which the pursuit of truth was a process of discussion that depended upon the understandings of two or more persons to carry the inquiry to deeper and unanticipated levels. Reasoning was a public art.

In the East, philosophy developed as a public art also. In the classical period of South Asia, the Hindu and Buddhist scholars pursued their religious and philosophical inquiries in public forums where they debated critical issues in logic, epistemology, and metaphysics. Hindu and Buddhist records are filled with accounts of famous debates, and most of their central texts are essentially written summaries of these oral dialectics. In both the West and East these ancient dialectical traditions are much diminished; however, the classical form of South Asian philosophical debate, which was carried to Tibet in the twelfth century, persists today as the *contemporary* philosophical praxis of Tibetan scholar-monks living and training at the few Buddhist monastic universities that have survived within the Tibetans' exile.

Buddhist dialectics achieved its defining synthesis during the period of Dharmakirti (seventh century), the great logician who formalized the rules of argument that had been practiced in India during the preceding six centuries. It is from Dharmakirti that the Tibetan scholars find the authority for their debate practices, which have remained virtually unchanged since Phyva-pa Chos-kyi Seng-ge (1109-1169) first adapted and promoted the system in Tibet.[1] Observers have long appreciated the Tibetan scholars' commitment to logical analysis and philosophical reflection. Stcherbatsky praised the Tibetans for their philosophical system "based on observation of facts and free logical proofs allowing and even inviting free criticism."[2] It is the classical system of Buddhist dialectics that provides for the Tibetans a system of discourse that features methodic reasoning based upon logic.

Valid cognition in Buddhism (Skt. *pramana*, Tib. *tshad ma*) includes the application of formal rules for reasoning. This reasoning may take the form of "syllogisms" (*rang rgyud kyi gtan tshigs*[3]) or what is termed "consequence" logic (Skt. *prasangika*, Tib. *thal 'gyur*). Generally, two scholars pair off—a sitting "respondent to the reasoning" (*rigs len pa*) defends a philosophical position against the logical challenges of a standing "person who clarifies the reasoning" (*rtags gsal gtang mkhan*) and who punctuates each logical challenge with a firm clap of his hands not far above the nose of the sitting defender. There is a saying common among young Tibetan debaters: "If we didn't base the debate upon

1. Vostrikov (1935, 151-76).
2. Stcherbatsky, "Philosophical Doctrine of Buddhism," in D. Chattopadhyaya (1979, 54).
3. Cf. Tsong Khapa (1997, 674). Also *rtags sbyor* (cf. Baso Chokyi Gyalsten, et al. 700) is a relevant term.

texts and reasoning, we'd be forced to debate with sticks and stones." Although mature scholars have debated in such a fashion for more than a millennium, debate is more frequently the specialization of younger scholars during their period of a dozen or so years of training in topics that include the processes of mental construction (*bsdus grwa*, or "collected topics"), modes of knowledge (*blo rigs*), tenets of the philosophical schools (*grub mtha'*), ways of using formal analytic reasoning (*rtags rigs*), and idealistic (*sems tsam pa*) and nondualist (*dbu ma pa*) philosophical traditions.

In the Tibetan monastic universities philosophical debate is an everyday, all day long affair. Debate is not merely a supplementary means of philosophical study and investigation, it is the perpetual *medium* of the university's activities. While the Tibetans' philosophical debating is based upon the philosophical practices of classical Buddhism, the Tibetans have reorganized it systematically and possibly place more emphasis upon it, having found numerous ways to exploit the medium for pedagogical purposes. In fact, classroom instructions are more or less appendages to the debates, and professors' (*gde bshes*) discussions of texts are directed to the principal debates they contain or that may be developed based upon them. Students orient to these instructions with an eye to what debates they can produce during the five or six hours of daily debate sessions (*chos ra*) that take place in the courtyards of the monastery before and after class. A graduate of the Tibetan Institute of Buddhist Dialects told me, "Debating is like a river. It's not just a class, it flows all of the time."

This focus upon debating commences with the very first years of a monk's studies. The initial instruction in ratiocination, which takes place during the first three years of study, involves the *Collected Topics* (*bsdus grwa*), which in its wider sense constitutes introductory dialectics (Onoda 1992, 38). The material is taught by means of debate forms, often to students who are not yet literate and who may have walked into the monastery directly from a childhood and adolescence as nomadic pastoralists. As Onoda (1992, 28) informs us, "The purpose of *bsdus grwa* is not only to know basic theoretical schema, but also to acquire the practical mastery of debating techniques which will be indispensable for further, more advanced study." The opportunity to engage in lively mental jousts with their peers raises in these adolescents a keen interest and determined commitment to study and preparation, and this serves to jumpstart their academic careers. One of the first steps in the cultivation of a philosophical imagination is getting a young scholar to begin to doubt daily experience and to begin to observe that things and the ideas of things are constantly conflated. The *bsdus grwa* literature, especially its being conveyed within live scholastic disputations, provides such an introduction by teaching, for example, that the meaning of a pot is not a pot and by pointing out the effects of the structural relations of logical categories upon thinking and belief. The *bsdus grwa* literature, which is a Tibetan innovation, plays a role in all Tibetan sects' studies. It was developed for the most part by Phyva-pa Chos-kyi Seng-ge at Sang-pu Monastery, which was founded in 1073 by Ngok Legpey Sherab (*rngog legs pa'i shes rab*), a Tibetan disciple of the Indian pandit Atisha (Onoda 1992, 23 and 69).

Extensive memorization takes place during the early stages of training, and even this involves public examination of how well one has memorized the texts. When a novice monk is tested, the supervising examiner may go out of his way to disrupt the monk's recitation to see how deeply ingrained is his memorization (Dreyfus 2002, 90). This moment of negation is an abiding presence throughout the training of a Tibetan scholar, whose thinking is destined to face frequent disruptions, sometimes in diabolical ways, in order to build a tenacious intellect that is able to accept some responsibility for what it knows.

This emphasis upon negative dialectics as an instructional methodology is largely a Tibetan innovation. Although public philosophical debates originated in India, it is likely that they were not as extensive there as they were in Tibet, especially within the Gelug monastic universities during the last two centuries. This contradicts those Indologists who claim that Tibetans contributed little of significance to Buddhism. In fact, Tibetans do not devote very much attention to the study of Indian texts. During three years of residence in Gelug and Sakya monasteries, I never once witnessed a Tibetan studying any Buddhist *sutra*, other than the short *Heart Sutra*, read primarily for ritual purposes.[4]

It was Sang-pu Monastery's emphasis upon philosophical scholarship that influenced the Kadampa tradition of Tibetan Buddhism, from which the Gelug sect was derived. Accordingly, the Gelug rely most heavily upon the study of *bsdus grwa*. In particular, Phyva-pa's reliance upon debating by means of the examination of logical consequences, instead of using the formal arguments more common to Indian logicians, led to the practice of negative dialectics becoming a distinctive feature of Gelug philosophical practice. Other Tibetan sects, who were more influenced by the *Pramanavarrtika* of Dharmakirti or by Sakya Pandita, did not adopt Phyva-pa's propensity for negative dialectics to the same degree as did the Gelugpa, although all traditions practice some form of public philosophical debate. Sera Je Monastery, created in 1481, today bases its study of *Collected Topics* upon the text by Pur-bu-chok (*phur bu lcog*, 1825-1901), which is a widely used debate manual. It may be said, then, that Sera Je Monastic University is squarely placed in the center of the Tibetan tradition of Buddhist negative dialectics.

During the second stage of a monk's academic career (at most Gelug institutions, years four through eight), the classes are devoted to a study of Maitreya's *Ornament of Higher Realization* (*mngon par rtogs pa'i rgyan*). During

---

4. I have observed the reading of the entire *kanjur* at a Kagyu monastery, but this was performed as a public celebration during which most members of the village sat picnicking outside the walls of the monastery listening to the reading while drinking large amounts of *chang*, the Tibetans' native beer. No one, not even the monks (some of whom shared in the drinking), paid the slightest attention to the content of the sutras.

this part of the curriculum young scholars are told that dull persons believe things without using logic,[5] whereas clever people always employ a reasoning-based knowledge. According to Dreyfus (2002, 181 and nd, 17), the goal of this study is not to undertake Buddhist practices or to engage in analytic inquiries, so much as it is to appropriate a narrative structure that can provide monks a means to place the entire course of their studies and Buddhist practice into a consistent and meaningful universe. Yet even here study proceeds by means of debating, during which their understanding of a topic is tested in a natural way. On occasion an entire class (some twenty monks) may develop an incorrect view that wins currency among them in a manner similar to how a rumor spreads. This mistaken view can continue for some time until they debate with students outside of their class, when the view is subjected to critical examination. In this fashion the practice of debating can play a corrective role in the learning process. For example, one *Ornament of Higher Realization* class came to the view that the nine gradations of reifying truth fit into the ten levels of a bodhisattva's progressive realization by dividing the fourth gradation of reificatory practice[6] into two parts, when the Sera Je textbooks consider it correct to divide the first gradation. The members of this class were corrected by their fellow students in the debating courtyard. Only after letting the debating continue for some time, since it was a pedagogically successful exercise, the Abbot confirmed the correctness of the perspective of those critiquing the class's wrong view.

When a teacher presents a portion of the text, he will engage each student in small debates about aspects of the reading. "Teachers debate in class to show students how to use debate to inquire into the relevant topics. The debates they propose are exemplary and students are encouraged to find their own" (Dreyfus 2002, 231). The students themselves will absorb new information with an eye for how it may play out in the debating that will follow later in the day, in the courtyards of the monastery. Preparing for the debating, and then testing one's views in debates, provides scope for study of considerable depth. As a neighbor of mine at Sera, Geshe Yonten Namgyal, commented to me, "One can read a philosophical manuscript for many days, and even think about it deeply, but when you put it aside and walk off you lose most of the meaning. Debate forces you to recall the meaning."

The third rung of monastic study at Sera Je and other Gelug institutions occupies two years of perhaps the most intensive study of a student's career, during which the Madhyamaka dialectics is read, memorized, absorbed, and debated. The negative dialectics of Madhyamaka philosophical analysis is well suited to Tibetan debate practice. For the most part, Tibetan scholars study these texts without pens, and instead of reading an extensive secondary literature, they

---

5. Here the term for logic was *tsad ma grub bzhin du dam bcha' ba rigs pa.*

6. They are speaking here of a positivist reification of the inherent essences of entities.

will examine exhaustively each of the topics on the debate grounds, covering all the vital theses of the curriculum and its principal text, Chandrakirti's *Introduction to the Middle Way* along with two commentaries (Tsong Khapa's *dbu ma dgongs pa rab gsal* and Jetsun Chokyi Gyaltsen's *dbu ma spyi don*). Argument and dispute far outweigh classes and lectures in importance. Newland (1996, 203) observes that the curriculum's focus on the debate manuals (*yig cha*) has displaced scholastic attention to fundamental treatises. That is, their study mostly involves contesting the ideas from various angles in heated dialectical discussions, fueled by the full hormonal energies of young adults locked in buoyant hand-to-nose intellectual combat.

That their study is driven by their concern for debatable matters was made evident one year during the class's study of *dbu ma dgongs pa rab gsal* by Tsong Khapa. The year commenced as usual with the preliminaries, the *ring song,* and the first practice gone-beyond (Giving), but then the Tibetan New Year (Losar) break came, which dragged on longer than usual due to exceptional teachings at the end of Losar. This put the entire class behind in their curriculum, and a number of students and the teachers of their tutorials (*dpe 'khri*) decided to skip the chapters on Ethics, Patience, Effort, and Concentration, since "There is not much debate in them." They proceeded directly to the main sixth chapter on Wisdom, which is rich in matters to be debated. Once half of the students had skipped to the Wisdom chapter, the others pressed their teachers to do so as well because they feared that they would lag behind in the debating and expose themselves to being embarrassed in the courtyard. That year the ethical teachings on "method" were eclipsed by the students' interest in juicy scholarly debates.

The final two stages of the curriculum involve several years of metaphysics (*abidharma*) and two to four years of studying proper discipline for monks (*vinaya*), topics which also are explored by means of debate in the courtyards.[7] Following this, monks wishing to receive their degrees (*ge shes*) will devote another year or two to review and then take their final examination, which itself is delivered by means of examination by public debate. In most cases the entire monastic program requires fifteen years to complete.

Exposing the world to dialectical investigation is a continuous practice to which young scholars are devoted with much enthusiasm. The first day I entered the Tibetan Institute of Buddhist Dialectics, a bright young monk, who could have been no older than twelve, challenged me with a logical syllogism emphatically punctuated with a confident clap of his hands. I have witnessed monks format debates over meals and during an argument in a game of handball. In his autobiography Rato Khyongla (1978, 110) has written,

> Many would remain and be so greatly interested that our debates lasted some-

---

7. For a more comprehensive review of the curriculum see Newland (1996) and Dreyfus (2002).

times to sunrise. Only when we heard the cocks crow would we stop, and I, as the one answering, could not leave as long as the challenging continued. But I do not recall ever having felt tired or hungry during those sessions. I had to concentrate my whole mind on the questions put to me, and the hours went by very fast.

These are not tales from the long-gone past, and the current generation of young Tibetan scholars continues to be energized by the process of daily philosophical debating. As the attendant of Song Rinpoche (who was fifteen years of age at the time of his attendant's remark; Hengst (2000, 63) describes, "He loves to debate so much that if he is eating and the debate bell rings, he won't even finish his food but will go to debate instead." Some contemporary monks are so keen to study that they will spend the entire month of New Year's holidays in retreat memorizing significant philosophical treatises, such as Tsong Khapa's *Legs bshad snying po* ("The Essence of Good Explanation").

"Debate" is not a fully appropriate term to refer to these activities. The term "dialectics," applied at least since 1902,[8] is sometimes used because participants are really collaborators in pursuing a line of philosophical reasoning more than they are intent upon winning the debate. They are dialectically engaged thinkers. The former abbot of Sera Me University, Geshe Lobsang Tharchin, has written, "The purpose of debate is not to defeat and thereby embarrass a mistaken opponent, thereby gaining the victory for oneself, but the purpose is to help the opponent overcome his wrong view." While this may be the ideal and not always the practice, there is serious attention paid to the disassembly of inaccurate mental constructs of reality and to the collaborative reassembly of a working system of reason. It is said that the right route to a true understanding is to face objections to one's thinking and refute them with reasoning. The application of logical challenge and consequent reflection is thought to enhance one's comprehension.

The Tibetan system of dialectics is a logical process of mental development, and the Tibetan monks who practice it are eager to follow a track of reasoning to see what it can accomplish and where it will lead. Tillemans (1999: 267) describes Tibetan debate logic as "through and through a set of rules for conducting a dialogue." Even when the participants have no personal commitment to the propositions, they delight in the process of clarifying the terms of a discussion and exposing theses to formal analytic challenges that have the capacity to carry the participants to logical conclusions they may not otherwise have realized. It is a creative activity that depends upon continually placing the thinking of participants at risk, a characteristic essential for any system of dialectics that is worthy of the name. The pedagogy of the Gelugpa sect's monastic universities are almost entirely invested in these public debates. Tibetan professors who visit the West to teach complain that it is nearly impossible to teach properly in European countries (including the U.S.) because of the absence of regular philosophical

---

8. Cf. S. C. Das (1902, 538).

debate. One geshe remarked in his broken English, "In India [where the monastic universities operate in exile] you can teach very well, very vast, debate, not like in Germany."

Some scholars of Tibetan Buddhism have questioned whether "dialectics" is the appropriate term for the Tibetan praxis of debate, since it does not always conform to what is meant by dialectics in the West. While there surely is no Marxian dialectic at work, it does have some features in common with Hegelian dialectics and with the more general dialectical tradition in the West. Hans-Georg Gadamer (cited in Dallmayr 1987, 134) has attempted to retrieve dialectics from what it has become in German idealism and reunite it with its traditional origins in dialogue: "What is involved in [dialectical] talk is not a mere fixation of intended meaning but a constantly renewed attempt—or rather the renewed temptation—to become engaged with something or someone, that is: to expose or risk oneself."[9] The pith of the Tibetan dialectical system is to be continually placing every philosophical position at risk. As one monk put it to me, "One reorders the reasoning according to what the consequences show." Every discussion involves the questions, "What is the consequence of that? What is the consequence of that? What is the consequence of that? (*thal, thal, thal*)," a reference to the frequent challenge within debate: "Is this not the consequence?" These scholars are like consequence-seeking logical machines set loose upon the world, and their dialectics draws out the ideas according to the consequences of the reasoning undertaken by the collaborating parties.

A hallmark of dialectics in the West has been the willingness of its practitioners to address not only philosophical subjects but to make the process of knowing itself a topic for investigation. This interest in the movement of knowing (alongside the interest in what is known) is the thinking "in awareness of itself" of which Hegel (1989, 25-28) has spoken. Does Tibetan dialectics engage in such a method of inquiry? Once dialectical thinking turns upon itself, the entire basis of philosophical reflection becomes open to radical (i.e., to the "root") investigation. Herbert Marcuse (1960, 10) has commented, "The dialectical system alters the structure and meaning of the proposition and makes it something quite different from the proposition of traditional logic." Another commentator (Bertell Ollman 1986, 42) adds, "The dialectics as such explains nothing, proves nothing, predicts nothing." In fact, its principal interest becomes the very process of thinking, particularly the way the structures of reasoning, as they reveal the world, entrap thinking itself. Frequently, Tibetan dialectics topicalize the process of thinking, and its greatest contribution may rest in these reflexive investigations. Even when it does not topicalize reflection, the emphasis upon debate itself keeps the processes of reasoning always in focus as an implicit, if not explicit, topic.

---

9. The cited passage is taken from an essay by Gadamer titled, "Text und Interpretation." In Philippe Forget, ed., *Text und Interpretation* (Munich: Fink Verlag, 1984), 27.

The philosophical tradition closest to this radical European sense of dialectics is the Prasangika Madhyamika (variously translated as "dialectical reasoning school," "consequentialist middle way school," or "dialectical nondualists"; Tib. *dbu ma thal 'gyur pa*). This tradition is especially concerned with the topicalization of the processes of reasoning. Although this school is not the subject matter of the present book, one illustration may be helpful. Common sense inquiry is accustomed to proceeding as if the notion that a substance has characteristics is obvious. The Dialectical Reasoning School calls into question the assumption that underlies this notion. They inquire whether something that is a characteristic of a substance is the same or different from it. If it is the same, then the distinction is unnecessary and therefore false; if it is different, then it cannot characterize it; hence, one cannot accurately think (or speak) of a substance "having" characteristics. In such a fashion a thesis is deconstructed, although not in the Hegelian sense by which a new synthesis follows from the antithesis. If anything, Madhyamika dialectics is more negative and radical than the Hegelian dialectic.[10]

But the real force of Tibetan dialectics rests in its capacity to expose any philosophical reflection to its consequences, and so to reflexively transform it in light of its emerging sense within the intersubjective situation. This "exposure" entails that philosophical propositions are always placed at risk. In its broadest sense of dialogue, and the associated exposure to unanticipated transformation, Tibetan philosophical inquiry is indeed dialectical.

Philosophical Culture

In a more practical and everyday sense, Tibetan dialectics means attending the debate sessions. It is here that young scholars develop and test their faculties of reasoning. At the Tibetan monastic university, there are several dozen professors who teach the same text to small groups of students. These students thus come to the debate grounds with slightly differing perspectives, and they are forced to test these perspectives against a variety of logical interrogations. At the same time, all the students have an opportunity to be exposed to these perspectives. Students pair off in twos and develop a logical apparatus for investigating the day's topics and each other's minds. Quite a few monks work out their "best shot" from the day's materials, and then present this during the debate session. They will roam around the debate grounds offering this "best shot" to any and all takers, refining it as they move along in light of the logical criticism they receive. There may be several "best shot" rovers at work, offering challenging problems to the monks at the session. These rovers, however, generally are not

---

10. Debate among scholars of the Dialectical Reasoning Middle Way School features some remarkable negative dialectics. Cf. Liberman (1996).

among the best debaters. Those who pair off together for an entire evening and take the time to refine their logical instrumentation in the new context and clarify an extensive lexicon of terms tend to develop the best debates, if they are not also the best debaters.

The practice of debate has the effect of making the mind very agile. When the mind holds tightly to its presuppositions, it does not easily let go of its interpretations. Tibetan dialectics provides frequent occasions that require that one to drop one's outlook at a moment's notice. This demands some mental acrobatics, which can provide some perspective and distance upon one's habitual patterns of thinking. At the early levels of study, debaters concentrate upon elementary features of logical instrumentation and critical reason. Monks learn these topics as if they were acquiring an extensive analytic tool chest, and they are trained to be very precise and quick. Students frequently ask each other about the various relationships of logical categories. For example (Goldberg 1985, 222-223), they may ask, "What are the four possibilities (mutual and partial inclusion and exclusion) of the two, nonvirtue and emotional affliction?" An answer, which must be delivered within a few seconds of the query, is that anger is both; a pillar is neither; a bodhisattva on the path of meditation has emotional afflictions but is not nonvirtuous; and the category "the ten nonvirtues" are nonvirtues but not emotional afflictions. Or, if one is asked, "Is 'one with vase' a nonnegative of vase?" one must reply in the negative because "one with vase" is not one with vase. Similarly, is category a category? Yes, because its specific forms or instances exist, for example permanent phenomena. Is "not a category" not a category? No, it *is* a category because its specific instances do exist (e.g., "the pair, a gold vase and a copper vase," which is certainly not a category). Is "specific instance" a specific instance? Yes, because a category that includes it exists (e.g., permanent phenomena). Is "not a specific instance" not a specific instance? Yes it is not, because a category that includes it does not exist.

Such exercises, along with their more advanced relatives in the fields of logic, epistemology, and dialectics may appear very abstract, but they are taken up with great enthusiasm by monks in training and constitute one of the centerpieces of mind-training Tibetan philosophical culture. In the vigorous form in which the monks practice debate, the problem is not a shortage but an excess of enthusiasm. As an advanced trainee explained to me, debate has three aspects: a *mental* aspect in which the mind is trained to respond quickly and accurately; a *vocal* aspect in which one learns to be articulate and to avoid being obscure; and a *physical* aspect, which provides opportunities for considerable exercise (including hand-clapping, vigorous gesturing, and shoving matches as monks compete for the floor in order to pose the next inquiry). While most young scholars take to the demonstrative aspects of public debate with enthusiasm, not all do. Geshe Lhundup Sopa (1996, 45) once commented, "Some people, when debating, are very shy. They have sharp minds and deep intelligence, but sometimes in a debating situation they don't do much; they're just too quiet. But some people have no shyness, and are able to debate in a playful way, joking and laughing. That's a very good way." A decade-long practice of public debating can produce a somewhat strapping personality, which fits well with the spirit of the Tibetan people more generally.

Scholasticism or Philosophy?

The mundane nature of these preliminary philosophical inquiries and the seemingly rote manner in which the defendants fire off their replies have led a few Western observers to criticize the practice of debate among members of the Gelug sect of being little more than a sterile scholasticism. Tillemans (1999, 118) describes Gelugpa logicians as "fairly unoriginal." Michael Walter and several other Tibetologists at Indiana University have termed the debate under examination here "ossified Gelugpa dialectics."[11] Matthew Kapstein (1987, 435) of the University of Chicago is even more severe:

> Study and critical reflection now serve only the function of instilling in the novice the propositions approved by the tradition, without the novice being in any way capable of determining for himself their truth or falsehood. Thus, the whole apparatus of debate and argument is merely a sham, disguising an elaborate conditioning procedure. . . . Thus, a tradition which spends much energy proclaiming the value of reason emerges as irreducibly authoritarian.

Is it that reason is a mere adornment for already worked out received notions, or do Tibetan scholar-monks have some capacity to change their beliefs and transform their understandings? While the accuracy of such criticisms merits investigation, such investigation cannot be confined to the critical analysis of texts; rather, one can best assess the originality or "ossification" of Gelugpa dialectics by participating in those dialectics. Before one can offer such condemnation, at the least one must experience what demands it places upon the philosophical imagination, what are the mental rhythms of the dialectic for its practitioners, and only then determine whether or not those philosophical practices carry one to investigations whose boundaries are continually being extended. It is here that a *sociological* method and not a *text-critical* method has its efficacy.

The implication in these criticisms is that these debates are performed much as actors read a script. Although occasionally the itinerary of a debate is well known, like a quiz, it is not always like that, and in actual practice there is considerable scope for creative reflection. And some of the creativity is designed into the structure of the pedagogy. The practice of debate trains one's mind to be as flexible and mentally agile as possible. Even with the first year of study's topics, one cannot just "parrot" replies. For example, there is a standard recita-

---

11. Personal communication.

tion of a definition for something that is "one with x." During the freshman debates one must provide this definition just prior to a recitation of illustrations, and there is an emphasis upon the speed of one's response. If one is asked about an "x" that is a rabbit's horn, it would be foolish to reply with the rote definition for "one with a rabbit's horn," for to provide any reply except an objection would be to debate seriously a topic that does not exist; such a mistake is considered to be a logician's disgrace. Since challengers are continually on the prowl for that inquiry that will catch the defender less than aware, such logical traps are numerous enough to constitute a minefield for any thinker who prefers to do his thinking by rote; therefore, one naturally tends to be vigilant about becoming routine. Furthermore, the challenges that one faces while debating forces one's theoretical understanding to be converted from abstractions to the more tangible knowledge that comes from practical activity.

To consider another illustration, one might apply the "four possibilities" query (inclusion, exclusion, etc.) from the *Collected Topics* to six pairs of phenomena, one after the other, and then slip in a pair of phenomena that are completely contradictory. If the respondent to the reasoning is not subtle, he will passively fall into a pattern and commence a search for four possibilities for two phenomena that have only one possibility, that of mutual exclusion. The slightest slip into mental habit will be cause for defeat; hence, routine recitation is discouraged skillfully by the way that Tibetan dialectical discussion is structured. While at the junior levels it may not lead to great profundities, it prepares debaters for the perils still to come.

It would also be incorrect to complain that the performance of these exercises is strictly rote and without an interest in the underlying meanings because most of the topics foreshadow vital substantive issues that students will encounter later in their philosophical careers. For example, the query regarding whether pot-and-pillar "is" (*yin*) an object of knowledge without having existence (*yod*)—nothing can be both a pot and a pillar at once—prepares the student for the Cittamatrin (*sems tsam pa*) and Madhyamika (*dbu ma*) thought regarding the status of emptiness which will come later in the curriculum; and the causes and results section of the topics on mental construction has a direct relationship with comprehending the laws of karma.

The late abbot of the Tibetan Institute of Buddhist Dialectics, Geshe Lobsang Gyatsho, has said,

> Some people say that a study of *bsdud grwa* is just for intelligence, or for developing the ability to be a smooth talker (*ka bde po*). This is not the case because there are so many things that one can learn about [Buddhist] practice in *bsdud grwa*. This depends entirely upon one's ability to spot the consequences for practice. If one is not able to observe the pertinent consequences for practice in one's study, if one cannot extract the practices, so to speak, then even a study of *Lam Rim* (*Graduated Path to Enlightenment*) would be of little use.

When lecturing about whether "father and mother" and "horse and donkey" are similar or dissimilar (and hence contradictories), this geshe explained that it depends upon perception, that is, how the perceiver comprehends them; hence, they could be similar or dissimilar, depending upon the situation. Such attentiveness to context is inconsistent with people who perform logical analysis merely by rote.

It is true that the dictum included in an introductory textbook on debate (Yongs 'Dzin 1979, 22b-25b), "By proving and refuting the meanings of these scriptures one will firmly grasp the Buddha's doctrine," implies that the ultimate destination of these philosophical investigations is preordained. But it is not to any extent greater or lesser than the paths of the Tibetan sects that do not emphasize dialectical inquiries. As with the case of tantric study and practice, one needs to assess what is the mental domain of the person who has succeeded in accomplishing a path of study before one determines whether his/her mental processes have ossified or not.[12] To this extent one must also reject the criticisms of some Kagyud and Nyingma monks who denigrate the Gelug and Sakya sects' emphasis upon debate and praise their own sects' accomplishments in the area of meditation. The ultimate goal of each sect is the same, only the training varies; and any study of Buddhist philosophical texts demands on the part of the reader some degree of familiarity with debate. One would have to criticize the Mahayana tradition in Tibet as a whole, and not strictly dialectics.

This is not to deny the importance of the criticism. Regarding the Svatantrika Madhyamaka curriculum, Goldberg (1985, 126) comments, "Mental constructs . . . classify events in terms of concepts, and by so doing they lose the unique aspects of the event and all information which is not available for a parameter of the concept held by the observer." This raises very important issues. Although the Tibetan system of philosophical investigation is logical, is it possible to provide a coherent organization of reasons without having a great deal of insight? Western traditions of philosophy and science also face this constraint upon formal analytic inquiry (and human knowledge generally). A Sakya monk once explained to me that the Sakya sect's emphasis in debate was "getting to the heart of the matter," while Gelug debate was preoccupied with precision in argumentation. This is a universal issue; that Tibetans are aware of it is proof enough that their philosophical imagination has not entirely "ossified." But *any* formal analytic practice is naturally inclined to formalization and routinization, and even sophistry, and this includes any practice of debate by Sakya, Nyingma, or Kargyud scholars.

Is philosophical reasoning possible only within a system, or can it benefit from the deconstruction of a system? What is dialectics, if not a continuous surpassing of the limitations of one's own system of reasoning? By this criterion,

---

12. Similarly, the mantra, "Om Mani Padme Hum," can be recited by rote or with a deep understanding of compassion and mental development.

one would have to give the Tibetan system high marks, for their scholars are continuously being shoved beyond the boundaries of their reasoning. While Tibetan philosophical discourse does not lack a certain coerciveness, it is not alone in succumbing to such a shortcoming. One needs to credit them for achieving great clarity in their debates; their system of dialectics provides for the confirmation of mutually accepted terms and grounds at each point. While it may at times also narrow their scope, they rarely talk past each other, a common flaw in Western academic discourse.

At a minimum, the Tibetan system is an excellent method of educating university-level students. By making a sport out of philosophical debate, Tibetans channel the energy of adolescents into the development of their rational capacity. In a similar way the energies of children are channeled productively into the memorization of scholarly texts which they will study later in their academic careers; their memorization becomes a verbal sport as these pupils play at the task by screaming as loudly as they are able. Since much of the older students' performance in philosophical debate is being judged by not by their elders but by their peers, their motivation to study receives the strong and effective reinforcement of not wanting to look foolish in front of their friends and colleagues. In fact, as a method of university-level education, the Tibetan achievement here is one of the outstanding innovations of any philosophical culture. As we will see, young Tibetan scholars are taught to think for themselves and to react to new perspectives quickly and with insight. Complacency is effectively minimized by teachers who drill them on their grasp of philosophical texts according to the method of discourse practiced in the debate courtyards. Rato Khyongla (1978, 93) recalls such an incident in his own career, involving his teacher, who was also the senior tutor to the Dalai Lama:

> He put to me a quick question. It was something I could answer immediately. He expanded his questions, and as they became deeper and darker, my answers became shallower and lighter. After a time, I could not give him a correct answer at all and became greatly confused. He suddenly changed to a different topic and though I tried to carry on a discussion, I could find no proper responses. The questions were very pointed, and he was critical of every answer I gave.

This is not a situation that is characteristic of a lack of philosophical creativity.

Valid Cognition (*tshad ma*)

Creative or rote, these Tibetan Buddhists retain an effective system of formal analytics, and it is within the public debates that the Tibetans learn and refine this logical praxis. This analytic praxis operates according to a clear-cut bivalent system (Goldberg 1985, 126) in which for every proposition put, the defender makes a positive or negative commitment. Debate ensues until both parties can agree that valid reasoning has established the proposition's truth or falsity; and the analysis proceeds from that point with the next dialectically pursued topic, which has its own bivalent resolution. Much of this tradition has its origins with the Sautrantika (Sutra Path School) and the Svatantrika Madhyamika (Dialectical Reasoning-based Middle Way School), and one of the principal texts for training in these rules of valid reasoning is Dharmakirti's *Commentary on (Dignaga's) "Compendium on Valid Reasoning"* (Skt. *Pramanavarttika*, Tib. *Tshad ma nam 'grel*). European critics of Tibetan dialectics perhaps have focused too much on the debating common to the earliest classes of the monastic curriculum—the *blo rig, tags rig*, and *grub mtha'* classes (nature of the mind, methods of reasoning, and philosophical tenets)—where gaining some basic mental agility is a primary objective. Though there are philosophical dimensions even in those early topics, their principal objective is training in logical practice, which as a technique is not quite yet philosophy; however, this is appropriate for early scholastic training. Later, especially during the Mind-only and Middle Way curricula, there is more philosophical content and the debates are more intriguing.

The system of reasoning in debates has five principal stages: (1) topic search, which may include the recitation of a text and the definition of terms; (2) clarification of the question; the questions taken up can be of several types, including questions confirming the answerer's memory, questions asking about the relations between two concepts, questions asking for an exegesis of an answer, questions asking for the answerer's judgment of the questioner's own reasoning (Onoda 1992, 39), questions raising a related topic that may be resolved in a manner contradictory to the answerer's judgment, etc.; (3) the challenge; (4) the response or defense; and (5) further refutation. The last refutation may be followed in turn by an extensive defense, which may be followed again by a more elaborate refutation. Dialectical partners may proceed collaboratively through any number of topics, but as soon as there is a point of contention a debate will ensue by way of providing reasons that validate or invalidate a formal proposition. Tibetan debates are not debates that always involve a challenger who holds one view and a defender who holds another, for according to the way that Tibetan debate is structured only the defender holds views. The challenger is free to change his perspective, and he can criticize the defender from multiple, even mutually inconsistent perspectives. A common feature of much contention is that a challenger will attempt to work a defender into accepting a minor commitment that is incorrect. By carefully demonstrating the invalidity of this position the challenger will hope to undermine the defender's confidence in his basic proposition.

The topic is generally proposed by the challenger, who will frequently suggest a given portion of a philosophical text and request a verbatim recitation of that text. Following this, the questioner may challenge the responder to provide definitions of one or more key terms in the cited passage. It is possible that a difference of opinion over the recitation (by memory) of the text or the accuracy of a definition may become the focus of an entire debate. Young Tibetan scholars, who spend many years training in valid reasoning, may devote most of the first two or three years of their study to this initial stage of logical analysis. Students expend much effort deciding what constitutes an accurate account of a textual passage. Geshe Gyatsho (cf. 62) advised beginning students to concentrate on requiring the respondent in a debate to provide the exact phrasing of definitions and explanations. Even slight mistakes in wording should become a topic for debate. In this way students are continuously being disciplined by each other on the debate grounds.

It is during the clarification of the question that a formal proposition is selected for debate. Debate will not commence until it is *clear* to all parties what precisely is the proposition for debate. Here is a translation of a portion of a debate that includes a brief clarification sequence:

> Challenger (T) Homage to Manjushri. According to the views of the Madhyamika, the Sravakas, and Pratyekabuddhas have completed renunciation and perfect understanding. You do not have the answer.
>
> Defender (L) The sign [i.e., that he does not have the answer] is not established.
>
> T You are the subject (*chos chen*). You have said that the sign is not established because you *can* put the answer.
>
> L I ACCEPT.
>
> T Then present it.
>
> L According to the Madhyamaka, it pervades that the Sravakas and Pratyekabuddhas must have achieved renunciation and perfect understanding because they have achieved it by the time they have reached the first bodhisattva level.
>
> T Your view, the basis of the debate, is that renunciation and perfect understanding are completed by the first bodhisattva level. Why does your reason pervade?

During the final turn of speaking the question has finally been clarified, so that the debate can proceed. During this stage of the debate, the participants are really only warming up. As will be seen in the succeeding chapters, they are erecting the logical scaffolding upon which their entire debate will be built.

The next stage (what would come next in the cited illustration) is the challenge. The challenger will formulate additional propositions that undermine the initial commitment of the defender. Frequently, these propositions will be an extension or further application of the initial proposition into new areas. All of these propositions take the same form: there is a subject, which is identified by the words *chos chen* ("subject") that follow it (see above); this is joined to a predicate (*bsgrub bya'i chos*) or clarification (*gsal ba*). Together they compose the thesis or promise (*dam bca'*). The proposition is completed when it is joined to a reason (*gtan tsigs*) or sign (*rtags*), which is identified by the word *phyir* ("because") that immediately follows it, completing the sentence. Much of the strategy of the challenge revolves around the effort of the challenger to have the defender commit to a proposition that is invalid or can be shown to be inconsistent with his position.

The defender will at all costs try to avoid such an inconsistency and will attempt to extend the debate. The final stage is the defense itself. The defender has four replies open to him: he can accept what the challenger has put to him, he can argue that the reason (or sign) is not established, he can claim that there is no entailment or pervasion of the reason in the subject, or he can call for further explanation by asking "Why?" (*ci'i phyir*, pronounced "chee-cheer"). "*Ci'i phyir*" is a routine query that by calling for further reasoning assists in overcoming a complacent acceptance of received notions, and it can take the inquiry to a higher level of philosophical investigation. As a systematic way of calling for further logical exegesis, it stands ready as part of the dialectical apparatus available to the participants. When reading Tibetan commentaries one will frequently find the *ci'i phyir* embedded in the text as a tacit reminder that the Buddhist texts had their origins in public philosophical debates. The principal exegetical texts of the Gelug school, such as Tsong Khapa's *Legs bshad snying po* or Jetsun Chogyi Gyaltsen's *Dbu ma spyi don*, a study manual to Chandrakirti's *Introduction to the Middle Way*, are written almost exclusively in these debate forms, and they feature either accounts of actual debates or textual discourse patterned upon such debates.

A defender will attempt to provide valid reasons for the theses he has made. If he cannot, he may prefer to put forward an invalid reason rather than admit that there is no logical entailment or pervasion in the proposition that he is committed to. This will place the analytic onus upon the challenger, who at least will have to work out a further refutation. Further refutation may be a succeeding stage, whereupon the challenge and defense repeat. This may include extensive elaboration of preceding themes, in accord with the participants' developing comprehension of the emerging dialectic.

Debate According to Two Authoritative Texts

As part of their introduction to debate, novice Tibetan scholars are given to study one of the standard summaries of proper forms of debate. Although these textual accounts are idealized versions which are not always followed in daily practice, they do set the standards for debate and as such are referred to from time to time later in a scholar's career. Here we review two of these textual summaries of proper debate, Yongdzin Jampa Tsultrim Gyatso's summary in his *Greater Collected Topics* and Sakya Pandita's "Method of Practicing Debate" in

Section Three of his *Entrance for the Wise*.[13] The text by Yong dzin is the standard debate manual for scholars at Sera Monastic University, a Gelug philosophical training college. The text by the greatest Sakyapa master is a principal
reference on debate for scholars of the Sakya sect. These two texts cover much
of the same material, and they shed considerable light on philosophical debate as
practiced by these two Tibetan sects who place considerable emphasis upon
formal public debate.

Sakya Pandita traces Tibetan debate to both Hindu and Buddhist sources.
He briefly summarizes the contribution to debate from the Nyaya tradition, but
ascribes the greatest authority to Dharmakirti. Yongdzin and Sakya Pandita (Sa-
pan) both describe the roles of the three principal participants. The first party is
the "disputant" (*rgol*); he is the challenger (*snga rgol*) who poses questions
about the thesis or promise. He corrects or sets in order (*'god pa*) the mistakes of
his opponent, clarifying the signs (*rtags gsel gtang khan*) by means of reasoning.
His opponent is termed the "defender" (*phyi rgol*) or "respondent to the reasoning" (*rigs len pa*), and he provides answers that refute the reasoning of the disputant. In Gelug debates there is usually one defendant, but in most Sakya debates there are two. A third party is the "witness" (*dpang po*) or judge who de-
cides who wins the argument and corrects mistakes. What distinguishes debate
from mere quarreling (*shags 'gyes*) is that these three roles are clearly defined
and never confused or mixed. According to Sakya Pandita (1984, 154-55), the
witness should summarize the debate for the benefit of the participants, and Sakya Pandita observes that an ignorant witness can inflict terrible damage upon a
debate; in such a case the participants are advised to write down what was said
and consult other learned scholars. According to Yongdzin, however, the witness need not announce a victor. It is common for debaters to consult their
teachers the next day for advice and assessment.

In daily practice the witness is frequently the supervising geshe or disciplinarian, who patrols the debating grounds where several hundred young scholars
may be debating simultaneously, mostly in pairs. Like a shepherd keeping a
vigil over his flock, these elder scholars will supervise here and there the students' correct use of formal analytic reasoning. On more than one occasion the
sight of this itself has struck me as constituting a major achievement in the history of human societies. When only one debate is held at one time, with most of
the scholars sitting silently in attendance, an entire audience can and does play
the role of witness. At Sera, the monks will alternate between hundreds of debates (one on one, two on one, etc.) occurring at the same time, one principal
debate that everyone attends more or less quietly, and group prayer with meditation. By rotating among these three activities each evening, the energies are

---

13. Sa skya Pandita, "*Rtsod pa'i tshul la spongs pa*" in his *Mkhas pa mams 'jugs
pa'i sgo* (Section Three), (Rajpur: Sakya Institute, 1984) 109-57. Readers are directed to
the English translation and extensive exegesis by David P. Jackson (1985).

allowed to vary. It is especially useful to suddenly draw people away from their engagement in the immanence of intellectual struggle. At the sound of a bell, the vigorous challenging ceases and a more quiet opportunity to reflect commences, permitting the young scholars to gain some perspective on what may have seemed have an inflated importance. The alternation between prayer and vigorous debate, one following the other in succession, is conducive to some flexibility of temperament.

In Buddhist thought there are three orders of philosophical inquiry. There are manifest phenomena, the validity of which can be decided by direct perception; there are hidden phenomena, or phenomena that may be ascertained only indirectly (e.g., the existence of fire where there is smoke, or the emptiness of inherent existence), whose validity is decided in dependence upon reasoning; and there are matters of belief (e.g., reincarnation), regarding which only scriptural sources have any utility. Reasoning may involve proofs or refutations, and these may be either accurate or "facsimiles." An accurate refutation is when a dialectician has put forward a reason (sign) that articulates correctly what are the consequences that follow or what is necessarily to be excluded. Fascimile refutations include what Sakya Pandita (147) terms one of the "three thorns" of Dharmakirti: the reason is not established as existing (in the subject), the reason is contradictory to the subject, or the reason is uncertain. Yongdzin asserts that flaws with the reason (unestablished, contradictory, or uncertain) are like a person attempting to fight using a weapon with a dull blade. Flaws in the logical pervasion are like an armless hero; he may be willing to climb a high mountain, but he lacks the means of doing so. A flaw in the correction or clarification (*gsal ba*), in which the consequence reasoning of a refutation is without effect because of lacking a correct logical predicate, is like poison given to a peacock, that is, it has no effect upon the peacock, who merely transforms poison into the bright colors of his plumage. On matters of belief one can apply logic only to the extent that one is able to analyze the scriptural passages and determine which ones contradict each other or are falsifiable by valid reasoning.

Sa-pan (Sakya Pandita) further cautions debaters to be very careful not to conflate the tenets or arguments of the various philosophical schools. Only when one keeps the position of each school of reasoning distinct will philosophical inquiry be productive. Sakya Pandita writes, "Keep the philosophical tenets clear! When one debates by means of reasoning, argue by clearly distinguishing which tenets one is following and which tenets one is not following."[14] This means that one should not conflate the arguments of commentators who agree only about a single tenet as if they were commenting from the same perspective, nor should one conflate minor differences among philosophers of the same school. Just as each region has its own successful method of agriculture, Sa-pan

---

14. "*Rigs pa'i sgo ne rtsod pa na/ grub mtha'i rjes su 'brang mi 'brang/ rnam par phye ste gsal bar tsod/,*" Sakya Pandita (1984, 127).

describes, if one were to mix together various methods in a single place, some of them would be inappropriate and they would not be successful. Similarly, "To confuse systems of reasoning together is to wander aimlessly" (Sakya Pandita 1984, 143). I have heard contemporary Tibetan teachers recall this advice on many occasions. Other frequent advice that may be traced to the debate manuals includes avoiding topics that have no relevance, not asking several questions at the same time, and employing more than one valid reason at a time. For a defender to respond to a challenger having any of these faults would implicate him in the error as well.

There is a great deal of counsel given on comportment. Yongdzin writes that one's behavior should be elegant. One's voice should be soft, clear, and meaningful, and one's face should be smiling, not angry or red. One should not speak too hastily, as if one has just been confronted with one's enemy. One's face should not be like a burning weapon, and one's voice should not sound like that of a ghost. Sakya Pandita (1984, 115) is similarly critical of speech in which the voice is too high, low, or mumbled, and he faults any antics such as laughing, speaking too quickly, prancing about, etc.

One should not praise oneself, denigrate others, torment others by exaggerating their faults, or destroy the self-confidence and brightness of an opponent. The Tibetan King *Khri song lde brtsan* has cautioned, "The victor should not be haughty." One's principal aim must be to locate the precise flaws in the other's thinking and to correct it. Yongdzin writes that one should eliminate the closed-mindedness of another and never employ obscure words and reasoning. Obviously, these scholars have some familiarity with these shortcomings. Yongdzin suggests that when a challenger makes an effective refutation, the defender should not become upset but should remain undisturbed, in the way a great mountain receives the wind. A revealing illustration may be found on the separately issued CD-ROM at the end of debate I.9 (6:18:03, when L' attempts to handle the public exposure of his inconsistency by retreating for a moment into a meditative stabilization).

Both commentators treat seriously the motivation of the debate participants. The worst motivation is to have only a desire to win, forgetting logic and becoming angered easily. Yongdzin counsels that one should not have the determination, "I must really defeat him!" as this will only increase one's attachment to one's self. The best motivation is to respect one's own desire for understanding and, with kindness, to clarify any incorrect thinking of another in order to assist him to understand the dharma. Sa-pan (1984, 127) emphasizes that one should be concerned to establish and clarify correct philosophical views, not with merely making some debating points. This is another reason why one should clarify the tenets that one is advocating: to debate without tenets is mere "craft" (*gyo sgyu*), not scholarship.

If one fails to perform a debate well, with the proper motivation, one's emotional afflictions will increase, according to Yongdzin. Such misguided thinking as wanting oneself to be higher and the other to be inferior will be a cause for binding one to ethical deficiencies. When one debates correctly, one will be satisfied with the way one's mind improves. One's grasp of scriptures will increase, and one will be capable of ascertaining, according to reasoning, the teachings of the Buddha and his commentators.

Debate in Actual Practice

The debating that takes place in the courtyards of a Tibetan monastic university diverges somewhat from the ideal just presented. This is largely because new students are socialized into the practice of debate by their fellow students, while the textual advice and the instruction of their teachers play lesser roles. Consequently, some of the dictums against laughing or speaking too quickly are disregarded; however, actual debate features considerable logical skill and devotion to the capabilities of the Buddhist system of valid reasoning.

In most debates the disputants alternate between what I call "doing form," during which the debate is formatted and the structures of a normative order are invoked, and "doing inquiry," in which the disputants lose themselves in an exploration of the philosophical questions that have arisen. The protagonist in a debate will collect logical commitments from the defendant in the hope that some inconsistency can be identified, while the defendant will attempt to avoid such entrapment much as a fencer parries a thrust, using even spurious means when valid means are unavailable. During a debate a complex web of interrelated propositions and commitments is constructed, and the debate may become entangled in it. When this occurs, the participants will reformat the debate along normative lines. In such a fashion, a debate may alternate back and forth between "doing form" and "doing inquiry," becoming slightly more freeform as the dialecticians become carried away with their ideas, and returning to strict convention as they recognize that they have lost some clarity and need to resurrect the structure of the debate.

As remarked above, in any given debate the participants will gradually come into synchronization with each other. They achieve this synchronicity by means of the formatting that they collaborate in performing. During the first step of a debate, the selection of a topic, the notions at first pass by quite rapidly. One party may even take note of the notions and propositions articulated by his opponent and propose them as his own. A good deal of semantic drift occurs as well, in which the significance of the terms may shift slightly according to the emerging context and in dependence upon how one's opponent uses the terms. As the debate moves into step two, the clarification of the question, an adequacy of communication on an intersubjective level is established in the form of a tightly structured and well-clarified logical dialectic.

As Goldberg (1985, 783) comments, the system pays special attention to "making clear the areas of agreement and disagreement between individuals so that they can form appropriate expectations of each other." It is not that the formal structure never changes (if it did it would not be a dialectic), but such changes are again formalized and dialogical work is undertaken to make them part of the intersubjectively validated debate structure.

Much of this work of formatting relies upon repetition. Repetition gives the participants the opportunity to display understandings and have them validated. "The ability of the questioner to gain mileage by misrepresenting the answerer's position is limited to some extent by the need to recheck the answerer's positions and to have the answerer explicitly accept the implication as being drawn from his position" (Goldberg 1985, 893-94). The repetitive and somewhat routine work of "doing form" also provides the debaters time to think and work out their logical strategies. The formatting is like the drummer's beat in modern Western music and is essential to the rhythm of the discourse. It is what participants are most comfortable with and can return to easily when the debate begins to become a little too cloudy. Also, it fills silence. It is as if the debaters are seeking the flow or energy of the dialectical process, which once established will operate on its own, much as a machine that needs to be turned on. The formatting provides the syntax for the debate and encourages the employment of those terms that have been best clarified.

During the third and fourth steps of the debate, the challenge and defense, both parties are more coy about clarifying what is principally at issue. Goldberg (1985, 188) describes this well:

> The answerer generally does not know for sure what the topic is until the questioner actually presents part or all of his proof. Since . . . the evidence search consists of asking similar kinds of questions, the answerer often cannot tell for sure whether the questioner is still looking for a topic and is satisfied with the previous answers, or whether the questioner thinks he has found a flaw in the previous answers suitable for a topic and is asking questions to gather evidence for a proof.

One can think that one has replied correctly, but one is never certain, for the process keeps one always in doubt. This obligates one to examine the situation from several possible perspectives, that is, more carefully than if one could quickly determine which one was correct, and never to relax one's attention. Further, over a long debate one can become uncertain regarding just what were all of the commitments one has made. It is here that interpretation and even bluff has its place. Putting together a successful argument at any stage of this evolving panoply of meaning and commitment requires considerable creative capacity.

Participants undertake "doing inquiry" in the form of an active and enthusiastic collaboration in pursuit of a philosophical topic or by applying a new idea (for one or both of them) to several familiar domains. Their corpus of understanding is never static, and as it grows they will apply it to new inquiries. An especially productive cooperation is one of the two types of debate that will quickly gather a crowd (the other type being a highly competitive debate skillfully performed). The monks on the debate grounds are always eager to learn something new.[15] As this logical dialectics is an active praxis, Tibetans apply it in any context, including when unfamiliar notions from Western philosophy are introduced. Tibetan dialectics is a philosophical culture.

Logical Strategies

Tibetan debaters employ both logical and rhetorical strategies. While a full account of the logical strategies utilized *in situ* in philosophical debate is taken up in chapter 7, I want to indicate here a few features that characterize Tibetan debate. It is important to recognize that a full description of these strategies requires more than attention to ideal types of logical argumentation; this is because the intellectual force of the debate for its participants depends upon the local and circumstantial detail of the logic as it emerges within the debate. Participants' logical strategies are dependent upon and oriented to the contingent details of the particular debate. Since this is a rapidly changing flux, the horizon of possible strategies, logical commitments, and beliefs is always in transition. An account that does not bring to the reader a glimpse of this *moving horizon* of logical possibilities, to which the participants *themselves* are oriented, fails to provide an adequate portrayal of Tibetan debate. I offer here a suggestion of what this conceptual horizon is like.

A debate commences with the commitment of the respondent to a logical proposition, and I have already discussed the interest of the challenger in working the respondent into a commitment that is in some way contradictory with his earlier commitment. Once a contradictory commitment is elicited, the "person who clarifies the reasoning" reasons his way from it back to the initial commitment, rendering it formally invalid. Here is an illustration (note: upper case indicates that the utterance is a standard token from the formal grammar of Tibetan debating):

Challenger (T) The unborn offspring in the mother's womb is not a human.
Defender (L) I ACCEPT.
T If you kill that unborn child, it follows that you are not stained with the fundamental sin of killing a human being.
L I ACCEPT.
T When you kill that unborn child, IT FOLLOWS THAT you are stained

---

15. Young monks would eagerly invite me to debate with them because, they explained to me, they were tired of the usual arguments and wanted some fresh logical challenges; however, I suspected that they were equally eager to secure an opportunity to defeat an American professor.

with the fundamental sin of killing a human being because it says in a
text on moral discipline, "One is stained with fundamental sin if one
kills an embryo."

L   I ACCEPT THAT it says that.

10 T   If that is so, IT FOLLOWS THAT the being in the mother's womb is a
human.

L   WHAT IS THE REASON? [*Ci'i phyir*]

T   Because it is one whose killing causes another to fall into the funda
mental sin of killing a human.

L   THERE IS NO PERVASION.

T   The reason does pervade because human is the main subject when it is
written, "embryo."

L   I ACCEPT.

T   FINISHED! [*Ts'a!*]

Once the defender has accepted the proposition of the challenger (line 9), it
remains for the challenger to reason back to the initial commitment (line 5). The
respondent is obligated to provide an answer, even though it is probably clear to
this defender that he would be defeated by an acceptance of the textual citation;
since it was an established fact, he could do nothing other than accept it. Although it is not the case in this instance, on many occasions if the respondent is
cognizant of the logical strategy of the challenger he will be able to provide a
response that will foil that effort, at least for a time. For this reason part of the
strategy of the challenger is to conceal his logical strategy. "If the answerer
knows what the questioner is trying to do, he is more likely to avoid making
guesses or careless or random applications of sources of knowledge which feed
into the questioner's plan. Therefore the questioner tries to order his material so
that the answerer does not know how it will be used" (Goldberg 1985, 773).

In this fashion the defender is occupied with constructing possible strategies
that the challenger might be employing, not unlike the projections of a chess
player. Working out several such possible strategies at once is part of the training. To add to the defender's troubles, a challenger may throw in some irrelevant questions to distract the defender and help obscure his own strategy.
Gradually, the defender will be worked into a corner where he cannot accept a
proposition without implying his ultimate defeat. Tibetan defenders are extremely elusive, however, and can generally come up with some reply that
forces the defender to do more logical work, possibly leading to a fresh logical
error of the challenger's own. In the above illustration (lines 12 and 15) the defender postpones his defeat briefly by requiring the challenger to carry through
all of the necessary logical entailments. Further (Goldberg 1985, 894), "Sometimes if the answerer thinks that the questioning may not be sharp, he will try to
foil him by refusing to give the correct answer unless the questioner gives incontrovertible proof."

Another strategy a challenger may take is to search for a proposition that will confound the defender, or he may call for the recitation of a pertinent text. This is a strategy employed frequently when it appears that the defender's basic commitment is a sound one. By finding some gap in the defender's knowledge, a victory of sorts may be obtained. The benefit is that even correct respondents have the opportunity to witness their shortcomings, which become objectively available to all those present. Defenders are not readily willing to have their shortcomings displayed, even when the challenger is being more helpful than antagonistic, and so they will provide almost any response to cloud the request. One of the most standard means of postponing the inevitable is to employ a request for reasoning, the *ci'i phyir* discussed previously. Line 12 of the illustration contains an instance in which the defender was able to postpone his making a contradictory commitment by employing this device.

At every level of study, these debate procedures maximize the learning opportunities for participants. During the elementary levels, such as when a challenger is calling for a recitation of the possibilities of inclusion and exclusion of various phenomena, the defender's strategy is to select replies that are difficult to assess. This forces the challenger to think and may *slow him down* enough to throw him off his rhythm of debating. Here, valid replies that appear to be incorrect are best. On the challenger's part, his demands that the respondent delve more deeply into the reply serve to force his partner out of any passivity into a more attentive state. For example, a request to "present" (*shog*) an illustration or explanation or to provide further detail about a body of instruction requires that a defender be an expert at least about his own responses. Occasionally, an opponent may not know a topic as well as it first appeared (to either of the parties). This technique is also carried over to ordinary classroom instruction, where challenging students to explain their understanding is employed frequently by teachers in order to discourage intellectual laziness on the part of students. Tibetan students do not have the protection of anonymity that many Western students enjoy.

Even those strategies that appear to be diabolical, in which propositions are put forward that deliberately sound correct but in reality are invalid (e.g., a proposition having an incorrect sign along with a correct entailment), are in fact superb devices for instilling in scholars some skepticism regarding the products of their mental deliberations. The most superb tool of all is the "consequence logic." Since it is dependent for its effectiveness upon the context in which it operates, it is a highly pragmatic device that is always shoving an opponent out of his logical perspective; in fact, it can quickly carry both parties into unanticipated realms of investigation.

Rhetorical Strategies

The most casual observer of a debate session will notice a discrepancy between the elegant comportment recommended in the manuals on the proper method of debate and what is actually taking place in the debate courtyard. In fact, the shouting is so considerable that a pair of debaters may not be able to hear themselves above the general din. The extravagant flourishes discouraged by the texts but widely employed anyway include disdain designed to force one's opponent to lose his confidence, derisive laughter, accusative vocal gestures ("Ahaaah!", "Oh!"), and certain antagonistic wrappings and twirlings of the challenger's rosary. It is said that when a defender is defeated, the challenger is entitled to circumambulate (*skor*, pronounced "kor") the defeated party three (*gsum*, pronounced "soom") times. Upon the occasion of a clear and hard fought victory, the challenger may take advantage of this privilege and prance about the defeated, gloating all the while, sometimes along with the derisive howls of the audience. During debates, challengers claim victory by shouting loudly, "kor soom!" even when the outcome of a debate is still uncertain. This too is designed to undermine the confidence of the defender. On occasion the challenger may circle his rosary above the defender three times in mockery. Another flourish that challengers employ is "Defeated" or "Finished!" (*tshar!*). This is shouted when the defender has been caught within a contradiction or when a challenger wishes to claim that there is a patent contradiction.

Up to a point, these flourishes are a legitimate means of inquiry, for they force one's opponent to exercise self-control and assist him to develop concentration. One is permitted and even encouraged to speak forcibly, provided that one's motivation is to improve the other's thinking and not merely to ridicule him. But if one puts forward too many "kor soom" or empty flourishes without any substantive intellectual content, the debate can become ugly. On rare occasions too much antagonistic flourish can lead to physical altercation, and the witness may need to intervene to put down the struggle. In one instance a monk who was excessively abused commenced a serious fight, for which he was expelled from the university. To the extent that such rhetorical flourishes flush out the "ego grasping" of one's opponent, they have the benefit of affording him an opportunity to work on his attachment to self, a principal theme of Buddhist investigation. One can only wonder if they ever foster egotism.

There is a bit of "poker" at work in these rhetorical devices. If a protagonist can convincingly employ these performance aspects, his opponent may lose faith in his own argument and a note of doubt may creep into his voice, even when there is not much substance to the protagonist's argument. What the opponent learns is to develop faith in his own reasoning and to rely upon his own judgment. Skilled debaters learn to develop the logical dialectic without losing their composure, to be strong and resolute without arrogance or conceit. When the rhetorical devices are rooted soundly in the logical infrastructure, it heightens the intensity of the investigation of the philosophical issues. Tibetan debate requires much concentration and self-control, because when one becomes excited, one's logic may become sloppy and lead to a defeat.

The defender also has his rhetorical armory, although his opportunity for training in humility and self-control is probably more extraordinary. Defenders are known for their poker faces in the midst of certain defeat, and on occasion the confidence of a respondent can so convince the challenger that the latter will overlook an obvious contradiction of his opponent. When a challenger has confidently prepared a line of valid argumentation and has finally put forward its climax in the form of a proposition, the defendant may calmly reply dismissively, "The pervasion is not established." This may spill the protagonist off of any unsteady pedestal. The metaphor of the peacock poison, provided by that challenger whose reason lacks logical pervasion is an apt description of a potential flaw in a defendant as well as a challenger: in Yongdzin's example the poison is not merely ineffective against the defender-peacock, he is able to metabolize the poison in a way that renders the colors of his plumage more glorious. This metaphor captures well the smugness of some defenders.

Since a defender is under an obligation to reply promptly, a frequent strategy of the challenger is to rush the defender to reply before he has thought the matter through. If the defender takes too long to give his reply, the audience will begin to ridicule him. This develops the capacity of debaters to think quickly, and accurately. It also requires that the debaters know their materials well. Once an audience begins to intervene, a defender can lose his composure, especially when the audience shouts together (in the manner of a sporting event), "Put the answer!" Rato Khyongla (1978, 110) gives this account:

> A monk would stand up, quote a verse, and demanding that I elucidate it, clap his hands. The assembled monks would start chanting loudly, "Give the answer!" and I would try to respond at once. . . . I remember one young man who, having asked his question [and receiving the reply] could not follow it up, and the prior scolded him publicly, enumerating his faults in detail. "You failed twice before and now can't even formulate a proper question. You are lazy and lax," he said, then struck him with a stick. In this way an audience or witness can intervene dramatically in the performance of a challenger. The risk of exposing one's philosophical abilities to public witness and criticism is one motivation for the many hours young Tibetan scholars invest in the study and recitation of texts. There is never any silence in a Tibetan monastic university, for even during "free time" monks are reciting aloud the texts that they will be required to discuss stanza-by-stanza and argument-by-argument. The harder that a monk studies, the fewer will be the number of logical defeats he will suffer and the less likely it is that he will become upset by contention.

I once witnessed a debate in which the challenger had the defender justly and fully trapped. At this point a rather large audience intervened to feign great surprise and criticism of the challenger's attempt to put forward such a supposedly illogical position, thereby emboldening the defender. The challenger lost his confidence and gave up his attack. At that, the crowd cheered in derision. This may appear to be a tactic far removed from logical analysis, yet such events can play an important role in the maturing of a scholar. The lesson for this challenger was to learn to rely upon valid reasoning alone and not upon the apparent efficacy of his rhetoric. There was another occasion when members of an audience deliberately ganged up on another debater, who was known for his capacity to anger easily. In this way the debater's temperament was being continually tested by his fellow scholars, another case of education by one's peers.

A close study of actual Tibetan debates demonstrates that their philosophical dialectics is an effective and coherent system of mental training and constitutes a powerful mechanism for logical investigation. Just what are the precise limitations of their logical praxis must also be investigated, as must investigation of the ways in which Tibetan Buddhist philosophical culture attends to such limitations and tries to remedy them. What is most extraordinary is that any culture has embraced so extensively such an austere system of formal analytic reasoning. It is emblematic of Tibetan philosophical culture in the Gelug tradition that they include as part of their daily liturgy the prayer, "In Praise of Interdependent Origination" by Tsong Khapa. This hymn lauds the central logical insight of Madhyamaka Buddhism, *pratitya-samutpada* (Tib. *rten brel*; also translatable as "mutual interdependence of concepts," cf. Nayak 1987, 16, or "interconnectedly dependent being"). That such a logical praxis is today being preserved and perpetuated as a centerpiece of a still contemporary philosophical culture, after 800 years in India and another 800 years in Tibet, is a remarkable human accomplishment. Further investigation of this philosophical praxis is fully warranted.

At the end of any monastery day, after the roar of the debating courtyard has subsided some time between 10 PM and midnight, and the pairs of debaters have all wandered off for some evening tea and an opportunity to debrief each other about the evening's debates, the air will give way to the murmuring of the monks reciting the textual passages they are attempting to memorize, just prior to going to bed. For a while the chanting and whispering of this memorization will come from all corners and shadows of the monastery, until long after most have fallen asleep the last one or two of these reciters will nod off themselves, and the night will give way to silence for a few hours until the long Tibetan bugles call the monks to their morning prayers some time between 4:30 and 5:30 AM.

Part II

Philosophical Praxis in the Tibetan Academy

Chapter 4

Organizing the Objectivity of the Discourse: Dialectics and Communication

> This discourse is therefore not the unfolding of a prefabricated internal logic, but the constitution of truth in a struggle between thinkers, with all the risks of freedom . . . where the common plane is wanting or yet to be constituted.
>
> —Emmanuel Levinas (1969, 73)

In its most basic form, dialectics describes the movement of the thinking between two persons whose reflections develop in collaboration and in contradiction with each other. Communication is the foundation of this relationship, since it is impossible for dialectics to take place without each thinker keeping attuned to the thought of the other. To this extent, philosophical dialectics is also social praxis and ethics.

The contradictions that emerge within such a dialogue are its soul. And that is because every thought that reaches any level of complexity is necessarily inadequate, and needs to be reminded of its inadequacy, in order to keep open the possibility of its further development. The negation of thinking produces criticism that exposes inadequacies and promotes repair. Negation can discredit error and disrupt narrow-mindedness, keeping thinking fresh for what has not been anticipated, for what is yet to be known. Of even the most sublime thoughts, dialectics keeps asking further questions. Philosophical reflection faces the predicament that this perpetual interrogation is both a blessing and a curse. The curse is related to the ready ease with which asking further questions, or making further challenges, devolves into distracting sophistry and pettiness that could merit the name philosophy only within a community of pedants. Here the question naturally arises whether there are points at which philosophical deliberation should be suspended, that is, where some rest may be taken so that thinkers can abide within the fleeting insight into truth that their philosophical reflection has enabled. Does thinking not sometimes find it prudent to regard in silent fullness what has unfolded? At such moments, further questions and continued intellection can become self-defeating, unnecessarily leading serious thinkers away from the depths to more shallow waters. Despite the dreams of logical positivists, no method can be relied upon routinely that would distinguish those occasions when further dialectics is required from those when the best recourse is silence; and that is why philosophy remains an art instead of a technique.

That thought may always be inadequate does not entail that there is no truth. Truth is something that exists alongside thinking, but it is not reducible to a thought. Thinking can carry thinkers to truth more readily when it operates as dialectics and not as stasis, for dialectics interjects sufficient instability and self-awareness to inhibit the establishment of reflection's enemy, which Tibetans term reification (*rgro 'dog*). In its simplest form, dialectics is a partnership between two thinkers that oddly employs a diabolical contrariness in service of each other's most vital philosophical needs.

Of course truth is not the only occupational interest of philosophical dialectics. As an empirical matter, philosophers engaged in their investigations are addressed not only to *truth concerns* but also to two practical domains of social action that always accompany philosophers at their worksite—developing and sustaining *a formal structure of argument* and *the organizational work of producing a local orderliness* that facilitates clear communication (or in fact, any communication). At some level all philosophy is collaboration, and the pragmatic concerns of people who must learn each other's minds are more vital than can be recognized by a cursory examination that limits itself strictly to what philosophy's formal analytics can reveal. The everyday work of people who philosophize requires that the local contingencies of the philosophical discourse be so arranged and so utilized that effective communication and understanding can take place. This local organizational work—the not always simple task of keeping their talk organized, and sensible to each other—accompanies their attention to the practical task of keeping organized the formal representation of their philosophical reflections, that is, the formal apophansis. Both of these two domains of practical activity, the local organizational work and the apophantic representation of the reflections, are collaborative enterprises. Therefore, on the agenda of those who philosophize together are *three* projects to which they are oriented, and such orientation is unavoidable. Philosophers address themselves simultaneously and collaboratively to these projects, each of which has sufficient integrity to prevent its being subsumed within the others:

Local Organizational Work—A Formal Structure of Reasoning—Truth Concerns

How does a debate becomes coordinated and how is a structure for analytic thinking developed, that is, how do Tibetan scholars clarify the philosophical issues they are addressing and how do they arrange their discussion in a manner that enables them to listen to each other carefully while they carry out their inquiries? We offer a close description of the philosophical practices of Tibetan scholar-monks and examine *in detail* how they concert themselves to produce a well-ordered philosophical debate. Tibetan debaters are addressed to numerous local contingencies that coordinate their discourse so that philosophical reflection can proceed. While it may be the participants' truth interests that motivate an inquiry, the work of Tibetan philosophers includes the repair of problems with the local orderliness of their dialogue, so that lines of clear communication can be built and sustained. Not infrequently, these local organizational matters receive their attention *before* philosophical issues. Participants in Tibetan scholastic debates are mutually oriented to each other's work regarding keeping the debate orderly and producing what would be recognizable by any knowledgeable Buddhist scholar to be a competent debate. Once these social concerns are addressed, and always alongside these concerns, the debaters turn their attention to philosophical interests and to winning the debate.

While most of the observations I will make are specific to Tibetan dialectics, some are applicable to the work of philosophers more generally, for all philosophical reflection includes formal analytic components of some sort. These investigations of Part II are motivated by a concern to present in detail the actual lived work of Tibetan philosophical debate and by an interest to elucidate some enduring philosophical anthropological issues, which are informed by the study of these Tibetan forms of reasoning. Readers concerned exclusively with only one of these two inquiries may need to exercise more than the usual patience; however, both inquiries can be served only by an examination that is addressed to empirical Tibetan materials that are finely detailed—"detailed" because ethnomethodological research has learned that adequate exhibits of ordinary society's distinctive orderlinesses depend exclusively upon the *details* of that ordinary lived work. We are above all preoccupied with the distinctive orderlinesses of ordinary Tibetan debating.

In most of these debates there are two respondents or defenders (L). The clarifier of the reasoning (T), or challenger, usually commences by asking a defender to explain something. T will elaborate on the basis of the defender's reply and call for further discussion. These contributions *gravitate toward the development of a formal structure of thinking*, and it is all a public performance. Although the matters here concern the most profound ontological issues, the first task that debaters face is to establish what Alfred Schutz (1971 Vol. II, 173) called "the mutual tuning in relationship," and this is through and through *a practical matter* that can only be achieved by means of a congregational exhibition of the debate's topic at hand. This congregational nature is distinctive of public performance. The relationship is a practical achievement of the debaters, with which they come to a "sharing of the flux of experiences in inner time, a living through a vivid present in common" Schutz (1971 Vol. II, 173). Only when they have tuned in to the topic *together* can they turn to ontology. Their gravitation toward some formal structure of thinking is an ethnomethod that debaters use in debate to synchronize their utterances and tune in to each other.

Organizational Matters

The ethnomethods of Tibetan dialecticians enable them to build up a formal structure of argument, the first step of which is this selection and ratification of the topic. The contingencies of this work require immediate organizational solutions, which are attended to before more universal issues come into the picture. That is, the participants are first addressed to the local organizational work of establishing some facilities for communicating, one of the three concerns of debaters—local organizational work, a formal structure of reasoning, and truth concerns.

Sociolinguists William Labov and D. Fanshel (1977, 70) suggest that the coherence of a conversation *is not found at the level of propositional statements*; rather, it is achieved among the actions of the interlocutors. Philosophizing can take place only after parties concert their actions to provide an interactional context for philosophical inquiry. The organization of the talk is directed to providing logical accounts of the philosophical matters at hand, but these formal accounts are themselves employed to keep the interaction organized, and there is an actively reflexive practice at work. Although keeping the talk organized and keeping the philosophical reflection organized are two distinct tasks, it may be said that they work hand-in-glove. *The formal structure of reasoning* finds its way about via the local organizational tools and the orderliness that the work of keeping the talk organized has provided; the formal analysis rides the interactional order, as it were. But that *organizational work of producing a local orderliness* exploits the formal accounts, utilizing those accounts' own organizational capacities. That is, to turn Labov and Fanshel's constructive insight on its head, conversational coherence can be established interactionally by means of those propositional statements that Labov and Fanshel denigrate somewhat dualistically; however, it is not only the truth-value of the statements that is vital here but the capacity of the propositions to integrate in an organized way the analytic contributions of the participants. Philosophy first finds itself always already embodied in organizational work. The philosophers' social logistics are not entirely coincident with the logistics that are essential to the reasoning; however, logic and reason are devices that assist the philosophers in their social task of organizing a philosophical inquiry. That is, the logical is the social, and logic and reason may be respecified as topics of social order.

We do not intend any sort of sociological reductionism here, for the philosophers do have truth concerns that invest themselves in the objective social forms that the philosophers have developed, and any adequate phenomenology must keep sight of those truth concerns. But the formal analytic accounts of the reasoning are devices which the participants can use to regularize their reflections. While it is the case that for a philosopher what is proven to be true by a formal unity of true propositions must be held to be true on Mars as well, it is yet undeniable that the "formal" in "a formal unity of true propositions" is a social achievement. It is the social praxis of the debaters that compels them to convey any intuited reflection to a formal unity of propositions, whose coherence and authority serves to organize the debate. As Durkheim once observed, the first logical categories are social categories.[1] Formalization facilitates communication and provides all parties equal access to the public deliberation. Bar-Hillel (1964, 120) observes that logic was a development that emerged from the social practices of Greek citizens who brought their disputes to a civil judge for some decision. In their search for legitimacy, they found that objective arguments were more persuasive than subjective feelings, and so they developed a variety of logical forms. Gradually such apophantics extended its sway to other regions. Bar-Hillel situates Aristotle's fresh contributions in this social environment that was concerned with developing objective standards of rationality. Putting one's argument in a syllogistic form, without losing its significance or purport (to the extent that is possible), rendered legitimate the rationalization of one's social interests. It is only from within a context constituted by the forms of social interaction which have been established that one can begin to attempt to dissociate a propositional formulation from those activities. In a fit of retrospective illusion, participants can promote their formal analytic achievements to a universal realm beyond the local contingencies of its production.

Any philosophical discussion reveals practices whereby debaters formulate the local deliberations in formal analytic terms in order to meet the demands of a transcendental reason. That formal reasoning becomes transcendental is a social as well as a philosophical phenomenon. Because it is also a social phenomenon, parties are directed not only to logical matters but also to aesthetic ones; that is, the elegance with which the philosophical rhetoric can come to embody the logical achievements is part of what motivates the participants. They are attracted to eloquence, to the beauty and simplicity of a formal orderliness, as much as they are motivated by the substantive issues. This is because the emerging structures of interaction, along with the social solidarity that facilitates their remaining attuned to each other's thinking, is affected by the aesthetics of their talk and their reasoning.

Logical formatting serves as a device which philosophers use to keep track of their thinking—that is, to retain in the objective memory of the occasion, or keep in play, the developing accomplishments of their philosophizing. They publicly objectify their thought enough to be able to correlate their interpretations. But we should not presume that they always know where they are heading. The rationality is a practical rationality and not an *a priori* one. It evolves not always as the conscious and deliberate efforts of philosophers to concretize their reflections; rather, the formal structure of reasoning evolves in a dialectical relationship with the thinking, and enables the philosophizing (cf. Liberman 1999a). A logical, supportive apparatus is built up *along with* the philosophical

---

1. Giddens (1972, 203 and 263).

insights; the apparatus may be motivated by those insights, in which case their compelling deductive force becomes a sort of dressing that ennobles those insights rather than being their origin, *or* it may be the formal analytic structure that makes some of those insights possible by providing a material semiotic matrix with which philosophers can coordinate new reflections effectively. A formally validated apophantic structure provides for "stable and presentable determinations" (Derrida 1994, 82) that serve as facilities for communicating clearly about philosophical matters. The expressive order is set up in tandem with the truth concerns, and the one is not found without the other. As Erving Goffman (1967, 39) observed, the expressive order comprises the social system to which the philosophers direct their contributions so that their thinking can remain coordinated: "A person incidentally subjects his behavior to the expressive order that prevails and contributes to the orderly flow of messages."

Merleau-Ponty (1968, 119) similarly describes the confrontation of ideas:

> A discussion is not an exchange or a confrontation of ideas, as if each formed his own, showed them to the others, looked at theirs, and returned to correct them with his own. . . . Someone speaks, and immediately the others are now but certain divergencies by relation to his words, and he himself specifies his divergence in relation to them. . . . Life becomes ideas and the ideas return to life, each is caught up in the vortex in which he first committed only measured stakes, each is led on by what he said and the response he received, led on by his own thought of which he is no longer the sole thinker.

It is the formal analytic matrix that carries the achievements of the debaters through the course of the debate, and the development of the formal analytic apparatus is a collaborative accomplishment of the debaters. The analytic forms and the philosophical insights keep each other company. But the truth concerns cannot be entirely subsumed within the formal structure of the reasoning. Tibetan debaters use *a formal structure of reasoning* to tame their reflections, to bring those reflections under the reign of formally validated structures, i.e. to socialize them. Formal analysis does not found truth, or valid cognition (*tsad ma*), but it accompanies it.

In our investigations, we are concerned to describe the ways that each Tibetan debater contributes to establishing the emerging logical validities, but this work of developing normative truth must be captured as the corporate and congregational endeavor that it is, and not idealized (even though most Tibetan philosophical texts themselves present only such idealizations). Edmund Husserl recognized that the coherence of logical judgments—the correspondence of one's judging with the judging of others as well as the capacity of one's own thinking to refer to the same object over time—is a function of certain conditions of intersubjective understanding. "The idea of objectivity implies that the intended object is valid at all times and for everyone, and is thus communicable" (Dieter Lohmar, in Embree, et al. 1997, 708). Or, as Merleau-Ponty (1962, xx) captures in a more embodied way, "Sense is revealed . . . where my own and other people's paths intersect and engage each other like gears." This is the site where our investigations are directed.

Habermas doubts that the concept of truth can distinguish between "true consensus" and "false consensus" since every truth itself has to be arrived at consensually,[2] and he acknowledges that reasoning is part of the bedrock of interpersonal communication. Reason has a moral force in part because it is a means with which a social collective makes possible clear communication. Formal reasoning is a constituent of the local organizational activity of parties; hence, formalization has a communicative purpose and is not exclusively a logical concern. The work of fitting one's reflections into the local validities that are emerging is a matter both of providing for the orderliness and contributing to the philosophical reflection.

In taking up the activities of philosophers related to the *formal structure of reasoning* and *the organizational work*, we are not overlooking the *truth concerns* that motivate these projects. Eugene Gendlin (1992, 23) recognizes the pragmatic importance of the philosophical forms, but he insists that "what the forms work *in* [namely, the truth concerns], 'talks back.'" Gendlin (1992, 35) wishes to celebrate our philosophical insights: "What is more than forms is not a fleeting moment between successive forms. If anything is ephemeral, it is the forms. Our saying, acting, and thinking is the steadier of the two, always moving in, with, and after all forms." It is important to note here that Gendlin speaks of "after," and not "before," since the forms provide the matrix for the philosophical reflection. Yet what is it that drives the debaters towards the logic of their deepest insights?

Gendlin conceives the originality of philosophers as consisting of the *way* that philosophers are able to exploit the tensions between the formal analytic work and their philosophical insight in order to do philosophy. Such originality has its own rigor and is not merely being led around by the nose of the local structural contingencies. Those contingencies are there, to be sure, but the philosophers work so that the contingencies bring the philosophical "intricacy along with them, so that it can lead to *further* steps that are not limited" by them (Gendlin 1992, 29). What philosophy that is accomplished does not get accomplished *in spite of* the forms, it gets accomplished *with* the forms. It cannot be done without the forms, but it takes some *philosophical expertise* to be able to do it *with* them. The "more than forms," of which Gendlin speaks, always accompanies the forms. And so part of our vital ethnographic task here is to identify just where philosophers are able to successfully pursue their truth concerns. This ethnomethodological analysis, then, is not a sociological reductionism; rather, all three projects, which are *the projects of the debaters*—truth concerns, a formal structure of reasoning, and the organizational work of producing a local

---

2. P. Sudarsan (1997).

orderliness—must be investigated, and the Tibetan debaters' ethnomethods regarding them must be described.

A Summary of Organizational Items

Tibetan philosophers have many tools at their disposal when, at their work site, they concert their efforts to produce a well-ordered debate. Many of these tools play a role similar to that of punctuation marks in grammar. Some of these organizational items are actual discrete utterances (when this is the case, they are printed in the upper case),[3] and the performative function of these utterances extends beyond their meaning. In two instances (TS'A and CHEE-CHEER), I have left the utterance in the Tibetan since the tonal properties of the utterances play a vital role in the rhetoric of the debate. The most important organizational items are listed in this table, and we will take up all of these items in the succeeding chapters during the course of our ethnomethodological description of Tibetan debating:

Organizational Items Employed by the Clarifier of the Reasoning

Hand-clap [">~", frequently accompanied by IT FOLLOWS THAT ...]
IT PERVADES
TAKE AS THE SUBJECT
BECAUSE
TS'A! [which means, "That is a contradiction"; frequently accompanied by
      a reversed hand-clap ("=v=")]
CONFOUNDED BY ALL THREE! ["*skor gsum*," which sounds like, "Kor
      Soom!" and signifies, "You are defeated!"]
Citations
Tokens
Reversals
Tautologies
Calling for a definition
Put-up or shut-up ["*ma yin rte-*"]
"Picking up" L's utterance
Ridicule, Pushing, Turning his back, etc.

Organizational Items Employed by the Defender

Commitment ["I ACCEPT."]

---

3. Note: the presentation in this volume utilizes capitalization in two ways—(1) within the descriptive text capitalized phrases are *organizational items*, and (2) within a verbatim transcript, the capitalization indicates that the phrase is a *formal token* used as part of the grammar of Tibetan dialectical logistics.

CHEE-CHEER ["WHAT IS THE REASON?"]
THE REASON IS NOT ESTABLISHED [Rejection of proof]
THERE IS NO LOGICAL PERVASION [Rejection of logical pervasion]
Calling for a definition
Stalls and Digressions
Citations

These organizational items of the clarifier of the reasoning and those of the defender are geared into each other; that is, they are the means with which the parties concert their work of debating. The clarifier of the reasoning will commence the discussion by means of a proposition, usually of the typical form, "IT FOLLOWS THAT ... >~" or, "IT PERVADES THAT ... >~"

The clap indicates that a *formal* move in the developing logic has been made:

IT FOLLOWS THAT it is nighttime. >~

The defender may then *accept* the proposal, which will then constitute a logical commitment he must keep: "I ACCEPT. "

Or, the defender may *reject* the proposal, which can be done in three ways: "CHEE-CHEER" ["WHAT IS THE REASON?"], "THE REASON IS NOT ESTABLISHED," or "THERE IS NO LOGICAL PERVASION."

In the case of the first mode of rejection ("CHEE-CHEER"), the defender indicates his preliminary disagreement with a proposition by requesting a logical justification for the formal proposal. The clarifier of the reasoning is then obligated to supply the necessary argument with a statement that includes the word "BECAUSE," as in

IT FOLLOWS THAT it is nighttime. >~
CHEE-CHEER.
BECAUSE it is not day.

And the defender will either accept it, or he will reject it using one of the other two formal tools for rejection: "THE REASON IS NOT ESTABLISHED." This declares that the clarifier of the reasoning has provided a reason that is false in itself, such as the statement,

IT FOLLOWS THAT is nighttime BECAUSE the sun never shines.

Or, the defender can reply, "THERE IS NO LOGICAL PERVASION." This reply acknowledges that the reason itself is true, but it denies that the reason has any logical relationship with the thesis, such as in the statement,

IT FOLLOWS THAT is nighttime BECAUSE it is raining.

Or in the argument, "TAKE AS THE SUBJECT a sound, IT FOLLOWS THAT it is permanent BECAUSE it is a produced phenomenon," the reply, "THERE IS NO LOGICAL PERVASION" is correct, since the assertion in the reason is true (sound is a produced phenomenon) but that does not entail that a sound is permanent.

Here is a brief exchange (from I.4), which displays several of the aforementioned formal tokens of Tibetan debate grammar:

```
         T    TAKE THE CASE OF the rope that looks like a snake. Listen! IT
3:38:36       FOLLOWS THAT it is the mere projection of a notion. >~
         L"   CHEE-CHEER. [BECAUSE OF WHAT?]
         T    BECAUSE that is how the citation says it.
    :37 L"    THE REASON IS NOT ESTABLISHED.
```

It is the burden of the challenger to elicit sufficient commitments from the defender to permit the challenger to ensnare the defender in a logical contradiction. When this occurs, the challenger will declare "TS'A!" and sharply clap the palm of his left hand with the *backside* of his right hand (cited in the transcript as "=v="). As we will see, frequently this is declared when there is no contradiction or when the existence of a contradiction is still an issue and a matter to be proven.

When the principal position for which the defender has been arguing has been proven to be erroneous, the challenger will loudly announce, "CONFOUNDED BY ALL THREE!" ("Kor Soom!"). This amounts to a public declaration of the defeat of the defender. One elucidation explains that it derives from the three criteria for valid reasoning in Buddhist logic—the *rtags chos don gsum* (reason, logical pervasion, and topic[4])—which the challenger is claiming the defender has failed to provide. Since it may be accompanied by the challenger circling his rosary three times around the head of a defender, it is polysemic in that *kor* also means "to circle." In its most appropriate usage, it identifies a point in a debate where a defender has failed to defend his position. It may be accompanied by the challenger circling his rosary around the head of the defender three times, or on rare occasions the challenger may circumambulate his sitting opponent. Occasionally, "Kor Soom!" may be cried even when the grounds for its declaration have not been fully secured.

These few organizational forms may be combined in hundreds of ways, and they have thousands of strategic uses. Here is a more lengthy excerpt (from III.4) that displays each one of the just described organizational items:

```
         T    IT FOLLOWS THAT [the Samkhya] say that a sprout that has
              manifested—
```

---

4. Here "topic" is a gloss for the reason's non-pervasion of the negative of the predicate.

        L"   Oh, that's right.
-001.5- T   —exists at the time of its cause. >~
        L"   They ACCEPT. The cause, oh, yes, yes. They say it exists. They say that it does exist.
        T   Yahh, IT DOES NOT FOLLOW THAT [the Samkhya] accept
-004-   that the sprout has already manifested. >~
        L'   / CHEE-CHEER
        L"   / CHEE-CHEER
        T   If the seed has already manifested, uh, it is necessary to say that
-005-   the sprout does not exist at the time of its cause. >~
        L'   They do not say so about the time of its cause.
        L"   THE REASON IS NOT ESTABLISHED indeed!
        T   IT FOLLOWS THAT they accept that the sprout that has already
-006.5- manifested, yah, is again produced. >~
        L'   / CHEE-CHEER indeed.
        L"   / CHEE-CHEER indeed.
        T   IT FOLLOWS THAT they accept that there is production again—
        L'   Mm.
        T   —BECAUSE they accept that the sprout exists in an unmanifested
-008.5- way at the time of its cause. >~
        L'   / THERE IS NO PERVASION.
        L"   / THERE IS NO PERVASION.
        T   Well then, you are indeed CONFOUNDED BY ALL THREE!

One of the most important aspects that makes Tibetan debating successful dialectics is *the capacity of each party to employ the terminology and reasoning introduced by the other party*. This is a skill that is practiced especially by the clarifier of the reasoning, who will "pick up" phrases and formal propositions used by the respondent. In this way Tibetan debaters are able to produce a common language and preserve the adequacy of their communication.

The clarifier of the reasoning will select from the respondent's utterances the most essential aspects, and then repeat them back to him or use them in his own analysis. By so doing he will elevate the respondent's contributions to the formal structure of the developing analysis, making them into *objective social phenomena*. He will do this even when he disagrees with them. The beauty of this device is that the challenger operates almost mechanically, picking up *whatever* is vital about what the defender contributes, whether the challenger thinks it is valid or not; and the challenger does it with *equanimity*. He plays the role of merely formalizing the accounts for the objective use of the participants. He will objectivate by repeating phrases, using the precise word selection and tone employed by the respondent.

Only a small number of Tibetan public debates reach full resolution of the issues under contention. For Tibetan scholar-monks it is the *process* of these dialectics that motivates them the most; winning arguments is a lesser concern. What is vital is to undertake a way of interrogating—the actual reply or final conclusion is less central to debate praxis. More precisely, their interest is to concert their efforts to produce a tightly organized, efficiently functioning formal analytic apparatus with which philosophical issues can be scrutinized. The better scholars are "better" at constraining the debating within the proper apophantic forms, and this is a primary goal of the local work of Tibetan debaters. In other words, their collaboration is preoccupied with the subjective side of the occasion; although the objective results of that collaboration are welcome achievements, and may be celebrated afterward, they are of lesser significance for collaborating scholars. For them philosophy is a state of dialectics as much as it is a collection of validated tenets, although this fact is unavailable to many Western scholars as a consequence of the textually based methodologies utilized by most Buddhist historians.

Tibetan debates generally commence with an open-ended discussion, and the examination proceeds for some time in a loosely structured manner. Gradually, as the parties find their way to contentious issues, the debate becomes more formally analytic and rigorously structured. Especially, the work of the clarifier of the reasoning is to tend the propriety of the debate, reformat loosely phrased positions into formal analytic ones and objectivate each of the defender's positions so that the differences of the debaters' positions are made evident to all of the participants.

Objectivation

The phenomenon of objectivating the philosophical observations of one's opponent is key to understanding Tibetan public debate. By objectivation I am referring to an actual social practice, not to an individual's theoretical practice. We have witnessed how the clarifier of the reasoning is able to sort out the key elements of the respondent's arguments (even when he disagrees with them) and formulate them publicly in formal, analytic terms. This provides the debaters with clear, evident summaries of the matters with which they are dealing; that is to say, it provides them with object-like, made-observable accounts of their developing investigation, and these accounts are the very material with which their philosophical reflection will proceed. Alfred Schutz (1967, 31-33) has observed that the notion of an objective phenomenon has both a negative and a positive meaning. Its negative meaning, according to which it is frequently understood, is that it is not the subjective meaning in the mind of an actor. But Schutz wishes to emphasize "the positive meaning" that the notion "objective" has, which is the meaning that is given "equally to all," the object taken up as a tangible event that has some facticity. Among such objects Schutz includes signs and expressions, or as Husserl (1970a, 682) suggests, word-sounds whose materiality is available to all. Objectivation refers to the act of making an object in common;

hence it is a social act in that it is a part of the work that actors do to organize the orderliness of their activities. Once a sign or account has been objectivated, that is, made an object, it becomes available for anyone to use as an "intersubjective thought object" (Schutz 1971, Vol. I, 12), that is, as a tool to facilitate communication. Parties may ignore or at least forget the work of this production, since the objective meaning becomes an achievement in hand. According to Schutz (1967, 134) objectivation includes an "already constituted meaning-context of the thing produced, whose actual production we meanwhile disregard." These objects and their meaning-contexts, so produced, are the keys upon which actors play the concerto of their activity.

Schutz relies upon Husserl's (1970a, 314) definition for an objective expression:

> We shall call an expression *objective* if it binds its meaning merely by its manifest, auditory pattern and can be understood without necessarily directing one's attention to the person uttering it.

Schutz's contribution is that he retained in his sight the fact that this objectivity is *practical* and that it is an *achievement* of actors. An objective expression comes to have an anonymous character, and its meaning is "intelligibly coordinated" by cooperating parties (Schutz 1967, 37 and 123). Husserl contrasts objective expressions with "essentially subjective and occasional expressions"; and he observes (1970: 321) that these occasioned expressions can come to be replaced with objective expressions, which implies that some work is performed to accomplish this. Husserl (1973, 57) speaks of objectivation as a process by which objects are designated and judgments presumed to be valid within a given community.

By formalizing thinking in this way, the individual thinker or a community can sustain and extend ordered analysis. Simply put, reason is a means with which thinking can be organized; objectivation and reason foster social integration. Although Husserl observed that objectivation is a dynamic process (cf. Husserl 1964, 184), Schutz takes the concept of objectivation further than Husserl did, and he is more attentive to the social practices that compose it. Especially, Schutz is interested in how actors collaborate among themselves so that the occasioned meanings of the terms they are using come to have a more anonymous, generally available sense. In these analyses we employ this notion of objectivation in order to describe the practical work of actors who concert themselves in providing reliable and reproducible terms, notions, and propositions, along with their meaning-contexts.

It is the nature of an object to be something observable and available in common to two or more parties, and it is the function of the objectivation practices here to make the key ideas of a debate commonly available to the participants. Only by formalizing some terms and having those terms ratified by shared usage, repeated in context along with the routines of reasoning in which they are located, etc., can those notions be shared in common by the collaborating philosophers. By building this social structure, the debaters are able to communicate with each other and clarify their differences. For a philosophical observation to be attended to, it needs to become part of the formal apparatus that is being objectivated, that is, that is being made available equally to all as the philosophical equipment with which the parties can do their work. In Tibetan debate the burden of this work of objectivation rests upon the clarifier of the reasoning, but it is collaborative work, and all of the debaters concert their activities in order to maintain the emerging objective social structure to which the parties are oriented and which consists of the very tools that the debaters use for establishing an orderliness.

By objectivating selected aspects of the philosophical discussion, the parties make their philosophical observations evident. Their methods of objectivation include repeating the statement of an opponent and reformatting it into more formal analytic discourse, in conformity with the grammar of Tibetan debate. A repeated or reformulated statement will be reproposed for corroboration, whereupon it becomes an object held in common and available for formal analytic applications. The dialogue of debate I.4 culminates with this objectivation:

3:40:54 T   Must it exist?! So if one "projects" a thought, it must exist, is it?
    :56 L"   The object of the projection needs to exist.
        T   Ohhh. So the object of projection, the object of projection must
3:41   exist? When the notion is "projected," it must exist?
        L"   It must.

By repeating the issue at hand T publicly emphasizes what is the formal commitment of L", at the same time making it more difficult for L" to renege on that commitment later. Further, by publicly objectivating their thought the clarifier of the reasoning and the respondent are able to correlate their interpretations so that they do not behave like two ships passing in the night. That is, the objectivity of their philosophical productions has the practical function of serving as the means by which their understandings can become more closely aligned, and it permits them to speak to each other more clearly. The products of the formal debate, as objectivated by the parties, have what Garfinkel has called "practical objectivity."

Let us examine a short excerpt from debate I.9, "The Mind that Realizes Emptiness." In this debate the clarifier of the reasoning is exploring the difference between *conceptual imputations* that are projected upon an entity[5] and *innate imputations* that are more deeply seated and refer to a reification that precedes conceptualization. T poses the formal question, and L' repeats it just to get a better hold of it:

---

5. An example may be believing that a certain woman's beauty is inherent in her.

T The text presents an example of the negation of the habitual reification of true existence that is *conceptually* imputed upon a referent object. In this system, that is not necessarily a realization of

6:05:55 emptiness. >~

L' If one refutes the habitual reification of true existence that is conceptually imputed, eh?

T desires a formal reply to his question and presses L' for it, but before replying L' attempts a small STALL[6] by calling for T to clarify which school's system of philosophical tenets he is speaking about:

T Oh, so.

L' In this system, eh?

T Right.

L' The habitual attitude of true existence conceptually imputed upon the referent object is understood to not have any existence. Yes, yes. Now, it would not necessarily be a realization of emptiness.

6:06 T According to this Middle Way Dialectical School.

L' Oh, it's not necessary.

Having won L''s commitment (to the idea that it is possible to formally negate the validity of an habitual attitude of conceptually imputing true existence without reaching the more deeply seated innate fixations, or actually becoming capable of implementing that philosophical insight within one's mundane everyday life, i.e., to realize emptiness), T wishes to elevate this commitment to the emerging objective, formal analytic structure of the debate. So he asks L' to publicly reaffirm this fairly subtle philosophical observation, so that the debaters can have that commitment in hand for their subsequent work:

T If one negates the habitual reification of the true existence conceptually imputed upon the referent object, then you say it is not necessary, right?

:03 L' It's not necessary.

Frequently, this request to reaffirm one's commitment will then be recast in more proper debate form, as in this excerpt from "Trainees With Penetrative Faculties" (II.3), where T recasts his query as a more formal, objective concern with the aid of an appended HAND-CLAP, and L" accepts:

T The commentary offers an explicit explanation, uh, the root text does not explain it so.

9:18:35 L" Oh, this is so.

---

6. Here upper case indicates that the action taken or words spoken are a standardized organizational item, used by Tibetan debaters to provide the orderliness of their local formal analytic affairs.

:36 T   So now, this is the way of explanation in the commentary. >~
    L"   O.K., I ACCEPT.

The clarifier of the reasoning may *keep repeating* the respondent's comments back to him, almost as an auctioneer keeps track of the bidding (the bid at an auction is another social "object" that permits participants to coordinate and align their participation). In this case the accounts of the philosophical argument play a role similar to the auctioneer's announcements. In this next excerpt from the same debate, they are speaking about a related topic, the fact that a person can have faith in the possibility of enlightenment (or freedom) without knowing very much about it:

9:21:08 T   It is said that it is not necessary to fully understand freedom. >~
    L'   This is not necessary. It is not necessary for having faith in freedom.
    L"   For just the generation of faith it is not necessary.
    L'   For the generation of faith in freedom, for a commitment to attain freedom, it is not necessary.
    T   For a commitment to attain freedom it is not necessary, is it?
    L'   It's not needed. It's not.
    T   For having faith in freedom.
    L'   It's not necessary. It's not necessary.
9:21:17 T   So, is it necessary that this person accept that freedom exists? >~
    L"   It is necessary that he accept that it exists, it's necessary.
    T   He must accept that freedom exists.
    L"   Yes yes.
    L'   One generates faith, doesn't one?
    T   Yes.
    L"   He can accept that freedom exists as a prerequisite to developing faith.
9:21:27 T   For developing faith uh, it is necessary to accept freedom. >~
    L"   It's O.K. to accept that.
    T   He accepts freedom.
    L"   It must be accepted.
  :33 T   It is necessary to accept it, isn't it? =v= [slight]. Since it is
-075.5-   necessary, uh, a commitment to obtain freedom is necessary. >~

Although the defenders' point is obvious at least by 9:21:27, the clarifier of the reasoning reformats it with a HAND-CLAP, and *repeats* it yet again, and then links it with the other portion of the defenders' contention, at 9:21:33. Observe that L' and L" are repeating each other as well as T, and so this "auctioneer's work" of keeping the business of the debate visible before the debating parties is a congregational effort. The substantive issue, the relation of philosophical understanding to faith, will be taken up later.

In this next excerpt (from "Nagarjuna's Proof," I.5), the clarifier of the reasoning and the defendants collaborate in this work of objectivating the philosophical issue, exhibiting the logical constraints they will be governed by, and keeping the object before them. They are taking up the refutation of existence according to an inherent essence, which is presented at the commencement of the first chapter of Nagarjuna's *Stanzas on the Middle Way*. At this point they are directed to the possibility of an entity being produced by something that is other than that entity:

	T	IT FOLLOWS THAT production from an other is refuted.
	L	We say that it does.
3:50:52	T	Like that. We have refuted any production from an other, and the sprout is not produced in any of these four possible ways [from itself, from an other, from a combination, or from neither]. When one realizes non-production—
3:51	L"	If production from an other is refuted, it must be that we have refuted true establishment on the basis of inherent characteristics, right?
	L'	No, that isn't necessary. If production from an other is refuted, IT DOES NOT necessarily FOLLOW that we have refuted true establishment on the basis of its inherent characteristics.
3:51:07	T	If production from an other is refuted, IT FOLLOWS THAT one does not have to have refuted true establishment on the basis of inherent characteristics.

Although L' and L" have a slight disagreement, *they keep in play* what it is they are disagreeing about by publicly sharing the same terminology. By the time T repeats the phrase "production from another" (at 3:51:07), the formulation has become so familiar it can stand as a token for the preceding discussion. It is typical for the debaters to build up an emerging argument by logical synthesis, using pieces of the discussion that have been objectivated. The philosophical construction expands as a number of relevant observations are synthesized within the objectivated complex; however, as the repetition of these objectivated agreements proceeds and the meaning-complexes of the terms become shared in common, they can be uttered more economically. Hence, after a period of synthetic building-up, an economy is fixed that permits the debaters to proceed with the remainder of the debate while holding in hand some capsulated summary or token of components previously objectivated. Husserl (1970, 640) describes this in more precise phenomenological language: "It is true of the 'conjunctive' (or better 'collective') synthesis . . . that it permits of nominalization, in which case the collective object constituted by the synthesis becomes the simply presented object of a new 'single-rayed' act, and so is made 'objective' in the pregnant sense of the word." Such tokens are objectively available to the debaters for use in their collective work, and the process assists the efficiency of their work as well the adequacy of their communication.

One of the practices that is most characteristic of Tibetan dialectics is the unrelenting way in which the clarifier of the reasoning will objectivate each commitment of the defender, *including* commitments that the clarifier or challenger himself may adamantly oppose. This practice keeps the current state of the debate in *full view* of all the parties, thereby ensuring clear communication. In this next illustration ("Reification of the Ego," I.6) the clarifier of the reasoning takes up the dissenting defendant at 4:46:35 and reformulates his position within the terms of Tibetan formal analytic grammar:

> T   If you accept that, then TAKE THAT AS THE TOPIC. IT FOL-
> LOWS THAT this is what the lower philosophical tenets accept
> 4:46:21   to be the view of an ego. >~
> L"   It's not necessarily the case. I don't accept it.
> :35 T   You must accept it. Listen please, professor. Listen. IT DOES
> NOT NECESSARILY FOLLOW THAT this formulation of a con-
> ceptually acquired view of an ego is accepted by the lower phi-
> losophical schools. >~

This competent reformulation of a position *with which T disagrees* helps to clarify what is at issue in the debate, in a fashion that minimizes any distortion of L"'s views. This next, more lengthy excerpt from the same debate explores the topic of "mineness" (such as "my" fingernail or possibly "my" watch—the issue being the ontological status of such mineness, a phenomenon that Buddhist inquiry finds to be without any substance). The debate provides more detail than we need to examine here; we are concerned now merely to observe that after a good deal of chatter in response to T's pushing for a reply (at 4:50:26), T finally *elevates* the general discussion *to the formal structure* that is emerging within the debate by means of his summary proposition (see asterisk at 4:50:44):

> T   TAKE AS THE TOPIC something reified by perception to be es-
> tablished by its own characteristics.
> L   Oh, exactly right.
> T   What is the reason why a perceived "mine" is not apprehended as
> 4:50:24   established by its own characteristics? >~
> L'   —/ [L' and L" speak simultaneously; and it is indecipherable]
> L"   —/
> :26 T   What is the reason?! >~
> L"   BECAUSE for that there must be the habitual reification of a per-
> sonal self.
> :28 L'   BECAUSE "I"[-ness] cannot be perceived. IT FOLLOWS THAT
> no "mine" can be witnessed BECAUSE an "I" cannot be per-
> ceived.

:30 T   Ohhh!

L"   It is said that having perceived a "mine" the eye and so forth having perceived one, the "mine" is reified as self-sufficiently existent and independent.

T   What are you saying? What is a perceived "mine"?

L"   When a "mine" is perceived, a personal self must be apprehended. Since here there is no reification.

L'   IT FOLLOWS THAT no "mine"[-ness] can be perceived BECAUSE no "I"[-ness] is perceived.

*4:50:44T   Yah. TAKE THE TOPIC the apprehension of something reified as established by its own characteristics and perceived as a "mine." Yah, yah. If a perceived "mine" is reified as existing according to its own characteristics, then IT FOLLOWS THAT an "I" is reified as existing by its own characteristics. >~

L'   I ACCEPT.

This congregational work of making formal, public objects of the assertions involves a good deal of back and forth checking and rechecking, and the temporality of this can resemble a game of ping-pong, such as in this excerpt from "Common Sense Truths," I.1:

T   Now, from the mundane, everyday perspective, to what does the "common sense" refer in the passage,[7] *"For the thinking of the common-sense mind of a person practiced at applying con-*

3:02:58   *ventions according to valid customary examination?"* >~

3:03 L" In general, common sense, customary conceptual thinking refers to the object.

T   What?

L"   It must be that it applies to the object.

T   Which?

L"   One speaks of the common sense object. How is it said?

T   When one says, *"applying conventions according to valid customary examination"*?

L"   Oh yes.

:07 T   It refers to the common sense object?

L"   Oh, it must be referring to the common sense object.

In the next case, from "Refuting Essentialism" (II.4), T similarly *keeps repeating* the proposition in order to check, align, and consolidate the mutuality of the understanding. The hand-clap (>~) serves as a token that indicates the formal summary status of the formulation to which it is affixed:

---

7. Here the italics indicate that the debater is citing a textual passage.

9:34:02 T   If we say that it is necessary, its lack of having a true essence, if
              we have cognized the lack of having a true essence, right?
         L'   Yes.
         T   So, if one has cognized the emptiness of the apparent inherent
              essence, which is the object to be refuted, then IT FOLLOWS
    :10   THAT one has cognized the lack of having a true essence. >~
-181-   L'   I ACCEPT.
         T   If we say that that is acceptable, right? Uh, so—if one has cog-
              nized the lack of having a true essence, then IT FOLLOWS
              THAT both the subtle entitylessness of phenomena and the subtle
    :17   selflessness of persons must be cognized. >~
-082.5- L   One has realized the selflessness, I ACCEPT.
         T   If we say that is necessary, right, uh, right? Ohh. This way. Uh, if
              we say that one has cognized the selflessness, uh, IT FOLLOWS
              THAT one cognizes both the subtle selflessness of a person and
    :27   the subtle entitylessness of phenomena. >~
-085-   L   I ACCEPT.

The short phrase, "If we say that" (T, -081-) reveals that the parties are not
merely philosophizing, they are addressing the practical organizational work of
doing philosophy. A reflexive hermeneutics is at work, and the debaters are
aware that they are engaged in a collaborative task of formalizing their inquiry.
    Similarly, in "Does Wisdom Formulate Emptiness As Existing?" (III.2, my
italics) the clarifier of the reasoning calls for the philosophical topic at hand to
be formally "presented," and L" responds in a manner that reveals that he is
aware of the practical, formal analytic work they are up to:

-016-   T   For example, something like a pot is said to be "posited by the
              mind" and "present through the force of appearing to the mind."
              How is this "mind" to be presented?
-017-   L"   What? Oh, I see. A pot, right.
         L'   (unclear)
         L"   *It can be presented* that a pot is constituted by something like a
              sense consciousness, right? Something like a sense consciousness
              can be proposed, right? There is a sense consciousness proposed, is
              there?

    In "How We Present the Mind that Realizes Emptiness" (I.9), T calls for L'
to "present" his position in formal analytic terms:

6:08:10 T   Oh, PRESENT how one refutes a mode of asserting an imputed
              conceptualization.
         L'   The /
         T   / The imputed conceptualization of a reified "true" essence,
              one who refutes the mode of asserting an imputed conceptualiza-

tion of a reified, "true" essence can be one who has a realization of emptiness, can he not?

:15 L' That's right.
T And one who refutes a mode of asserting an imputed conceptualization of a reified, "true" essence can be one who has not realized emptiness, isn't it?
L That's right.

After considering and agreeing about the observation that one can formally, or abstractly, refute a false belief without necessarily understanding it, a reference to the fact that apophantic reasoning can remain correct but shallow, T calls for L' to "formulate" their insight in a formal way (at 6:08:18 below). At first L' stalls by referring to a particular school of philosophical tenets, but T promptly (at 6:08:21) HAND-CLAPs in L''s face, exhorting him to make an immediate reply. T and L both recognize that part of their philosophical activity includes the practical work of reformulating their discussion using formal analytic objects:

6:08:18 T Oh, now HOW DOES ONE FORMULATE THIS?
L' According to the analysis of the Syllogism-based Reasoning School /
:21 T   / >~
L' According to the analysis of the Syllogism-based Reasoning School there is an imputed conceptualization of a reified "true" essence, isn't there?
T Oh.
L' There is also an innate proclivity to objectify an entity, but here there is no apprehension that considers thoroughly the essentialist reification of an entity's being that is produced by this innate proclivity to objectify. And such a subtle realization in terms of an awareness of the essentialist reification of an entity's identity by the innate proclivity to objectify is required.

In debate I.2, T publicly comments about when L does and does not satisfy this requirement to speak in formal analytic terms, observing, "This is the point to be proven formally, right?" (*da bsgrub bya gcig yin da*) and "This is not the way to formalize our talk" (*bzhag pa'i skad cha 'di ma red*) when he wishes to direct the discussion along more formal analytic pathways. In "The Customary Truth of Common Sense Practices," I.1) there is a call for formal analytic formulation that occurs at the very outset of a debate, and the practical character of the philosophical work of the debaters is evident:

2:58:27 T So first, what is there to prove?

> L'   What? When we consider what appears to an ordinary person's consciousness. [5.0 seconds of silence] Mm. [3.0 seconds of silence]
>
> T   >~
>
> L'   There is a way to fix the formulation about whether or not a customary truth is based upon what appears to an ordinary person's consciousness.

"Fixing formulations" is their philosophical business. Their concern for the proper formulation is a concern for social order as a production problem. Using formal analytic formulations is not exclusively a logical concern, it is also a concern for constructing a communicative or social organizational structure that is efficacious.

There is a variety of repeating that involves more than the verbatim repeat of one's partner's utterance. It is a concerted repeat that so resembles the rereading of a script that I speak of it as a REHEARSAL. In a rehearsal both parties keep going over the same analytic ground together. From the same debate,

3:08:20 T   Does it not necessarily PERVADE that a customary truth must be the distorted common sense perception of a mundane, everyday consciousness? IT PERVADES that it must be distorted common
    :26   sense; or DOES IT NOT PERVADE? >~

> L"   IT PERVADES THAT it is a distorted common sense.
>
> T   What?
>
> L'   IT PERVADES, it is said.
>
> T   It pervades, right?
>
> L"   It is said that it pervades.

T objectivates L's reply by persisting in his repetition of the question. By T's next turn, the two of them are working together efficiently:

> T   If it pervades, right? Yah, now IT PERVADES, right? It's a distorted common sense appearing to a mundane consciousness. TAKE AS THE SUBJECT the reification of an entity as having inherently true existence. Yah. IT FOLLOWS THAT it is distorted common sense!
>
> :38 L"   It is said that IT PERVADES that it is distorted common sense, but you don't say, "It's a distorted common sense appearing to a mundane consciousness."
>
> :40 L'   IT IS ACCEPTABLE THAT it is distorted common sense.
>
> T   IT FOLLOWS THAT it is distorted common sense. TAKE AS THE TOPIC the reification of an entity as having inherently true
> :44   existence. IT FOLLOWS THAT it is distorted common sense. >~
>
> L'   IT IS ACCEPTABLE!

Efficient partnership is promoted by T and L synchronizing their utterances together in a rhythmic way, and because rehearsals are so well known to the parties they facilitate this *rhythmic* alliance. Indeed, the function of REHEARS-ALS is not only the objectivation of the discussion but the establishment of a rhythm for the debate, and the rhythm echoes, or embodies, the conceptual alignment. Here (II.2) such rhythm is established at 9:11:23-29:

9:11:19 T   It is said that one will be unable to obtain liberation by relying upon a correct understanding of the Four Truths and the Sixteen Attributes as it is explained in the two principal Abidharma texts. [T ties robe around his waist.] Now, in order to obtain liberation from cyclic existence, this text explains that this system, uh —/

:26 L'   / It is said that one must realize emptiness.

T   It is said that one must have a realization of the reality of suchness.

L'   It is.

T   Isn't it?

-086-   L'   It is.

9:11:29 T   Therefore, oh, so it's said, uhh, *"By relying upon a correct understanding of the Four Truths and the Sixteen Attributes as it is explained in the two principal Abidharma texts,"—*

L'   Mm.

T   —uh, IT FOLLOWS THAT one cannot thereby obtain liberation

9:11:37   from cyclic existence. >~

L'   Yes, indeed.

T   One cannot thereby obtain it, right?

L'   One cannot obtain it.

T   Because one would not be able to obtain it, uh, oh, so, uh, IT FOLLOWS THAT to actually liberate oneself from cyclic exis-

:47   tence, it is necessary to realize the meaning of emptiness. >~

-091-   L'   I ACCEPT!

:48 T   It is necessary to have this realization.

L'   It is necessary to have this realization.

By means of these rehearsals (at 9:11:29, :37, :47, and :48) T and L' have clarified the topic for the debate and learned where they stand. Rehearsals are like familiar signposts, and they may be used to recover the common ground should the debate stray from the topic. A debate cannot succeed until both the clarifier of the reasoning and the defendant are listening to each other closely, and although at times it may appear tedious to a novice observer, rehearsals may be performed with great skill and in a fashion that permits the debate to remain a dynamic event, one that can provide context and a structure for their reflections.

A similar device that bears elegant rhythmic properties is the REVERSAL. This is when a party, usually the clarifier of the reasoning, repeats a proposition

in an incorrect form, receives a rejection, and then promptly *reverses* the terms
of the proposition (rendering it correct) in order to receive the defender's assent
(I.5):

3:48:13 T   The reasoning is not correct. >~
         L   YOUR REASON IS NOT ESTABLISHED.
         T   . . . IT FOLLOWS THAT the reasoning is correct.
         L   I ACCEPT.

Not only does the reversal here sustain *the rhythm* of the debaters' utterances, it
displays a dialectic in which the parties are able to listen to each other, which is
what makes it "dialectic" worthy of the name.

In objectivating philosophical views, the positions are reformulated to meet
the demands of a transcendental reason, a function that is both logical and social. Once a position has been objectivated it is then made available for ratification by the parties, and a proposition so ratified wins authorization as being formally valid. Authorization provides dignity to the parties' philosophical deliberations. Either the clarifier of the reasoning or the respondent may nominate
candidates for such Authorization. There is a third stage[8] that follows the Authorization, and that is a process by which the formulation duly authorized becomes *disengaged* from the process by which it was developed.

Objectivation → Authorization → Disengagement

The work whereby an insight becomes formalized, synthesized, objectivated, and ratified *necessarily* comes to be forgotten by the collaborating philosophers, and the formulation, syllogism, or argument that is the product of
their work is elevated to part of what composes "universal" reason, transcending

---

8. Most ethnomethodologists are suspicious of heuristic schema such as this, and for
good reason. Garfinkel has advised, "Try to work without trying to theorize generally
from the very outset. 'Ethnomethodological indifference' is important advice, but it is
merely a slogan; you'll be damn lucky if you can do it." In many sociological analyses,
theorizing provides a convenient narrative means for ordering the sensibility of the local
work of parties, but the real work is to describe the organizational devices that the parties
themselves use to order the sensibility of their affairs. The real order is methodogenic
(Garfinkel 2002, 71), an ethno-order that depends upon member's methods and is not at
all a literary achievement of the analyst. Nothing should be introduced from the outside
that would substitute for a description of that local orderliness. In this instance, the local
orderliness is described in its specific details, and this schema, developed only *after* the
ethno-order has been identified and analyzed, is intended merely to assist the reader in
finding his or her way about these very complicated social affairs. They serve especially
as a pertinent heuristic device for indicating the temporal order in which the parties' local
organizational work proceeds when they collaborate in producing an instance of universal
reason.

all local circumstances. This apparently objective, abstracted, and indifferent logical calculus seems to share the "immortality" of a Durkheimian social fact (Garfinkel and Wieder 1992, 203-4; Garfinkel 2002, 65) in that it becomes a taken-for-granted object whose site of production is forgotten. It becomes a so-cial fact (*fait sociale*, Durkheim 1964). The illusion is fostered that the reflec-tions were compelled strictly by the formal analysis and that the only contingen-cies were formal logical ones.

The impersonality with which Disengagement can occur is conveyed by one of the most common locutions found in Tibetan debate—the "*zer,*" which means "so it is said." This syllable is affixed to a considerable portion of the proposi-tions that a Tibetan scholar-monk proposes in a debate, and it has the sense that what is said is undoubted, generally accepted wisdom and not merely the view of a particular thinker. By employing it, a debater removes himself from his own statement. In this next excerpt (III.4) L" articulates his personal view at -124-, but he dignifies his assertion with the attribution that it is a well accepted notion, and such attribution is achieved by means of the "*zer.*" It is also typical of Ti-betan debate for the challenger to readily dismiss any defender assertion; the challenger will pick up a defender's assertion and immediately challenge him to defend his view, as at -125.5-.

-123.5- T   That is for a Dialectical School proponent. >~
Audience   It is. It is.
       L"   It's not. It cannot be the Dialectical School.
       L'   TAKE AS THE SUBJECT a sprout. IT FOLLOWS THAT it is not produced from self—
-124- L"   That is not the way to refute a Dialectical School proponent, THEY SAY [*zer*].
       L'   —"BECAUSE its production would be purposeless and endless" is not a refutation for the Dialectical School. This is for Vaibhasika proponents, these are the Vaibhasika proponents!
-125.5- T   Oh >~ Why is it not for the Dialectical School ?
       L'   What?
       T   Why is it not for the Dialectical School?
       L'   "Why is it not for the Dialectical School?"
2:19:08 L" BECAUSE they already do not accept that it has been established according to its own essence.

Disengagement involves practices in addition to this use of the *zer*. The sig-nal practice, by which Tibetan debaters accomplish, in a collaborative way, the Disengagement that allows an objectivated truth to become accepted as univer-sal, is for the debaters to orchestrate their utterances in a rhythmic manner that lends to the apophantic discourse an apparently independent character.

In setting up a temporalization for the dialectics, the debaters give reason the aspect of running itself; here aesthetics and logic are inextricably mixed.

This social process is described in exacting detail in chapter 6, "Rhymes and Reason." Ethnomethodologically speaking, it is the organized accomplishment of what Merleau-Ponty (1964b, xiii) calls "*le prejugé du monde*," the bias that what is a local social production has universal application as a fact of life. It is ironic but expectable that Tibetan philosophers, whose philosophical practice is centered upon deconstructing reifications, should rely so heavily upon a universalizing practice that requires a degree of social amnesia about the causes and conditions of their philosophical productions. This Disengagement is achieved by the collaborative work of the parties. It is a vital part of philosophical practice and the important final stage in the production of "universal reason," a pattern that typically includes these three stages, which we have just described.

Chapter 5

Reason as a Public Activity

Human thought is consummately social: social in its origins, social in its functions, social in its forms, social in its applications. At base, thinking is a public
activity.

—Clifford Geertz (1973, 360)

The public character of reason in Tibetan philosophical culture is by now obvious. However, there is a tendency in both European and Tibetan intellectual
cultures to view reason as something that stands independent of social practices.
Even when Tibetans deny that truth is something static and expressible, their
denial is argued in formal terms and reasonings. In this way there occur peculiar
debates in which Tibetan scholars will employ logical validation to prove that
logical validation is not ultimate, or they will attempt to prove apophantically
that emptiness cannot be reduced to any formal representation (see debate III.2).
Despite a naive but commonly held belief in the independence of formal reason—that is, the assumption that what is reasoned to be true rests upon absolutely secure grounds, which are independent of any particular cohort of philosophers—logical reason is indeed, and necessarily, a public activity. It is the
perspective of ethnomethodology that meanings, especially formal ones, are not
personal possessions but public events; this outlook is founded upon a long tradition of sociological research and reflection that includes Emile Durkheim,
George Herbert Mead, and Jurgen Habermas, among others.

The Interactionist Tradition of Investigating Reason

Mead (1962, 133) has argued that the referent of the notion "mind" itself is a
social activity: "It is absurd to look at the mind simply from the standpoint of
the individual organism; for although it has its focus there, it is essentially a social phenomenon." Throughout the investigations of this volume we have been
concerned to identify and describe the relation between logical validation, or
what we have termed the *formal structure of reasoning*, and social validation,

including what we have been calling the *local organizational work* of providing the orderliness that permits adequate interaction and communication to occur. These two domains are in fact not separable from each other. Their separation is an analyst's convention, for the reason that logic is used as a social organizational device. Since logic is not exclusively a social device, it deserves conceptualization in its own domain, but where will one find a logic that exists without concerns for local orderliness and social validation?

We have already discussed Bar-Hillel's account of the emergence in the environment of the Greek *polis* of formal syllogistic reason.[1] The formal analytic practices developed there by the Greeks were developed as social practices. They developed as the discourse of juridical advocates, most especially when such advocacy became the specialty of professionals. In India as well, a number of the terms used in logical treatises written by classical scholars—terms such as "position" (*paksha*) and "thesis" (*pratijna*), which were taken over by Tibetan scholars (*phyogs, dam bca'*)—were derived from legal procedures as defined in classical treatises concerning law and politics (Dreyfus 2002, 205).[2] Therefore, significant portions of the philosophical practices of two civilizations were derived from the social contexts of jurisprudence and not by the contemplation of truth concerns by isolated philosophers operating individually. During the time of Plato, philosophy was imagined as a public, social activity. Plato himself was suspicious of writing and conceived of philosophy as a practice, a dialectics, an activity, a process, and not as stasis. It was Aristotle who codified philosophy as a straightforward method, but he was still operating in the practical world of the Greek *polis*, where the argumentation was mostly juridical. Those logicians who followed Aristotle increasingly turned away from analyzing arguments and investigating the semantics and structure of natural languages, and instead turned to analyzing and interpreting Aristotle's own formal analytic achievements (Bar-Hillel). But according to Heidegger (1991, 4 and 33), "Centuries were needed for the principle of reason to be stated *as a principle,*" that is for the modern development of logic as logistics to become established, in the seventeenth century. Sociological researchers are concerned to relocate formal reason in its natural social origins (cf. Collins 1998) and to refocus upon the natural languages, and sociologists are less given to the naive acceptance of the received notion that reason stands upon its own grounds, independent of the contingencies of human agency. This, of course, is blasphemy in some philosophical circles.

The anthropologist Clifford Geertz (1973, 360) is well known for the observation that is the epigraph of this chapter: "At base, thinking is a public activity—its natural habitat is the houseyard, the market place, and the town square."

---

1. See page 85.
2. Dreyfus is citing E. A. Solomon, *Indian Dialectics.* Ahmedabad: Institute of Learning and Research, 1976.

Harold Garfinkel (1977b) elaborates upon this idea that thinking is a public activity:

> Accountable thinking and knowing must be put back into the world. And as soon as one begins to look for such objects in the world, one is simply overwhelmed by them. It is a strange policy which requires that all credible thinking be sought for in the heads. I mean as biologist's heads. You can bowdlerize the whole enterprise of thinking and knowing by putting it together in a manageable package by speaking of "mindful displays," "thoughtful speaking," "thoughtful action," "planful action," providing for its observability (since you need to do that) and once you have pinned it down via the devices that are provided for, that are "observable," then stuffing it into a head somewhere alongside other things in the head like ears, Eustachian tubes, electrical discharges, etc. The question here, however, is why would anyone want to turn his back on the very places where thinking and knowing are first encountered as the most obvious facts of life, namely in the looks of ordinary things. Nothing is available by introspection. We are dealing with the produced looks of things. It is worldly matters we are concerned with.

What Mead and Geertz address in only a general way, Garfinkel is attempting to specify, and the respecification of formal reason as a worldly matter requires that one capture thinking—and here, reason—as the "produced" event that it is, that is, as a social activity. Our aim is not some sort of general notion of how reason is a produced achievement of philosophers; rather, our purpose is to identify and describe in its lived details the just-so's and just-what's of real and actual reasoning in this empirical setting.

Ethnomethodology's "empirical" is not an empirical that involves constructing experimental settings that are far removed from any indigenous settings. Ethnomethodology's "empirical" is reserved only for natural settings, and by this is meant the settings of the parties being studied themselves. That is because the meaningfulness of the world of the persons being studied must be preserved and not submerged beneath the language and relevancies of modern European and American social scientists (here again, what is valid bears a social component). We heed Adorno's advice (2000, 120) "not to operate with ready-made, thought-out concepts in isolation, but to confront concepts with that from which they arise." We are not interested in an investigation of Tibetan reasoning study that loses the phenomenon itself, in the way that Wittgenstein (1972, 66) implied when he quipped, "In order to find the real artichoke, we divested it of its leaves." For example, what would be the point of running Tibetans through preprogrammed experiments in logic, when it is far more instructive to capture their philosophical practices in their indigenous setting, a setting, incidentally, that has endured in one form or another (counting its original life in India) for sixteen hundred years? Rather than subject them to our language and its vanities, the more challenging course of action is to expose ourselves to their language.

The notion of reason being a public activity is rejected by many Anglo-American philosophers and cognitive scientists, who see thinking as something that only takes place inside people's heads, and for the most part Tibetological investigations of Tibetan philosophy have followed this prejudice. We are not claiming that there are no internal physiological processes associated with "mind," "thinking," "reason," etc. We are only arguing that the study of internal mental processes do not have the capacity to tell us what we need to know *most* about thinking. As Mead (1962, 125) commented, "The whole process is not a mental product, and you cannot put it inside the brain." Understanding and reason are social processes. As Durkheim (1983) queried, "How could reason, in particular, have arisen in the course of the experiences undergone by a single individual?"

Wittgenstein (1972, 133) contended that "understanding is not a mental process," and he described well the social origins of understanding when he summarized concisely, "Meaning is like going up to someone." It is not only "like" that, meaning *is* going up to someone. And Levinas (1993, 142) makes the identical point in reference to formal reason itself: "Beyond the thematization of the Said and of the context stated in the proposition, *apophansis* signifies as a modality of the approach to the other person. The proposition is proposed to the other person." Without a social context, reason would be without motive. Wittgenstein was especially critical of psychologistic reductionisms. "We talk of processes and states and leave their nature undecided. Sometimes perhaps we shall learn more about them we think" (103). In the final paragraph (1972, 172) of the main section of *Philosophical Investigations*, Wittgenstein concluded emphatically (his exclamation), "Nothing is more wrong-headed than calling meaning a mental activity!"

Mead (1962, 78-9) suggested that any "process" at work must in fact be external: "The interpretation of gestures is not, basically, a process going on in the mind; it is an external, overt, physical process going on in the actual field of social experience." One of the reasons that Mead believed that understanding was not primarily an internal mental process is that understanding is not always a conscious activity, but it is always a social one. Mead (1962, 80) wrote, "The basis of meaning is thus objectively there in social conduct. . . . Meaning is a content of an object which is dependent upon the relation of an organism or group of organisms to it. It is not essentially or primarily a psychical content (a content of mind or consciousness), for it need not be conscious at all." Most of the things we understand are the result not of logical processes but of intuited social demands.[3] Adorno (1992, 12) accused philosophy of "concept fetishism," and he emphasized the importance of *mimesis* in understanding, which is humans copying other humans, not out of feeble-mindedness but as persons naturally living within the social solidarity of a community of actors. Persons develop their understandings congregationally, that is, people concert themselves

---

3. See the description of intercultural communication in chapter 6, "The Hermeneutics of Intercultural Communication," in Liberman (1985).

in order to achieve some harmony, which is a *prerequisite* for understanding. This perspective is consistent with what the phenomenologist Maurice Merleau-Ponty (1973, 44-45) envisioned when he attempted to replace the notion of a primordial *cogito* with a more intersubjective orientation. Merleau-Ponty recommended abandoning the Cartesian postulate that consciousness is mainly consciousness of a self and instead suggested starting with a consciousness that is neither self nor others: "The essence of consciousness is communication, where one cannot determine what is ours and what belongs to others" (Merleau-Ponty 1973, 49).

Meaning is locatable, as Garfinkel says, out there in the world as "worldly matters," or as Mead described it,

> Meaning is thus not to be conceived, fundamentally, as a state of consciousness, or as a state of organized relations existing or subsisting mentally outside the field of experience into which they enter; on the contrary, it should be conceived objectively, as having its existence entirely within this field itself.

When Garfinkel suggests, "Thinking takes place not in the heads but in the world," he is attempting to redirect sociological methodology to human experience in its natural setting, where the phenomena of thinking, understanding, mind, and reason can be witnessed as the world's work.

Hence, Mead and Garfinkel situate meaning in the field of experience—the world toward which and with which actors are mutually orienting themselves to each other—and that is where we are situating reason here. As Anne Rawls (1996, 25) has asked, "How could reason, in particular, have arisen in the course of the experiences undergone by a single individual?" Only the extreme individualism that is characteristic of the European Enlightenment could have led philosophers to conclude that the primary locus of reason is individual consciousness. The political theorist Fred Dallmayr (1996, 96) has concluded, "Far from reflecting a subjective-intentional design, understanding always has the character of mutuality or of an experience one undergoes with others." Or as the Hegelian commentator Robert Williams (1992, 191) explained, "Reason is intersubjective and embedded in a social-intersubjective context." What Williams, like Mead, calls the "relational aspect" is a proper focus for investigations of reason: "The relational aspect and dimension of intersubjectivity is not contingent, but rather part of the structure of rationality itself" (Williams 1992, 196). Even Husserl, whose investigations proceeded mostly from the standpoint of a constitutive subjective ego, admitted during the last period of his career that reason was intersubjective and even communal: "Reason is the specific characteristic of man . . . in the necessity of allowing individual-personal reason to come to ever more perfect realization only as communal-personal reason and vice versa" (Husserl 1970b, 338). If we are going to learn about reason, we will have to leave our idealistic and individualistic reductionism behind and turn to the practical relations most people have towards, and with, their philosophical objects. I would contend that this method is more empirical than those of self-labeled "empiricists" who have so thoroughly idealized reason that they have lost the phenomenon.

When thinking is reduced to "inner processes," it is not an empirical methodology at work but an overly theorized representation of human experience. In what is an achievement made possible only by the social processes of disciplinary scholarship, this theorized representation is given foundational status and placed at the center of all ensuing research. But it is merely an unexamined axiom whose value persists so long as the presumption is socially confirmed by researchers, without a thorough examination of its truth or efficacy. The rejection of ethnomethodology as a subjectivist project (which is hardly the case, since it is solely oriented toward objective productions, in the Durkheimian sense of objective facts) is another illustration of the social forces that are the context for reason. The structuralists and positivists who control the disciplinary machinery of contemporary sociology (which includes dominance, albeit contested, of the discipline's major publications, the boards of national granting agencies, etc.) demand that research be carried out only within the accepted language and narratives of constructionist social science, including an overly theorized view of individual rationality. This is so despite the fact that the alternative tradition for investigating reason, which we are following here, has a sociological pedigree that is equally impressive.

The Grounds of Reason

Some claim that the real work of philosophers is the providing of logical validation, and any social influences upon validation are to be kept to a minimum. The problem is that the social function that validation plays is ubiquitous, and the time when a pure calculus can operate without social consensus never arrives. It may be argued that research into the social conditions of formal analysis is itself a reductionist method, a sociologism if you will. I would agree that the real work of logical analysis rests in the provision of formal validation; however, these vital tasks of logical analysis are always socially prescribed and mediated. The "formal" in formal analysis refers to social prescriptions.

Heidegger (1991, 72) defined reason as "the faculty of principles, that is, of fundamental principles, of the giving of foundations." What are the circumstances of this giving of foundations? A concern for truth is certainly the motive for reason, but this concern is by no means done justice simply by the dutiful application of a mechanistic reason. It is the real work of philosophers neither to *over*estimate nor *under*value fundamental principles (Heidegger 1991, 13). Serious reflection relies heavily upon, but ultimately is not reducible to, fundamental principles. Characterized in another way, philosophers find themselves poised between the perfunctory routines of formal logistics and the groundlessness that such formal analysis will ultimately reveal "as soon as we take what the principle says seriously in relation to the principle itself" (12). That is, the bona fide work of philosophers, including Tibetan philosophers, is the giving of valid reasons, but when does the giving of grounds itself leave off? It is impossible to keep going on forever providing the grounds of grounds, yet every ground requires its own justification and every criterion its own criterion, *ad infinitum*. Or, as Heidegger (1991, 18) formulated it, "If we nevertheless insist that the principle of reason—and it above all others—has a reason, then we are faced with the question: what reason is the reason for the principle of reason?"

Where and when to break off the work of giving valid grounds is a locally organized accomplishment. When does the giving of grounds leave off? My Tibetan debate materials make evident that it leaves off when a fellow thinker says, "Oh, now I see!" Meaning is like going up to someone. Or as Wittgenstein (1972, 84) asserted, "Well, how do I know?—If that means 'Have I reasons?' the answer is: my reasons will soon give out. And then I shall act, without reasons." It is the destiny of reasons to "give out," sooner or later.

This is very evident in this passage from debate II.4:

9:33:14 T   Why is it that the establishment of inherent essence is not refuted?
-067.5- L' An apprehension of a single instance of establishing an inherent essence is not necessarily the refutation of the establishment of inherent essence. Do you understand?

The entreaty "Do you understand?" is an attempt to negotiate a reasonable end to L"s giving of reasons. In this way the giving of grounds is a collaborative accomplishment. The challenger, if he wishes, can demand more reasons, as in I.2:

3:16:08 T   PRESENT a formulation of the reasoning that follows from this. >~

Genuine dialectics requires that thinkers remain closely tuned to each other because they must engage in this collaboration about the reasonable ends to philosophical exegesis. Observe the social agenda that is implicit in the word "right?" in this excerpt (from III.2). Empirically speaking, the word "right?" is ubiquitous in reasoning dialogues.

(-008-) L" Right? There is the subtle or rough modes, right? One is rough, right? Another is subtle. This is the way they appear to the mind.

The provisions for when the giving of grounds ends is an interactional contingency and not exclusively a logical one. Again, in I.5:

3:46:27 T   Then, uhh, can you formulate the reason that proves for the Dialectical Reasoning School that there is no inherent production in any of the four possible ways?

> :33 L" The existence of an entity is not produced from the continuum of
> its own self because such a self would already exist. It is not pro-
> duced from an other because it already exists, we say it like this,
> right?

The ubiquitous "right" reveals that these people *are talking to each other*, that is, reasoning *together*.

Deciding the point at which reasons give out is usually done in a collabora-tive way, and what constitutes sufficient grounds for warranting truth is a so-cially negotiated and socially contextualized affair. Heidegger (1962, 197) rec-ognized the phenomenological reality of formal assertion as a shared communi-cation; and "that which is 'shared' is our Being-towards what has been pointed out." The truth of assertions, understood in an existential manner, is a social event. If the giving of grounds tends toward becoming a foundationalism, that is because every effort must be made to gain secure knowledge (1991, 17), and the task of securing knowledge (as well as deciding what constitutes security) is social. Heidegger (1991, 39) poses the question, "Are we humans the ones who demand that our cognition in each case render reasons? Or does reason itself, from out of itself as reason, make such a demand on our cognition? But how can reason make a demand?" Properly situated, reason is simply the office of human reflection, more a functionary, frequently a guide, but never a commander in chief. The genuine work of philosophers is to secure knowledge without mecha-nistically routinizing reflection, and in this project they are sentenced to hover between the tedium of validated grounds and the vertigo of groundlessness: the philosophers' skill rests in when and how they employ the principle of reason, and so philosophical merit has social conditions.

All reason, including "universal" reason, operates amidst a local tradition. Jurgen Habermas argues that logical grounds are always used discursively to redeem truth claims; grounds can be circumscribed only through argumentation in language (Sudarsan 1997). There is a continuous need for agreement about when to stop providing grounds, and this agreement is necessarily consensual and collaborative, that is, reason is a public activity. Social sanctions assure that thinking remains confined within the authority of those judgment forms. What qualifies as sound or flawed is a locally warrantable event.

The public character of Tibetan debate is especially apparent in the partici-pation of the audience in the formal disputations. All of the classical Indian and Tibetan texts that describe how to perform a proper debate include the audience as one of the participating parties, and they were there in the Greek *polis*. The audience is a full participant in the objectivation and authorization that occurs in this excerpt from III.4:

> ```
>         T   IT FOLLOWS THAT they accept that an already manifested
> -069-       sprout is established at the time of its cause. >~
>         L"  CHE-/                      // They can accept that.
> ```

L'   / I ACCEPT, indeed. //
Audience   They accept that. They accept that.
2:16:32 T   (At the time of its cause) they accept that it is produced. >~

Here the audience participates in issuing the warrant for validating the assertion. In II.2, the audience intervenes to provide a solution to a semantic dispute about whether or not Bhavaviveka is considered to be a Middle Way scholar. Bhavaviveka is a Middle Way Scholar of the Syllogism-based Reasoning School, but he is not a scholar of the Dialectical Reasoning Middle Way School. The challenger attempts to get the defenders to agree to a proposition that is technically wrong (if correct to the extent that it is true for just one but not both of the two Middle Way schools), that is, that Bhavaviveka is not a Middle Way Scholar. The audience is aware of the rosy trail that T offers L' and L", a path that will lead to a contradiction that can already be foreseen, and they smile when T's attempt to secure the agreement is successful (at 9:12:35). T implicates L' and L" deeply by getting them to accept a citation of a principal text, but at that point (9:12:(54)) the *audience* intervenes to provide the solution, which L' adopts in the final line:

T   TAKE AS THE SUBJECT Bhavaviveka, IT FOLLOWS THAT he
        is not a Middle Way scholar.
9:12:35 L'   I ACCEPT!
L"   I ACCEPT! [Audience members smile.]
T   BECAUSE that's what it says in the text.
. . .
T   Ohh. *"Just as it cannot be asserted that a Middle Way scholar
        who accepts that entities are truly established on the basis of
        their own essences is not a Middle Way scholar."*
L   Yes.
:53 T   So it is said in the text! >~
Audience   A Syllogism-based Reasoning Middle Way School scholar.
-110- L'   What did he say?
T   It says that in the text, does it not?
L'   He is a Syllogism-based Reasoning Middle Way School scholar,
        isn't he?

The role of the audience is not always so benevolent. On occasion, an observing Tibetan scholar will interject a line of reasoning that is distracting to the philosophical issues about which the challenger and defender are collaborating. But such distractions, the multiple meanings and interpretations, and such contentiousness are part of the "jungle" to which Bar-Hillel refers (see 37), but since they *are* the real environment of natural philosophical discourse they must be included in any scientific research and examined in rigorous ways. Each party—the challenger, the defender, the members of the audience, and the judge or arbiter (sometimes the disciplinarian)—is oriented to all of the others, and all are reflecting together and reading each other's readings of each other as if they were thinking in a hall of mirrors. Where ambiguities exist, definitions will be formalized in order to clarify them so that intelligent collaboration can occur, and the audience will be consulted during this process:

> L"   The mind is afflicted with the ingrained habit of many routine con-
>   ceptualizations.
> T   Oh, yes?
> L"   The mind-habit "mine" is presented in this way.
> T   [To audience] What is he saying? Well, "mine" is a reified appre-
>   hension of something so that it is perceived to exist according to its
>   own characteristics. IT FOLLOWS THAT that "mine" must have
>
> 4:45:17   an apprehended basis. >~
> L"   I ACCEPT.

Here (from I.6) T has turned to the audience to solicit some advice ("What is he saying?"). And he then tries to pin down, by means of the apophantic forms (in upper case), some acknowledged formal basis for discussion.

The way that ideas are defined and synthesized, and then redefined, and also the way that definitions are sustained *and kept visible* before the parties, is all part of the public work of the reasoning. Inspect the way the dialectics is working toward the stabilization of the meaning of the term "penetrative faculties" in this excerpt, from II.3:

9:21:50 L"   A person with penetrative faculties can come to have an under-
>   standing based on faith, / right?
> T   / Now that's right, isn't it? Uhh, a person
>   with penetrative faculties, yes, yes. A person with penetrative fac-
>   ulties, right? For example, uh, how must we say it?

This work is very intricate, enough to make it difficult to describe in detail. The parties are attempting to circumscribe a semiotic field and to do so in a way that makes any achievement of theirs a public acquisition. Husserl (1970a, 639-40) wrote extensively about the synthesis of ideas and of the way that a synthesized idea-complex will be reduced, in an economy that can facilitate reflection: "The 'conjunctive' synthesis . . . permits of nominalization, in which case the collective object constituted by the synthesis becomes the simply presented object of a new 'single-rayed' act, and so is made 'objective' in the pregnant sense of the word." Collaborating parties can then carry on their work with a more economical and nominalized version that summarizes the itinerary of their philosophical work. Formal analytic reason is prone to these nominalizations (cf. Levinas 1981, 62); what is still to be appreciated is that the creation and establishment of such an *economy of notions* is yet another social practice.

This is not to say that truth submits to whatever an audience wishes to make of it. The purpose of the principle of reason is to provide some means by which clear and original thinking can take place, in the context of contingent social affairs. Just as in the rule of law it is hoped that the most prejudicial distortions of a political climate can be overcome, so it is with the principle of reason. Not infrequently, the audience at a Tibetan public disputation will attempt to sway the defender, and they may deliberately goad him into accepting an incorrect proposition, shouting "It must be!" (II.3, -121-) or "Acceptable, acceptable, acceptable!" (III.4, (067)). On such occasions the originality rests in consulting the principle of reason and *resisting* the influence of the audience. Those occasions when the formal apophansis is decisive are especially worthy of ethnomethodological attention, but even on those occasions the reasoning takes place in a social context, and so the interpretation and application of the formal reasoning must be examined as a worldly affair.

Dilthey was fully aware of the need for a hermeneutics of understanding, and he advised, "The context in which thinking is active forms the latter's irremovable precondition" (cited in Boeder 1997, 138). Mead (1962, 89-90) similarly emphasized that reason cannot exist without a context:

> As the logicians say, a universe of discourse is always implied as the context in terms of which, or as the field within which, significant gestures or symbols do in fact have significance. This universe of discourse is constituted by a group of individuals carrying on and participating in a common social process of experience [Mead's footnote: a common world exists . . . only in so far as there is a common (group) experience] and behavior. A universe of discourse is simply a system of common or social meanings. [Mead's footnote: Our so-called laws of thought are the abstractions of social intercourse. Our whole process of abstract thought, technique and method is essentially social.]

Truth statements are legitimized by the context, and the scope, quality, and extent of that legitimation is a contingent social accomplishment. Ethnomethodology seeks to identify such occasions, as they occur naturally, and describe what for the parties themselves are the intricate details. Ethnomethodology has drawn heavily from Bar-Hillel's study of indexicality, from which it has learned that meanings are only what they are in a specific social context. Meanings are not our personal possession but are a public event.[4]

The Social Bases of Apophansis

Although dialectics may be conceived as strictly a conceptual process, performable by a single thinker, the notion of idea engaging idea implies the introduction of a second thinker. Dialectics in either its Socratic or Hegelian sense im-

---

4. For a more extensive discussion, see Liberman (1999a).

plies the negation of one's notion and will not suffer any self-sufficient truth that claims to be able to rest on its own foundations. The negation of one's notion destabilizes the complacency of reason and returns every notion to the process of thinking truth. As we have seen, Tibetan dialectics shares at least this much with these two forms of European dialectics; however, because its negative dialectics remains intimately associated with live, public forms of dialectics, the relationship between reason and dialogue is better recognized.

Randy Collins (1998, 53) has concluded that "Logic is deeply social." The dialectical forms of philosophical scholarship we have been identifying specify just how reason is a social activity. The challenger poses a question to the defender, and the defender replies. After he replies, the defender looks at the challenger. There, in his look, is everything social that reason could be: he looks to learn what it is he means, he looks to gauge the correctness or incompleteness of his reply, he looks to glean from where in the talk the warrant for his reason will come. And what does the rejection of one's ideas accomplish for one's understanding? Here again, the philosophical passageways are provided by the social organization of the interaction. There are philosophical issues, to be sure, but the vision of truth itself is provided by the social conditions for philosophical collaboration. The philosophical and the social cannot be severed. The apophantic forms make possible the clarity of positions, but negation hurls the imagination into that abyss between certainty and groundlessness of which Heidegger spoke and which is conducive to witnessing reason as a process. Hopkins (1983, 516-17) speaks of Gelug dialectics:

> By presenting a system in structural form, what is gained is clarity and sharpness in differentiating positions, resulting in ease in applying such tenets in meditation. Still, in the debating courtyards of the monastic universities, the sources for these now seemingly hardened positions are examined in detail with the result that those who pursue the topics in depth realize the almost fluid nature of the sources while reconstructing and examining the patterns of [scholars'] thoughts as they formalized these systems.

Securing the warrant for a valid reason, or what we termed above "authorization" (see page 99) is an abiding social activity. The apophantic forms must be publicly displayed so that their correctness can be validated, challenged, and adjusted. We have observed how the formal structure of an argument is a continual building-up. Formal reason is concerned with having "something on which to build" (Heidegger 1991, 100). Philosophical reflection is made to stand as an achievement, objectivated and then authorized, and as authorized it can be combined with other philosophical achievements. But all of this takes place in language, in the world, and with collaborators (even if for some philosophers the collaborators are silent). The formal procedures, the *apophansis*, is what facilitates the collaboration, or as Levinas has instructed us (see 104), *apophansis* is a modality of the approach to the other person. The lawfulness of reasons provides a philosophical framework for sharing understanding, and so it is a social praxis.

The apophantic forms, the formal analytics, are logical and social phenomena at once, which is to say that *the logic is used as by the parties as an organizational device*. That does not make the logic ultimate, not for Levinas, not for Heidegger, not for Nagarjuna, and not for Tsong Khapa. But the logic is necessary to the process.

To separate the logic out from the social is to be left with only an idealized, reductionist reason, which represents no one's philosophical practice. Instead, we need to turn toward the wild "jungle of daily discourse," and face directly the forms of language and reason there. The complications multiply, to the point that it is not only difficult to communicate the details we can identify, it is difficult to identify them. But simply lifting a formal philosophical assertion out of the context of its production and building our inquiry into reason around that is not a practice that will assist humankind. "This glib talk—superficially and off the cuff—of *axioms, principia*, and fundamental principles in a homologous sense is indeed precarious" (Heidegger 1991, 19). In fact, the desire for a homologous reason is another social demand, more than it is a philosophical one. Moreover, Heidegger (1991, 19; see also Paz 1956, 87) viewed the penchant for clear and distinct thinking to be the "basic trait of the history of Western thinking"; that is, it is a culturally and historically contingent philosophical praxis.

The third stage of Tibetan philosophical practice we have identified, the *disengagement* of the philosophical products from the process of their production, is the critical step that permits the objectivated accomplishments of philosophers to become "universal" truths. Nevertheless, what is universal is a contingent production—it is a local construction that obtains public ratification. Social sanctions assure that thinking remains confined within the authority of the judgment forms, and these forms disguise the social work of the local production of universal truths. Mead (1962, 90) allocated such universality to its proper location:

> Ways of acting under an indefinite number of different particular situations—ways which are more or less identical for an indefinite number of normal individuals—are all that universals (however treated in logic or metaphysics) really amount to; they are meaningless apart from the social acts in which they are implicated and from which they derive their significance. The [invariability] is strictly relative to the situation in conduct within which the reflection arises . . . and never transcends the social conduct within which the method arises.

A few present day sociologists and psycholinguists are prepared to enter the jungle of natural reasoning. Lance Rips, et al. (1999, 172-73) have studied the way conversational moves (e.g., request for justification, justification, rebuttal, etc.) fit together in reasoning dialogues, and they concluded that intelligibility is the important factor driving the formalization of guidelines: "Argumentative dialogues display features that unite the arguers' individual contributions." Reasoning partners are addressed to the social work of concerting their thinking. Observe the dialectics that operates in the alternation of utterances in this excerpt from I.9. The two parties are closely attuned to each other, and they are adjusting their understanding with each new contribution:

> T When one has realized the emptiness of this pot, since we agreed that one does so on this basis. Truly, oh yes, do we say that IT DOES NOT NECESSARILY FOLLOW that one understands the
> 6:03:33 way in which the pot still exists with some functional efficacy? >~
> L' When one has a realization of emptiness/
> T   /Oh. At the time one has a realization of emptiness.
> L' One says it is not necessary.
> :37 T It *is* necessary isn't it?
> L' Mmm-hm.

It may be said that when both parties are listening to each other this well while they are concerting their utterances, a genuine dialectics is taking place. Contemporary sociological scholarship should investigate the conditions of successful dialectics and examine the practical and collaborative work of fitting together ideas and developing philosophical insights in reasoning dialogues.

The formalization of reason is an ethnomethod for the local organization of affairs and a social production practice that provides an orderliness which permits thinkers to philosophize. In the next chapter we will examine more closely how developing a smoothly functioning formal analytic order facilitates communication, fuses the contributions of the several parties and transforms the philosophical praxis into a potent and collaboratively sustained tool. Local semiotic systems are transformed into clear and distinct apophantic structures that provide for public observability and public validation. It is natural for these philosophers to wish to preserve the consistency of these emerging structures. These structures are logical in that they constitute a formal order of reason that relies upon the principle of formal validation, but they are also social in that it is these very apophantic structures that make possible philosophical *communication*. It is impossible to measure where the social motivation for preserving the consistency of the structures leaves off and the logical motive takes over. Here the logical is the social—as Mead and Geertz insightfully declared, but only as generalizations. Our concern here is to identify *just how* and *just where* the logical is social, by providing precise ethnomethodological descriptions of such occasions in their naturally occurring details.

Chapter 6

Rhymes and Reason:
Reason as the *In Vivo*, Concerted Work
of Tibetan Philosophers

Logical objectivity derives from carnal intersubjectivity on the condition that it
has been forgotten as carnal intersubjectivity, and it is carnal intersubjectivity
itself which produces this forgetfulness by wending its way toward logical objectivity.

—Maurice Merleau-Ponty (1964a, 173)

In Tibetan philosophical debate, the dialectical forms mandate that reasoning be
a collaboration by the parties. The structure of interaction in their debates provides numerous opportunities for the thinking of two and more persons to engage each other—to transform the other's thinking and to be transformed by it.
The success of dialectics in the Tibetan academy can be judged by the readiness
with which this encounter with the thought of the other, in the opposition and
conjoining that occurs there, results in a growth and transformation in the thinking of each party. In making the actual debates the object of our investigation,
we are able to capture the life of Tibetan philosophy *in vivo*, that is, in the lived
process of its production. This method makes available to us the full range of
social interaction that is available to the Tibetan scholars themselves, and interactional matters lost to those who analyze only the textual records of Buddhist
philosophical practice can be recovered and examined.

We have described already some of the features that help to facilitate communication among the parties, including the concern by the challenger to pick
up the precise wording of the defender and to incorporate it into the developing
structure of argumentation, the collaborative building up of fully formed formulations of the theses under examination, the objectivation of accounts, cooperation and assistance in locating and completing pertinent citations from authoritative texts, etc. All of these tasks, during which participants in these debates act
congregationally in order to ensure their successful and sonorous completion,

are done for the sake of philosophical as well as spiritual ends. But they are not accomplished for philosophical and spiritual ends alone. The structures of philosophical discourse that Tibetan scholars congregationally produce are at the same time an *aesthetic* interest of the parties. Any objective social researcher must ask the question, what are the principal objectives of the people being studied? In most Tibetan debates the exploration of ideas, the formal establishment of truths, and the winning of an argument are accompanied by an additional objective that frequently comes to eclipse them—the production of a smoothly functioning, competent debate. In fact, competence here entails smoothness: *the debate must flow*. The oppositions and convergencies of the reasoning must harmonize in a way that is aesthetically pleasing and that retains a clarity of thought and a predictable rhythm in its logical phrasing. The mental flows of the two parties must be conjoined, even when there is strong disagreement, in fact especially when there is strong disagreement; and the debate will be judged not only by its product or by who wins but also by the beauty and steadiness of the rhythm of the argumentation.

Among the organizational items that Tibetans use to make their dialectics work are devices that compose the choreography of their debates. David Michael Levin (1985, 99) has argued that analytic studies should pay more attention to the work of "orchestrating and choreographing our bodily postures, gestures, attitudes, and comportments."[1] Tibetan scholar-monks are animated physically, and the grammar of their arguments is embodied also in their gestures and body positioning.[2]

In his study *Creativity*, Mihaly Csikszentmihaly (1996, 107) observes that "it is not what people do that counts but *how* they do it," and at some point the flow of creative activity becomes "autotelic" (113), that is, the doing becomes an end in itself. Is the production of a smooth, "clean" debate an aesthetic achievement or a logical one? Or does such a question cause us to abstract ourselves from the haecceity of the phenomenon at hand?! We will discover that for the Tibetans the smooth flow of a philosophical debate, beautiful and efficient at once, is what identifies a properly functioning formal analytic practice. Csikszentmihaly (1996, 124) comments further, "The link between flow and happiness depends on whether the flow-producing activity is complex." And George Herbert Mead (1934, 87) acknowledged how important the harmonizing of complexities is for the experience of beauty:

> If one can bring in a number of [stimuli] and get a multiform reflection of all these attitudes into harmony, the artist calls out an aesthetic response which we consider beautiful. It is the harmonizing of these complexities of response that constitutes the beauty of the object.

---

1. In a previous linguistic ethnography, I described the importance of bodily gestures and speech prosody for ordinary communication (Liberman 1982, 330-337).

2. This will be evident to anyone who views the videotaped presentations on the CD-ROM that is included with this volume.

It is a principal objective of Tibetan debaters to concert themselves so that one utterance is conjoined seamlessly into the next utterance. When they are successful, the complexities of their inquiry become harmonized, and it is as if they are speaking as one. Randy Collins (1998, 47) has spoken about a "deepening rhythmic entrainment" in the coordination of utterances between conversationalists. When Tibetan debaters are well tuned in to each other, and their utterances are "entrained," it is not two "I's" at work but a "We" that functions as a congregation. Analyses of Tibetan debate that preserve the isolated individuality of the participants throughout the descriptions will miss the phenomenon that Tibetan debaters live.

Of Repeats, Rehearsals, Rhythms, and Reversals

We have observed that repeats are ubiquitous in Tibetan philosophical debates. Parties formulate accounts of the reasoning and then repeat those accounts often, as if they were engaging in a game of ping-pong. We have examined as well how the repeats offer the parties a way to objectivate their accounts and to coordinate the conceptual components of the philosophical discussion. But the repeats do not only make a given discussion a publicly available matter, they also afford the parties a way to establish an organic rhythm. Finding the right formulation for a philosophical issue is *accompanied by finding a rhythm for speaking about it.* The conceptual coordination is an embodied phenomenon, and the embodiment takes place in the synchronization of the utterances, in the verbal dance of the parties, and in the claps, shouts, and gestures of the challenger. A study of Tibetan debate cannot overlook these matters, for they are of prominent interest to the parties themselves.

Repeats permit the parties to keep the ideas in play, as if there was a ball in the air between them that must not be allowed to fall to the ground. The inclination to verbatim repetition is so habitual that it operates even where it seems to have little function. It is not a strictly conceptual phenomenon we are dealing with here, it is an energy; but this energy is a social fact that has important consequences for the philosophical work. Tibetan debating is never just about the ideas, as a formal analytic tradition might have it (whether the tradition be social constructionism, constitutional phenomenology, or analytic philosophy). A strictly formal analytic outlook misses the important lesson that Durkheim elucidated in his *The Elementary Forms of Religious Life,* regarding the contagiousness of the social forces that are embodied in ritual. Durkheim (1915, 361) writes, "Some have tried to explain it with the well-known laws of the association of ideas." It is not that there are no ideas or that the ideas are not important, but the ideas are accompanied, in varying degrees, by the "collective effervescence" of interacting parties.

At the outset of a philosophical dialogue, repeats provide the parties a way to get a rhythm going and to come into some sort of alignment, even if the direction in which the rhythm will take them is uncertain. Here is a simple illustration (from II.4):

       T IT FOLLOWS THAT one must identify the object to be refuted, that entities are established as if they had inherent essences.
9:30:03 L' We do say that one must have identified it. One must, one must.
       T One must identify it?
       L' One must.
  :07 T If we say that one must, right? An example, right? Ohh, . . .

Another illustration involves the repetition of "CHEE-CHEER" ("WHAT IS THE REASON?"). Nothing new philosophically is gained by the repetition, but it does permit the parties an opportunity to cultivate a rhythm. The parties (in III.2) come into sufficient alignment during the repeat when L' and L" happily sing the second "CHEE-CHEER" in a chorus of rejection.

-034.5- T IT FOLLOWS THAT the wisdom that realizes just-how-it-is, yah, formulates emptiness as existing concretely. >~
  -035- L" CHEE-CHEER.
       L' CHEE-CHEER. For the system of the *Great Digest*? For the system of the *Great Digest*? You're—
       T IT FOLLOWS THAT the wisdom that realizes just-how-it-is, yah,
  -036-   formulates emptiness as existing concretely. >~
       L' /CHEE-CHEER.
       L" /CHEE-CHEER.
       T IT FOLLOWS THAT emptiness is formulated as existing concretely . . .

This rehearsal of the rejection energizes the debate, and within the rhythm of that energy T is able to proceed with building up a more complex formulation. Rehearsals are not dumb, mindless repeats but a deliberate effort to set up some common ground and to establish a rhythm for the debating. They can add elegance to a debate's choreography, a phenomenon overlooked by most classical Tibetologists. Even a brief double-check, during which the challenger can ask "Is it?" and elicit the defender's "Yes-yes," assists the parties in developing a pace for concerting their speech. Similarly, in I.3 and in III.1 the parties find simple ways to come into alignment:

       T Among the four possible ways of producing inherent existence, the most important one to refute is the refutation of production
3:26:13   from another. >~
       L" Yes. Yes.
       L' Production from another is most important.

T The refutation of production from another is the most important of
:18   the four possible modes of production. >~
L" THAT FOLLOWS.

What is taking place is that by means of verbatim repeats the parties are
revving up the engine of their dialogue, which assists the parties in finding a
way to collaborate in the development of their verbal contributions. The repetition provides a way for every participant to get on board the train of verbaliza-
tion of the reasoning as it leaves the station (II.6):

T *"If we speak of matters pertinent to the meaning that is so difficult
to understand."* This is said, isn't it?
-006.5- L" Oh, yes yes.
L' The way one witnesses the dharma body, and the way one witnesses suchness, right?
L" The way one witnesses the dharma body, and the way one witnesses suchness.
9:47:51 T There are some scholars who recognize no difference between
them, right?
L' Some scholars recognize no difference. But there is a distinctive
way of witnessing the dharma body.
L" According to our philosophical system [i.e., the Middle Way
view], there is a difference, we say.
-008- T Although there is no difference in the way the systems witness
suchness, / there is a difference in the way of witnessing the //
dharma body, we say.
-008.5- L'   / Though there is no difference there, the way of witnessing the dharma body. //
9:48   T Now. There is no difference in the way of witnessing suchness.
But there is a difference in the way of witnessing the dharma body.
:03 L This is what our system says.
-011- T So, now why does our system say this?

The duet at -008-/-008.5- is effective in energizing the debate. Another way
to warm up the engine is for the challenger to use an intrasentential repeat, as in
I.1, where T pleasingly reverses the order of the two principal semes:

T Therefore, *the valid conceptual cognition* spoken of here, <u>during
the discussion of patently wrong common sense</u>—right?—<u>during
the discussion of patently wrong common sense</u>, *the valid conceptual cognition* referred to must be a mundane, everyday
3:07:23 conceptual cognition. >~

By such means the parties gain enough momentum to proceed on their way to a
philosophical examination with sufficient focus and synchronicity of discourse.

Here is a slightly more extensive illustration of how the parties in I.1 ("The Customary Truth of Common Sense Practices") concert themselves in the establishment of a rhythm. The function of the logical token NOW IT DOES NOT FOLLOW serves as a means to jumpstart an effective rhythm for the developing logic; that is, its efficacy rests not in its semantic content but in its rhythmic contribution:

> T   NOW IT DOES NOT FOLLOW. A common sense thought like that is posited by the eye-consciousness, is it?
>
> L'   The eye-consciousness. Sense-consciousness.
>
> T   NOW IT DOES NOT FOLLOW. Yah, isn't it necessary that a cognition reasoning validly establishes that a sense-consciousness is an incorrect consciousness?
>
> L'   A sense-consciousness. Mm.

This is followed moments later with some serious work to establish a tempo for the debate. The rehearsals (e.g., 3:01:21) permit the debaters to move their argumentation forward in lockstep:

> T   NOW IT DOES NOT FOLLOW. For an ordinary, everyday person who is practiced in applying conventions, the reflection of an im-
>
> 3:01:12   age in the mirror is not said to be true, it is said to be false. >~
>
> L'   I ACCEPT that it is, indeed.
>
> :15 T   That sort of customary truth is necessarily determined by a con-
> :19   ceptual cognition that is valid. >~
>
> L'   Yes.
>
> :21 T   That sort of customary truth, right?
>
> L'   / If you present customary truth that way it's all right.
>
> L"   / A common sense mind.
>
> T   What?
>
> L'   Yes yes.
>
> T   NOW IT DOES NOT FOLLOW. Yah, TAKE AS THE SUBJECT
> :30   a common sense mind. Why must it be established by valid conceptual cognition? >~
>
> L'   For that sort of common sense mind.
>
> T   What about that common sense mind?
>
> L'   It is the realization that the reflection does not exist in the way that it appears. Now that mind, huh?
>
> :35 T   That common sense mind.

By the end of this work, the parties' utterances are well coordinated, and they are ready to take up the philosophical work in a collaborative way. The thinking of parties is not conjoined automatically; rather, debaters must engage in active organizational work that provides for the weaving together of their thinking. This organizational work is one component of competent philosophical discussions.

Parties will employ facile repeats only to keep the tempo of the discussion alive and preserve the alignment of their utterances. Here (I.7) the parties collaborate in formatting what is a chaste debate form. Although it may seem repetitious to a fault, it is a fault only if one is judging the work by its substantive achievements and ignoring the aesthetic success the parties are having in structuring the interaction and tuning in to each other. The repetitiveness may be redeemed by the philosophical work that is to follow, for which the building of a smoothly functioning rhythm has prepared the way.

> L' If it is a valid cognition, we say that IT DOES NOT PERVADE THAT it is an inferential valid cognition.
>
> T Oh, if it is a direct valid cognition IT DOES NOT PERVADE THAT it is an inferential valid cognition. We say it like that, right?
>
> L' Oh, CONSIDER a valid cognition.
>
> T Oh.
>
> L' IT DOES NOT PERVADE THAT it is an inferential valid cognition.
>
> T What.
>
> L' Oh, CONSIDER a valid cognition. IT DOES NOT PERVADE THAT it is an inferential cognition.
>
> T CONSIDER a valid cognition. IT FOLLOWS THAT it pervades that it is not necessarily an inferential valid cognition.
>
> L' Like this.
>
> 5:47:36 T >~ So, said like this, IT FOLLOWS.
>
> L' THAT IS ACCEPTABLE.
>
> T IT FOLLOWS THAT it pervades.
>
> L' Yes.

Repeats, of course, can be used not only to establish the pacing of a debate but also to slow it down or give one of the parties more time to think about a proper reply. Duets can be employed in similar ways. We have briefly referred to the duets that parties will perform during which parties will recite portions of a citation together, and even repeat the recitation (II.2):

> L' *"While it is possible that an analytic person could have / a doubt like that,"*
>
> L" */"a doubt like that."*
>
> T *"While it is possible that an analytic person could have // a doubt like that,"*—
>
> L' *//"a doubt like that."*

At times such performances become a dance of repeats, and as such they can contribute much to the aesthetics of a debate. Reversals provide similar aesthetic benefits. Here T makes a negative assertion about the correctness of Bhavaviveka's interpretation of Buddhapalita's reasoning, *repeats his negative assertion, then repeats it in a positive form,* and yet again offers the negative version, while L remains in alignment all along (I.5):

3:48:13 T   The reasoning is not correct. $\succ\sim$
          L   YOUR REASON IS NOT ESTABLISHED.
          T   The reasoning is not correct.
          L   YOUR REASON IS NOT ESTABLISHED.
          T   IT FOLLOWS THAT the reasoning is correct.
          L   I ACCEPT.
          T   IT FOLLOWS THAT the reading is not correct.

Such reversals permit the establishment of a crisp, clean rhythm in the dialogue. These reversals can be quite elegant, and on occasion it can seem as if the dancers of the rhythm have performed a pirouette. Such verbal pirouettes are performed in partnership, and they add beauty and clarity to a dialogue.

The debaters face two objectives here—developing the philosophical inquiry and organizing the debate. For this reason, sometimes the parties appear to take the long way about in coming to a formulation, such as reciting the incorrect negative version of a proposition before reciting its positive version. It may seem that they could save time by proceeding to the correct positive version straightaway; however, the roundabout way in which they work serves to clarify the positions, making public objects of them, *and it affords them with a means of providing a synchronized rhythm* for their debate. Similarly, before calling for an elicitation a clarifier of the reasoning may assert, "You cannot correctly PRESENT it," only to follow up the respondent's rejection of the idea that he is unable to so present with something like, "Then PRESENT the way. . . ." The point is to establish a tempo for the debate. In such fashion debaters cooperate in setting the stage for serious debating, but whether they will actually be able to do the work of formal analytic reasoning on that stage is serendipitous: the philosophizing may or may not come, but the way has been prepared. Reasoning in Tibetan debate occurs in the midst of a choreographed dialectics.

What David Abram (1996, 81) says of two birds singing to each other is also true of Tibetan debaters:

> Each voice, each side of the duet, mimes a bit of the other's melody while adding its own inflection and style, and is then echoed by the other in turn—the two singing bodies thus tuning and attuning to one another, rediscovering a common register. . . . This melodic singing is carrying the bulk of the communication in this encounter, and the explicit meanings of the actual words ride on the surface of this depth like waves on the surface of the sea.

After a rhythm is established and a debate proceeds, the parties will attempt to tighten the rhythm further. In this way a debate can gain considerable speed, and speed is an indicator of a well-performed debate. The parties will not merely repeat the same utterances, but gradually enlarge their philosophical formulations. In that way the rhythm is not as circular as it is in the nature of a spiral.

We have observed how the challenger will pick up the formulations of the defender even when he disagrees with them. During this practice, the challenger labors to pick up the wording of his opponent as quickly as he possibly can. On occasion, he will repeat the defender's wording and then quickly call for an explanation, a move that resembles aikido in that the challenger escorts his opponent's argument very rapidly in the direction that his opponent has suggested. Here are two brief illustrations, from III.2. Here T comes right back at L' *with L''s very own phrase*, "Emptiness is a non-affirming negation," along with a question that challenges L':

T	EXPLAIN HOW is it that the wisdom that realizes how-it-is does
-043.5-	not cognize emptiness as existing? >~
L'	Emptiness is a nonaffirming negation. Emptiness is a nonaffirming negation.
T	If emptiness is a nonaffirming negation, DOES the wisdom that
-044.5-	cognizes just-how-it-is, yah, not cognize emptiness as existing? >~
L'	Oh. That emptiness is an affirming negation. If the mind is analyzing a non-affirming negation, IT PERVADES that an established subject is *not* implied.

It is *the speed* in recycling the phrase that makes it effective. When T can pick up L promptly with speed, a debate can gain velocity:

L"	There is one way of thinking according to which *there is a cognizer of such existence*, isn't there?
T	IT FOLLOWS THAT for the wisdom that realizes just-how-it-is,
-060.5-	in the face of the realization of just-how-it-is, *there is a cognizer of the existence of emptiness.* >~

The promptness of the repeat offers evidence that T has heard L" clearly, that is, that the debate is proceeding with adequate communication and is in fine form.

In I.6, T adjusts his proposal to comply with L"'s contention, and here he does it so *quickly* that L" must pause a moment to be certain that there is no stratagem hidden in the move:

L"	Oh yes. It is said that an "I" cannot be perceived, right?
T	IT FOLLOWS THAT it is perceived, BECAUSE there is a per
4:52:08	sonal self. >~
L"	I contend that THAT DOES NOT PERVADE.
T	Oh. If it is the reification of a "person," IT DOES NOT PERVADE that an "I" is perceived. >~
L"	[pause] I ACCEPT that it does not pervade.

If L" was more competent, he would have been able to reply seamlessly, without the hitch of a pause, and that is what most debaters attempt to achieve. Here is an occasion where the defender meets the query promptly, and the challenger repeats the defender's reply (at (097)) in order to objectivate it *and to sustain the rapid pace* of the dialogue (from II.4):

	T	Between the subtle entitylessness of an entity and the subtle selflessness of a person, one of them must be cognized first.
	L'	Yes.
-096-	T	Ohh. We say that the subtle selflessness of the person must be
9:35:15		cognized first. What is the reason? >~
	L'	Because it is the easier subject.
(097)	T	Because that subject is easier. One should first work to establish the easier of the subjects.

And again (from II.1), T rapidly picks up L"'s comment from 9:04. The fine form of the debate is evident in the speed with which T accomplishes this, at 9:04:06. This comprises beauty in Tibetan debate since good form resides in the speed with which a challenger can incorporate the philosophical contributions of a respondent (see asterisk).

9:03:52	T	IT FOLLOWS THAT one must have a cognition of emptiness
:56		upon realizing what is erroneous about the reflection of a face in the mirror. >~
-065-	L'	/ CHEE-CHEER ["WHAT IS THE REASON?" I.e., "No."]
	L"	/ CHEE-CHEER
-066-	T	If one has posited what is erroneous about the reflection of a face in the mirror, why has one not posited what is erroneous according to the Middle Way tenets? >~
9:04	L	THAT DOES NOT NECESSARILY FOLLOW. [Everyone speaks at once.] But there is a cognition. A person who has not cognized emptiness has some cognition of what is erroneous./
*	T	/A person who has not cognized emptiness sees the reflection of a face in the mirror.>~
:06		
-067.5-	L	I ACCEPT. He does so posit.

Parties carefully concert themselves to achieve some acceleration in the rhythm of their dialogue. They wish to proceed as quickly as they can while still managing to keep hold of the logical forms. One way that an acceleration of the rhythm of a debate can be accomplished is to employ and repeat citations. In I.9, T has cited previously, "*Subsequent to being subjected to the three—the basis, its appearance to awareness, and the path of analyzing and meditating upon it,*" which is a reference to how one properly contemplates emptiness. In this case, the excerpt on the CD-ROM (see Illustrative Debate I.9) can be consulted to appreciate the acceleration, as L' and T engage in a dance with the citation. It is the repetition of the citation that produces the acceleration in the rhythm of the debate:

6:09:13 T   There is what we speak of as the refutation of an object of attachment generated by an imputed conceptualization of an habitually reified "true" essence, isn't there?

       L'   *"Subsequent to being subjected to the three—the basis, its appearance to awareness, and the path of analyzing and meditating upon it."*

    :15 T   Oh, in accord with *"Subsequent to being subjected to the three—the basis, its appearance to awareness, and the path of analyzing and meditating upon it,"* there is a type of refutation of an object of attachment produced by an imputed conceptualization of a reified "true" essence. It's the same.

    :18 L'   Exactly, exactly, exactly.

       T   And there must be a realization of emptiness. >~

       L'   I ACCEPT that there must be.

       T   Oh, because "There must be?" IT FOLLOWS THAT there must not be! Right? BECAUSE *"Subsequent to being subjected to the three—the basis, its appearance to awareness, and the path of analyzing and meditating upon it,"* that is the way that the analyses of the lower tenets establish how entities are apprehended to exist by virtue of their own defining characteristics. In his system there are such fixations. >~

       L'   Yes, sure.

       T   When one refutes that sort of reified fixation, *"Subsequent to being subjected to the three—/*

       L'   / That's right. //

       T   // *the basis, its appearance to awareness, and the path of analyzing and meditating upon it,"* IT DOES NOT FOLLOW THAT it is a refutation of the object of attachment produced by an imputed conceptualization of a reified

6:09:32   "true" essence. >~

       L'   I ACCEPT.

       T   [Quickly spoken] IT DOES FOLLOW, BECAUSE it is a refutation of the object of attachment generated by the habitual, imputed

6:09:35   conceptualization of a reified, "true" essence. >~

       L'   THE REASON IS NOT ESTABLISHED.

       T   IT FOLLOWS THAT for such a person as this the object of

    :37   attachment produced by an imputed conceptualization of a reified, "true" essence is not refuted. >~

       L'   I ACCEPT.

At the end, T has preserved the speed of the debate *while picking up L''s philosophical position* and reformatting it at 6:09:37; the debate continues in this fashion with considerable effect. In the next chapter, we will examine this debate in careful detail.

Finally, it is obligatory for the challenger to *pick up* the contribution of a defender even when a debate has become very heated and its pace has become rapid. The success of the challenger's performance very much rests upon his ability to incorporate his opponent's argument while he rapidly carries the issue to an absurd formulation. The rhythm achieved by these repeats, rehearsals, and reversals is a vital part of a Tibetan philosophical debate that one ignores only at the price of losing the phenomenon of Tibetan debating.

The Mechanics of Tibetan Formal Analytics

In its more perfect moments, logical argumentation in Tibetan debate is a semi-autonomous, self-propelling mechanism that carries the participants along within in its own dialectical rhythms. When the debating is going well, the social organizational work that formats the dialectics will be transparent. Even though these dialectical forms are constructed by the participants, once they emerge as a social structure in their own right they acquire a transcendental character, and the parties orient themselves to those forms as an independent social fact.[3] This transcendental object that their formal dialectics becomes is

---

3. It was Durkheim who argued that social facts have an objective reality; however, this reality is not that of a concrete object. However much social structure transcends the individuals who produce it, "social structure" cannot be seen, for it is only a notion; yet the emerging social structure to which the parties are oriented is what provides them with the tools for establishing the orderliness. It may be said that the local practices of the parties stands in a dialectical relationship with the very social structure that they generate. The social structure, which is their practical achievement, makes possible efficient, organized social interaction. (The circularity of the reasoning here is an innate circularity.)

Nagarjuna, (1995, 129) in his *Mulamadhyamakakarika* (*Fundamental Wisdom of the Middle Way*) offers a metaphor that is useful here. He questions the notion "A mover moves" because it is the very *in vivo* process of moving that defines the mover, without which he is not a mover. There are not two movements, only one:

When without motion,
It is unacceptable to call something a mover,
How will it be acceptable
To say that a mover moves?
For him from whose perspective "a mover moves,"
There would be the consequence that
Without motion there could be a mover.

Similarly, there is only *one* activity of producing social structure, and apart from that *in vivo* activity there is no social structure. While commenting upon Nagarjuna's text,

readily accepted as a candidate for universal reason. In chapter 4, we discussed how the parties show tremendous concern for converting their talk about philosophical matters into formal formulations (see 98-104). One of the fundamental aspects of their praxis of philosophical debate is to convert any discussion, no matter how casual or confused, into some formal analytic representation of itself. In II.4, T displays this concern to cull philosophical order out of the discussion, which he succeeds in doing here by the end of the exchange (see next page, at 9:33:55). First, let us examine the preceding lines:

> L' When we establish the subtle emptiness, we ask whether the refutation of the habit of reifying the inherent essences that appear to awareness is necessary or not. It is not necessary. If it is not necessary, then the literal wording of your textual citation from *The Elucidation of the Thought* is not suitable for being accepted. We have to do some sorting out of the meaning of these words.

9:33:45 T Uh, right? Ohh. One refutes the object to be negated, that is, the object of attachment that develops when there is an apprehension

-075-   of an inherent essence, / right?

L'   / One does not necessarily refute essentialism.

The import of the discussion is that if one negates a given, particular object of attachment, it does not necessarily follow that one has appreciated or refuted essentialism generally. This discussion also references the Tibetans' epistemological investigations and their soteriological interest in overcoming attachment to objects of desire. Their notion is that when one understands philosophically that objects lack any inherent essence, then the mystique that a desired object has for one will be deconstructed and the force of any obsession that attracts one to it reduced. T transports the principal philosophical elements into a *formal proposition* that includes a logical token ("IT FOLLOWS THAT") and a handclap, and he receives a formal commitment from L' at -078.5-:

Chandrakiri in his *Madhyamakavatara* (*Entry into the Middle Way*; cf. Huntington 1989, 176) offers an additional metaphor that is helpful to sociologists, that of a car or carriage:

> One does not consider a carriage to be different from its parts, nor to be identical, nor to be in possession of them. . . . If the carriage were simply the composite of its parts, then it would exist even when the parts were disassembled. . . . It follows that the carriage no more exists after assembly than it did among the disassembled parts.

That is, "car" is a label that is imputed upon a collection of contingent phenomena, and it has no status independent of those contingencies, just as "social structure" has no existence apart from the contingent practices that compose it. Incidentally, this is the ontological import of the "as" in the singular locution, "in and as the immortal ordinary society," encountered frequently in Garfinkel's writing (e.g., Garfinkel 1991, 14, Garfinkel 2002, 92fn, 99, 138, 207, 211, 246, and 247, and Garfinkel and Wieder 1992, 175).

T   Um—
L'   —One does not necessarily refute essentialism.
T   Um, right? IT DOES NOT FOLLOW THAT one has actually
:55   refuted the object to be negated, that entities are established as if
          they had inherent essences. >~
-077.5- L'   It's not necessary. It's not necessary.
T   We say it is not. Right? Yah-yah. If one *has* refuted the object to
          be negated—that entities are established as if they had inherent
9:34   essences—we say, IT FOLLOWS THAT one must cognize its lack
          of having a true essence. >~
-078.5- L'   I ACCEPT.

There is a progressive development to these formal analytic devices. At first
a formulation will be made with a simple hand-clap (">~") that indicates that the
argument has a place in the formal order of the debate. Subsequent to this, the
hand-clap will be joined by a formal analytic token, as above at 9:34 (see capitalized phrases) or as in I.6:

T   TAKE THIS AS THE SUBJECT [*De'i chos can*]. Those appre-
          hended objects, how do they arise? Knowing sir, now explain
          properly, please. >~

With the use of the token *and* a hand-clap, T is able to conscript L' into chaste
logical deliberation.

It is here that the debaters' concern to add some rhythmic pacing to the
presentation of the formal propositions is manifested, and repeats begin to have
considerable efficacy in structuring the dialogue. At first, this is more the task of
the challenger than the defender, but after the claps and tokens are geared into a
rhythm, the parties collaborate in the synchronization of that rhythm. Once the
rhythm has been set and both parties are proffering their utterances in time with
each other, the formal analytic mechanism has reached peak efficiency. The
progression may be idealized in this way:

Hand-clap→ Hand-clap + Token →
Hand-clap + Token + Rhythm → Synchronizing the rhythm

Once the utterances of the participants have been serialized in conformity
with the established rhythm, it may be said that a smoothly functioning formal
analytic practice has been produced. This collaborative work of the parties may
be compared to the winding up of a toy, such as a child's small play car whose
rear wheels can be wound up and then quickly set on a level surface and then let
go, whereupon it will run on its own for some distance. While it is the participants who do the work of "winding it up," once it is set in motion it seems to run
as if it is on autopilot. When that takes place, there is a successful debate. That
is, a successful formal analytic practice is recognized as much by the rhythm at

work and by the aesthetics of the choreography as by the logic it contains; however, the important point here is that *the rhythm and the logic facilitate each other*. The logic is made to dance, and under conditions where there is no "time-out" for independent and unconstrained reflection. Here, thinking may be truly witnessed as a congregational activity.

These formalizing tokens are well established and have been discussed. They include "TAKE AS THE SUBJECT" and "NOW IT DOES NOT FOL-LOW," and they permit the clarifier of the reasoning a way to get the formal analytic mechanism going. Once the time for serious philosophizing has come, it is poor form to use informal terms of address, such as "Now it's this way, is it not?" (*Da lta 'di red pas?*). The clarifier may not be able to establish a clean rhythm in his first couple of attempts, and he may return to one of the tokens along with a brief formulation in order to recoup some of the previous philosophical itinerary. The implication of the use of tokens is that it is not merely a local agreement that has been achieved; rather, it is its claim to be a more universal reason. At times it may seem that the use of the token is strictly iconic: "NOW IT DOES NOT FOLLOW, to cite the proper text. . . ." The clarifier of the reasoning may even invent a phrase just so that he *can* have the opportunity to append a formalizing token (e.g., "IT FOLLOWS THAT there is this concern"), only in order to take that initial step toward rhythmically driven formal analytic discourse. From that point the clarifier will reformat the previous turns of talk for their formal inclusion in the developing analytic form. This practice has the capacity to clear up the discussion and reformulate it so that the parties are in accord about the basis of the dispute and know where they stand.

The clarifier may need to rev up his own engine by means of an intrasentential repeat, before proceeding to dialogical forms, as in II.4:

> T   Uh, TAKE THE MATTER of a reflection in a mirror AS THE TOPIC. How is it said? Ohh. TAKE THE MATTER of a reflection AS THE TOPIC. It is without inherent essence BECAUSE its being is interconnectedly dependent. The perfect defender will
>
> 9:34:41   cognize this selflessness. >~

And this may be done poetically, as in this passage where T inverts his semes:

> T   "It is necessary no matter which person, when anyone has cognized emptiness. For anyone, no matter which person."

In our next example (I.1), by employing a token and a hand-clap T promotes the discussion into a formal analytic statement at 3:06:30:

> T   In "*the falsity of ignorant habits of routine conceptualization*," the words "*the falsity*" bear an implied reference to a verb of action,

that is, the activity of a mistaken understanding. The word "falsity" (*'khrul par*) is the object upon which the verb acts, is it not?

L" Now it must be said that a mistaken understanding is unable to realize the falsity.

T IT FOLLOWS THAT a mistaken understanding is not able to
3:06:30 recognize the falsity. >~

L" A valid conceptual cognition. I ACCEPT—I ACCEPT—I AC-
.CEPT—I ACCEPT.

Once the discussion has been formalized in this way, it remains for T to establish a rhythm for the analysis, so that the dialogue can *gather speed and energy*. In I.5, T and L' collaborate in the construction of a formal analytic account, but it is T who must carry most of the burden of adding the hand-claps and setting the pacing:

3:50:13 T The text says, "There is no production from self." TAKE AS THE SUBJECT a reason like that.

L' Oh yes.

:19 T How to say it, how to say it. TAKE AS THE SUBJECT a reason like that.

L' TAKE AS THE SUBJECT a sprout. It is not inherently produced.

T A reason like that. A sprout that one must ascertain as not produced in any of the four possible ways.

:27 L' Oh yes.

T We must ascertain a sprout that is not inherently produced. >~

L' When he establishes the characteristic reason of the subject sprout, we say.

T TAKE AS THE SUBJECT a sprout that one must ascertain as not produced in any of the four possible ways. If one ascertains that, then one necessarily ascertains that it is not inherently produced. >~

T has successfully formatted the topic *and* established a rhythm for the formal analysis.

This next excerpt involves an important question that Tibetan scholars address frequently. Since many Buddhist schools of philosophical tenets hold that the *innate* proclivity to reify notions is far more prevalent than what is termed "objectification by mere *conceptual* imputation," and since the former habit of objectification is thought to be the more intractable of the two, Tibetan scholars ask why it is necessary to divert so much energy to removing habitual tendencies toward *conceptual* imputation? In this next excerpt (I.9 6:08:(32)-47) L' has taken up the position of the Syllogism-based Reasoning School, and T incorporates L"'s topic into the formal structure of the debate. T and L' find their way to a decent rhythm for their discussions:

6:08:30 T   Oh, TAKE THE TOPIC the analysis of the Syllogism-based Reasoning School regarding the customary mode of reifying an essential nature. When one negates such an object of attachment, in this system why then must one also refute the object of attachment that is a conceptually imputed reification of a truly existing

:39   essence? >~

      L'   IT FOLLOWS THAT one must BECAUSE according to their system, there is a reified apprehension of a "true" essence that is a habit of conceptual imputation.

:42 T   In this system, there is a reified apprehension of a "true" essence that is a habit of conceptual imputation. When one negates the object that is projected, must one refute the object that is projected

:46   by a conceptually imputed reification of true existence? >~

      L'   I ACCEPT THAT one must.

      L"   Now here it is, right?

      T   And that hardly undermines anything.

      L'   [L' and L" speak at once] This is exactly right. It's surely this way.

That both defenders can concert their reply so that they answer *together* is another good indication that the debate is proceeding in a clean, efficient manner. T's invocation of formal debate forms at 6:08:39 prompts L' to respond in kind, and they are able to synchronize their utterances. By the time they are done, the dialectics is ready to operate under its own head of steam.

Tautologies are the bane of any logician, and yet we find that *tautologies have useful organizational functions* in Tibetan debates since they are a means by which the parties can establish or reestablish the rhythm of a philosophical dialogue. The video excerpt III.4 2:15:33-38 includes a tautology that has no logical function but permits T to recover some of the synchronization of the debate after several sloppy previous turns:

2:15:33 T   Therefore, the sprout that is said to be already manifested—

      L'   Mm.

-048.5- T   —yah, is now said to be manifested already. >~

      L'   / Yes.

      L"   / Oh, this is so, isn't it?

-049-   T   It is said to be produced already. >~

      L'   / Yes.

      L"   / Yes.

Tautologies may not make logical sense, but they do make organizational sense in that they assist in the establishment of a rhythm of discourse that facilitates the flow of reasoning. A cleanly flowing formal analytic dialogue is a practice for clarifying the reasoning in a debate. It permits the parties to come to a mutual understanding of the key terms and references and to employ them in productive ways while retaining the conceptual alignment. Above all, it permits two parties to concert their utterances so that the analytic flow can proceed without impedance. Once the formal analytic mechanisms of a debate are set up in this way, the philosophical investigations can proceed in an efficient manner.

An examination of the video record on the CD-ROM for I.1 3:08:15-3:09:03 will reveal that the formal analytic mechanisms of this debate energize the parties and permit them to build their investigation dialectically. The debaters have taken up the issue of whether there can be any customary truth in everyday life (*kun rdzob bden pa*) that is free from distortion, and they conclude that it is not possible, that is, that customary truth must always involve distorted common sense (*log pa'i kun dzob*):

3:08:20 T   Does it not necessarily PERVADE that a customary truth must be the distorted common sense perception of a mundane, everyday consciousness, DOES IT PERVADE that it is ordinary wrong
     :26   common sense; or DOES IT NOT PERVADE? >~
     L"   IT PERVADES THAT it is a distorted common sense.
     T   What?
     L'   IT PERVADES, it is said.
     T   IT PERVADES, right?
     L"   It is said that IT PERVADES.

This alternation of utterances, which rehearsal of the topic allows, serves to set up a rhythm that lends vitality to the debate. T makes of their discussion an enduring formal analytic accomplishment, and the dialogue proceeds apace:

     T   If IT PERVADES, right? Yah, now IT PERVADES, right? It's ordinary wrong common sense appearing to a mundane consciousness. TAKE AS THE SUBJECT the reification of an entity as having inherently true existence. Yah. IT FOLLOWS THAT it is distorted common sense!
     :38 L"   It is said that IT PERVADES that it is distorted common sense, but you don't say, "It's ordinary wrong common sense appearing to a mundane consciousness."
     :40 L'   IT IS ACCEPTABLE THAT it is ordinary wrong common sense.
     T   IT FOLLOWS THAT it is ordinary wrong common sense. TAKE AS THE SUBJECT the reification of an entity as having inherently true existence. IT FOLLOWS THAT it is distorted common
3:08:44   sense. >~
     L'   / IT IS ACCEPTABLE!
     L"   / IT IS ACCEPTABLE!

In the next illustration of smoothly functioning apophansis, the formal analytic discourse comes to operate *as if it were on autopilot*. It commences with T formatting the comment of L' (cf. II.3 9:22:(01)-(22), "Are Logical Theses Necessary?" on the CD-ROM):

> L' But for the Dialectical Reasoning School the proponents of lower tenets are not persons with penetrative faculties, they are not.
>
> T Here we are taking up the case of the Dialectical Reasoning School's system. For example, uh, according to the Dialectical Reasoning School IT DOES NOT PERVADE that the Buddhist Particularist proponents, uh, are persons with penetrative facul-

-083- ties. >~

L' synchronizes his reply, and the dialectical rhythm of the debate is set up:

> L' IT PERVADES that they are not.

-083.5- T IT PERVADES THAT the Buddhist Particularist proponents are not persons with penetrative faculties, right?

> L" It pervades that they are not.

T continues the pacing by extending the analytic framework to another of the lower schools of philosophical tenets, and L" and L' keep pace with the rhythm. The rhythm, in evidence on the video excerpt, is very compelling and is indicative of Tibetan debate at its smoothest:

9:22:11 T Oh. Consequently, IT PERVADES also for the Sutra Followers School? >~

-084.5- L" It pervades.

> L' It pervades. It pervades.

T now offers a rehearsal strictly for the sake of the timing, and L" adds his own suggestion of an additional school of tenets, permitting the rhythm of the analytic forms to be extended further:

> T IT FOLLOWS THAT it pervades that there are no persons with penetrative faculties for the Sutra Followers School also.

(086) L' Indeed, THAT IS ACCEPTED. I ACCEPT.

> L" And for the Mind-only School.

The elements of the formal propositions of the Tibetans' dialectical inquiries are public objects, in that they are objects to which the debaters congregationally—and embodiedly—orient themselves, objects that provide the means with which the collaborating debaters bring their argumentation into synchrony.

Fine form in these proceedings involves the ability for the parties to collaborate in the work of keeping-the-rally-of-the-concepts-going, and it is especially competent for the challenger to *incorporate quickly* the notion of the defender when that notion is one with which he disagrees. Here in I.4, T is attempting to force L into a more rigorous formal analytic structure, but they are squabbling over which illustration should be examined to elucidate their interest in how one's concretized mental fabrications are erroneous:

> T   You can discuss the reflection of a person in the mirror, or TAKE THE CASE OF the perception of a rope as a snake. Uhh, quiet. Quiet, quiet, quiet.
>
> L"   The rope as a snake is not the correct illustration.
>
> L'   It is correct to discuss the reflection of a person in the mirror.
>
> L"   TAKE the example of the reflection of a person in the mirror.
>
> 3:36:44 T   No. No. No. We're speaking of a wrong view here. An erroneous view, we're speaking about. Erroneous. Erroneous.
>
> L"   A rope-snake is not what is generally recognized as what is erroneous.

In his next turn, at 3:36:50, T formalizes the perspective of the defenders, *even though he disagrees with it*, and in formalizing it so, he keeps the rhythm of the debate proceeding while clarifying the formal commitment of the defenders. It is competent debate praxis, and it is aesthetically pleasing when this objectivation of a commitment is accomplished with considerable speed:

> 3:36:50 T   Ohhh. TAKE the example of a rope-snake, IT FOLLOWS THAT it is not generally recognized as what is erroneous. >~
>
> L"   It's not, they say.

Much of the success of a debate depends upon the facility with which the challenger can incorporate the defenders' contributions and turn them into part of the abiding formal analytic structure of the debate. Formal thinking is demanded, not mere talk. Even when an informal discussion proves fruitful, one party will inform the other, "You still have to prove your point properly from the beginning." This may require that the challenger become quite demanding in his insistence that the defender revert to proper analytic forms. As in the previous example (T's first turn in I.4), the challenger may have to silence a defender who is not following the correct debate protocols. During debate I.6 (discussed on page 98 at line 4:46:35) T must quiet L before invoking formal analytic mechanisms: "Listen please, professor. Listen. IT DOES NOT NECESSARILY FOLLOW THAT this formulation of a conceptually acquired view of an ego is accepted by the lower philosophical schools. >~" Similarly, the competitiveness of the discussion in debate III.2, "Does Wisdom Formulate Emptiness as Existing Concretely?" has become so keen that no one can speak (or think) correctly, and so T attempts to organize it more formally, which permits him to clarify the discussion. The parties are enmeshed in a heated argument, but with some firmness T is able to regain control and introduce the formal analytics while ensuring that the defender's comments play a central role in the emerging analytic order. The topic is whether the notion of emptiness can be grasped adequately by a logical formulation:

-031- L' It is said that there is no such formulation that formulates emptiness as existing concretely in the face of the realization that cognizes the nature of things. Do you follow? According to the *Great
Digest* -/

T   /(In the face of the realization...)
-031.5- L" No no.
L' Now we discuss it, do we?
T Now we don't need too much talk!
L" This is said—one does not formulate it as existing concretely; it's
the same. It is formulated, but it is not formulated as existing concretely.
T IT FOLLOWS THAT the wisdom that realizes just-how-it-is,
-033- does not formulate emptiness as existing concretely. >~

Finally, T has properly formatted the discussion.

L" I ACCEPT.
L' It does not formulate that.
T =v= TS'A!
L' The realization that cognizes such does not formulate that.

A rhythm has been set in place, and T is able to proceed apace with the
formal analysis:

T IT FOLLOWS THAT the wisdom that realizes just-how-it-is,
-034- yah, does not formulate emptiness. >~
L" CHEE-CHEER.
L' CHEE-CHEER!

The defenders are now in fine form in their rejection of T's proposition;
however, T comes right back at them and calls for an explanation:

T How then is emptiness formulated?
L" The mind formulates it.
L' What?
L" There is a realization of emptiness.
-034.5- T =v= TS'A indeed! IT FOLLOWS THAT the wisdom that realizes
just-how-it-is, yah, formulates emptiness as existing concretely. >~
-035- L" CHEE-CHEER.
L' CHEE-CHEER.

They have come to a full rehearsal, and this permits the formal analytics to
retain its rhythm.

L' For the system described in the *Great Digest*? For the system of
the *Great Digest*? You're—
T IT FOLLOWS THAT the wisdom that realizes just how it is, yah,

-036-   formulates emptiness as existing concretely. >~
      L'   /CHEE-CHEER.
      L"   /CHEE-CHEER.
      T   IT FOLLOWS THAT emptiness is formulated as existing con-
            cretely—
      L'   What?
      T   —BECAUSE the wisdom that realizes just how it is formulates
-036.5-   lates emptiness as existing. >~

T remains within the rhythm of the dialectics while he provides the defenders the complete reason they ask for, which is the fact that there is emptiness;
however, since emptiness itself does not have any inherent existence, the defenders reject T's proposition. What is of interest here is that the discussion has
proceeded almost as if it was running *by itself* without the cohort of debaters:

      L'   ... THE REASON IS NOT ESTABLISHED. Does such a realiza-
            tion pose it so? You were just saying so, were you?
      L"   What? It must be said that THERE IS NO PERVASION. Now
            what?
      T   IT FOLLOWS THAT the wisdom that realizes just-how-it-is
-038-   formulates emptiness as existing—
      L"   Mm.
-038.5- T   —BECAUSE the wisdom that realizes just-how-it-is cognizes
            (*rtogs*) emptiness. >~
      L'   THE REASON IS NOT ESTABLISHED.
      T   CONFOUNDED BY ALL THREE!!

The success here is that T has compelled the defenders to be more formally
analytic, and this can have important substantive consequences for a debate.
Defenders fall into compliance with the debate protocols as a way to insure that
their views will become heard.

On occasion defenders may require considerable scolding by the clarifier of
the reasoning, in order to coerce them to keep their insights confined to the formal protocols. But the use of these formal protocols helps to guarantee their
views a hearing. Here (I.4) T first silences L in order to format the discussion in
formal public terms. In this excerpt, T displays considerable faith in the capabilities of Tibetan formal dialectics:

3:41:04 T   Ohh! Now, if it's that way—quiet. Wait, you'll see. Now, when we
            begin to analyze correctly, we must identify the formal compo-
            nents of our analysis. If we don't formalize our analysis, there will
            be no place for a discussion. Right? If the thought that apprehends
            an essence has posited something, then it is said that a mind has
            posited, right? But if the thought that apprehends an essence has
            posited something, a notion is not necessarily projected? First,

:17   this distinction. >~

    L"   Except for speaking on faith, you are not presenting anything.

:20   T   Eahh! Don't speak this way, you must argue with proper distinctions.

    L"   Except for saying that it's a thought that apprehends an essence, you're not arguing anything.

     T   I'll examine that. Don't speak of extraneous matters. You need to speak properly.

T believes that if L" is patient, the dialectics will be capable of giving a full and public hearing to every issue that L" wishes to be examined, and the views of L" are indeed fairly and publicly summarized in T's next turn:

    L"   What?

     T   When a thought that apprehends an essence posits and when a mind posits, it's the same thing. If there is a mind that posits, there doesn't need to be an object, right? If there is the projection of a notion, then there must be an object, right?

    L"   Oh. There must be.

     T   Well then, here there must be!? Ohh, like this? ...

Part of Tibetan dialectics is for the dialogue to proceed in a smooth rhythm of its own. It is as if it was a dialectical machine that needs to be permitted to churn and chew each philosophical notion in its own fashion, and it can function well only when the parties cooperate in establishing for the formal analytics its own temporality, which is one that moves swiftly and efficiently.

Overlaps, Duets, and Speaking-as-One

Tibetan debates involve considerable choreography of utterances, formal gestures, and body language. Parties will complete each others' statements or citations and serialize their utterances so that at times it appears to be that one commentary is being voiced by two or three participants, and sometimes this can include the audience. This serialization might commence clumsily in the way that a high school marching band awkwardly serializes a tune until all performers can find their place in the emerging rhythm; after the rhythm is developed and the pace tightens, the serialization will become more adroit. At such times the debate may seem more like an opera, but that is not only because the participants know the parts so well; Tibetan debaters strive to serialize their contributions so that the staccato of a well functioning analytic mechanism can carry out its work. This is how they produce a universal, Durkheimian social object, whose reality is made to seem independent of that of the participants.

Let us examine some cases in which the respondent completes the utterance of the clarifier of the reasoning, the clarifier of the reasoning completes the utterance of the respondent, both speak simultaneously, and the respondents speak simultaneously, and then inspect some instances in which the debaters serialize their utterances and choreograph overlaps so that the parties can still hear each other and come to speak as one. In II.4, the respondent completes the proposition of the clarifier of the reasoning:

9:29:21 T   Now that's why, right? Um, the emptiness of an entity's having an inherent, true essence—how must we say it?—having identified that, uh—
-018-   L'   The mind must come to ascertain well the object of refutation, that is, the seemingly true essence of an entity.
        T   Oh, this is right. If one does not apprehend this, because/
        L'   / it is said that one cannot have a thorough apprehension of what the emptiness is empty of.

Later in II.4, the clarifier of the reasoning returns the favor and completes the respondent's syllogism:

        L'   Oh. TAKE AS THE SUBJECT a sprout. It is not produced from self—wait a moment—TAKE AS THE SUBJECT a sprout, it is not produced from self/
-122-   T   / IT FOLLOWS THAT production again is both purposeless and endless.
        L'   Uh.
        T   BECAUSE it exists as established according to its own essence. That is the correct Defender's retort.
        L'   Mm.

In III.1, the challenger and defender speak simultaneously:

        L"   Here is the method for immanent attainment of the uncommon meditative absorption in cessation, isn't it?
:40   T   NOW IT FOLLOWS. BECAUSE OF THAT, it is said. There is what is called the wish / to obtain this uncommon meditative absorption in cessation // isn't there?
        L"   / to obtain this uncommon meditative absorption in cessation.//
        L'   Yes yes.

The use of simultaneous speech in the next example is more elegant, and the aesthetics of the choreography may be well appreciated by examining the video presentation on the CD-ROM, II.3 9:23:04-30 (see also photo II.3 9:23:28), in which the parties concert their utterances as if they were performing a dance. In taking turns, the parties achieve a lively syncopation that lends considerable vitality to their investigation of the Sutra Followers School's understanding of emptiness, and they sing the simultaneous utterance at -099-:

9:23:04 T   Ohh, for the Sutra Followers School a truth of cessation, a coarse truth of cessation is accepted?

-097- L'   THAT IS ACCEPTABLE.

T   If it is said that the coarse truth of cessation is a true cessation—

-098- L   Yes.

T   Then according to our system of tenets, how is it that we say it?

L'   What? The ultimate truth.

T   THAT the Sutra Followers School's valid cognition cognizes

-099-   ultimate truth / MUST FOLLOW.

L'   / MUST FOLLOW

Audience   / MUST FOLLOW.

L"   IT DOES FOLLOW

L'   IT DOES FOLLOW. IT DOES FOLLOW. Take the existence of the mind that cognizes the emptiness of being a self-sufficient, substantially existing person.

9:23:17 T   A course truth of cessation, ohh.

L'   TAKE THIS, the existence of a truth of cessation, a coarse truth of / cessation.

T   / cessation. TAKE THIS, the realization of the valid conceptual cognition of the Sutra Followers School.

L'   There is the cognition of emptiness of being a self-sufficient, substantially existing person, isn't there? First there is the cognition of the emptiness of being a self-sufficient, substantially existing person—

T   Mm.

L'   —then there is said to be the realization of an emptiness that removes such a manifestation. / It is said that to consider this removal to be an ultimate cessation contradicts the system as explained by Tsong Khapa and his two disciples.

:30 T   / So, ...

In this next example (I.4), the two defenders concert their utterances so that they reply simultaneously. In their reply they seem to be speaking as one:

3:34:28 T   The Syllogism-based Reasoning School says that an object's existence is not merely the external projection of the mind?

L'   Although there is no object whose mode of being is to really exist entirely on its own, without being posited through the force of appearing to the / mind, // there is no contradiction when the—

:34 L"   / to the mind//

> L'   —Syllogism-based Reasoning School asserts that a phenomenon
>   exists as something / beyond the mere // projection of a notion. ///
> L"   / beyond the mere //   ////
>   These are illustrations of rough and subtle objects of refutation.
> L'   This is why, this is why—
> :43 T   Ohh, now.

Many respondents make an effort to project the completing phrase of the utterance of either the challenger or a fellow defender, so that he might be able to chime in at the end of the utterance. This adds to the sonority of a debate and provides an environment for social solidarity. From II.3—

> 9:27:50 L'   When one discusses how one comes to obtain the uncommon
>   meditative absorption in cessation, it is said that it emerges
>   from the absorption that manifested at the Fifth Stage
>   / and occurs during the Sixth Stage.
> -010-   L"   / and occurs during the Sixth Stage.
> 9:28   T   Now, there must be prerequisites for such an attainment at the
>   Sixth Stage, right?
> -011-   L   Yes yes.

The communicative structure here contributes a good deal to what the parties will be able to achieve philosophically. Although the aesthetic phenomena here do not in themselves constitute formal analytic reasoning, they are its necessary accompaniment and a way for one to identify that a debate is proceeding in a rigorous way.

In his essay, "Making Music Together," Schutz (1971, Vol. II, 160) describes how cooperating parties "have to be oriented in their course with reference to one another." The key phrase here is "in their course," for it is *as* the flow of the interaction that the congregation finds itself. Schutz (1971, Vol. II, 176) attempts to describe in the language of constitutional phenomenology how individuals come to share a vivid present together:

> Either party has to foresee by listening to the Other, by protentions and antici-
> pations, any turn the Other's interpretation may take and has to be prepared at
> any time to be a leader or follower . . . each, simultaneously, shares in vivid
> present the Other's stream of consciousness in immediacy.

Or rather, the stream belongs to the congregation, to the debate; and the parties synchronize their activities with it. While the synchronization assists the communication of meaning, it is a vital interactional expertise that may be exercised even when there is no adequate understanding. Schieffelin (1998, 1) comments, "Coordination, organization and rhythmicity (and hence sociality) are possible even without mutual understandings about what is going on." This phenomenon of synchronization or rhythmic entrainment, though ignored entirely by Tibetological research, is an important topic for sociological investigation.

In this next example, during the beginning moments of the debate the parties work successfully to build up a rhythm for the debate by serializing their utterances, a regime within which each party has a say. This "round-the-rally" format permits the parties to tighten up the rhythm in an attractive way, and the speed produced by such tightening of the rhythm is emblematic of a competent debate. This work can be better appreciated by inspecting Illustrative Debate II.3 on the separately issued CD-ROM. The excerpt commences with some repetition and with the defenders serializing their reply at 9:17:27:

> L' Now, the connection among innate awareness, compassion, and the awakening mind is explained explicitly, is it not?[4]
>
> T Oh, yes yes. There is an explicit explanation isn't there? Now, is a person with penetrative faculties referred to in the explanation of how they are connected; or is it referring to a person with dull faculties?
>
> 9:17:27 L' There are explanations for both.
> -014- L" There are explanations for both.

T now offers two rehearsals of the point, in order to get the debaters in synch.

> T So this, right?
> :30 L' So it is said that there are in terms of both of these.
> :32 T In terms of both, correct? >~
> L" Yes yes.
> T Now this, huh, for example.
> L' Although the site of the principal discussion is this reference to persons with penetrative faculties, it also discusses persons who have dull faculties.
> T These words are from the *Autocommentary*, right?
> L These words are from the *Autocommentary*.
> T So now, there are explanations in terms of both?
> L Yes.
> T Since there are explanations in terms of both, for example, now this, this is said?
> L Yes.

The debate has achieved an effective rhythm, and T now employs a textual citation to sustain it. Both respondents participate in reciting the citation and developing its elucidation:

> 9:17:43 T To quote from the beginning to the end, oh, *"One who has compassion"*—

---

4. The reference is to chapter one of the *Madhyamakavatara*.

L Yes.

T —"*protects all others who suffer from the nature of suffering and other emotional afflictions, without a single exception,*"[5]— Oh, so.

L' "*He familiarizes himself with this.*"

L" "*He familiarizes himself with this.*"

T "*Even though one has the commitment to generate the mind of awakening, if one does not engage in the practice of nondual innate awareness, one will not succeed,*" right?

L" He is compassionate.

L' "*All suffering, without a single exception.*" That is—"*All suffering, without a single exception,*" and he familiarizes himself with emptiness.

:56 T Though that is so, . . .

The attention that Tibetan scholars pay to concerting their utterances so that there is "round-the-rally" participation, the operatic quality of their overlaps, and so forth, are the abiding preoccupation of Tibetan debaters. When a debate is functioning well, the clarifier of the reasoning and the respondent can overlap each other continuously and yet still hear what each other is saying. This is evident by the fact that during periods of continuous overlap, parties will recycle the utterance of the other so that each comes to speak the other's words, in a manner that can be said to be two (or three) people speaking as one. Their task is to choreograph their utterances so that they fit into the developing rhythm.

The next illustration is one of the most elegant demonstrations of speaking-as-one I have recorded. It should be reviewed on the CD-ROM (I.7 5:43:26-38), although since the T and L" are overlapping each other throughout, much of it sounds like white noise. Observe how T and L" are able to hear each other's utterances, despite the fact that they have been speaking simultaneously. But in this short excerpt there is some meticulous choreography in the serialization and overlapping of the utterances, which at times is an arpeggio. I have marked with special fonts the passages that each party picks up from the other's speech. The debaters are speaking of the example of the magician's illusion and are considering the reasoning of a spectator who realizes that what appears cannot exist in the way that it is being presented. (They are explaining that although the spectator may know through logical reasoning that there is no horse there, he nevertheless sees the appearance of a horse—i.e., reasoning can remedy one's subscribing to an illusion without affecting one's perception of an illusory construction; the implication is that everyday life is like that, in that the illusive character of our constructions is intractable, even though we know better. The task is to de-

---

5. The *Autocommentary* text (6.4) is *'Di ltar snying rje can ni gzhan gyi sdug bsngal gris sdug bsngal ba nyid kyis sems can sdug sngal bar gyur ba ma lus pa yong su bskyab par bya ba.*

construct one's illusions by applying formal analysis.) That the parties are able to speak together amidst the tumult and velocity of the debate here is an extraordinarily skillful accomplishment. But even more interesting is that when the parties are able to speak-as-one this well, it seems as if they are also thinking as one. This is an excellent exhibit of thinking as the activity of a congregation:

5:43:26 L" By the two, the magician and the appearance—the *illusory horse*—right?

:27 T By those two   /the mind constructs//

:28 L"   / an *illusory*   // *horse*, right?

:30 T The *illusory horse* ///is constructed by the mind.////

:31 L"   /// Oh, the *illusory horse* //// is the way it is formulated, right?

:32 T Oh yes.

L" By those two.

:33 T Mm hm.

L" Here, uh/

:34 T   / **That one, and also** //

L"   //the way it is formulated, **that one, and also**, so—///

:35 T   /// So, and the way/ it is formulated. //

L"   / and the way it is //formulated by analytic reasoning.

:36 T Yaah, the two ways of cognizing are different.

L" *Now this way* it's alright.

:38 T *Now this* is the *way* the two are explained. >~

The Temporalization of Utterances in Debate

Levinas (1981, 70, my emphasis) has observed that when persons find an accord in their interaction prior to (or alongside) thematization, this accord takes the form of an arpeggio:

> The signifyingness of the one-for-the-other is . . . an accord or peace between planes which . . . are in accord *prior to thematization*, in an accord, a chord, which is possible only as an arpeggio. Far from negating intelligibility, this kind of accord is the very rationality of signification in which . . . the ego receives the other.

By "arpeggio" Levinas may not mean a rhythmic phenomenon necessarily, but that is one way in which an arpeggio can find expression. The rhythmic forms found in, and as, Tibetan debate is an order that is not reducible to thematization, but it is closely affiliated with thematization.

Although James Edie (Merleau-Ponty 1973, xviii) has described "an affective tonality, a mode of conveying meaning beneath the level of thought, beneath the level of the words themselves," most philosophers have ignored this pragmatic dimension of philosophical discourse. The topic calls for sociological inspection. When dialectics is functioning at its optimum level, it involves not only contradiction and contrariness but also harmonics in which two mental continuums can be congregated as one, and the debate can proceed within its own pulsations. By being rhythmically synched the understanding of the social actors can become mutually shared (Schieffelin 1998, 1). This conjoining requires parties' social collaboration in choreographing their inquiries, and motivates in part the formality of those inquiries.

The Tibetans' formal analytic work is embodied work. The hand-claps, cries, spins, and gestures of contradiction of the challenger add theatrical punctuation to the argumentation. There is also a choreography of their prayer beads. At times, the challenger will rub his 108-bead string back and forth between the palms of his hands as if it is digesting the possible consequences of a logical proposition; he will pull and stretch the string at each end as if to cock a bow that will propel his argument (taking his aim directly at the defender); or he will circle the rosary around the head of the respondent three times when the respondent has offered an absurd argument. Before making a pivotal assertion, a challenger may raise his left leg as high as his shoulder, before snapping it down in time with his hand-clap. Because the argumentation is embodied it bears rhythms, and these rhythms may be synchronized so that all parties are able to keep moving together within the same dance. Synchronization of utterances is a principal ethnomethod that Tibetans use to produce a well organized debate. Their efforts to produce a smooth flow of synchronized utterances bear both aesthetic and logical motives, and it would do the phenomenon an injustice to try to separate these two motives. The more competent debates seem to run by themselves, propelled by the energy of their own rhythms. When this occurs, the analytic praxis seems beautifully impersonal and remote, a Durkheimian object. As I have already observed, that is the intent, for the implication is that the reasoning being produced has some universal significance: it is the disengagement that promotes an authorized, locally objectivated truth to a universal truth.[6] Locating the universal in the specific is the achievement of any art, and so it may be said without exaggeration that these Tibetan debaters are philosophical artists.

In this illustration from II.3 (see Illustrative Debate section on the CD-ROM), a crisp synchronization of utterances has been established. L" *sings* his reply at 9:20:50, and in a pleasing arpeggio T repeats the utterance immediately as if he was reciting an incantation; that is, he speaks as if he himself was removed from the saying:

---

6. See 92-94.

	T	Does there exist a faith in freedom?
9:20:49	L"	Of course. He has such faith, does he not?
	T	Oh, there is a belief, right?
:50	L"	There are thoughts along the lines of freedom being wonderful.
	T	Oh, there are some thoughts that freedom is wonderful, right?
	L"	Yes.
:51	T	However, it is not necessary that he fully understand freedom in order to generate faith in freedom, is it?
:55	L"	Oh, it is said that it is not necessary.
	T	Why is it necessary that a mind that is intent upon achieving free-
-066.5-		dom fully understand it? >~
9:21	L'	Oh. This is necessary, isn't it?

The debate continues within its own timing, as may be witnessed by the speed of T's demand for clarification (put-up or shut-up) of the comment that L" offers at 9:20:55, and the equally speedy (although not very informative) response of L'. It may be that on occasion the requirement to maintain the temporalization causes some responses to be less than informative. But frequently, maintaining the tempo of the dialogue is as important as advancing the discussion in substantive ways.

We will now examine extensive portions of two debates, in an effort to capture closely this phenomenon of setting up a timing for the utterances. It is an important phenomenon to describe because it stands at the pinnacle of achievement in Buddhist public debate, a philosophical form that has endured for at least fifteen centuries. The reader is invited to refer to the video and audio excerpts included on the CD-ROM (see Illustrative Debate III.4, -029- to -070-).

Our first selection of excerpts is from "The Samkhya View of Production from Self" (III.4), a debate that follows from the seminal first sloka of Nagarjuna's *Fundamental Stanzas on the Middle Way* (my emphasis):

Neither from *itself* nor from *another*
Nor from *both*,
Nor *without* a cause,
Does anything whatever, anywhere arise.

Here Nagarjuna is referring to the fact that one cannot have both causality and inherent essences, for if entities had essences that were intrinsic, they would be incapable of transforming themselves into anything else. A typical example is a seed that becomes a sprout. If the seed had an inherent essence, it would endure always and so a sprout could never arise. And in the event that the seed did cease, there would be nothing remaining that could cause a sprout. Nagarjuna is refuting causal realism, not causality itself, for a thing is able to cause something but without either the cause or the effect having an intrinsic nature. This is a refutation of essentialism; causes and effects are interconnectedly dependent.

Nagarjuna's refutation examines the four possible ways in which essentialist production could occur—from itself, from another, from both, or from neither. The Samkhya School of Hinduism contends that an essence resides in the seed, which shares its continuum with the sprout; therefore, they contend that there is production from self. Buddhist scholars are concerned to refute this position. Here the debaters take up this example of the sprout. T commences with the formal TOKEN for formatting a syllogism, and after L' joins in the rhythm with his vocal gesture ("Mm") T offers a hand-clap (at -029.5-), to which both defenders reply in unison, in conformity with the developing syncopation:

2:14:47 T   Oh, right, right. TAKE AS THE SUBJECT a sprout like that.
         L'   Mm.
-029.5- T   Yah, for them it does not exist in an unmanifested way at the time
              of its cause. >~
         L'   / THE REASON IS NOT ESTABLISHED.
         L"   / THE REASON IS certainly NOT ESTABLISHED.

T has provided the formulation first in its incorrect, negative formulation. After he receives the defenders' concerted rejection, he then provides the correct, positive formulation of the same topic. The defenders are able to chime their agreement together, thus sustaining the debate's temporalization. This rapid alternation between the negative and the positive formulations permits the debate to establish its own rhythm as an autonomous object, that is, independent of the debaters who have produced it:

         T   TAKE AS THE SUBJECT a sprout that has already manifested.
         L'   Mm.
         T   Yah, IT FOLLOWS THAT the Samkhya accept that it exists in an
-031.5-   unmanifested state at the time of its cause. >~
         L'   / I ACCEPT.
         L"   / Indeed. I ACCEPT.
-032-   T   CONFOUNDED BY ALL THREE. An already manifested sprout,
              yah, according to how the Samkhya put it—
         L'   Mm.
-033.5- T   —IT FOLLOWS THAT they accept that it is produced again. >~
         L'   / CHEE-CHEER. ["WHAT IS THE REASON"]
2:14:59 L"   / CHEE-CHEER.

The utterance of "CONFOUNDED BY ALL THREE" at -032- is done more for the sake of the tempo than for announcing any error in the defenders' reasoning, although it is ominous for the dialectical argumentation that is to come. L' keeps up the timing with his vocal gesture ("Mm"), T draws out an incorrect absurd consequence about the Samkhya position (at -033.5-), and the defenders harmonize their rejection of T's proposal. With such proper ruffles and flourishes as these, the debate is in fine form.

After twenty seconds or so of confused debating, during which the rhythm momentarily falters, T successfully reestablishes the synchronization of utterances by using a tautology at 2:15:33. The defenders harmonize their reply:

2:15:33 T   Therefore, the sprout that is said to be already manifested—
       L'   Mm.
-048.5- T   —yah, is now said to be manifested already. >~
       L'   / Yes.
       L" / Oh, this is so, isn't it?

T solidifies the tempo here by rehearsing the approval of the tautology, and then at -050- he introduces a new argument that attempts to draw out the inconsistency of the Samkhya position which accepts some form of manifestation of a sprout in the essence of a seed without it yet manifesting to the point that it may be actually witnessed by someone looking. The defenders chime their assent that such a sprout may be seen (since their assent is incorrect, it may be an artifact of being lulled into a conformity with the tempo), but T contests it at -051.5-, and for the moment they are unwilling to go along:

-049-   T   It is said to be produced already. >~
       L'   / Yes.
       L" / Yes.
-050-   T   They accept that it becomes an object of eye-consciousness. >~
       L'   / Yes.
       L" / Yes.
:41   T   But IT PERVADES THAT what exists in an unmanifested state at
-051.5-   the time of its cause does not become an object of the eye-consciousness. >~
       L'   Oh, what exists in an unmanifested state at the time of its cause—
       L" IT DOES NOT PERVADE. IT DOES NOT PERVADE.
       L'   IT DOES NOT PERVADE.
       L" NO PERVASION.

The rhythm of the debate is well established, and T has become quite animated. He repeats himself in order to gather even more steam before offering a summary proposition at -055.5-, and the defenders are paying very close attention to him:

2:15:48 T   Yah, what exists in an unmanifested state at the time of its cause—
       L" Mm.
       T   —yahh, such as a sprout, what exists in an unmanifested state at the time of its cause,
       L" Mm.
       T   yah, the eye-consciousness.
       L" Mm.

	T	IT DOES NOT FOLLOW THAT they accept that it is an object of

    T   IT DOES NOT FOLLOW THAT they accept that it is an object of
-055.5-   the eye-consciousness. >~
2:15:56 L" Oh.

        L' Unmanifest at the time of its cause, what is unmanifest at the time
           of its cause can be, can it not?

        L" It cannot be.

T has communicated his argument, and the defenders realize their mistake.

    T seems to be agitated by L"'s admonition prior to 2:16:07, and he begins to review the argument while accelerating the pace of his speaking. The formality of T's argument assists him in organizing a return to the rhythmic regime of the debating, and it is remarkable that T is able to provide a summary account in the heat of battle, so to speak. For their part, the defenders find a way to sustain the timing (2:16:10-21) by their concurrences.

2:16:00 L' Something that is unmanifest at the time of its cause cannot be an
           object of an eye-consciousness.

        L" What exists so at that time cannot be an object of an eye-
           consciousness. Here you need to / specify better.//

    :07 T   / (   ) // TAKE AS THE
           SUBJECT an already manifested sprout.

        L' Mm.
-061-   T Yah, they accept that it exists in an unmanifested state at the time
           of its cause. >~
2:16:10 L' Yes.

        L" (This is so.)

        T   Oh if it has phenomenal existence like that they accept that IT
-063-   PERVADES THAT it has existence at the time of its cause. >~

        L' Yes.

        T   If it has phenomenal existence, at the time of its production IT
           PERVADES THAT they accept that it is established by way of its
-064.5-   own intrinsic essence. >~

        L' What?

        L" IT PERVADES. IT PERVADES.

    :21 L' IT PERVADES. IT PERVADES. IT PERVADES. IT PER-
           VADES.

        T   CONFOUNDED BY ALL THREE. IT FOLLOWS THAT they
           accept that such an already manifested sprout is established at the
-066.5-   time of its cause by its own intrinsic essence. >~

        L' What is he saying?
Audience   ACCEPTABLE ACCEPTABLE ACCEPTABLE.

        L" IT IS ACCEPTABLE.

        L' IT IS ACCEPTABLE.

T rehearses his proposition, and the defenders again agree. While this repetition permits the debaters to objectivate the assertion, its primary function is to sustain the tempo:

T   IT FOLLOWS THAT they accept that it is established by way of
:27   its own intrinsic essence. >~
L" / I ACCEPT, indeed.
L' / I ACCEPT, indeed.

Now T attempts to draw an absurd conclusion from the defenders' position (-069-), and even the audience goes along. The audience participation here, also in time with the rhythm of the debate, is an indication of the successful production of a competent debate.

T   If you accept, IT FOLLOWS THAT they accept that an already
-069-   manifested sprout is established at the time of its cause. >~
L" CHEE- /   // They can accept that.
L'   / I ACCEPT, indeed.//
Audience   They accept that. They accept that.

T next makes the absurdity of their commitment more obvious by replacing the word "established" with "produced." Although the Samkhya accept inherent production from self, they do not accept that such production occurs at the time of its cause, that is, when there exists only a seed. Both defenders reject the *reductio ad absurdum*:

2:16:32 T   At the time of its cause they accept that it is produced. >~
L' CHEE-CHEER!
L" They do not accept that it is produced so!
T   What?
L" It exists in an unmanifested state.

The formal analytics of a smoothly functioning debate has particular nervous properties. The participants concert their utterances as rapidly as they can while still remaining in synchrony with each other, as if they were dancing the philosophy. They must do this while making publicly evident the positions being discussed, and this is accomplished by the challenger objectivating the contributions of the defenders with extraordinary quickness. I have observed some special occasions when aged, senior scholar-monks come to debate philosophical matters with each other. Usually, these have been spontaneous occasions during which the lamas have been genuinely motivated by the issues at stake. The debates were undertaken with much playfulness; however, it seemed to me that when these elder lamas attempted to temporalize their arguments and collaborate in developing a smoothly running analytic practice, they were playing at being youthful, perhaps half in reminiscence.

In our final debate, "Was Bhavaviveka a Middle Way Scholar?" (II.2), the repetition is not so much circular as it is a spiral, since the discussion accretes additional material each pass the parties make over the topics. We have already discussed the duets that occur at the beginning of this debate, and also the initial rehearsals that are performed around the textual citation from Jetsun Chogyi Gyaltsen's *Overview of the Middle Way*. This sets up the rhythm of the debate, and finding the right formulation is most effective when it is accompanied by finding the rhythm. The objectivation of the key aspects is accomplished with syncopation, as in

```
9:08:38  T    >~
-034-    L'   Yes there is.
         T    Is there?
         L'   Yes.
```

Following this, the debaters undertake more serious work in timing their overlaps, so that the pace of the debate is achieved by this sequence of concerted activities:

> duet → citation → well-timed overlaps → synchronization of utterances

They proceed to include the audience in the pacing of the debate, which leads to general celebration of the well-performed debate (see the ending of this debate). Not only is a competent inquiry built up, the debaters have successfully choreographed an aesthetically pleasing formal analytic mechanism; each is enhanced by the other.

The first half of this debate is devoted to understandings of emptiness that are less profound than those of the Dialectical Reasoning Middle Way School and yet more profound than the antidualism of the Categorialist Hindus. The view of emptiness of the lower schools of Buddhist tenets are considered penetrating but still less sagacious than that of the Dialectical Reasoning Middle Way School. The lower schools have developed various subtle views and rough views of the emptiness of inherent essence. The rough view of the emptiness of phenomena of the school under consideration is related to the observation that although the phenomena we witness are apparent in the forms that we see, their true nature does not rest in such forms because those forms are only collections of atoms. Entities are said to be only the aggregate of atoms which are presumed to be directionally partless. In this debate the parties address the difficulty ,that although scholars of the Mind-only School view themselves to accept a middle way view (all Buddhist subscribe to some "middle way," since it was the message of the Buddha himself), they are certainly not members of the "Middle Way School" as it is understood by the Dialectical Reasoning Middle Way School. The debate is thus somewhat technical and occasionally merely terminological. But the performance of a well-designed rhythm in the utterances contributes to the dialectics displayed here, and so merits inspection.

By 9:09:38, when the challenger presents a key citation from the *Overview of the Middle Way*, a monastic textbook, the debate has already found its rhythm. This rhythm is sustained by the defenders' overlaps at -056- and -057-, with which L" completes T's utterance and L' offers a gratuitous repeat:

9:09:38 T   So. There is that explanation, isn't there? Ohh. *"The aggregate of directionally partless atoms that is evident is apprehended as existing inherently, and the valid reflection that apprehends that it is empty of having a separate identity is explained to be a rough discernment of a phenomenon's lack of existing in the way it is conceptually reified. That is according to how it is presented by the Mind-only School."*[7]

-055.5- L'   Mmm.

L"   Oh I see.

-056- T   —ahh, That one, ohhh, is said to be / unacceptable.

L"   / unacceptable.

T   Hence, it is said, "The Middle Way scholars present a course of argument against that way of explaining a phenomenon's lack of existing in the way it is conceptually reified," and / IT IS NEC-

:55   ESSARY TO PRESENT IT. >~

-057- L'   / When the Middle Way scholars present their course of argument, yes.

T now keeps the pace of the dialogue quick with a gratuitous check:

T   Is there?
L' Yes, yes.

With the rhythmic pacing now begun, T builds up some steam by repeating his statement twice:

T   Now, because this is the case, ohh. When relying upon the realization that proceeds from the correct understanding of the Four Truths and the Sixteen Attributes—

L' Mm.

9:10 T   Uh, ohh. Relying upon the realization that proceeds from the correct analytic of the Four Truths and the Sixteen Attributes as it is explained in the two principal texts of Abidharma—

L' Mm.

---

7. Lobsang Chokyi Gyaltsen [Jetsunpa], *Overview of the Middle Way.* *"rdul phran cha med kyi brtsams pa'i rags pa dang/ de 'dzin pa'i tsad ma rdzas gzhan gyi stong pa'i stong nyid pa'i rags pa gzhi ma grub par khas len pa'i phyir,"* 117, which varies slightly from T's verbatim citation.

T's repetition is more than just going in circles, for he adds a few concepts; hence, it is more of a spiral, according to which the debate gradually accumulates concepts and reaches finer logical organization. But this is not only about the formal reasoning, the debaters' concern is also to establish a right pace for the formal analytic work they are doing. T continues to augment his statement and to maintain the pace:

-060-   T   —one will be unable to obtain liberation from cyclic existence or to obtain the path of seeing and the subsequent paths [the path of meditation and the path of no-more-learning], and so forth; one cannot obtain these paths. It is said that in our system of tenets we do not accept this method, right?

-062-   L'   We do not accept it.

      T   It is said that we do not accept it. Now, there is an illustration presented in the text that follows from this dispute with the Mind-only scholars?

      L'   I ACCEPT.

      T   Is there?!

      L'   I ACCEPT.

Not only is there agreement, the agreement is made as a move in a dance. The repeats are not merely for clarification (though they contribute to that), they are for the rhythm.

Half a minute later T offers a similar citation from another seminal text:

9:10:49   T   *The Great Commentary* says this, right? Professor, please listen. Right? "*The aggregate of directionally partless atoms that is evident is apprehended by valid reflection to be empty of having a separate identity.*"[8] Ohh, "*The path of seeing and the subsequent paths come after,*" ohh.

:56   L'   It is the interpretative text.

      T   When we present the system of the Mind-only School, it is an interpretative text/

:58   L'   / a definitive text.

The view cited in the text is considered by the Middle Way School to be interpretative (that is, a view whose words cannot be taken literally, so must be subjected to interpretation), but the Mind-only School considers the view to be definitive. Since T wishes to present the system of the Mind-only School, it is

---

8. Tsong Khapa, *Dbu ma gongs pa rab gsal,* (*The Great Commentary on the Middle Way*), Mongolian Edition, folio 27B; "*rdul phran cha med dang/ de bsags pa'i phyi don dang/ de las rdzas tha dad pa'i 'dzin pa gnyis bkag pa yang tsad mas 'grub cing.*" Cf. also, Gyaltsen *loc. cit.* 117, "*rdul phran cha med kyis brtsams pa'i rags pa dang/*" and "'*dzin pa'i tshad ma rdzas gzhan gyi stong pa'i stong nyid,*" 118.

necessary for T to observe that it is considered by them to be a definitive text; hence, L' corrects him at :58, and T accepts the correction, but he does so *without losing the pacing* (which otherwise might have been at risk, like a missed beat) during the repair; in fact, the tempo is consolidated by T's objectivating the point and by his rechecking with L' following -079-:

9:11 T A definitive text, but the Middle Way scholars consider it to be a text that has to be interpreted. Presented in this way, uhh, it is said that though according to the Mind-only School it is a definitive text, the Middle Way School explains that the meaning requires
:06 extensive interpretation. >~
-079- L' Yes indeed.
T Now, this we say, do we not?
L' I ACCEPT that it is.

T next begins to offer some exegesis of the citation, and the parties participate in this explanation together by sustaining the rhythm with a duet at -081-, by T reciting the pertinent textual reference (already referred to earlier), and with a member of the audience attempting to join in T's recitation of the textual reference:

T Now, this text discusses liberation from cyclic existence.
L' Mm.
T Ohh.
L' The thought of the Middle Way School.
T It is said that *The Great Commentary* explains that there must be a realization of the meaning of emptiness.
-181- L' / It is said that there is a realization.
L" / It is said that there is a realization.
T *"If one relies merely upon the realization that proceeds from a correct understanding of the Four Truths and their Sixteen Attributes-"* //
Audience // [attempts to complete the citation along with him.]

T next repeats his previous statement (at -060-), and the defenders take their turn to comment upon it:

T It is said that "one will not be able to liberate oneself from cyclic existence."
-082.5- L' This explanation is the one based upon the two principal Abidharma texts.
L" It is said to be the explanation of the two Abidharma texts.
L' Basically, this is said to be the explanation based upon the two principal Abidharma texts.

By this time the debate has heated up and an enduring rhythm has been established. T proceeds to repeat the topic and prepares for serious work by tying his robe around his waist. The near overlap at 9:11:26 demonstrates the efficiency of the synchrony as L' echoes the words of T, and the turns of speaking rapidly alternate through -086- and beyond:

9:11:19 T   It is said that one will be unable to obtain liberation by relying upon a correct understanding of the Four Truths and the Sixteen Attributes as it is explained in the two principal Abidharma texts. [T ties his robe around his waist.] Now, in order to obtain liberation from cyclic existence, this text explains that this system, /

:26 L'   / It is said that one must realize emptiness.

T   It is said that one must have a realization of the reality of suchness.

L'   It is.

T   Isn't it?

-086- L'   It is.

For a multimedia presentation of the developing rhythm, helpful for fully appreciating the way the pacing is working, closely consult the accompanying CD-ROM (Appendix section, chapter 6 files: II.2 9:11:43-9:12:44). We will pick up our examination of the debate just following that minute and offer some exegesis of the theatrical tempo during the latter half of the debate, including the conclusion. The parties are discussing whether or not the Syllogism-based Reasoning School scholar Bhavaviveka is a Middle Way scholar, a point that has its technicalities since he is not a Middle Way scholar who subscribes to the view of the Dialectical Reasoning Middle Way School, to which the debaters belong. Our interest lies not with resolving this minor issue but with the animated way in which the parties perpetuate the temporalization.[9] The cries of "TS'A" of the challenger punctuate and energize the debate, and the defenders' short utterances are rhythmically placed:

-117- L"   According to our system he is not a Middle Way scholar. Before—
9:13:18 T   —TS'A! TAKE AS THE SUBJECT the Master Bhavaviveka, is he a Middle Way scholar?!

L'   / According to our system he is not a Middle Way scholar.

L"   / According to our system he is not a Middle Way scholar.

. . .

(121) T   TS'A. TAKE AS THE SUBJECT the Master Bhavaviveka, IT
9:13:36   FOLLOWS THAT he is a Middle Way scholar. >~
:37 L'   I ACCEPT.

---

9. Consult the audio clips II.2, -117- to -118-, (121) to (122), -131.5- to -132.5-, and (147) to -156- on the CD-ROM.

:40   T   TS'A.

. . .

-131.5-   T   =v= TS'A. TAKE AS THE SUBJECT the Master Bhavaviveka.

        L'   Yes.

        T   Uh, ohh. IT FOLLOWS THAT he is not a Middle Way scholar.

-132.5-   L'   "It follows he is not." CHEE-CHEER. CHEE-CHEER!

. . .

(147)   T   Yah, TAKE AS THE SUBJECT the master Bhavaviveka!

        L'   Yes.

9:15:09   T   Yahh, IT FOLLOWS THAT he is not a Middle Way scholar. >~

-148-   L'   / CHEE-CHEER!

        L"   / CHEE-CHEER!

The simultaneous reply by L' and L" is performed as a chorus with aplomb. In his turn at 9:15:13, T very quickly picks up L''s qualification "in this system" and includes it in his objectivation. But in his next turn (:15), he satirizes L''s view; however, L' and L" are happy to go along with the satire and pacing, so T makes his view more blunt by declaring the defenders' defeat ("CONFOUNDED BY ALL THREE!") at -149-. L' scolds him for exceeding the decorum of a proper debate. Accordingly, T attempts to properly resummarize the issue of the debate (at 9:15:20 and ff.), and the rhythm is quickly recovered.

        T   Though he is a Middle Way scholar.

        L'   In this system he is not a Middle Way scholar.

9:15:13   T   It was said that he is not a Middle Way scholar as explained according to this system.

        L"   Oh, this is right.

:15   T   IT FOLLOWS THAT this is a fine distinction. >~

        L'-   / I ACCEPT.

        L"-   / I ACCEPT.

-149-   T   CONFOUNDED BY ALL THREE!

        L'   Now you must debate within the distinctions we have established here!

        T   O.K., please listen. According to the Middle Way system, IT FOLLOWS THAT a middle way scholar is a person who abides in

9:15:20   the middle way view of this system. >~

        L'   / I ACCEPT.

-151-   L"   / I ACCEPT.

        L"   I ACCEPT, I ACCEPT.

        T   A person who abides in the middle way view of this system must necessarily be a person who has realized the middle way view as

:24   explained by this system. >~

        L"   It is necessary.

Audience   It is necessary. It is necessary. [L" and audience answer in unison;
            everyone is smiling.]

The participation is now quite gleeful. It is important to one's understanding
of Tibetan philosophical debate that one appreciates that the debaters' smiles are
their response to the energy set in force by the speed of the debating and are not
just the effects of the logic upon them. Yet amidst this glee, T continues to work
to develop an absurd consequence that follows from the defenders' position, and
so the logical tasks are never forgotten. T presents this absurd consequence at
9:15:38:

          L'   In the view of the middle way as it is explained in this system.
          L"   I ACCEPT.
-152.5-   T   According to the Middle Way system, IT FOLLOWS THAT a
               middle way scholar is a person who abides in the middle way view
    :30   as it is explained by this system. >~
          L"   It is necessary. It is necessary.
          L'   Indeed, I ACCEPT.
-154-   T   Oh. CONFOUNDED BY ALL THREE! Yahh, oh so. IT DOES
               NOT FOLLOW THAT a person who abides in the view that all
               things, including form and so forth, do not exist according to their
               own inherent characteristics is a person who necessarily abides in
               the view as it is explained in this [Dialectical Middle Way] system.
9:15:38   >~
          L'   All things, oh.

The rhythm is now so well established that members of the audience are
able to participate at will without disturbing the flow of the debate. The debate
has become a transcendental object for the participant. T repeats his absurd formulating, but the defenders hold firm in their negation of it:

-156-   T   IT DOES NOT FOLLOW THAT a person who abides in the view
               that all things do not exist according to their own inherent charac-
               teristics—
          L'   Uh-huh, yah.
9:15:47 T   —is necessarily a person who abides in the view as it is explained
               in this system. >~
          L'   He should be.
Audience'   He should be.
Audience"   It does pervade.
-158-   L"   CHEE-CHEER indeed!
Audience'   It does pervade.
Audience"   It is the same. [Audience yells all at once.] Both are the same.

Finally, the debate is coming to a close with all the participants, the audience included, feeling intoxicated with the cadence of the dialectics they have produced. Next, at 9:16:24, T stretches his proposition from 9:15:47 by proposing an even more absurd formulation, emphasizing the excellence of the middle way view of the Dialectical Reasoning Middle Way School. At first L' rejects it, in line with his previous rejections; however, it seems to be dawning upon the defendants that not all followers of the correct view of even this school have actually realized the full significance of suchness [*de kho na nyid,* "just the way it is"]. Accordingly, L' revises his commitment by asserting that a follower merely needs to formally accept the view:

	T	IT DOES NOT FOLLOW THAT, this fine distinction, that a person who abides in the middle way view as it is explained in this system necessarily realizes "just the way it is" as it is explained
9:16:24		by this system. >~
-168-	L'	THE REASON IS NOT ESTABLISHED.
	L"	There is not necessarily such realization.
	L'	It is only necessary that he accept it.

T anoints that reversal with a double-TS'A (9:16:26), and he is breathless by the time he poses his final irony (9:16:36), in the form of a most absurd formulation of the notion introduced by L' that a follower who only accepts the view while remaining clueless about its true import nevertheless "abides in the view." That such a clueless person could abide in the view is an irony that L' happily, if surprisingly, embraces, for the reason that it is indeed possible that some very confused people can come to accept excellent philosophical tenets. At -171-, the ease with which L' assents to T's highly ironic formulation of L"'s position, *without L' breaking the cadence,* causes the parties to laugh out loud. The smiles and general celebration occur because the parties are pleased with their successful production of a tight, smooth, formal analytic mechanism. In this instance, their achievement of embodying the argument in rhythm is more important to them than is winning.

9:16:26	T	What? =v= TS'A ! =v= TS'A indeed! A person who, not having realized that all things, including form and so forth, do not exist according to their own inherent characteristics, accepts that all things, including form and so forth, do not exist according to their own inherent characteristics [out of breath] is a person who abides in the view, and IT FOLLOWS THAT he is a person who abides
:36		in the middle way view as it is explained in this system. >~
-171-	L	I ACCEPT.
	T	=v=

9:16:39   [Bell rings signaling end of debate. All parties laugh together with considerable congeniality—consult the video display on the CD-ROM.]

Many debates have these moments of celebration. They are the collective effervescence that Durkheim (1915, 405 and 441) observed takes place when social solidarity has been established. "It is by uttering the same cry, pronouncing the same word, or performing the same gesture in regard to some object that they become and feel themselves to be in unison" (1915, 262). It may take simple forms, as in the phrase, "We all say it like this" (*'Di 'dre zer lab so*), or it can take the form of a metanarrative comment upon how well the debate is proceeding: "Now you're debating properly." In these instances the social solidarity is derived from the congregational practice of effective rhythm.

Chapter 7

Strategies in Tibetan Philosophical Debates

It pervades that your thinking is the distorted common sense that appears to a mundane consciousness.

—Tibetan debater

Whether dialectical reflection occurs within the stream of one's own thinking or in dialogue with the thinking of another, there are critical moments when one runs up against the negation of one's ideas. Though inconvenient for the idle thinker, negation can be remarkably productive philosophically, for negation tends to be attracted to the weakest portions of one's thinking. The negation of one's philosophical commitments can lead to their reexamination and expose their weaknesses, producing a better understanding of both the topics at hand and the elements of one's own convictions. Negation can take the form of disagreement, which forces one to turn one's attention again to the logic and order of one's thinking. Or it can be composed of argumentation on behalf of a competing perspective, the construction of a different edifice of syllogisms, and so forth. However, when the perspective that bears the negation encounters closely the content of the opposing thought, intersecting it so to speak, negation then tends to settle upon inconsistencies.

Tibetan debaters are *afficionados* of exposing inconsistency, and their philosophical praxis is largely characterized by the comprehensive and methodical monomania with which a clarifier of the reasoning—turned into a *Homo apophantikos* and using various strategies of negations—probes through the commitments of a defender and sifts for inconsistencies. The Buddhist idol who personifies this praxis of negation is that of the Tibetan *yidam*[1] Manjushri, the god of wisdom, who bears in his right hand an extremely sharp sword made of silver that is incessantly slicing through the web of one's obscuring thoughts in order to discover truth. It is the cry of this god that Tibetan debaters cite when they utter the "DHII!" that commences each debate. The flaw in the constant searching and slicing of inconsistencies, a flaw that reveals the delicate nature of dia-

---

1. A *yidam* is a form of a deity that is used as an object for meditative stabilization.

lectical reasoning, is that one cannot permit that keen dialectical machine to run perpetually—and yet one turns it off only at the peril of breeding myopia anew. However, without taking pause to listen to the course of another's thinking (that is, without silencing one's own ratiocination), no adequate communication can take place, and without communication there can be no dialectics. For one to hear or learn anything new, one needs to suspend one's own logical praxis for a time, that is, the dialectics must be shut off occasionally. For dialectics to have its own life, it must provide life to what opposes it. In the Tibetans' brilliant preoccupation with uncovering inconsistencies, there is *both* clarification of thinking and a compulsive sophistry. Whether the two practices are separable is here a matter for sociological inquiry. The logical abilities that will be described in this chapter do produce very sharp intellects, capable of outwitting associates (I know this from personal experience with being outwitted). But how does it serve wisdom? Or better, how can these abilities that always accompany philosophical practices be placed in the service of better knowing truth? These questions will explored in Part III. First we will review the strategies employed by Tibetan debaters, in order to gain more appreciation of what Tibetan philosophical debate actually entails *in its course.*

Logic as Sport

Tibetan scholars who engage in philosophical debate resemble martial artists. Like two wrestlers who have entered the ring, Tibetan monks commence their dialogue by circling each other's thinking, at first probing and pawing in tentative and general ways. But it is a sport of the mind that they engage in. Aikido may be a more appropriate metaphor than wrestling, for Tibetans prefer to use an opponent's own thinking to defeat them rather than to build an independent competing argument. Though frequently challengers will lead defenders down a rosy path straight into inconsistencies, they much prefer to follow the defender down that path, coaxing him when it is necessary, while playing the merry escort. But contentiousness is always lurking nearby in their strategic battles of wits, and such negations serve to keep the thinking pot well stirred, when the turbulence itself does not cloud the thinking.

   Here is an example of a challenger escorting a defender to a commitment only to immediately contradict it (II.3). T commences with a textual citation:

-023-   T   *"Even though one has a commitment to generate the mind of awareness* [bodhicitta], *if one does not engage in the practice of nondual innate awareness, one will not succeed."* Can you accept it just like that? Yahh.

         L"   This. This.

9:18:11 L'   This is, right?

-025-   T   For example, the root text explicitly discusses a person with penetrative faculties.

L' In this, yes? One with penetrative faculties is explicitly explained.

L" / One with penetrative faculties is explained.

L' / One with penetrative faculties is explicitly explained. One with penetrative faculties is explicitly explained.

T If that is so, why does this citation explicitly refer to persons with dull faculties?

It is the task of the challenger to secure commitments that can be exposed as bearing some inconsistency, and it is the task of the defender to select commitments that are consistent with each other. It is a common practice for challengers to solicit commitments that are patently incorrect, and so it is not uncommon for a proposition to first be posed in an incorrect form. In III.4, near the outset of the debate, T proposes *four incorrect commitments* in succession (at 004, 005, 006.5, and 008.5), each marked by his hand-clap. The debaters are discussing the relationship between the seed and the sprout, exploring the moment when it can be said that there exists a sprout with its own inherent essence and examining whether any moment of production (by a cause, of a result) can be identified:

-004- T Yahh, IT DOES NOT FOLLOW THAT [the Samkhya] accept that the sprout has already manifested. >~

L' / CHEE-CHEER [WHAT IS THE REASON? I.e., No.]

L" / CHEE-CHEER

-005- T If the seed has already manifested, it is necessary to say that the sprout does not exist at the time of its cause. >~

L' They do not say so about the time of its cause.

L" THE REASON IS NOT ESTABLISHED indeed!

-006.5- T IT FOLLOWS THAT they accept that the sprout that has already manifested, yah, is again produced. >~

L' / CHEE-CHEER [WHAT IS THE REASON?] indeed.

L" / CHEE-CHEER indeed.

T IT FOLLOWS THAT they accept that there is production again—

L' Mm.

-008.5- T BECAUSE they accept that the sprout exists in an unmanifested way at the time of its cause. >~

L' / There is no pervasion.

L" / There is no pervasion.

T Well then, CONFOUNDED BY ALL THREE indeed!

Although the Buddhists contend that production "again" is implied by the Samkhya belief in the sprout already existing in an unmanifested form in the seed, the Samkhya do not themselves accept such a conclusion, and so L is correct in asserting that it does not pervade that for them the unmanifest existence of the sprout in the seed entails production again. The Samkhya Hindus wish to hold on to their belief in a self-nature inherent in the sprout, but to do that they must contend that this nature is something that was always there as part of its essence, and so that sprout must already exist somehow within the seed. But if it already exists in the seed (the Buddhists want to argue) then there is no need to produce the sprout, and its production "again" is unnecessary. The Buddhists use this logical consequence of the Samkhya position to defeat them in debate. Here the opponent is a Buddhist who is merely speaking correctly about the Samkhya tenets, and so T's cry announcing the defenders' defeat, "CON- FOUNDED BY ALL THREE," is not appropriate; however, it puts the defend- ers on notice that they have entered a slippery slope. A declaration of CON- FOUNDED BY ALL THREE keeps L off balance, even when it is not justified. L has navigated four incorrect propositions successfully, but the debate is only beginning and there are many more incorrect proposals to come. The incorrect proposals will be alternated with correct ones, and here T is more or less daring the defenders to recognize the difference.

Shortly following the above passage, T attempts two REVERSALS, in each case putting *the incorrect form first, followed by the correct version.* This is done with considerable speed (see video for III.4 2:14:47-59), and the alterna- tion is almost machine-like; but the defender does not bite the bait. At first T plays the amicable escort:

2:14:47 T   Oh, right, right. TAKE AS THE SUBJECT a sprout like that—
         L'   Mm.
-029.5- T   —Yah, for them it does not exist in an unmanifested way at the time of its cause. >~
         L'   / THE REASON IS NOT ESTABLISHED.
         L"   / THE REASON IS certainly NOT ESTABLISHED.
         T   TAKE AS THE SUBJECT a sprout that has already manifested.
         L'   Mm.
         T   Yah, IT FOLLOWS THAT the Samkhya accept that it exists in an
-031.5-   unmanifested state at the time of its cause. >~
         L'   / I ACCEPT.
         L"   / Indeed. I ACCEPT.

That is the first reversal. Here is the second:

-032-   T   CONFOUNDED BY ALL THREE. An already manifested sprout, yah, according to how the Samkhya put it—
         L'   Mm.
-033.5- T   —IT FOLLOWS THAT they accept that it is produced again. >~
         L'   / CHEE-CHEER.
         L"   / CHEE-CHEER.
-038.5- T   … When it exists as unmanifested at the time of the cause it is customary to label that "production."

L' /Yes.
L" /Yes.

Should L accept an incorrect proposal, T may or may not inform him of his error. That is, T may prefer to amicably lead him on a bit further ("Oh, right right . . .") into an even deeper contradiction. T will line up the incorrect proposals alongside the correct ones, sometimes asking both of them in a REVERSAL, trying to catch L thinking weakly, and it will be L''s task to discern the fool's gold from the genuine. The correct responses may be obvious when one reads an account of a debate, but the defender does not have the luxury to study an account or transcript of the debate; he must decide while residing within the claustrophobia of the dialectics. Much academic study of Tibetan debate, both by Tibetan scholars and by European commentators, misses the in-the-course looks of the logical terrain for the defenders.

Here (II.6) T secures the defender's erroneous agreement and repeats it to solidify L's commitment, only to loudly declare his error (CONFOUNDED BY ALL THREE!), citing the pertinent textual passage:

T   Although it is said that one directly realizes the grossest level of *rough* abandonment IT FOLLOWS THAT [at the second stage] one does not directly realize the abandonment of grossest *innate*
-046.6-   truth habits. >~
9:51:10 L' I ACCEPT.
-042- T   It's not so realized, is it?
       L' I ACCEPT
       T   If it's not so realized, DHII! CONFOUNDED BY ALL THREE! [Circles L''s head with rosary beads.] IT FOLLOWS THAT it is realized. IT FOLLOWS THAT it is realized. It is Jetsun Chokyi Gyaltsen's human embodiment of Manjugosha who presents the splendid thought —
       L' Oh yes.

Recitation of "CONFOUNDED BY ALL THREE!" is a formal move in a debate, and its use is ubiquitous. It is the means by which the challenger offers public scorn of an inconsistency that has been proven, or is about to be proven, to be patent error. More literally, CONFOUNDED BY ALL THREE! ("KOR SOOM!") makes three logical claims simultaneously—that the defender is presently unable to deny the validity of the challenger's reason, at least not without falling into some sort of nihilism; that the defender is unable to claim that there is no pervasion, the reason being pertinent to the subject;[2] and that the defender is unable to accept the argument or syllogism without publicly displaying an

---

2. In other words, that the predicate of the consequence is entailed by the reason. Cf. Hopkins 1983, 444 and 682.

inconsistency in his formal commitments, since he has already accepted the opposite of the consequence. According to Phyva-pa Chos-kyi Seng-ge (1109-1169), the principal developer of Tibetan reasoning in debate, if the challenger's reasoning is correct the defender will be able to make no response at all (Onoda 1992, 72). In brief, it is a claim that the defender is tied up in knots and his positions doomed no matter which way he turns. More performatively, whereas the backward hand-clap (TS'A) merely announces a single isolated inconsistency, CONFOUNDED BY ALL THREE! is a public declaration of defeat in a debate.

An Ethnography of the Hand-clap

While CONFOUNDED BY ALL THREE! is the culminating gesture of a debate, the most frequent punctuation is the hand-clap [>~]. Its principal role is to indicate that a formal proposal has been tendered, or is being tendered. It serves as a tool of Tibetan rhetoric and, when used skillfully, adds considerable energy to a debate. In fact, it turns much Tibetan debating into a physical sport. The hand-claps punctuate arguments effectively, and formal proposals can be strung together one after the other and can be nicely temporalized by the effective use of hand-claps. Frequently, there will be so much hand-clapping (both forward as well as the back-handed slap of TS'A) that a challenger's hands will grow red and swell up after several hours of the daily debating. Students learn how to perform effective hand-clapping as a practice, independent of their studies of logic. Having skillfully learned the art of choreographing a debate with the hand-claps, clarifiers of the reasoning must then hang their developing mastery of the syllogisms and dialectics onto the claps. By clapping, one is making the claim that one is a competent dialectical logician, and this in turn places pressure upon young Tibetan scholars to improve their logical skills while motivating them to perform competently. Students are told that only inferior debaters clap excessively or inappropriately, and so they exercise some resolve to hang only bone fide formal proposals onto their hand-claps.

The gesture itself is a token of contentiousness, since the hand-clap commences with a large wind-up (the right arm reaching high into the air behind one) and terminates after a rapid descent on top of the open left hand which is placed only a few inches from the nose of the sitting defender. When used skillfully it is a formal punctuation that can be intimidating, especially when a respondent feels some insecurity about his own position. In this way, a degree of athletic coordination is cultivated alongside mental coordination (no nerds among the intellectuals here), and some welcome corporal release from their scholarly duties is won.

There are other physical components to the debating, including frequent loss of voice (especially when hundreds of debates are occurring in the same courtyard at the same time). When a respondent is particularly adept or a debate is especially interesting, more than one challenger will gather to present a defender with increasingly difficult arguments. At times these challengers will compete for the floor and wrestle each other for position, and this can lead to very strenuous exercise. Frequently two, three, or four persons will struggle together, and after twenty minutes or so sweat will drip from their clothing. Sometimes, when two scholars are engaged in an hand to hand contest for the position of challenger, a third, weaker contender will slip in to propose his argument to the defendant. One friend of mine complained that every second week he had to purchase a new monk's vest to replace one that had torn during such struggles. Of course many monks enjoy this aspect, and it increases the eagerness with which they prepare for the debate sessions. The best method for sustaining the floor is to offer logical arguments that captivate the audience that has gathered around to listen, for if one has a very keen line of inquiry the others will keep their silence in order to learn where it is leading.

The hand-claps are the physical scaffolding that organizes the argumentation. They convey the seriousness with which a challenger expects a defender to adhere to the logical structure that is being built collaboratively. They discourage fuzzy thinking, and when the thinking does grow fuzzy, hand-claps will be employed to clarify and firm up the respondent's logical commitments. And they serve to keep the debate on the move. The defendant is compelled to attend to the next issue directly, and the punctuation provided by the claps produces a rhythm that the defender is obliged to sustain, although on occasion he may choose to disrupt the tempo intentionally in order to throw the challenger off of his rhythm. Similarly, the challenger will not hesitate to follow up one proposal bearing a hand-clap with another, or swiftly follow up one CONFOUNDED BY ALL THREE! with his next argument, hardly giving the respondent time to consider where the alleged error might possibly lie. It is to the challenger's advantage to keep L off his balance, to keep pushing forward (e.g., "CONFOUNDED BY ALL THREE. IT FOLLOWS THAT . . .").

Such pushing forward can become a cavalcade of proposals, each punctuated by a hand-clap. There may be three incorrect proposals, followed by a correct one, and then two more incorrect ones. Or, the challenger may use the tempo provided by similar replies (yes, yes, yes, or no, no, no) to lull the defender into compliance. Having set up a syncopation of "yes" replies, T can then propose something controversial, and L must be ready and able to recognize it at once. The cavalcade of a challenger's queries may alternate incorrect-correct, and again incorrect-correct, until a pattern as been established, whereupon the challenger can attempt to propose an incorrect-incorrect sequence. One thing is for certain—a participant's focused attention cannot lapse for a moment.

As mentioned, it is not the style of Tibetan debaters to contest directly, so much as it is to roll with the punches, and that is why the metaphor of aikido is apt. It is the joy of every clarifier of the reasoning to get the respondent to work his way into an inconsistency naturally, by force of the momentum of his own thinking. The clarifier will follow up and explore the shortcoming of whatever notions a respondent proffers, as in III.4:

	L'	Here there is no such person who cognizes an entity that is not produced from itself.
-112-	T	PRESENT what would be the correct Defender's retort regarding this. >~
	L'	There is a Buddhist, how is it said? There *is* some such Buddhist.
	T	PRESENT IT. If there is such a one, then surely you can PRESENT that one.
	L'	. . . There is probably a bearded Vaibhasika proponent. There may be some Vaibhasika like that...
2:18:35	T	Yah, possibly the Vaibhasika, or not?
	L'	. . . What? [speaks very rapidly] What is not produced from itself, oh, can exist according to the Vaibhasika proponents!
	T	Oh, so the Vaibhasika proponents are the ones. Such a *reductio* is tailored for the opponent.
2:18:45	L'	Oh, yeah!
-118.5-	T	PRESENT the reasoning for there being such a Vaibhasika proponent. >~
	L'	There can be. Why can there not?
-119-	T	=v=

Each time the respondent offers a comment, the clarifier invites him to engage in further explication of that topic, just as an aikido master will propel an opponent further along the vector of his own energy, flowing with the opponent in the direction the opponent has initiated until a blunder naturally occurs. The hand-clap at -118.5- and the back-handed slap at -119- imply that the respondent has waded into waters too deep for him to navigate.

Prior to the debate session or when one is waiting in line for a turn to challenge a defender and has time to plot out some basic moves, the strategizing may be like that of chess; but once the debate is engaged it is much more like surfing. That is because one has precious little time to consider moves and must react almost instantaneously to the direction and changes that take place, always accommodating oneself to the principal vectors of reasoning that have been set into motion. This dialectical flow is the natural element of Tibetan scholars. They move along this flow together in an interlocking dialectics, each replicating each other's replies in a mirror-like logic, only the mirror is one that renders the replies slightly more bizarre and distorted than at first they seemed. In this work, both parties must maintain their composure while following the dialectic to its sometimes absurd conclusion. Debate affords young Tibetan scholars the opportunity to learn how to be resolute without arrogance. Although conceit does exist on the debate grounds, it only serves to make the frequent defeats bitter, and so conceit is counterproductive.

Some debaters make a sport of attempting to defend successfully incorrect thesis or prevail while adopting the tenets of a "lower" school of philosophical tenets. Lopez (1998, 168) remarks, "Particular fame was attained by those monks who were able to hold the position of one of the lower schools in the doxographical hierarchy against the higher." The practice of enduring severe interrogation, even when one is correct, affords an opportunity to learn firmness and even a certain tenacity or aggressiveness in pursuing one's positions. As one new Tibetan professor once explained to me, "You need to 'push' because if you don't, you won't find a way to present your own version of how it is." Dialectics requires that one's own version is heard, and in this task there are duties and responsibilities for both the challenger and the defender, and "pushing" is one of the duties. If one is too reticent it will be impossible to "make a way" for one's ideas. Here again, the secret lies in a judicious use of pressing one's point. Once the matter has been articulated and objectivated, it is prudent to allow some room for exploration and creative examination. Fear of defeat and years of so-phistic skill can confine the more creative aspects of dialectics.

On the other hand, the firmness and resoluteness occasionally can amount to intellectual courage. As "the flow" of the dialectic speeds up, a defender must track the REVERSALS *while maintaining the syncopation* of the formal ana-lytics, without making a misstep. A reversal (see 121-22) can come at any time. Reversals provide for a ready temporalization of the flow, and no matter how fast the pacing is, the respondent must reply accurately, converting his dis-agreement into agreement in verbal pirouettes. This requires alertness, especially while a challenger retains his own firmness and resolute control of the direction of the discourse. If the pace exceeds what the respondent's ability can handle, he can slow it down a little by replying with a CHEE-CHEER [WHAT IS THE REASON], just as a challenger can gain some time by calling for a definition or asking the respondent to PUT-UP OR SHUT-UP, that is, to present an explana-tion of his acceptance of any proposal. A CHEE-CHEER can be tendered even to proposals that are patently true, as in I.7:

> T   For example, IT FOLLOWS THAT the mode of appearance of
>   smoke produced by a fire is the illustration for our conceptual way
> :32 of reasoning in terms of an inferential valid cognition, is it not? >~
> L"   CHEE-CHEER [WHAT IS THE REASON?]

The respondent's negation of such a hackneyed truth is sheer contentiousness, which is likely to prompt the challenger into a more formal analytic mode, with an increasing use of syllogisms and hand-claps. But it does gain L" some time.

An Ethnography of Absurd Consequences

The principal instrument that Tibetan debaters use for following a defender's
commitments to an inconsistency is the signal practice of Buddhist philosophical
debate, ARGUMENT BY ABSURD CONSEQUENCE. As we have been observing, it is the preference of Tibetan Buddhist logicians to argue not by means
of syllogisms that compete with the reasoning of an opponent but by carrying
the opponent's own thinking to an absurd conclusion. When a challenger is
faced with a defender who is reluctant to proceed with him to an impending
contradiction, the challenger will become more assertive by engaging in the dialectical practice known as the *phul ba*, that is, the "forcing" of an opponent to
accept a consequence that will be shown to be logically inconsistent with his
commitments. This assertiveness is similar to the debating device of calling for
the defender to present an explanation of his understanding, but since it has as
its objective a particular absurd consequence it is more specific and is compared
to shooting an arrow at the core of the opponent's argument.

Argument by absurd consequence is a philosophical preference that the Tibetans have elaborated but which has its origins among some of the Mahayana
dialecticians of India, who believed that connecting inferences directly with the
thinking of the other was a better philosophical strategy than constructing new
edifices of syllogisms that operate at a distance from the other's perspective.
Take the classical case of the refutation of the Hindu Samkhya's essentialist
belief in a real Self. The essentialist argument of the Samkhya regarding the case
of a seed that produces a sprout that bears an inherent essence is probed for its
weaknesses, and the Samkhya's own thinking about the impermanence of essences must lead to the absurdity that the essence of that sprout must exist *before* the seed has been watered and germinated in some soil: what can be said of
the Samkhya argument that the sprout is there unmanifested in a seed that never
sprouts? In this way Buddhist dialecticians have tried to work with the central
lines of argument of their opponents rather than construct competing arguments.
While the Tibetans have inherited this practice by way of Mahayana philosophical treatises, they also have elaborated it extensively in their practices of philosophical debate in the monastic universities. The Dialectical Middle Way
School is termed the *prasangkika* school in Sanskrit, which literally means the
"consequence" school, and that is because their preference is to argue by means
of their opponent's logical consequences. This is well typified by the seminal
philosopher of the Middle Way School, Nagarjuna, in the arguments of his
Treatise on the Middle Way. There he does not argue straightforwardly for what
he believes but reviews the impossibility of all the contending views. An entity
has no essence because its existence is to be so interconnected with the existence
of other entities that one cannot say it is either different than them nor the same.
In Nagarjuna the dialectic proceeds via negations, but it is by no means a nihil-

ism, as Tibetan philosophical literature has taken pains to emphasize, although Christian Indologists generally missed the point. The strategy of Nagarjuna, and his Indian and Tibetan followers, is to place the thinker into a quandary and to bring that quandary to life along with its full complexity. This aspect has been cultivated in one way by the Tibetan dialecticians and in another by the *chan* (Chinese) and *zen* (Japanese) descendents of Nagarjuna's Middle Way philosophy.

The Tibetan commentarial literature is unanimous in its recommendation of argument by absurd consequence. For example, *The Four Interwoven Annotations* (*Ba so chos kyi rgyal mtshan* et al. no date, 700-702), a well known compendium of four Tibetan scholars commenting upon Tsong Khapa's *Great Treatise on the Stages to Enlightenment* (*Lam rim chen mo*), argues that intelligent scholars are able to reason directly with inferences gained by analyzing the consequences of their thinking, without using logical syllogisms (*rtags sbyor med tshul*), whereas more simpleminded scholars will require the use of formal syllogisms (*sbyor ngag*).

In Tibetan philosophical debate, the aim of a challenger is to place the respondent into a position where he is unable to say yes and unable to say no, entitling the challenger to proclaim CONFOUNDED BY ALL THREE! The principal aim, however, is not to taste victory and bestow defeat but to carry thinking into a philosophical quandary within which philosophical insight can grow. The Tibetans are connoisseurs of argumentation by absurd consequences, and they have developed a literature about the proper use of consequences which has enumerated the species and varieties of consequences about as extensively as the Inuit have enumerated varieties of snow. Although Tibetans use syllogisms when necessary, their preference is for consequences, particularly consequences that employ an other-approved inference (*gzhan la grags kyi rjes dpag skyed byed kyi thal 'gyur*):

> Consequences have greater usage than other-approved syllogisms because they must be stated in all instances of generating an inference in another in order, at least, to break the pointedness or the vibrance of the other party's adherence to a wrong view. (Hopkins, 1983, 482)

That is, the employment of absurd consequences is a method of forcing the contradicting logic upon the very heart of an opponent's reasoning. Such reliance upon absurdity lends to Tibetan philosophical discourse a certain flavor of irony,[3] and Tibetan argumentation can become very humorous. This humor only increases the attraction that public debate has for Tibetan scholars.

The negative temper of irony is obvious, and this temperament is well denoted by the most frequent refrain that marks the inauguration of a new topic or

---

3. Their irony is akin to the irony of postmodern discourse, perhaps because that, too, relies heavily upon argument by absurd consequences.

proposal in a Tibetan debate, NOW IT DOES NOT FOLLOW (*Da ma yin par thal*), the "*thal*" in this statement meaning "consequence" or "follow." This statement is difficult to translate into English, where frequently (especially when citing short passages to untutored English readers, including some of the interactive exercises on the CD-ROM) I am forced to translate the phrase as "NOW IT FOLLOWS," that is, in the positive mode, which is not a poor illustration for summarizing the contrast of Anglo-American positivist philosophical culture with the Tibetan philosophers' penchant for dialectical negation.

Here is an example (I.1) that demonstrates how a clarifier of the reasoning will hone in on the vagary of a defender's responses and also PICK UP the concepts that the defender is using and further push the envelope that contains them. In this debate they are discussing the example of the reflection of a face in the mirror; the defender has asserted that "A customary truth is based upon what appears to an ordinary person's consciousness," and the clarifier has been probing him for what he means by that. The clarifier wants to maintain that the truth or untruth of an image in the mirror is a matter for the correction of perception by conceptual cognition. The defender disagrees and explains, "What appears in the face of this sense-consciousness can generally be established to be false." Having raised the notion of a "sense-consciousness," T follows that up with a question, which is preceded by the negative temper of his opening refrain:

2:59:36 T   NOW IT DOES NOT FOLLOW. A common sense thought like
              that is posited by the eye-consciousness, is it?
         L'   The eye-consciousness. Sense-consciousness.
         T   NOW IT DOES NOT FOLLOW. Yah, isn't it necessary that a
              cognition reasoning validly establishes that a sense-consciousness
              is an incorrect consciousness?
         L'   A sense-consciousness. Mm.
         T   Some conceptual cognition must establish that, or not?
         L'   Not necessarily.
2:59:46 T   One does not require such a cognition reasoning validly to say that
              the reflection is untrue?

The defender here has not yet clarified his thinking, and T is pressing him, while L' is attempting to find a way to think the matter through. L''s repeat in the third line and the translation of "eye-consciousness" to "sense-consciousness" is an attempt to *stall* for time to think. The product of this stall, "sense-consciousness," is PICKED UP by T (in conformity with proper Tibetan dialectical practice), and T uses it in the elaboration of his argument. It is important to observe that the building up of a line of reasoning here is not so much calculated deliberation as it is T being serendipitously provided with his tools by the developing structure that is being used by the debaters to organize the debate. Here logic is partly a function of the social organization and not simply the outcome of an ideal course of deductive philosophical reasoning. L' is interested in gaining time to think, not offering a term with which to format or clarify the debate; but his term, once uttered, becomes part of the developing structure of the discourse and finds its way into the formal argument being put together by the clarifier of the reasoning.

Not infrequently, argument by absurd consequence will occur in the form of the challenger deliberately suckering the defender into an inconsistency. Examine the rosy trail that T offers here in this extended excerpt from II.1. They are discussing the two illustrations of the emptiness of the reflection of a face in the mirror and of a pot. Since L has argued that the composite of appearance and emptiness of the reflection of a face in the mirror does not entail its emptiness of inherent existence, T follows L's logic by proposing for L's consideration the composite of the appearance and emptiness of a pot. In order to preserve the appearance of remaining consistent, L is pushed to assert that neither would that case entail the (pot's) emptiness of inherent existence:

8:59:(30)T   When its composite of appearance and emptiness comes to be established, yah, IT DOES NOT FOLLOW THAT the subtle falsity [i.e., the emptiness of inherent existence] of a pot is established. >~
-016-   L'   No, no, no.
      L"   I don't think the subtle falsity must be established, does it? It is not necessary that the subtle falsity is established.

T keeps his proposals moving in the direction of L"'s own logic, but applies that logic to an absurd consequence at (8:59:44), which L rejects. Following that, T proposes the positive version of the same (at 8:59:45) and L accepts:

      T   If that is not necessary, the establishment of the pot's true existence—please listen. At the time one realizes that the pot's actual mode of being is not in accord with how it appears to exist by virtue of its own inherently true essence, IT DOES NOT FOLLOW
8:59:44   THAT there is a realization of the pot's subtle falsity. >~
-018-   L'   CHEE-CHEER [BECAUSE OF WHAT?; i.e., 'No']
:45   T   TSS'A! IT FOLLOWS THAT a falsity is established in connection
:47   with the pot.
-019-   L'   I ACCEPT. Your TS'A is groundless! In this case we are not speaking of the composite of appearance and emptiness.

T believes he has exposed L"'s inconsistency; however, L' (probably correctly) tries to explain that there is simply a problem with the terminology. T then tries to clarify the discussion, but his reprise only escorts L' back to the same inconsistency, who tries to avoid it (cf. 9:01:(01)). First, T repeats his positive formulation, *picking up the tempo*, and L assents:

      T   On the basis of the pot—the subtle falsity of the pot is realized at the time one cognizes the lack of accord of the actual mode of

8:59:54   being of the pot and its appearance. >~
-020-   L   Yes.

A minute later T tries to clarify the dispute, gathering together most of its elements:

        T   Take the case of a pot. When one realizes that it does not exist in the way it appears to be existing as an external object and cognizes
-032-   the composite of its appearance and emptiness, IT FOLLOWS
9:01   THAT one must establish what is erroneous about the pot. >~
        L   No. This is not necessary.
        T   IT MUST FOLLOW. On the basis of the face's reflection.
        L   That is the ordinary, everyday sense of erroneous. It's an example. It's a different matter. It's an example of how ordinary falsehood is recognized. It's how an ordinary falsehood is recognized.
        T   Now, professor. This. Wait a moment. On the basis of the reflection of an image in the mirror, uh—
        L   Yes.
        T   —when one establishes the composite of the appearance and emptiness of the reflection of an image in the mirror as not existing in the way it appears—

Far from being perturbed, L *smiles* at T's persistence in forcing his absurd consequence and smiles at the competent acceleration of the pace of debating.

        L   Yes.
        T   —does one necessarily establish what is erroneous on the basis of
:15   the reflection of an image in the mirror? >~
        L   [Both L' and L" smile] It's an example of how an ordinary falsehood is recognized, and example of how a falsehood is commonly known.
        T   Yah-yah-yah. Hey hey! Now wait a second. If one has realized that the reflection of a face in the mirror has given rise to a mistaken understanding—
        L   Yes.
        T   —IT FOLLOWS THAT IT PERVADES THAT one realizes what is erroneous about of the reflection of an image in the mirror.
        L   THIS DOES PERVADE.
9:01:27 T   =v= You are in contradiction with the text!
        L   IT DOES PERVADE. IT DOES PERVADE.
        T   IT FOLLOWS THAT IT DOES NOT PERVADE that the reflection is realized like that. Jetsun Chogyi Gyaltsen Palsang Sangpo [4] has explicated this very nicely.

---

4. The author of the principal textbook of the debaters' monastic university.

L   Uh, you are correct.

9:01:34 T   >~ THIS FOLLOWS. The great author's text, *Overview of the*
-039-   *Middle Way*, how is it said? In the *Overview of the Middle Way*,
right?

L   Yes.

T   Uh, "*IT FOLLOWS THAT a person whose mental continuum has
never experienced a cognition of emptiness is able to realize what
is erroneous about the reflection of an image in the mirror by
means of a cognition that has conventional validity. Realizing such
an error does not imply the realization of the mistaken* [i.e., essen-
tialist] *understanding which is also involved.*"

T has successfully trapped L into a commitment that contradicts the position
expressed in a well-known textbook, and L''s entrapment took place not regarding the emptiness of the pot, where L was particularly wary, but regarding the
emptiness of the reflection of a face in the mirror, where L was less vigilant. The
clap at the outset of the line at 9:01:34 is skillfully placed *before* T's utterance,
to emphasize the closure of the trap, so here the aesthetics of the embodiment of
the debate renders additional rhetorical value.

Our next example (III.2) is an illustration of a classic case of T suckering L
into a contradiction, so we will revisit this debate (see 140 ff.) in order to follow
the progression of the argument closely. The debaters are examining the ways
that two different philosophical schools describe intentionality, that is, the projection of meanings onto the objects of the world. The Syllogism-based Reasoning School claims that objects are "present through the force of appearing to the
mind" (*blos dbang gis bzhag*) and the Dialectical Reasoning School says that
objects are "posited by the mind" (*blos bzhag*). T and L are collaborating in the
task of determining the truth about intentionality.

-016- T Now [this matter of] "being present through the force of appearing
to the mind" and "being posited by the mind." For example,
"something like a pot is said to be posited by the mind" and "present through the force of appearing to the mind." How is this
"mind" to be presented?

L" . . . It can be presented that a pot is constituted by something like a
sense-consciousness, right? Something like a sense-consciousness
can be proposed, right? There is a sense-consciousness proposed,
is there?

L' The way that it comes to appear can be different.

It is the task of T to clarify the debate, so he takes up L'''s observation and
formalizes it:

T Yah, TAKE AS THE SUBJECT something like a pot. Yahh, IT
FOLLOWS THAT it is posited by an eye-consciousness that

-021-   apprehends a pot. >~
        L' I ACCEPT.
        L" It is posited, isn't it?
        T   Right?
        L" It is indeed posited.

As T has the debate progressing in an amicable way, he changes the object of their illustration, to which L' and L" offer their accord *while collaborating in building the debate's rhythm*; T also changes the characterization of the subject that is perceiving the object. But since T retains the *same structure* of reasoning he has been employing, the defenders accept the proposal:

        T   In that case, for example TAKE AS THE SUBJECT something
            like the nature of things (*chos nyid*).
        L' [Rapidly] Emptiness, emptiness, emptiness.
        L" We can present the idea of something like emptiness.
-022.5- T   IT FOLLOWS THAT it is posited by the wisdom of an Arya's
            meditative equipoise >~
        L" THAT IS ACCEPTED.

And T firms up that assent, again maintaining the rhythm of the debate.

        T   Is it?
        L" Yes yes.
        L' Yes yes!

Next T expands his proposal further, again changing the object that is the illustration:

        T   If it is said to be posited, TAKE AS THE SUBJECT the nature of
            things, yah, IT FOLLOWS THAT the wisdom that realizes just-
            how-it-is (*ji ltar ba*) posits it. >~
        L' /I ACCEPT!
        L" /I ACCEPT!

Securing that assent, T extends his proposition a bit further still, substituting "posit" (*bzhag*) with "formulate" (*'jog*), successfully suckering both defenders, who are happily moving along with the direction and rhythm of the debate, into accepting an absurd consequence:

        T   Well then, TAKE AS THE SUBJECT something like the nature of
            things, IT FOLLOWS THAT it is formulated (*'jog*) by the wisdom
-024.5-   that realizes just how it is. >~
        L' I ACCEPT.
        L" I ACCEPT.
-025-   T   Positively, TS'A! =v= You are contradictory! IT FOLLOWS
            THAT there is no such formulation. IT FOLLOWS THAT accord-

ing to the thought of our highest, most excellent guide, Khedrup
Gelek Palsangpo, there is no such formulating. THIS FOLLOWS.
Suchness, as it is composed in the *Great Digest*—
-026.5- L" Oh yes.
       T   Is it not!?
       L' Hm.

With his TS'A, T publicly announces the absurd contradiction and adds a
suitable textual reference. The absurdity exposed by T here is that any Aryan
being in meditative equipoise who is directly witnessing suchness is not formulating anything, for that would involve the application of conceptual structures
that would alienate the meditator from his immediate realization of "just the way
it is" (i.e. suchness, *ji ltar ba*). The phenomenon itself is somewhat contradictory—deliberately resolving to not be deliberate—and a good deal of the Buddha's discourses address this quandary.[5] T formalizes the quandary, articulating
the contradiction bluntly, "*'jog kyang mi 'jog*"—"although it is formulated, it is
not formulated." It is one thing to discursively present a contradiction in reasoning, but it is a more significant accomplishment to carry that contradiction into
experience *and bring it to life* in front of the thinkers. One is reminded of Levinas's comment (1981, 23), "Truth is an exhibition of being." T's philosophical
work in this debate includes his bringing that quandary to life and exhibiting its
workings, and the use of absurd consequences is one of his tools.

       T   Although there the nature of things may be formulated as arising
           through the force of appearing to the mind, it is not formulated so
           (*'jog kyang mi 'jog*). It's this way is it not? It is not formulated so,
           and although the wisdom that realizes just how it is formulates the
           nature of things through the force of the mind, yah, the wisdom
           that realizes just how it is does not formulate the nature of things
           as existing in that way.
-029- L" Oh, there is no concretized formulation.
       T   . . . IT FOLLOWS THAT the wisdom that realizes just how it is,
-033-   yah, does not formulate emptiness as existing concretely. >~
       L" I ACCEPT.
       L' It does not formulate that.
       T   =v= TS'A!

Note that T's formal proposal at -033- is in substantial contradiction with
the proposal at -024.5-, to which the defenders gave their assent, thus justifying
T's TS'A. This is a well-constructed contradiction, built up within clean dialectical structures, and the contradiction flows naturally out of those structures.

---

5. See, for example, the discussion of "The Questions of Maitreya Chapter" of the
Sutra on Perfect Wisdom.

Having the defenders on the ropes, so to speak, T slightly modifies his proposal, *keeping the important quandary directly before the eyes* of the debaters:

> L'   The realization that cognizes such does not formulate that.
>
> T   IT FOLLOWS THAT the wisdom that realizes just how it is, yah,
>
> -034-   does not formulate emptiness. >~

To accept this would be to err too far in the direction of anti-intellectualism, so the defenders rightly exchange their acceptance for a rejection. T then immediately prompts them to explain themselves, using the explosive syllable "tey-" (*ste*), a mode of query closely associated with PUT-UP OR SHUT-UP. This forces the defenders to cope with the quandary:

> L"   CHEE-CHEER.
>
> L'   CHEE-CHEER!
>
> T   How then is emptiness formulated? [*stong snyid 'jog ste-*]
>
> L"   The mind formulates it.
>
> L'   What?
>
> L"   There is a realization of emptiness.
>
> -034.5- T   =v= TS'A indeed! IT FOLLOWS THAT the wisdom that realizes just-how-it-is, yah, formulates emptiness as existing concretely. >~

The quandary is here kept alive before the defenders, who try to stall by inquiring about which interpretive system is pertinent here. T doesn't pay their stall any mind, but keeps the quandary visible:

> -035- L"   CHEE-CHEER.
>
> L'   CHEE-CHEER. For the system of the *Great Digest*? For the system of the *Great Digest*? You're—
>
> T   IT FOLLOWS THAT the wisdom that realizes just how it is,
>
> -036-   yah, formulates emptiness as existing concretely. >~
>
> L'   /CHEE-CHEER.
>
> L"   /CHEE-CHEER.

T will comply with their call for a reason (CHEE-CHEER). It is not important here to resolve the matter conclusively, or to win or lose the debate. The aim here is strictly to bring the contradiction to life:

> T   IT FOLLOWS THAT emptiness is formulated as existing concretely—
>
> L'   What?
>
> T   —BECAUSE the wisdom that witnesses [*gzigs*] just how it is, yah,
>
> -036.5-   cognizes [*rtogs*] emptiness as existing. >~
>
> L'   "IT FOLLOWS THAT such a realization so cognizes," THE REASON IS NOT ESTABLISHED.

In our next illustration, the debaters argue about the status of a particular Syllogism-based Reasoning School scholar who is the subject of much criticism by Tibetan academics. Although he is a well-known early proponent of the Middle Way School, they fault his limited understanding of the emptiness of inherent existence. In this debate (II.2) T leads L' up a rosy trail with a truism:

> T   IT FOLLOWS THAT to actually liberate oneself from cyclic
> 9:11:47   existence, it is necessary to realize the meaning of emptiness. >~
> -091- L' I ACCEPT!

T repeats the truism in order to *establish the pacing of the debate*, as L' consorts with him in this work pertinent to organizing the orderliness of the debate:

> 9:11:48 T   It is necessary to have this realization.
>   L'   It is necessary to have this realization.

Then T lays the groundwork for suckering L' into a false commitment, by emphasizing how the Middle Way scholars have a correct view of emptiness:

> T   That's why, uh, according to the explanation of this system, it is
>   positively necessary that a person abiding in the Middle Way view
> :52   fathom the meaning of emptiness. >~
> Audience   What are you saying?
> -093- L' A person abiding in the Middle Way view must do so.

Now T is ready to propose the case of a Middle Way scholar who in fact does *not* have a correct view of emptiness:

> T   Because of this, uh, ohh, so it is said. For example, TAKE AS THE
>   SUBJECT Bhavaviveka—
> L' Yes.
> T   —Uh, according to this system he is not a person who abides in the
> 9:12:02   Middle Way view. >~

T proposes this case in the negative and incorrect form, the preference of these dialecticians who advocate absurd propositions. It is likely that L will be declared wrong no matter which answer he selects; however, constrained by sustaining conformity with his previous commitments, he declares incorrectly,

> L'   He is not.
> L"   He is not, it is said.
> L'   No no.

The "it is said" of L" is an effort to invoke an imagined universal acceptance of their answer. T is hardly swayed, and he repeats the proposal in order to *formalize their commitment*, prior to a public declaration of its error:

> -096-   T   TAKE AS THE SUBJECT Bhavaviveka.   IT FOLLOWS THAT

:07   according to this system he is not a person who abides in the Mid-
         dle Way. >~
L'   / I ACCEPT !
L"   / I ACCEPT !
T   However, CONFOUNDED BY ALL THREE! This contradicts
         the text! >~

The text T is referring to is Tsong Khapa's *Essence of True Eloquence*
(*Legs bshad snying po*), which specifically confirms that Bhavaviveka is a
Madhyamaka scholar, though it does indeed treat him as a misguided member of
the Middle Way School.[6] Being locked into his previous commitment, L' is
placed in the awkward position of defending himself even though T is right:

L'   . . . There is no basis for your asserting, "He is a Middle Way
         scholar." It cannot be said that he is a Middle Way scholar.

And so T formulates L''s position in an argument by absurd consequence
and turns to look at the audience as if ridiculing the reply:

T   TAKE AS THE SUBJECT Bhavaviveka, IT FOLLOWS THAT he
         is not a Middle Way scholar. [T moves to clap, his foot raised high,
         but he holds off, waiting for L''s response.]
9:12:35 L'   I ACCEPT!
         L"   I ACCEPT!

T completes the full syllogism, including the subject (TAKE AS THE SUB-
JECT), the predicate of the thesis (IT FOLLOWS THAT . . .), and the reason
(BECAUSE), but T is being entirely ironic, practically wallowing in the absurd-
ity of it, because he knows the text does not say this:

T   BECAUSE that's what it says in the text!
L'   That is different! [much audience talk, as they are discussing the
         strategy of T's move]

And then T rubs this absurdity in L''s face by turning the previous comment
into a grossly apparent falsehood:

T   IT FOLLOWS THAT it is BECAUSE it is the position of our kind,
         uncommonly great emanation of Manjushri, the respected second
         Buddha, Losang Drakpa himself!

---

6. *Drang ba dang nges pa'i don rnam par phye ba'i bstan bcos legs bshad snying
po*, 233-34. The text raises the matter in the form of a query that is rejected by Tsong
Khapa n.d. b: "'di pa ltar na legs ldan la sogs pa'i rang rygud pa rnams don dam par
dang bden par brub pa'i don kas len dbu ma par mi 'jog gam snyam na . . . mkhas pa de
dag . . . dbu ma pa ni yin no."

Losang Drakpa is the original name of Tsong Khapa. Unfortunately, L' cannot deny it without falling into contradiction, so T puts an end to his misery:

L'   Yes.
9:12:41   T   You are in circles. DHII! CONFOUNDED BY ALL THREE!

T then begins to educate L' about what the text presents, comparing the wayward Middle Way scholar Bhavaviveka to a wayward monk who remains a monk even though he has violated his vows. L' accepts the instruction:

T   . . . If you ask what is the explanation according to this text, *"Even though a monk who has vows violates them and acts inappropriately, by merely violating some vows, it should not be said that*
9:13:03   *he is not a monk. It's just like that,"* it says. >~
L'   Oh. This is so.

Following this, T offers the proposal again. L', caught and exposed in his corner, submits, and T announces the contradiction (TS'A):

T   TAKE AS THE SUBJECT the Master Bhavaviveka, IT FOL-
:36   LOWS THAT he is a Middle Way scholar. >~
:37   L'   I ACCEPT.
9:13:40   T   TS'A.

And from this point the debate proceeds with an exploration of the thought of Bhavaviveka.

In this case it is uncertain whether such logical antics are useful to an enhancement of the defenders' understanding; however, it did bring them face-to-face with the dilemma at hand. Our next case (I.1) takes up the matter of the limits of conventional wisdom for gaining access to the understanding of the emptiness of essences, and it further illustrates the Tibetan penchant for playing with absurdities. The topic is from a passage by Tsong Khapa (1988, 183) from his *Elucidation of the Middle Way Thought*, a meaning commentary on Chandrakirti's *Introduction to the Middle Way*:

3:06:19   T   Tsong Khapa wrote, *"Such a valid conceptual examination [tha nyed pa'i tshad ma] is incapable of establishing the falsity of ignorant habits of routine conceptualization that contaminate our awareness."*
L   Yes. This is right.
T   In *"the falsity of ignorant habits of routine conceptualization,"* the word "falsity" bears an implied reference to a verb of action, that is, the activity of a mistaken consciousness. The word "falsity"[7] is the object upon which a verb acts, is it not?

---

7. The *'khrul pa* in *'khrul par.* T emphasizes the "*-r*," which indicates an action.

L" There is mistaken common sense examination [*'jig rten pa'i tha nyed pa'i tshad ma*]. Now it must be said that this is unable to realize the falsity.

T IT FOLLOWS THAT it is not able to recognize that there is a
:30 mistaken [i.e., essentialist] understanding. >~

L" I ACCEPT—I ACCEPT—I ACCEPT—I ACCEPT.

L and T have reviewed the matter, and T has promoted their conclusion to formal status. Now T is ready to propose his ARGUMENT BY ABSURD CONSEQUENCE, which takes an extremist view that valid conceptual reflection is powerless to examine false essences. Though conceptual reflection, while valid in common sense terms, is still a distorted consciousness, it nevertheless has a capacity for analysis that can be of great utility:

T TAKE AS THE SUBJECT a distorted consciousness that has reified an entity as having an inherently true essence. IT FOLLOWS THAT a valid conceptual examination is incapable of recognizing
:34 it. >~

L' No no.

L" CHEE-CHEER [WHAT IS THE REASON?]

It is an interesting dilemma that probes how conceptual reflection, which is basically erroneous, can possibly recognize the truth of how entities lack inherent essences; in other words, is it possible for the blind to lead the blind? Although the defenders are correct to reject the extreme proposal, since there is indeed a role for conceptual reflection (especially in Tsong Khapa's thought), it may be a logical consequence of this rejection that valid conceptual examination comprehends the truth of entities perfectly satisfactorily. And if that is the case, it must understand emptiness as well. But if a conceptual consciousness can recognize truth, then perhaps an ordinary consciousness can do so as well, so T proposes a humorous but patent absurdity, *turning his back* to the defenders in ridicule, which stirs them into vigorous replies:

3:06:35 T [To L"] TAKE AS THE SUBJECT a distorted consciousness that has reified an entity as having an inherently true essence. IT FOLLOWS THAT this is emptiness! >~ [T turns his back to L' and L".]

:37 L' / CHEE-CHEER! CHEE-CHEER!

L" / Now here there is no doubt. This is a distorted consciousness.

L' Now no, that's why it's a word trick. It's a word trick. *"A valid conceptual examination is incapable of establishing the falsity."* That's why "the falsity"—

T [to L"] It is not, it's not. Professor, here Jetsunpa has expressed some doubt!

When L" claims there is "no doubt," T offers the rejoinder that the author of their college textbook himself has a doubt. Referring to L" as "Professor" while berating his response is a further indication of the sarcasm of the moment. Whether sarcasm has any role in serious philosophical reflection is an issue that will be taken up later.

Our next illustration, from debate I.9, includes a similar simple absurdity, and the inquiry hovers about the adequacy of the Syllogism-based Reasoning School's understanding of the nonexistence of inherent essences. After securing L"s agreement to a preliminary matter (at 6:07:49), possibly giving L' a false sense of comfort. T proposes the absurdity that the Syllogism-based Reasoning School's analysis of existence does not refute any essentialism:

	T	Like the Mind-only System, the Syllogism-based Reasoning School—right—has not identified the referent object that is *innately* produced. Within the terms of the designation of their philosophical tenets, uh, there is still some sort of habitual reification of an entity's "true" essence, right?
6:07:49	L'	Right.
	T	Merely such a refutation does not establish the realization of a
:51		phenomenon's lack of existing with *any* true identity. >~
	L'	THE REASON IS NOT ESTABLISHED!
	T	Now in this system (unclear).
	L'	That's not right. That's not right.

T now sharply presents (see photo of T for I.9 6:07:53) an ARGUMENT BY ABSURD CONSEQUENCE. Observe that T is moving with the flow of the debating, casting a supremely *absurd consequence* as the natural extension of L"s previous contention:

	T	If that reason is not established, for this system, right? IT DOES NOT FOLLOW THAT one needs any realization of emptiness in
6:07:59		order to refute some sort of true existence of a pot. >~

This is a great absurdity. It suggests that since L' has no standards at all regarding refutations of reified existence, it must be possible to refute true self-identity or essences while being entirely ignorant of the meaning of emptiness. If a mere formal assertion about emptiness, without any realization of emptiness, can refute inherently existing self-identity, then any actual realization of emptiness is rendered superfluous, an idea that must be rejected:

	L'	CHEE-CHEER, CHEE-CHEER!
6:08	T	It must be, does it not? IT FOLLOWS THAT it is not necessary BECAUSE the reified apprehension of a pot's "true" existence [that the Syllogism-based Reasoning School refutes] is merely
:03		an imputed conceptualization. >~

L'   THERE IS NO PERVASION.

There is no pervasion because though it is true that the reification, or essentialist fixation, that the Syllogism-based Reasoning School refutes is an imputed (and not innate) conceptualization, it does not pervade that achieving such a refutation is not to any degree a realization of emptiness.

In the case (I.4) where T and the defenders are arguing about which example of conceptual projection to consider, the illustration of the rope-snake or the reflection of a face in the mirror, with each side advocating the example that better favors their own position, L" attempts to argue that T's illustration "is not what is generally recognized" as an illustration of erroneous projection:

L"   TAKE the example of the reflection of a person in the mirror.
3:36:44 T   No. No. No. We're speaking of a wrong view here. An erroneous view, we're speaking about. Erroneous. Erroneous.
L"   A rope-snake is not what is generally recognized as what is erroneous.

So T takes L"'s contention and formally proposes it as an ABSURD PROPOSITION. In this case, however, L" stubbornly holds to his standpoint, ignoring the absurd consequence.

:50 T   Ohhh. TAKE the example of a rope-snake, IT FOLLOWS THAT it is not generally recognized as what is erroneous. >~
L"   It's not, they say.
T   IT DOES NOT FOLLOW THAT the reflection of a person in the mirror is not a good example of what, generally speaking, is recognized to be erroneous.

Note that T prefers to present his view in a double negative, rather than straightforwardly stating his preferred position. Tibetan debate can do that to a scholar.

Our next short excerpt (from I.9) demonstrates T's persistence in calling for explanations from the defender. They are discussing the extent to which one who realizes emptiness still cognizes the ordinary world. T explains,

T   If we speak of when the mind that realizes emptiness is completed, and one comes to cognize the interconnectedly dependent being of an object, there has been a previous refutation of an inherently true essence, right? If the awareness of this negation has not dissipated, and we are able to retain it while also recognizing just how an entity abides with a functional efficacy, that time we must be cognizant also of what is common to the customary apprehen-
6:05:14   sion. >~ [T folds his arms]

T's exegesis here is an attempt to explain how the negation of inherently true essences does not entail nihilism, since one is able to witness the continuing interaction of phenomena in the world. However, L' considers the case of one who might be fully absorbed in a contemplation of emptiness, and may not be cognizant of any customary apprehensions:

> L' When we realize emptiness we don't need to pay attention to the customary apprehension.

T rejects this, since it leaves such a person open to a charge of denying the world, but T's rejection proceeds not by providing a competitive argument or syllogism but with a call for L' to explain himself. L' offers a fairly lame reply, suggesting that one merely contemplating emptiness may fall short of a "complete" analysis; but T mocks this, first by offering an absurd proposal (at 6:05:31) and then by an exclamatory sentence (:33):

> :18 T Oh! If we do not, EXPLAIN HOW one analyzes the view.
> L' Merely discerning emptiness and "completing an analysis of the view" are different are they not?
> 6:05:24 T Oh. "Completing an analysis of 'the view'" he says. This is *extremely* wrong-headed! CONFOUNDED BY ALL THREE! IT FOLLOWS THAT the cognition of emptiness and the generation of a mental continuum of Middle view not a completion of the
> :31 Middle Way analysis of the view. >~
> L' I will concur.
> :33 T How can that possibly be how it is?! . . .

The absurd consequence T has drawn from L''s position is that a Middle Way scholar who contemplating emptiness would not have completed a Middle Way analysis of the view. T, however, quickly calls for L' to explain his position further, a likelihood that T, in a mockingly formal way, suggests is improbable:

> 6:05:41 T Now, why do you speak of it this way? It must be that you have an example of someone who has realized emptiness but does not yet recognize that that entity lacks any existence on the basis of a true essence. IT FOLLOWS THAT you do not.

Our final example (II.2) of an ARGUMENT BY ABSURD CONSEQUENCE demonstrates the playfulness with which Tibetan philosophers entertain ironies. T has been discussing the view of one who accepts the philosophical tenets of the Middle Way school:

> T IT FOLLOWS THAT all things, including form and so forth, do not exist according to their own inherent characteristics. Ohh, so. A person who abides in that view accepts the *thesis* that all things,

including form and so forth, do not exist according to their own
inherent characteristics, so IT FOLLOWS THAT he necessarily
-164-   understands that all things, including form and so forth, do not
9:16:09   exist according to their own inherent characteristics. >~
Audience: It is not necessary, it certainly is not necessary.
   :12 T   If there is not necessarily such an understanding—
       L'   I say such an understanding is not necessary!
       T   =v= TS'A indeed!
       L'   It is not necessarily the case.

What is intriguing about this discussion is that it is quite true that one can
have the correct philosophical positions and even study them for decades without really integrating those intellectual understandings in any effective way in
one's own life's practice. As Stephen Batchelor (2000, 74-75) has commented,
"No matter how much you have thought about emptiness, the living experience
of it may have passed you by. Somehow a step has to be made across the gap
that separates reason from experience." L' is here suggesting some humility for
philosophical work. T, however, extends L''s position into the absurdity that it
bears on its surface, drawing L''s position out to apply it to a much more elementary task of appreciating impermanence; but both defenders hold firm:

       T   =v= TS'A indeed! IT FOLLOWS THAT a person who abides in
               the middle way view as it is explained in this [Dialectical Middle
               Way] system is not necessarily a person who understands im-
9:16:17   permanence. >~
-166- L'   It is not necessary. It is not necessary.
       L"   It is not necessary.
   :18 T   If it is not necessary, TS'A indeed!
       L   How is it a "T'SA"?
   :19 T   TS'A indeed!
       L   Yahh.

T formulates his account of L''s position yet one level of absurdity deeper:

       T   IT DOES NOT FOLLOW THAT this fine distinction—that a per-
               son who abides in the middle way view as it is explained in this
               system necessarily realizes "just the way it is" [suchness, *de kho*
   :24   *na nyid*] as it is explained by this system. >~
-168- L'   THE REASON IS NOT ESTABLISHED.
       L"   There is not necessarily such realization.

Occasionally an absurdity will be sustained when its acceptance further
highlights an irony that is in some way revelatory. A third defender, heretofore
silent, attempts to explain the distinction between accepting a philosophical position attained on a logical basis and immediate insight into truth, something

akin to the distinction between knowledge and wisdom. But T is not ready to quit his position, and he presses forward (at 9:16:36) with yet a deeper, marvelously well-drawn concluding utter absurdity that synthesizes within a final formulation all that has transpired:

L'''   It is necessary that he <u>accept</u> it.

9:16:26 T   What? =v= TS'A ! =v= TS'A indeed! A person who, not having realized that all things, including form and so forth, do not exist according to their own inherent characteristics, accepts that all things, including form and so forth, do not exist according to their own inherent characteristics [out of breath] is a person who abides in the view, and IT FOLLOWS THAT he is a person who abides in
9:16:36   the middle way view as it is explained in this system. >~

By this time the defenders are in full celebration of this irony and the insight into a philosopher's life that it bears, and so they sustain the patent absurdity T has just wonderfully proposed for summarizing their position. Although it seems absurd that there can be a person who accepts profound theses as true and so is a proper member of his school of philosophical tenets, yet fails to realize their true import, it is a philosophical insight of considerable expanse. The ability to channel such an insight into one of the three conventional defender's responses—in this case (at -171-) the single-syllabic *'dod* (I ACCEPT)—demonstrates an economy of signification that is typical of Tibetan philosophical rhetoric. When the meaningfulness of debaters' reflections is refracted within the logical infrastructure in philosophically perspicuous ways, the acme of Gelugpa philosophical practice has been achieved:

-171-   L   I ACCEPT.
        T   =v=

[All parties laugh, indicating they are pleased with this performance, see video on the CD-ROM, "Ethnomethods" section: ("Argument by Absurd Consequences": "Master Bhavaviveka").]

Running a Tight Ship

In Tibetan debate the challenger strives to retain control of the direction of the deliberations, and he does so ostensibly to insure that the digressions are few and parties remain focused on the philosophical issues at hand. Especially, the clarifiers of the reasoning attempt to reformat the dialogue in analytically formal ways. They will not permit unformulated reflections to play too great a role in the debate. They will warn and cajole a respondent into keeping within the formal structures of the discourse, cautioning him, "Don't raise a different topic," and "If we stick with the vital point . . . ." If a respondent begins to stray or wander outside of strictly formal terms, a clarifier will admonish, "Now we don't need too much talk," or as T does in this illustration from I.6 (see line 4:46:48):

4:46:39 T   Oh yes?! What is the correct way to define a conceptually ac-
             quired view of an ego?
       L"   Generally speaking, they think like that, right? They do not fathom
             the Middle Way Dialectical Reasoning School's view.
   :48 T   Listen. Listen. Except in response to the logical reasoning I for-
             mally present to you, don't say anything. TAKE AS THE TOPIC
             the reification of a person as permanent, partless, and autonomous.
             IT DOES NOT FOLLOW THAT it is the conceptually acquired
4:47   view of an ego. >~
       L'   We say that it is a conceptually acquired ego view.
  :(04) T   Oh. Listen please, professor. Listen. Why is it an acquired view of
             an ego?
       L'   Because it is the conceptually an acquired view of an ego for the
             lower schools of philosophical tenets.

The "Listen listen," may take polite forms, such as "Oh yes, oh yes, but please listen!" or impolite forms, such as "Yah-yah-yah-yah. It's not like that. Now listen to this, forget that. Shh!" More often than not, such control is used on behalf of a reassertion of the formal logical apparatus that is being developed for the ideas at hand. A challenger might remind a defender, "You still need to prove your point from the beginning." Or ask him, "Now explain properly, please." In debate I.4, T is perfectly ready to take up the matters that L" is proposing, but he repeatedly admonishes L" to wait until they can do so in a systematic and formal analytic way that is appropriate for a philosophical debate:

3:37:42 T   It must be that it exists while being posited by the mind.
   :45 L"   Precious Lord, when it is merely "the projection of a notion," one
             says that the object must exist. Why are you saying it that way?
        T   Yesss. We'll find it's just the same. IT FOLLOWS THAT the exis-
             tence of the rope-snake is not exclusively by means of the projec-
             tion of its notion?
       L"   I ACCEPT.

The words "*We'll find*" refers to T's intention during their dispute to patiently and methodically scrutinize each aspect of the discussion.

   :51 T   If it is not, =v= you contradict the textbook! THIS FOLLOWS! It
             does. You say it is not merely an imputed notion.
   :56 L"   That's the way it is.
   :57 T   According to the thought of the great master [Tsong Khapa], who
             composed *Illumination of the Thought,* it is.
3:38   L"   That is the adornment of all rejections [i.e., "Absolutely not"].

With this insult, the debate is beginning to degenerate, and so T attempts to regain his firm hold on the direction of the debate, specifying the particular citation being analyzed:

> T Quiet. Quiet. Quiet. Hold on! Please hold on! Wait. *"At dusk, a plaid-like twine of different colors when coiled like a snake may present to the mind the appearance of a snake. At that time it is said that the mind merely projects a notion."* >~ This unique example is given, is it not? *"At that time the mind merely projects a*
> :13   *notion,"* it is said!
> :16 L" That's why/
> T   /It does, it does.
> L" Which?
> 3:38:20 T Is there a mere projection of a notion when one perceives the rope as a snake? We say that there is.

L" now wishes to engage in a more informal, "man to man" kind of discussion. But T will hear nothing of it, and he abruptly scolds L" and attempts to whip him into speaking only by means of employing the chaste forms of proper debate, an effort which meets with some success:

> L" Here, when we speak about the system that discusses the mere projection of a notion, there are a great many things to say about the mode of establishing objects.
> T We're talking about the mere projection of a notion. There is no talking about other things. IT FOLLOWS THAT it is merely the
> 3:38:30 projection of a notion. >~
> L" Which one? The case of the rope-snake?
> T The rope-snake. TAKE THE CASE OF the rope-snake. Listen! IT
> :36   FOLLOWS THAT it is the mere projection of a notion. >~
> L" CHEE-CHEER. [BECAUSE OF WHAT?]
> T BECAUSE that is how the citation says it.
> :37 L" THE REASON IS NOT ESTABLISHED.

L" has at last been driven to make his utterances conform with the correct grammar of debate, but T still senses the need to retain a tight hold of the reins:

> :38 T It is there! So, be quiet and pay attention! Pay proper attention. Ohh. Yahh . . . There is a plaid-like object that appears differently.
> L' This is right.
> T At that time there is a collection of the rope and its parts. Oh, yes, the basis, the basis. "Snake" is posited upon this basis, which does not have the slightest bit of such existence. "At that time the mind merely projects a notion," it says. Then, that is compared to the example of a "person."

As we discussed in Chapter 4, a challenger will begin to invoke the formal tokens of debate (e.g., TAKE AS THE SUBJECT, etc.) in order to regain control, and the use of these tokens in this way is ubiquitous. This brief excerpt from III.1 demonstrates how the formal token "BECAUSE OF THAT" (*De'i phyir*) is employed by T to prevail in a small struggle for the turn to speak:

9:30:30 L'   Now- /

        T   / It is mentioned // in the text.

        L'   // It is mentioned.

        T   I need to speak! BECAUSE OF THAT, ohh, the wisdom-gone-beyond—how to say it—that manifests is the truth developed from having completed training in wisdom.

Such use of logical tokens demonstrates that they are not strictly for the use of formal analytic reasoning but are also *local organizational tools* that parties use for making the interaction orderly. The boundary between their function as a means of formal analytic reasoning and their function as tools for organizing the interaction is indistinct. This is for the reason that formal analytic reasoning itself is fostered by clear and competent communication, which is only achieved by deliberate social practices. Genuine dialectics can proceed best in a social context that fosters the clear articulation and hearkening of notions. Although I would consider it unsound to suggest that the domains of either philosophy or sociology be reduced to the other, there are many moments when the event in question is naturally a phenomenon for both faculties, during which the interests of each are the means to the interests of the other.

We have mentioned the organizational item available to challengers that we have termed PUT-UP OR SHUT-UP, and this is a device that may be used to keep a defender focused on the analytic tasks at hand. In III.1, when L "accepts" T's proposal that the uncommon meditative absorption of the Sixth Stage of a bodhisattva's progress occurs through the practice of the wisdom-gone-beyond, T immediately presses L for an explanation: "Therefore, how is the method of the exceptional practice of wisdom-gone-beyond PRESENTED? Now how is it PRESENTED?" This interactional device reduces the frequency with which a respondent will agree to a proposition gratuitously, since it is always possible that he will have to explain his reasoning for any consent. One must be prepared to provide an understanding for *any* term or notion one uses, on call.

Here are two typical illustrations:

-000-   T   If we take the example of a person whose mental continuum has
8:58:31   never experienced a realization of emptiness, IT FOLLOWS
               THAT one can present a characterization of the mind to which the
-005-   appearance of inherently true existence arises. >~

        L   THAT IS CORRECT. This can indeed be presented.

        T   PRESENT an exegesis of the mind to which arises the emptiness of any such inherently true existence. (II.1)

And

    T   Regarding a person with penetrative faculties who has faith in this and that, oh, it is not necessary to realize emptiness in order to ac-

9:21:46   cept such things. >~

-078.5- L   Oh, this is not necessary.

    T   Now PRESENT the reasoning for this. (II.3)

After a challenger calls for a respondent to PUT-UP OR SHUT-UP with his reasoning, it is not unusual to discover that there is no meat on the bone, so to speak. Here (II.3) the clarifier will not permit loose discussion and becomes very sharp with the respondent when he intuits that the respondent cannot support his assertion:

(034) T   So both are never explained together explicitly in the same text.

       L" What? But both are explicitly formulated. In general we have an explanation, an explicit explanation of both. The text—

       T   Whether there may be explanations generally is not the concern. Nowhere is there an explicit explanation of both together.

       L" It is said there is no explicit explanation of both together.

L"'s ready capitulation prompts a TS'A from T. A TS'A may be used not only when the defender gives up his thesis, but also when he modifies a thesis, changes a reason, speaks in an ambiguous or irrelevant way, or repeats himself when the repetition in no way contributes to the rhythm of a debate.

    In our next illustration (II.1), L comes to challenge the sufficiency of the citation recited by T, and so T immediately invites L to remedy the imagined insufficiency, which L is unable to do. The quibble over the citation is preceded by a couple of amicable exchanges:

    T   IT DOES NOT FOLLOW that the method for realizing that the reflection of a face in the mirror is erroneous is to realize that the reflection of a face in the mirror does not exist as inherently true

9:02:24   in the way that it appears. >~

-048-   L   No, no, it's not. This does not pervade [i.e., he agrees with statement]. *"IT FOLLOWS THAT one does not realize that it does not exist in the way that it appears to be established as truly existing—"* [cut short before completing his citation].

    T   If it is said that IT FOLLOWS THAT *"A person whose mental continuum has never experienced a cognition of emptiness"*—

    L   Oh yes.

    T   —*"is able to realize what is erroneous about the reflection of a face in the mirror by means of a cognition that has conventional validity. Realizing such error does not imply the realization of the erroneous conceptual consciousness that is also involved."*

        L   That's not all there is to the citation.
        T   Oh yes. So explain the meaning of this citation.
9:02:38 L   The citation is not only this.
        T   What is meant by "does not imply?"

When asked to come up with an account of the citation, L is only able to
hesitate; in the face of this hesitation, T is ready to push him harder, almost in
the way a strong hand might squeeze the back of another's neck while directing
him to the issue to be faced. Later in the same debate, T is still pushing L to face
his commitments.

        T   The reflection of a face in the mirror in the continuum of an ordi-
             nary person is posited by the mind as erroneous.
        L   It is. It is.

T now proffers an absurd consequence:

        T   IT DOES NOT FOLLOW THAT the lack of accord of the appear-
             ance of the reflection of a face in the mirror and its mode of being
9:04:53   is posited. >~

It is absurd because of course there is a discrepancy between the image in a
mirror and a real face. So L properly rejects the suggestion:

-077-   L   CHEE-CHEER [BECAUSE OF WHAT?]

If challengers have at their disposal the strategic move of PUT-UP OR
SHUT-UP, defenders have the strategic use of calling for the reason—CHEE-
CHEER. T now poses the proposition correctly:

        T   So, the lack of accord between the appearance of the reflection of a
   :55   face in the mirror and its mode of being is posited. >~
-077.5- L   Yes.

And with the debate now well tethered to the formal analytic practice, T
composes a fuller summary of what this debate has concluded up to his point:

        T   IT FOLLOWS THAT the mind that has posited the lack of accord
             between the appearance of the reflection of a face in the mirror and
-078-   its mode of being is not complete according to the Middle Way
9:04:59   proponents' way of formulating what is erroneous. >~
9:05   L   We say it is not complete.

A professional Tibetan debater will formally summarize the products of
their discussion, in this way gradually building up the formal analytic representations of their achievements. And he will do so even if it should involve notions
with which he disagrees.

After L concurs with the summary, T then recycles L's concurrence, along with a demand that L PUT-UP OR SHUT-UP by explaining just what their summary description entails. A hand-clap punctuates his demand (at 9:05:05):

<blockquote>

T   If it is not complete, when we come to posit the lack of accord between the appearance and mode of being of a pot, how do the Middle Way proponents present what is erroneous about the pot that appears to a mind? >~

L   It is an example of how everyday truth is known. Generally, it is an example of how everyday talk is known.
</blockquote>

-079-
:05

This is a very small contribution to an explanation, so T presses L for a fuller exegesis:

<blockquote>

T   How is it that it is an example of how everyday truth is known? What have they done?

L   This, right? Because it's the way everyday truth is known. [Everyone speaks at once.] The worldly attitude that accepts anything just the way it appears is incapable of cognizing its nonexistence.
</blockquote>

This way of proceeding stirs up the participants' motivation to engage in the dialectical discussion.

The purest form of PUT-UP OR SHUT-UP is the logical-cum-interactional token "*ma yin ste*—," which means, "EXPLAIN WHY IT IS NOT—." It seems that much Tibetan debating naturally flows toward this token *ma yin ste*—. This is because a negative dialectics is continually probing the reasoning in its effort to uproot inconsistencies. The *ma yin ste*—, the "why not?" is always lurking in the background. The "why not?" in the final line of this excerpt from II.6 was uttered incredibly *swiftly*:

<blockquote>

T   We say, for example, the path of liberation at the first level—

L'   Yes.

:12 T   —is capable of invoking the direct antidote to the grossest innate truth habits. >~

L'   Oh it can? THE REASON—it is capable of invoking that—IS NOT ESTABLISHED.

T   Oh yah?!

L'   THE REASON—it is capable of invoking that—IS NOT ESTAB-LISHED.

T   And why is it not capable? [*ma yin ste*—]
</blockquote>

In I.6, T is very tenacious in insisting that L' provide an explanation. Note the "why not?" at 4:49:(58) and the calls for explanation at 4:50:00, :07, and :12. [The final explanation may be observed on the video I.6 4:50:11-12, and the pained expression of L' is evident in the photo (see Appendix of the CD-ROM, I.6 4:50:15)]

T   Please listen, professors. Now, how to say it? TAKE THE TOPIC a visual perception, etc., a sense perception, that apprehends a reified phenomenon that is established by own characteristics. IT

4:49:56   FOLLOWS THAT it is not something perceived as "mine." >~

L"   / I ACCEPT.

L'   / I ACCEPT.

T   Why not?

L"   IT DOES NOT FOLLOW.

4:50   T   Why is the "mine" not something to be perceived? Please listen. Why is the "mine" not something to be perceived?

L"   "Why is the 'mine' not something to be perceived?" Now, there is this "I," this "mine," how to say it, this "mine," uhh, this.

:07   T   Why is the "mine" not something to be perceived?

L"   Will you please listen? Are you asking, why is the perception of a "mine" not a reification of a phenomenon established according to its own characteristics?

T   Oh yah.

L"   I ACCEPT THAT it is that way.

:12   T   So explain it! >~

L"   [Pained expression] Why is it not the object of a perception? Like this. This. Ohh.

T   "Mine," yes? "Mine"!

:17   L"   [Eyes closed in concentration] "Mine."

L'   Yes, "mine."

T   "Mine," yes? TAKE AS THE TOPIC something reified by perception to be established by its own characteristics.

L   Oh, exactly right.

T   What is the reason why a perceived "mine" is not apprehended as

:24   established by its own characteristics? >~

L'   / [L' and L" speak simultaneously,

L"   / and it is indecipherable]

4:50:26   T   What is the reason?! >~

L"   BECAUSE for that there must be the habitual reification of a personal self.

:28   L'   BECAUSE "I"[-ness] cannot be perceived. IT FOLLOWS THAT no "mine" is witnessed BECAUSE an "I" cannot be perceived.

:30   T   Ohhh!

T's persistence in pressing the defenders to account for themselves (note the hand-clap at 4:50:26) pays off, in that he forces them to contribute an idea that is philosophically productive, namely that I-ness is not perceivable, and so neither can be mine-ness.

The always possible PUT-UP OR SHUT-UP serves as a vigil against weak or irresolute replies, and it does so even during the intensifying rhythmic collaboration that we have termed an arpeggio. An examination of the audio record of II.3, 9:20:48-58 (-064- to -066.5-) on the CD-ROM, which contains a display of an arpeggio, during which T invokes a PUT-UP OR SHUT-UP:

-064-	T	Does there exist a faith in freedom?
9:20:49	L"	Of course. He has such faith, does he not?
	T	Oh, there is a belief, right?
	L"	There are thoughts along the lines of freedom being wonderful.
	T	Oh, there are some thoughts that freedom is wonderful, right?
	L"	Yes.
:51	T	However in order to generate faith in freedom, it is not necessary that he fully understand freedom, is it?
	L"	Oh, it is said that it is not necessary .
-066.5-	T	Why is it necessary that a mind that is intent upon achieving
:57		freedom fully understand it? >~

PUT-UP OR SHUT-UP can be invoked out of the blue, when a defendant least expects it. In fact, challengers take some delight when a defender is caught by surprise. Also, it is a recourse available to challengers in the midst of a battle, as a weapon with which to engage their opponent:

	T	In our system, if there is a mental positing there must be an object. And if there is a conceptual projection, an object does not necessarily exist. It's like this, right?
	L"	You can take this notion and depart! [Audience laughter.]
3:43:48	T	Now you PRESENT. >~ You PRESENT how it is. (I.4)

This responsibility of the clarifier of the reasoning bears to keep the respondent moving along the formal paths of philosophical reflection they are working with can require the clarifier to engage in certain forcing techniques. As we have just observed, the PUT-UP OR SHUT-UP is a ready quick retort to a vacant and gratuitous concurrence by a defendant, but there are other devices available. In I.9 (6:02:55-6:03:16), the respondent took too much time to reply, and the challenger responded to the silence with a nudge: "Now is it yes or is it no?" Such efforts can be more gentle ("Now it's not so difficult") or more insistent ("You have to say yes!"). As my Tibetan colleague advised, if one doesn't push to some extent, one will be unable to present his issue. When the respondent is only moving along with the surface structure of the debate, agreeing without really knowing the issues at stake, pushing is justifiable. As we have just seen, it is possible to push simply by repeating the question until a satisfactory answer is obtained. To each of a series of turns in which the defendant is fudging his answer, the challenger can simply and calmly repeat his query, as if the defendant's reply was little more than warm air.

In I.4, L' attempts to stall the discussion by asking about which school's tenets are under consideration (even though L' raised the issue in the first place):

3:35:20 T   The mere projection of a notion, and, uhh, the mere establishing
             through the force of appearing to a mind—are these two the
    :27   same or different? >~
        L'   "The mere projection of a notion." In whose tenets?

T insists that L' answer the question. The two defenders cannot agree on the correct answer, so T keeps pushing the issue:

    :31 T   Is it distinctly different from "the mere projection of a notion" or
             not?
        L'   There is no difference at all.
    :36 L"   Generally, there is a slight difference.
    :38 T   Now is there or is there not?

Increasing the pacing of a debate is another way for the challenger to put pressure on a defendant. Although a defendant will join in the speed when the dance is safe and playful, he may try to slow the pace down as soon as he senses danger, and a struggle over the pacing of the debate may ensue. As soon as a defender hesitates, a challenger may pounce on him, making it difficult for the defender to think clearly. It is not unusual for a defender to not fully appreciate the scope of one of his replies and instead to reckon its fate in the logical and interactional items that ensue, and to which his answers have given rise. It can confound a thinker to face such pressure, especially when the pressure comes in the form of CONFOUNDED BY ALL THREE! since a public declaration of his defeat just when he reaches the climax of his argument can be very distracting. Similarly, when a challenger turns his back to the defendant, breaking off his eye contact, there is an implication that the logistics are so well in place they can handle the job without the challenger's attentiveness. The challenger tying his robe around his waist can have a similar effect (see video clip on CD-ROM). It is a piece of choreography that implies that one means business, and it is like a debater taking his gloves off before he gets down to the more serious work of pressing his argument on a defendant.

These strategies can undermine the confidence of a respondent. Order in debate demands firmness; however, firmness by itself is no guarantee of being correct. For this reason defendants must be resolute in the face of abject forcing. Challengers may deliberately test a defendant's resolve by applying many or all of these techniques, and members of the audience may ally themselves with the challenger just to see how centered and durable a defendant can be in his thinking. At times Tibetan debate can require a good deal of courage, and the cultivation of intellectual courage must be considered a good thing.

Strategies Employed by Defendants

Other options available to a defendant are less than courageous, and these include qualifications of his commitments, the facile suggestion that his notions are widely accepted truths (so widely accepted that fuller explanation is thereby rendered unnecessary), and various methods of stalling for time to reflect. We will briefly review these phenomena.

Qualifications permit the respondent to offer a commitment that is so broadened that the danger of being trapped in an error is lessened. The difficulty with this strategy is that it can muddle a debate and require the clarifier to undertake some serious formal analytic work to reclarify the positions. Invoking an "in general" leaves room to allow an exception without rendering one inconsistent, as in I.1:

> T   Now, from the mundane, everyday perspective, to what does "common sense" refer in the passage, *"For the thinking of the common sense mind of a person practiced at applying ordinary*
> 3:02:58   *conventions?"* >~
> 3:03   L" In general, common sense, customary conceptual thinking, refers to the object.

To which T asks later,

> :27 T   . . . Now, how do you explain this? >~
> 3:03:33 L' [Silence 7.0] In general, the customary sense determined is determined by a conceptual cognition that is valid.

When asked whether the projection of a notion and establishing through the force of appearing to the mind were the same or different (I.4), the defendant replied, "Generally, there is a slight difference." Other ways of qualifying one's commitment include, "It has to be a little bit" and "Something like that." On occasion, a defender will be scolded for qualifying his reply, as the challenger does twice in debate II.3:

> T   So both are never explained together explicitly in the same text.
> L" What? But both are explicitly formulated. In general we have an explanation, an explicit explanation of both. The text—
> 9:18:54 T Whether there may be explanations generally is not the concern. Now where is there an explicit explanation of both together. >~

And

> L' In general, it's about a person with penetrative faculties.
> L" It's penetrative faculties.
> L' Basically, the nature of some persons is to have dull faculties. But, in general, they are able to have penetrative faculties.

9:26:19 T   We don't need any "in general" in this discussion of the penetra-
             tive faculties!

Finally, there is a form of qualification that takes advantage of the fact that
usually one is not able to articulate completely and exhaustively the full scope of
a matter. What can be told is necessarily a synopsis or an icon of the state of
things. And so, one is able to "defer" the full explanation until some later time.
Although that later time never arrives, its presence for collaborating parties is
nevertheless vital to their acceptance of the full truth of a matter. It is the ghost
in the closet that authorizes parties to conclude that sufficient grounds for an
assertion have been presented.[8] Accordingly, defenders will excuse themselves
from making a fully adequate account of their position, implying that when the
circumstances permit it (when there is more time, etc.) such can be done without
difficulty. There are many varieties of this sort of qualification, but here is one
illustration:

         T   IT FOLLOWS THAT there is completion BECAUSE that must be
              what is meant by speaking of the attainment of the most excep-
-062-   tional practices. >~
         L'   The thorough capacity, the capacity for single-pointed meditative
              stabilization must be thoroughly completed. For example, now if I
              can put it simply, for example, right? At the First Stage one thor-
              oughly applies oneself. When one attains the Second Stage, there is
              said to be a . . .

The ostensible effort to speak clearly and concisely for the benefit of the opponent ("Now if I can put it simply"), is used by the defender as license to be thin
with details in his account of spiritual development.
    A common way to draft one's commitment is to invoke the protection of the
umbrella of commonly accepted belief, so that it is not just one's own view but
what "we say" or what "they say." Accordingly one does not reply, "I AC-
CEPT" (*'dod*) but "It is said that it is ACCEPTABLE" (*'dod zer*). We have
briefly discussed the "*zer*" (see 105 and 163), and it may be a way that a defendant will respond to a challenger, the suggestion being that the challenger will
be counted among a very lonely group of scholars if he does not go along with
the respondent's position. In I.4, the respondent, being forced to decide whether
there was a difference between projection and establishment by appearing to a
mind, qualified his answer, so the challenger kept pushing. In his next turn to
speak, the defender, instead of qualifying his reply with an "in general," requali-
fies it with the "*zer*":

3:35:31 T   Is it distinctly different from "the mere projection of a notion" or
             not?

---

8. The ubiquity of deferring is well described by Jacques Derrida (1982).

L'	There is no difference at all.
:36 L"	Generally, there is a slight difference.
:38 T	Now is there or is there not?
L'	They say [*zer*] that there is no difference.

The *zer* is uttered with great equipoise, as if it was only natural that the whole world is backing his position. It is like a certification or a chorus of "Hail to the way it is said!" with all heads nodding eagerly. It is a weak but common retreat into the protection of accepted notions—for example, *'di dre zer lab so*: "We all say it is like that."

Accordingly, a defender will claim not merely that the bodhisattva's work of removing obstructions to understanding is "not complete"; instead, he will assert, "We say it is not complete." By so doing, the defender exaggerates the forces on his side of the dispute. Defenders will employ the *zer* even for their own original comment, no matter how idiosyncratic it may be. And yet deference to received notions is somehow related to the work of formal reasoning, since debaters will announce that "There is a way to fix a formulation about *x*," or "There is some explication about that" (*skad cha bshad kyi yod sa red*). The implication is that there exists (already) a widely accepted method for formally analyzing the matter at hand; that is, it is a way to universalize philosophical practices. "Universal reasoning" requires social confirmation.

The clarifiers of the reasoning may summon the imprimatur of accepted truth for their assertions. When they summarize the products of a debate they will adorn those summaries with a comment such as "We present it this way," in order to universalize it. And it can be used as a strategy by challengers to sucker defenders into accepting a faulted proposition ("It is said that . . ."). Tibetan debaters draw upon a (supposed) received body of notions accepted by all the world as a resource for universalizing their own reasoning. It seems that apophansis everywhere is surrounded by a context of "what is acceptable," and the ideal of independent, *a priori* truth is never found to be quite as independent as is imagined. This is not to deny that there are *a priori* structures for knowledge; however, in any given cited instance, a process of social confirmation is always nearby. Numbers may exist *a priori* (and 2+2 always equals 4), but they are always produced in the context of a human activity, namely counting, and judicative propositions are always produced in judging activity.[9] Social processes operate alongside logical ones.

When in I.1 (2:59:40) the challenger suggests about his proposal, "Is it not necessary?", what is this "necessary"? Is it logic, or is it universalizing social practice? Is not formal analysis always accompanied by a context of received knowledge ready to be invoked and which contributes to the authorization of

---

9. John Scanlon (1997, 576).

each step of the analysis?[10] My apologies to my philosopher friends, but sociology here has some disappointing news for them—all traditions of formal reasoning have equivalent universalizing procedures. It is not only the Tibetan scholars who are reliant upon a body of received notions. Edmund Husserl (1973, 30-31) speaks of the universal ground of belief in a world presupposed by not only the praxis of life but also by the theoretical praxis of cognition:

> An actual *world* always precedes cognitive activity as its universal ground, and this means first of all a ground of universal passive belief in being which is presupposed by every particular cognitive operation. . . . . The world as the existent world is the universal passive pregivenness of all judicative activity, of all engagement of theoretical interest . . . . The world as a whole is already pregiven in passive certitude.

Although Husserl is not invoking a sociological analysis here, the context of such passive certitude can include the practice of social confirmation. Philosophers are obligated to pluck their ideas out of the ooze of social intercourse and clean them up, but it seems always that the smell of the social environment lingers. That fact does not absolve us critics of reason from the task of criticizing unjustified appeals to naively accepted beliefs. For reasoning to remain original and creative, the influence of the natural contexts of thinking must at times be subverted.

Another strategy employed by defendants are STALLS, and they come in a great variety of forms. It is a fair impulse for a defender to seek a moment to reflect upon his answer before uttering it. But even in instances where a defender is certain of his answer, he may become cautious when a challenger begins forcing a point, and the defender may choose to stall to consider whether there is any unnoticed logical gambit at work. And so stalls are evident throughout Tibetan public debates.

Stalls by Repeat

Perhaps the most common and easiest stall, stalls by repeat, provide a safe if only momentary haven for a defender to collect his wits:

9:08:52 T   Yes, this reply. Ohh. We say, PRESENT the method of the explanation that is consonant with the thinking of his *Great*
-039-   *Commentary.* >~
        L'   Now this, right? Ohhh. The method that is consonant with the thinking of the *Great Commentary*, is it not? (II.2)

And,

---

10. As Durkheim (1985, 485-86) has described, "The concept which was first held as true because it was collective tends to be no longer collective except on condition of being held as true: we demand its credentials of it before according it our confidence."

6:08:06 T   Now in order to refute an imputed conceptualization, is it or is it not sufficient to refute just a part of it?!

       L'   To refute a mode of asserting an imputed conceptualization.

       T   Mm-hm. So? (I.9)

Instead of a verbatim repeat, the challenger's query can be reworded, as in this more general waffle in which T's hand-clap calls L' to attention:

       T   When one has cognized the emptiness of a self-sufficient, substantially existing person, why must that cognition be a truth of cessation?

9:23:38 L'   Because, oh, since it is said to be a penetrative faculty, a penetrative faculty, how is it said? At the time one cognizes the meaning of emptiness, uh—

    :43 T   Right, now what are you saying? >~ (II.3)

Gary Alan Fine (2001, 34) observes that this strategy of stalling by repeat is commonly used by high school debaters in American forensic societies, who repeat phrases and insert unnecessary words in order to give themselves a moment to think and to collect themselves.

Stalls by Asking a Question

The question may be as simple as "What did you say?" Or it can be a request for a minor clarification, or as in the next topic, by asking for which school of philosophical tenets the query is about.

Stalls by Asking about (or Referring to) the School

The request for a clarification about which school of tenets ("According to whose tenets?", "In which system?", etc.) is common:

3:35:20 T   The mere external projection of a notion, the mere projection of a notion, and, uhh, the mere establishing through the force of appear-

    :27   ing to a mind—are these two the same or different? >~

       L'   "The mere projection of a notion." In whose tenets? (I.4)

This is one competent question that is always available to a defender, and it is an excellent stall, in that it can gain a defender a bit of time; moreover, not infrequently it is a pertinent question to ask, important for insuring that the parties are communicating clearly. Here (II.4) it is used sensibly:

9:30:08 T   We say that all phenomena are conceived merely by imputations,

 -027-   right? If we have realized this, uh, then it is necessary that we

9:30:18   realize the view of "just how it is." >~

       L'   . . . Are you referring to the Dialectical Middle Way School or to the Syllogism-based Reasoning Middle Way School?

9:30:26 T   The Dialectical Middle Way School.
-031-   L   If it's the Dialectical Middle Way School, then one must.

Its use is frequently overdetermined by the valid interest to pursue truth and an interest in protecting oneself. But gaining a moment to compose one's answer in the face of pressure is hardly a gross transgression of reason (from I.9):

> T   Oh, now HOW DOES ONE FORMULATE THIS?
> L'   According to the analysis of the Syllogism-based Reasoning School /
>
> 6:08:21 T   / >~
>
> L'   According to the analysis of the Syllogism-based Reasoning School there is . . .

In a second illustration from I.9, L' repeats the query twice and calls for a clarification of which system is being considered. And given the sufficient time provided by these stalls, L is able to proffer a proper reply:

> T   The text presents an example of the negation of the habitual reifi-cation of true existence that is *conceptually* imputed upon a refer-ent object.   In this system, that is not necessarily a realization of
>
> 6:05:55   emptiness. >~
>
> L'   If one refutes the habitual reification of true existence that is *con-ceptually* imputed, eh?
>
> T   Oh, so.
>
> :56 L'   In this system, eh?
>
> T   [pregnant pause]
>
> L'   The habitual attitude of true existence conceptually imputed upon the referent object is understood to not have any existence. Yes, yes. Now, it would not necessarily be a realization of emptiness, would it?

The question "In this system, eh?" at 6:05:56 is unnecessary. It is not an instance of needing philosophical clarification; it is simply a strategic move to gain time to compose a reply, and in that it was successful. Here again social practice, in prevailing over philosophical practice, operates in service of the latter.

But there are many cases where the defender's request for clarification of the school of tenets is little more than a blind fudge. In II.1 (-017-), the defender suggests, "It must be this way for one of the systems." Such technical discus-sions that sort out the fine distinctions among the schools are readily available for use in diverting the direction of a debate.

Stalls by Citation or Textual Erudition

If a respondent wishes more time to think, it is always appropriate to call for a full recitation of any textual reference that is made. Tibetan debaters are expected to have memorized most of the important passages of their scholarly texts. In fact, young scholars face rigorous public examinations during which they are requested to recite from memory extensive passages verbatim, much in the way that European students are tested for spelling in spelling bees. For this reason, it is not unreasonable for a respondent to request a verbatim recitation, and his challenger may even welcome the opportunity to display his erudition. This can gain for the respondent considerable time, and in the process a defender can even portray himself as an exemplary scholar who sustains a keen interest in precision.

Similarly, a respondent can distract a challenger with any technical discussion about terminology or the proper identification of the source text of a citation ("These words are from the autocommentary, right?"), a favorite pastime of Tibetan debaters. For a philosophical culture that does not use indexes, there is some functionality to this exercise. But when the defender in II.2 stalls for time by identifying the chapter in which a citation is *not* located, it is utterly useless:

(020)   L" It's not in the *Tsad 'gog* chapter [of *Dbu ma spyi don* by Jetsun Chogyi Gyaltsen].

Besides these obvious stalls, there can be a general intransigence on the part of defenders that resembles a wrestler (who is probably losing the match) dragging himself along the mat in ways that do not present any openings for his opponent to act upon. When such intransigence develops into obstinacy, we have the worst of Tibetan debating. One form that obstinacy can take is when a defender tries to interrupt the smooth flow of a challenger's presentation in order to throw him off of his balance. We have observed how the development of a certain temporalization of the utterances can energize a debate and contribute to the force of a clarifier's attempts to analyze a problem. If that rhythm is disrupted, the clarifier may lose his momentum and unnecessary damage may be done to the debating. That may be successful as a strategy, but it is usually not productive philosophically. In its capacity to alter the rhythm of a conversation, reciting a full citation when it is unnecessary can be akin to the timeout of lighting a cigarette.

On the other hand, it should be observed that interruption is an important moment of dialectics. When one's own thinking is rushing headlong into its own favored dominions, it is likely to grow too full of itself. On such occasions disrupting the temporal flow can offer some negation that can temper overconfidence and afford opportunities for new perspectives. More than infrequently, the divergencies introduced by the challenges of another person may be salutary.

Ridicule

Argument by absurd consequence is naturally related to irony and ridicule, and irony is the precipitate of many Tibetan scholarly disputations. When dialectics operates within the reflections of a single thinker, irony can provoke exposure of the shortcomings of quite a few notions that may have had good standing for a long while. Especially, irony rears up when glimpses into the natural limitations of analytic reasoning are to be had. But when dialectics proceeds as the contesting inquiries of two persons thinking and speaking in dialogue with each other, it is natural for the irony to be directed at one or another of them. And so ridicule has been part of Buddhist monastic debate, and the philosophical discourse that it fostered, from the days of the monasteries in India. When Dharmakirti refuted the Hindu Samkhya's essentialism by taking up the matter of the essence of a sprout, which the Samkhya claim abides inherently in the seed but in an unmanifested way, Dharmakirti raises the illustration of the inherent but un-manifest essence of a fly that lands on a blade of grass. Since given acceptance of the doctrine of rebirth (to which both the Buddhists and Hindus subscribe) this fly is destined to be reborn as an elephant a hundred times, according to the Samkhya it must already possess within it the essence of these hundred elephants; hence, Dharmakirti asks how it is possible for a single blade of grass to bear all of that weight? In this way, the absurdity of the Samkhya's inherently contradictory argument is held up to ridicule.

The founder of the Gelug sect of Tibetan Buddhism Tsong Khapa himself was not very restrained when it came using ridicule against his philosophical opponents. In his *Great Treatise on the Stages of the Path to Enlightenment* (1997, 757), he devotes a page to criticizing the beliefs of another Indian philosophical school, the Charvaka. These are atheists who reject the doctrines of rebirth and karma, believing that events occur only by random chance. The Charvaka argue that such chance is demonstrated by the illustration of the peacock, observing that the beautiful colors of a peacock arise naturally, without effort on anyone's part. Tsong Khapa takes up the Charvaka illustrations and argues that if events were strictly serendipitous and did not involve any cause and effect, then there should be at least a few crows who have resplendent, colorful eyes on their tails.

Such humorous but absurd arguments as these have a favored place in Tibetan philosophical culture. Tsong Khapa's student Khedrup, himself an author of several important treatises, seems always eager to berate his opponents, occasionally calling them "colossal idiots" (Khedrup n.d., 474). And his readers are sometimes left to ponder when the dividing line between genuine dialectics and sophistry has been crossed, and also to consider what the proper uses of irony may be. With the forefathers of modern day Tibetan scholars showing no reluctance to engage in insult and ridicule, it is not surprising to witness it on the debate grounds of contemporary monastic universities. I once observed the monastery's disciplinarian (a senior monk elected to the post for a single year) cock his ear to listen to some of the ridicule being spoken. When I expected him perhaps to warn the monks against using abject insult, instead I observed on his face a mild, tolerant smile, possibly himself taking some pleasure in the young schol-ars' humor or enthusiasm for their activity.

Ridicule is used as one more weapon in the arsenal of a challenger who is attempting to hone in on his opponent's weaknesses, and it can contribute to an opponent's insecurity. But a defendant may respond in kind, as we have seen: "Now you are full of consequences" and "You have cited such an impressive passage!" If a challenger can mock a respondent, "Now you are going to be a professor, but you are speaking nonsense," "Your lips have been completely twisted the wrong way!" (see Illustrative Debate I.4 3:35:46 on the CD-ROM), and "You have contradicted the text, whose contents seem to have slipped from your memory," the defender can suggest, "That is the adornment of all rejec-tions!" An opponent's mocking can even have a salutary benefit when it serves as the motivation for the opponent to sharpen his thinking, as in I.7. L" berates T at 5:46:07:

5:46 T There are two valid cognitions. I am speaking of the horse appear-ance that is produced by a magical spell, which upon analysis is understood not to exist.

L" Which analysis is this?

T On the basis of reasoning, we recollect that the illusory horse does not exist.

5:46:07 L" This is a puny sort of reasoning that lacks specificity. We don't describe it that way. We describe it in terms of causes and exam-ples, or in terms of its self-nature, or in terms of causal results, or in terms of being truly established, or in terms of being imperma-nent. If we speak of the existence or nonexistence of an entity only on the basis that its appearance is due to a magical spell and so is nonexistent, without discussing the ontological reasoning that it is meant to illustrate, then there is no reasoning.

Of course T is not pleased to be reprimanded, so he contests L"'s account, and they struggle for the floor:

T No. We don't say like that. There is the continuum of an apprehension /[unclear—both speak at once]// the continuum of something apprehended.

L"   / It's the same.   //

T This is the conventional way of describing it, is it not?

:26 L" Oh.

T then attempts to satirize L" with a hackneyed stock account of inferential reasoning, but L" won't abide such satire and, absurdly, deliberately denies (at :33) that such a patent truth is so:

> T   For example, IT FOLLOWS THAT the mode of appearance of
>   smoke produced by a fire is the basis for our conceptual way
> :32   of reasoning in terms of an inferential valid cognition, is it not? >~
> L' / Yes, yes.
> L" / CHEE-CHEER [WHAT IS THE REASON?]

T is so incensed with L"'s insubordination that he is driven to reflect more deeply, and he comes up with a quite penetrating insight which pertains to his observation as a philosopher that the quality of some reasoning cannot necessarily be judged by its strict conformity with proper analytic forms:

> T   Terminology is not absolutely necessary for there to be reasoning.
> L" This is not right. This is not right.

Ridicule can come in the form of outright hostility or friendly teasing that is designed only to gently prompt one's partner into competent participation. In I.6, the clarifier of the reasoning requests of the respondent an exegesis of the appearance of a personal ego. After a few weak responses, the clarifier mocks, "So, why don't you give the text's definition for an ego this time?" to which the audience laughs. But the respondent still does not provide a competent account, so the clarifier uses more formality in order to bring about compliance—

> 4:43:29 T   TAKE THIS AS THE SUBJECT. Those apprehended objects,
>   right? How do they arise? Knowing sir, now explain properly,
> :33   please. >~

L" attempts to negotiate for some leeway, but T only presses him harder and mocks him, to the delight of the audience. What is amusing about T's ridicule (at :42) is that he asserts the respondent's ignorance by using a token *from the formal grammar of debating*, hand-clap and all:

> L" I won't give you the exact wording, but I'll present an account
>   from my understanding. But it will be the same.
> :42 T In giving your understanding of the definition of one's ego, IT
> :46   FOLLOWS THAT you don't know the precise wording. >~
>   [laughter]
> L" I have some wording. Really.

The intensity produced by such formalized ridicule motivates L' to reflect on the topic and contribute a serious and insightful exegesis:

> L' When one perceives either the "I" or "mine" that has become one's
>   object of observation, it is explained that the afflicted conscious-

ness that reifies an "I" that exists according to its own characteristics reckons that there is an ego.

A skilled debater may feign surprise at a valid proposition of a respondent, just to determine the degree of commitment the respondent has to his idea. For example, two debaters might be discussing how production from self and production from another do not exist ultimately, but that there is production from self in a conventional sense, for if you plant a seed a sprout will rise. Such production does not rest in the seed/sprout in an ultimate sense but is dependent upon causes and conditions that exist quite beyond any inherent essence it may bear. At this point, a challenger may ask a defendant whether there exists production from another in a conventional sense. The correct answer is no, for even in the commonsense world entities are not said to be produced by entities that are other; otherwise, a seashell could produce a sprout. When the defender proffers the correct reply, a challenger might feign shock and even anger, pressing the defendant further in hope of throwing him off of his pedestal. Further shock and dismay, perhaps a sarcastic gesture to the audience, might follow a second denial; and if the defender does not have a deep understanding of the matter, he might come to question his own position. This can provide the means for the cultivation of disciplined thinking. There are a few analogous devices for defenders. When a geshe participates as a defender in a public debate, he will wear his pointed scholar's hat. He is obliged to remove the hat and keep it on his lap when the challenger presents a citation from a venerable text. If the citation is pertinent and makes the challenger's point, he will keep the hat sitting on his lap; however, if the argument is inconclusive, he will replace the hat on top of his head. If he wishes to engage in some playful competition, he will be inclined to replace the hat in nearly any circumstances, in an effort to undermine the challenger's confidence and present an additional obstacle to the challenger's philosophical task.

The use of CONFOUNDED BY ALL THREE! which we have already analyzed plays a role in such gambits, and its employment can amount to institutionalized ridicule. As we remarked, it is not only a logical assessment, it is a complicated move embedded in an interactional context. Although ridicule is not a major component of Tibetan philosophical debate, it is a spice that flavors the dialectic from time to time and occasionally adds some amusement to their scholarly tasks.

Pulling the Rug Out from under a Defender

Upon detecting the direction of an opponent's analysis a master debater will encourage that direction, energizing it further, in the hope of escorting the opponent to an absurd consequence. It hardly matters whether the direction is analytically correct or not, and the clarifier of the reasoning is able to play both sides of an issue, for unlike a defender he has no obligation to remain consistent. The speed with which a clarifier can change directions can be awesome at times, and this unpredictability itself keeps some defenders guessing. Just when it seems apparent to a defender what the clarifier's intention is, that intention will change, leaving the defender high and dry. I term this phenomenon PULLING THE RUG OUT from underneath a defender. In many debates, offering some opposition to a philosophical position will reinforce an opponent's will. When a clarifier senses some energy building up in a defender about a particular thesis, he may contest it a little just to let that force to build up a bit further and have the defender's resolve about his thesis strengthen. Then when the defender is arguing with vigor, the clarifier can secure a firmer commitment than he might have otherwise; then, later in the debate, the clarifier will return to the issue and examine it from a competing perspective and endeavor to entrap the defender in a contradiction. Such dialectical strategies can become elaborate and elegant.

Debate II.3 is one of several debates that investigate when an understanding of emptiness is necessary and whether this understanding is formal analytic or not. This debate's thesis amounts to being a logical thesis about not needing logical theses, and reason is ruled neither in nor out. Here we will review some of the initial moves of that debate, portions of which we have already seen in connection with other debate properties. First, let us look at a paradigmatic portion of that debate, and then we will examine closely the debating that precedes it and also a few passages that follow it:

> T   IT FOLLOWS THAT there is an explicit explanation of the pene-
>   trative faculties.
> 9:19   L"   They have an explicit explanation of the penetrative faculties.

Having secured L"'s agreement, T PULLS THE RUG OUT, asserting just the opposite, and L" is compelled to contradict his statement and conform. L' does not seem to mind and rather enjoys the dialectical turn, for he smiles at the strategic move:

> 9:19:03 T   Oh. IT DOES NOT FOLLOW THAT there is an explicit explana-
>   tion of the penetrative faculties. Right? [L' smiles] Now, BE-
> -039-   CAUSE the method of the commentary is to address the way a
> :06   person with dull faculties thinks. >~
>   L"   When it speaks of "practicing compassion" it refers to a person
>   with dull faculties.

Let us examine this exchange again by beginning from several turns previous to 9:19:06. T's question has its origin at line -013-:

> -013-   T   Now, is a person with penetrative faculties referred to in the expla-
>   nation of how they are connected; or is it referring to a person with
>   dull faculties?

9:17:27 L'   There are explanations for both.

-014-   L"   There are explanations for both.

Having secured their preliminary reply, T repeats his query to firm up the commitment, and the debaters engage in a collaborative summary rehearsal of their agreement:

    T   So this, right?

:30 L' So it is said that there are in terms of both of these.

:32 T   In terms of both, correct? >~

    L" Yes yes.

And they rehearse this:

    T   ... So now, there are [explanations] in terms of both?

    L   Yes.

    T   Since there are [explanations] in terms of both, for example, now this, this is said?

-017-   L   Yes.

With this in hand, T next takes up the pertinent citation from a text, Chandrakirti's *Autocommentary* to his own work, *Introduction to the Middle Way*:

9:17:43 T   To quote from the beginning to the end, oh, *"One who has com-passion"*—

    L   Yes.

    T   —*"protects all others who suffer from the nature of suffering and other emotional afflictions, without a single exception,"*[11]—Oh, so.

    L' "He familiarizes himself with this."

    L" "He familiarizes himself with this."

And the debaters dance around this citation in a friendly collaboration, by the end of which they have come to a degree of solidarity. T returns to his question:

9:17:57 T   You say it is about one with penetrative faculties, but we can see that it is referring to those with dull faculties, right? >~

-023-   L   This is the dull faculties. This is different, isn't it?

Next comes the passage we considered above on 166-67 ("Logic as Sport"):

-025-   T   For example, the root text explicitly discusses a person with pene-trative faculties.

---

11. The *rang 'grel* text (6.4): *'di ltar snying rje can ni gzhan gyi sdug bsngal gris sdug bsngal ba nyid kyis sems can sdug sngal bar gyur ba ma lus pa yong su bskyab par bya.*

> L'   In this, yes? One with penetrative faculties is explicitly explained. /
>   One with penetrative faculties is explicitly explained. One with
>   penetrative faculties is explicitly explained.
> L"   / One with penetrative faculties is explained.
> T   If that is so, why does this citation explicitly refer to persons with
>   dull faculties?
> -027- L"   Now this, huh? Oh, there can also be this.

It is evident that T has the defenders looking in both directions at once. In
fact, he wishes to highlight the ironies of the issue, but in doing so he is leaving
no ground for L' and L" to stand on. He then embarks upon a related issue,
whether the textual exegeses of the matter are explicit or implicit, and he poses
his query in the form of a REVERSAL[12]:

> T   In the root text there is an explicit explanation, in the commentary
>   there is no such explicit explanation, right?
> L"   Oh, there's no such explanation.
> T   The commentary offers an explicit explanation, uh, the root text
>   does not explain it so.
> 9:18:35 L"   Oh, this is so.

With L" having agreed to both sides of the issue, T firms up the commitment:

> :36 T   So now, this is the way of explanation in the commentary. >~
> L"   O.K., I ACCEPT.

And then T combines the two inquiries. Here L" goes along, but he is a bit
evasive and offers a qualification ("in general"), and he is scolded for attempting
to qualify his commitment[13]:

> T   So both are never explained together explicitly in the same text.
> L"   What? But both are explicitly formulated. In general we have an
>   explanation, an explicit explanation of both. The text—
> T   Whether there may be explanations generally is not the concern.
>   Now where is there an explicit explanation of both together. >~
> L"   It is said there is no explicit explanation of both together.

T now formally declares L"'s inconsistency, and it is following his double
TS'A that the paradigmatic passage we have just cited appears. It is a successful
tactic to follow up a TS'A *immediately* with another proposition. Admonished in
that way, L" becomes very compliant, and he offers his assent to T's proposal,
only to have T PULL THE RUG OUT from underneath him just as soon as he

---

12. See 128-129 and 169; see also the "Ethnomethods" section on the CD-ROM.
13. See 182ff., "Running a Tight Ship."

does (see video clip for II.3 9:18:54-9:19:27), which brings us back again to the crucial turns we examined at the start:

9:18:56 T   There is not, is there? >~ /Therefore, =v= TS'A! =v= TS'A indeed! Now also, IT FOLLOWS THAT there is an explicit explanation of the penetrative faculties.

9:19   L"   / Ohhh. They have an explicit explanation of the penetrative faculties.

     T   Oh. IT DOES NOT FOLLOW THAT there is an explicit explanation of the penetrative faculties. Right? [L' smiles] Now, BE-

:03   CAUSE the method of the commentary is to address the way a person with dull

:06   faculties thinks. >~

     L"   When it speaks of "practicing compassion" it refers to a person with dull faculties.

And what is more, T rubs it in:

9:19:15 T   Here there is a discussion of the dull faculties, isn't there? >~

     L'   There is a presentation of dull faculties.

-042-   T   Oh, therefore, =v=

L", somewhat exhausted, retorts in his defense,

     L"   Now you want to challenge hard (*ngar shog*), is it?

But T keeps pushing:

     T   There is an explicit explanation of the dull faculties, isn't there? >~

     L"   I ACCEPT that there is. [L' smiles]

While the debate is making progress in collecting commitments, at this point L" is more or less helpless in the hands of this skillful debater.

In our next illustration (I.1), the challenger presents a citation that he actually intends to criticize. It is not so difficult to get a defender to agree with an authoritative citation, and having done so one can then test the person's understanding about its difficult points. T begins,

3:08:15 T   *"It is inappropriate to contend that there are both correct and distorted customary truths since there can be no correct customary truth. Since it pervades that if it is common sense it is distorted,"*[14] the citation says.

---

14. The citation is a conflation of two passages from Jetsun Chogyi Gyaltsen, *dBu ma'i spyi don skal bzang mgu'i rgyan*, Bylakuppe: Sera Je Computer Project, 1997, 268 and 284—and so, strictly speaking, it is inaccurate. The pervasion referred to is the view of an opponent; however, L" does not catch the mistake because the last three words are spoken with such deep certainty that a "yes" is made almost compulsory.

    L" Oh yes.

:20 T   Therefore, yah, does it not necessarily PERVADE that a customary truth must be the distorted common sense perception of a mundane, everyday consciousness? IT PERVADES THAT it is dis-

:26   torted common sense; or does it NOT PERVADE? >~

T's question has mostly to do with the fact that common sense presumes that the reifications it works with exist by their own independent essences, and since it fixates on these mental constructions, it is necessarily a distorted consciousness. L" replies appropriately, and the parties rehearse the issue,[15] publicly exhibiting the details of the reasoning:

    L" IT PERVADES THAT it is a distorted common sense.

    T   What?

    L' IT PERVADES, it is said.

    T   It pervades, right?

    L" It is said that it pervades.

    T   If it pervades, right? Yah, now it pervades, right? It's a distorted common sense appearing to a mundane consciousness. TAKE AS THE SUBJECT the reification of an entity as having inherently true existence. Yah. IT FOLLOWS THAT it is distorted common sense!

3:08:38 L" It is said that it PERVADES that it is distorted common sense, but you don't say, "It's a distorted common sense appearing to a mundane consciousness."

:40 L' IT IS ACCEPTABLE THAT it is distorted common sense.

Here the rehearsals permit the debaters to gear themselves into one another, and the debaters are working together in fine form (see video, I.1 3:08:20-50):

    T   IT FOLLOWS THAT it is distorted common sense. TAKE AS THE SUBJECT the reification of an entity as having inherently true existence. IT FOLLOWS THAT it is distorted common

:44   sense. >~

    L' / IT IS ACCEPTABLE!

    L" / IT IS ACCEPTABLE!

Now, just when everything is proceeding straightforwardly, T pulls the rug out from their collaboration:

    T   IT DOES NOT FOLLOW THAT it is distorted common sense. IT FOLLOWS THAT a person whose thinking does not understand emptiness does not necessarily realize that it is a distorted con-

3:08:49   sciousness. >~

---

15. For the discussion of REHEARSALS, see 124-25.

T is raising the problem that if a valid examination is a matter of common sense reflection and therefore is itself a distorted consciousness, it would be incapable of establishing itself as being distorted; hence, its being distorted cannot be established. Although this seems like some logical gymnastics, it poses the serious question of how a clueless person can make any headway in his philosophical endeavors. The respondents appreciate the point:

:50 L' IT IS ACCEPTABLE.
     L" IT IS ACCEPTABLE.

But that places them in contradiction with the text, so T uses the text against them, teasing them about it, even though they were merely agreeing with his contention:

T   The text says that it is necessary, and you have contradicted the text, whose contents seems to have slipped from your memory.

L'   The citation refers only to what appears to mundane consciousness.

T   Yah. This is a contradiction due to memory lapse, is it not?

L"   What?

T   If it is common sense and it pervades that it is distorted common sense, TAKE AS THE SUBJECT *"the reification of an entity as having inherently true existence."* Now, yahh, *"That FOLLOWS*
3:09   *BECAUSE of this reason."*[16]

L'   There is a statement like that.

L"   Oh. Oh. This is right.

And so the defenders have reversed their position. T can then proceed to criticize them from the other direction, since he himself believes that the authoritative citation, to which they have acceded almost gratuitously, is flawed.

It is due to the challenger's effective use of "pulling the rug out" that their consideration of matters was not performed as a dry recitation but as a lively presentation of quandaries and contradictions. This Tibetan style serves to keep participants motivated and attentive, and it exposes the dusty corners of a course of what might otherwise be little more than routine reflection. Monks delight in witnessing the ironies that their thinking contains, and they collaborate in exposing and savoring these ironies, which can generate considerable energy among the debaters. Tibetan debaters work deliberately to direct these energies into a well synchronized, smoothly flowing course of dialectics. When the dialectics is going well, the energies are flowing freely and there is a synergy that is brought to their intellectual concerns.

---

16. "THAT FOLLOWS BECAUSE of this reason" is a verbatim citation from Jetsunpa 1997, 269.

Dangling in the Wind

In our final example, we witness a masterful performance, by the end of which the defendant is ready to say yes to anything. The reader may wish to review the turn-by-turn video presentation of the debate, "The Mind that Realizes Emptiness" (on the CD-ROM, Illustrative Debate section: Debate I.9), alongside a reading of this text. Because of the brilliance of the debating it contains, we will examine excerpts from substantial portions of it. Their topic is the relation between the formal analysis of emptiness and an actual realization[17] of emptiness. Our debate commences with the clarifier of the reasoning (T) posing the initial question to the respondent (L):

> T   One speaks of the realization of emptiness, right? Can you have
>   that realization [*rtogs*] occur without realizing that an entity lacks a
>   true identity? >~
> 6:02:53 L' Can a realization of emptiness occur without realizing that an en-
>   tity lacks a true identity, huh?

In order for the reader to follow this debate intelligently, it is necessary to introduce the debaters' topic, emptiness. For Mahayana Buddhists, emptiness is not something that exists "in general" like a phenomenon in the world, to which they pay some sort of nihilistic obeisance (although many of the interpretations by European commentators before the mid-twentieth century treated it that way). Rather, emptiness is always an emptiness of something *specific*, such as the emptiness of my pen. My pen does not bear its own existence intrinsically as if its reality was derived from an inherent essence or a Platonic idea; instead, it consists of the transitory aggregation of plastics, metal, ink, etc., along with a cultural context and the projection of a label and the notion, "my pen." Its penness is therefore due to an adventitious confluence of events and not due to an essence that rests inherent *within* it, so it is "empty" of having any independent essence. Similarly, it lacks as part of its intrinsic identity any "mineness," though should someone pocket my pen I might feel a strong attachment to it and think of it as though its self-nature did include this "mineness." The Buddhist notion is that we reify our notions and then become obsessed with those reifications, which in turn leads to a strengthening of our desire, which can lead to suffering. Here the debaters are considering the correct way to approach an understanding of emptiness. Since the matter is a profound one, the respondents repeat the question, shaking their heads as they pause to consider the issue.

The question suggests another important aspect—one *can* be a proponent of a view of the emptiness of inherent existence on the basis of a *strictly formal* (and hence general) understanding of emptiness, without actually having any

---

17. "*rtogs*" can mean "realization," "understanding," or "cognition." It is to be distinguished from its near-homonym "*rtog*," which means "thought" or "conception," that is, a more exclusively intellectualized awareness.

empirical realization of the more subtle aspects of emptiness. This issue amounts to a consideration of the issue of the relation between the formal analysis of the emptiness of essences and the actual realization of emptiness.

Since the question is pregnant with many possible meanings and practical applications by T, it is difficult for L' to know just what T is going to do with the question. To gain an instant to think about it, L' repeats the question. The defender and the clarifier of the reasoning each repeat the question to get a better hold of it, and then the clarifier (T) begins to press for an answer, demanding, "Now is it yes or no! >~" and "Now it's not so difficult," and then,

6:03:14 T   You have to say yes. According to the texts, it *is* this way, isn't it?
       L'   Yes, it *is* this way.

With the practically forced assent in hand, T then tries to firm up L''s commitment, but L' is only willing to offer a qualified consent:

       T   You're saying yes, are you?
       L'   If it is formulated on the basis of a perceived entity.

The parties come to agree that emptiness must pertain to a specific phenomenon, and they suggest the example of a pot as a phenomenon to consider. T then proposes a second proposition:

       T   Now. When one has realized the emptiness of this pot, since we agreed that one does so on this basis. Truly, oh yes, do we say that IT DOES NOT NECESSARILY FOLLOW that one understands the way in which the pot still exists with some functional
6:03:33   efficacy? >~
       L'   When one has a realization of emptiness/
       T   /Oh. At the time one has a realization of emptiness.
       L'   One says it is not necessary.
   :37 T   It is necessary isn't it?
       L'   Mmm-hmh.

This second question refers to the important fact that the view of emptiness is not a nihilism. It does not deny the "functional efficacy" that phenomena empty of inherent essences can have in the everyday world. Incidentally, this is the import of the famous line from the *Heart Sutra*, that runs, "Emptiness is form, and form is emptiness." "Form" refers to the fact that something is recognized to exist, so there is no nihilism operating; and "emptiness" refers to the abandonment of any essentialism, and so no positivism or naïve realism is operating either. A correct view of emptiness cognizes everyday events while understanding the emptiness of the phenomena that are in play; however, a limited view of emptiness may not sustain such a cognition of mundane events.

The center of the debaters' activity here is that the clarifier is laboring to develop a fully adequate formal account of emptiness, in order to deepen the parties' understanding. T is fitting together, piece by piece, the essential elements of a competent account of emptiness. Here it includes the observation that emptiness is not an emptiness in general and that the specific phenomenon concerned must retain its functional efficacy. In such a fashion, T is fulfilling his philosophical responsibilities by assembling an adequate formal analytic version of emptiness:

> T   When one reflects upon the meaning of interconnectedly dependent existence, on the basis of the pot/
>
> L'   /Yes.
>
> T   When undertaking an analysis of the emptiness of the way one customarily apprehends and reifies a referent object. Oh. Yes. When one refutes a referent object's inherently true existence,
>
> 6:03:50   then one posits its emptiness, doesn't one? >~ Depending upon whether one does or does not realize the correct limits of emptiness [i.e., what is to be negated and what is not], right, when one considers and reflects upon what is an acceptable way of formulating the functional conventional existence of the entity, which does have efficacy, without forgetting having negated the previous habit of reifying the entity's being, there *is* what we call a realization of
>
> :59   emptiness. >~

T is trying to locate the fine line between negating too much and negating too little. One does not want to deny the reality of a beautiful woman, for example, yet it is a truism that beauty rests in the eyes of the beholder. Similarly, although a truck is merely an adventitious collection of parts, such as tires, doors, a chassis, a steering wheel, etc., and so does not bear its own existence as an *inherent* essence, it can still run over someone, so its functional efficacy must be appreciated by any philosophical analysis that focuses upon its emptiness. This is a summary of the realization of emptiness that Tsong Khapa (1357-1419) elucidates in several of his treatises.

The defender (L') here is tenacious and won't grant T anything, frustrating T in his attempt to get all of the elements of an adequate formal account of emptiness together so that it can be authorized as a true proposition. Moreover, *having already earlier committed himself* (at 6:03:(36)) to the notion that realizing a pot's functional efficacy is not necessary for realizing its emptiness, L' holds out against T's position. Although he is forced into his rejection by virtue of his *structural obligation* within this debate, L' is still able to mine his situation for what it can offer to philosophical reflection, and he squeezes out of it a valuable insight regarding the distinction between the formal and the actual realization of emptiness. What is noteworthy about L''s achievement is that in rejecting T, he is recycling an insight that is related to the pivotal insight at 6:02:(52) with which T himself commenced the debate; hence, in disagreement there can be agreement. Here the disagreement is at the surface structure, and the collaboration lies in the deep structure of the dialectics, in a sort of "countersophistics that at every moment runs the risk of replicating the *reply*: reproducing in a mirror the logic of the adversary at the moment of the retort" (Derrida 1994, 156). This, too, is dialectical practice, albeit it is hidden within (and perhaps by) the formalities of their discourse. The respondent's vital insight is won serendipitously perhaps, driven by both the surface and deep structure of the dialectics, but even great philosophical insights may be serendipitous:

6:04   L'   YOUR REASON IS NOT ESTABLISHED. There may or may not be a realization of emptiness. One who understands only the assertion of emptiness merely posits an emptiness, yes.

      T   Are you sure? In *The Three Principal Aspects of the Path*, right? [18]

      L'   Oh yes.

This is actually a very astute observation on L''s part, and one which fully recognizes the limitations of formal analytic accounts; that is, proving that an assertion is correct may or may not be accompanied by a full understanding of its implications. But by being so contrarily clever L' begins to anger T, who presses harder and brings in the big guns of an authoritative citation from Tsong Khapa's *The Three Principal Aspects of the Path*, to clarify and bolster his contention. I have added the preceding four stanzas in order to set the vitally important philosophical context for T's citation of Tsong Khapa's stanza:

T   "[*Without the wisdom that realizes the way things abide,*
Even though one has cultivated renunciation and the altruistic mind,
One will be unable to cut the roots of mundane existence;
Therefore, one must apply oneself in the methodology for fathoming entities' interconnectedly dependent being.

Whoever views all phenomena
To exist only by causal relations, without exception,
And destroys all tendencies to concretize them
Has then entered the path that is celebrated by Buddhas.

One who sees the incontrovertible interconnectedly dependent being of what appears
And has an understanding of its emptiness that is not merely dependent upon theorization
Yet views these two to be separate events
Has still not realized the thought of the Able.]

18. The citation is from Tsong Khapa 1985a. 16-19, my translation.

> *But when the recognition of functional efficacy and the realization of emptiness do not alternate in one's consciousness but are cognized simultaneously*
> *And one witnesses only the incontrovertible interconnectedly dependent being, then*
> *Such ascertainment thoroughly destroys the customary modes of reifying apprehended objects.*

6:04:14   *And at that time we say the analysis of the view is completed."* >~
     L' I ACCEPT.

Following such an erudite and profound citation, L' is obliged to accede to T's position. T repeats the citation a couple of times, flaunting it before the defendants, in an effort to consolidate the position within the debate's structure. His performance *contributes a rhythm* to the debating, *marked by hand-claps*:

     T   —[very rapidly] When the previous negation of the establishment of inherently true existence, of the customary mode of reification, is not forgotten, then is what we call a realization of [a specific]
6:04:41   emptiness then needed? >~
     L' It's like this. In that case a realization of emptiness is not needed.
     T   First of all, if one consults the text, it goes like this:

> *"But when the recognition of functional efficacy and the realization of emptiness do not alternate in one's consciousness but are cognized simultaneously,*
> *And one witnesses only the incontrovertible interconnectedly dependent being, then*
> *Such ascertainment thoroughly destroys the customary modes of reifying apprehended objects,*

6:04:56   *And at that time we say the analysis of the view is completed."* >~
     L' Yes.
     T   This is what we understand to be the analysis of the view, the analysis of the Middle Way view. The present realization of the emptiness view is due to a realization of a Middle Way analysis of
6:05   the view. >~
     L' Yes.
     T   This is the Middle Way view. This is how we present the mind
6:05:03   that realizes emptiness. >~
     L' Yes.
     T   Right?

The challenger (T) works to objectivate *every* commitment, even those with which he may disagree. This provides for the parties clear communication, perhaps better than takes place when two Western scholars debate one another at an academic conference. By employing such interactive and formal logical mecha-nisms, Tibetan debaters almost never play the role of two ships passing in the night. The generalized versions of their philosophical inquiries that such objec-tivation produces may occasionally dumb down an inquiry, but it does provide for a communication in which all parties, including the audience, know what is at stake. This is thinking produced as a public activity. Here the work of validat-ing a universal reason is social and not merely logical; or rather, the logical here *is* the social. T proceeds with his work of building up a competent account of the topic:

> T If we speak of when the mind that realizes emptiness is completed, and one comes to cognize the interconnectedly dependent being of an object, there has been a previous refutation of an inherently true essence, right? If the awareness of this negation has not dissipated, and we are able to retain it while also recognizing just how an en-tity abides with a functional efficacy, at that time we must be cog-nizant also of what is common to the customary apprehension. >~
> 6:05:14 [T folds his arms]

T's folding of his arms reveals his own appreciation of what he has accom-plished; however, L' continues to confound T by *refusing* to go along:

> L' When we realize emptiness we don't need to pay attention to the customary apprehension.

This animates a little dance by T, visible on the CD-ROM, a dance that in Tibetan debates frequently accompanies a challenger's presentation of his for-mal propositions. T presses L' for a full explanation by asking him to PUT-UP OR SHUT-UP:

> :18 T Oh! If we do not, EXPLAIN HOW one analyzes the view.

L' offers merely a pedantic reply, suggesting in a fuzzy fashion a difference between a "complete" analysis of the view (cf. citation) and merely cognizing emptiness in a preliminary, analytic way. But T will have nothing of it and ridi-cules L''s reply:

> L' Merely discerning emptiness and "completing an analysis of the view" are different are they not?
> 6:05:24 T Oh. "Completing an analysis of 'the view'" he says. This is *extremely* wrong-headed! CONFOUNDED BY ALL THREE!

T is frustrated with L', so he quickly follows up his ridicule by presenting in the same breath an ARGUMENT BY ABSURD CONSEQUENCE (6:05:31). This is a glimpse of real Gelug dialectics:

> T   IT FOLLOWS THAT the realization of emptiness and the genera-
>   tion of a mental continuum of the Middle Way view are not a
> :31 completion of the Middle Way analysis of the view. >~
> L'   I will concur.

This proposition is absurd because it is practically the denial of a tautology—a Middle Way practitioner who generates a mental continuum that cognizes emptiness is the very definition of the completion of the Middle Way
view. Note that the reference here is to an experience and not to a formal assertion.

> T   How can that possibly be how it is?!

T proceeds with the work of philosophers, that is, the work of assembling
an adequate formal analytic account of (in this instance) emptiness, adding the
important distinction between the habitual reification of inherent essence that is
conceptually imputed and those reifications or fixations that are innate. Conceptual imputations are projections that humans engage in, especially philosophers,
and covers cases where people are victimized by their own intellection. These
imputations are acquired ones. Innate reifications are those fixations that all
creatures have, including cows whose intellection presumably is minimal. The
former fixations are the easier to abandon, while the latter are nearly intransigent
despite diligent efforts to remove them. The distinction is an important component of any adequate formal account of emptiness.

> T   Now, why do you speak of it this way? The text presents an exam-
>   ple of the negation of the habitual reification of true existence that
>   is *conceptually* imputed upon a referent object. In this system,
> 6:05:55 that is not necessarily a realization of emptiness. >~
> L'   If one refutes the habitual reification of true existence that is con-
>   ceptually imputed, eh?
> T   Oh, so.
> :57 L'   In this system, eh?
> T   [pregnant pause, as T waits for L' to commit one way or the other]
> L'   The habitual attitude of true existence conceptually imputed upon
>   the referent object is understood to not have any existence. Yes,
>   yes. Now, it would not necessarily be a realization of emptiness,
>   would it?
> 6:06 T   According to this Middle Way Dialectical School.
> L'   Oh, it's not necessary.

T's proposal (at 6:05:55) is competent, but L' STALLS by calling for which
school of philosophical tenets T is considering (:57). This stall is a move in the
game, and it gains L' time to consider how to handle the newly introduced element. T *pushes* the matter, and so L' goes along, and T repeats the point (at 6:06)

in order to firm up the commitment. An abiding aim of Tibetan debate praxis is to secure clear and firm commitments.

At this point, the topic of conceptual imputation leads L" to introduce his own idea, and he raises the case of the Syllogism-based Reasoning School (specifically, the Sautrantika Svatantrika Madhyamaka), which has a less sophisticated understanding of emptiness that concerns itself more exclusively with conceptual imputation:

6:06:14 L" According to the view of the Syllogism-based Reasoning School, it is the view of emptiness that is the negation of a reification of true existence that is *conceptually* imputed.

Since the challenger (T) is obligated to "pick up" any matter that a defender introduces, objectivate it as well, and analyze it in a formal way, T carries out an exegesis of L"'s topic, comparing how one cognizes emptiness in the Syllogism-based Reasoning School and the Dialectical Reasoning School. First, he summarizes the gist of a college textbook's account of the Dialectical Reasoning School, and the reference to such an authoritative text prompts L"'s agreement:

T In our system, the central point of the commentaries is that unless we recognize this object that is *innately* apprehended, right, we do not realize emptiness. The emptiness posited on the basis of a *conceptually* imputed apprehension of true existence—a negation that proceeds by way of an analysis of conceptual imputations—is insufficient for realizing emptiness. This is the real point of the
6:06:36 *Overview of the Middle Way.* >~
L' I ACCEPT.

Then in response to L" raising again the perspective of the Syllogism-based Reasoning School, which is more germane to the defenders' position, T also summarizes the view of that school:

L" The Syllogism-based Reasoning School has its own understanding of the referent object.
6:07 T This is so. Ohh. Their analysis, which proceeds from considering referent objects to be merely a collection of directionless, partless atomic particles, teaches us only a rough sort of emptiness.

Some lower schools of Buddhist philosophical tenets have a physical theory of emptiness that depends upon recognizing that an aggregation of atoms that composes an object, such as a pot, does not involve an inherent identity—only partless atomic particles could be so inherently existing; however, even atomic particles have directional sides (north, east, etc.; European scientists would speak here of protons and electrons, or perhaps quarks), so actually they are not ultimate either. Since this collection is a transitory assembly of atoms, which are ultimately separable, it cannot have an intrinsic essence. This is a discernment of emptiness that is somewhat less sophisticated than an understanding of the inter-connected dependence of notions upon each other, with no single idea capable of an independent, intrinsic existence.

At this point it seems that the thinking of T and both defendants are coming into alignment at long last. But as we have just seen it is an identifying charac-teristic of Tibetan philosophical debate that *just as the parties seem to come to a consensus* the challenger will pull the rug out. T extends the consequences of L'''s position to imply that the profound Syllogism-based Reasoning School analysis provides *only* for refutation of conceptual imputations; that is, since L' is arguing that a cognition of the emptiness of conceptual imputations may not entail the actual realization of emptiness and since he suggests that the Syllo-gism-based Reasoning School may have some proponents who conform to that description, T concludes (absurdly) that it is L'''s position that all persons of the Syllogism-based Reasoning School who analyze true entities as apparent collec-tions of directionless, partless atomic particles negate only *conceptual* imputa-tions.

> T   For this reason IT FOLLOWS THAT such a basis for realizing
>   emptiness only permits the realization of a lack of true existence of
>   the *conceptual* imputations that are projected upon a referent ob-
>   ject. >~
> L'   CHEE-CHEER [WHAT IS THE REASON?]

L' rejects this, since although the Syllogism-based Reasoning School's un-derstanding is less sophisticated, it is going too far to claim that they are unable to correct *any* innate fixations. But T keeps pressing. At 6:07:49, L' throws T a bone in the direction of T's contention:

> T   In that way, the Syllogism-based Reasoning School—right—has
>   not identified the referent object that is *innately* produced. Within
>   the terms of designation of their philosophical tenets, there is still
>   some sort of habitual reification of an entity's "true" essence,
>   right?
> 6:07:49 L'   Right.

But then T tries to *extend* the concession too far by proposing (at 6:07:51) another absurd consequence, which L' emphatically rejects:

> T   Merely such a refutation does not establish the realization of a
> :51   phenomenon's lack of existing with any true identity. >~
> L'   THE REASON IS NOT ESTABLISHED!

That is, those of the Syllogism-based Reasoning School do have some cognition of that, only perhaps not enough of it. T responds by extending the consequences of L''s argument to the point of blasphemy:[19]

> T   If that reason is not established, for this system, right? IT DOES
>   NOT FOLLOW THAT one needs *any* realization of emptiness in
> 6:07:59   order to refute some sort of true existence of a pot. >~
> L' CHEE-CHEER, CHEE-CHEER!

That is, if a mere formal assertion about emptiness, without any realization of emptiness, can refute true, inherent self-identity, then a realization of emptiness would become superfluous. It is a fine dialectical move, and T presses this absurdity, which incorporates parts of L''s previous reasoning. Here T has L' on the mat and is trying to pin his shoulders down:

> 6:08 T   It must be, does it not?
> L' It must.
> T   IT FOLLOWS THAT it is not necessary BECAUSE the reified
>   apprehension of a pot's "true" existence [which is refuted by the
>   Syllogism-based Reasoning School] is merely an imputed concep-
> :03 tualization. >~
> L' THERE IS NO PERVASION.
> T   But it is an imputed conceptualization, is it not?
> L' THERE IS NO PERVASION.

With L''s shoulders not yet on the mat, but hovering an inch or two above, T in a pounce asks him to PUT-UP OR SHUT-UP, but he leaves him no time to reply before he launches into a profound discussion of the relation of the refutation of imputed conceptualization and truly realizing emptiness:

> 6:08:10 T   Oh, PRESENT how one refutes a mode of asserting an imputed
>   conceptualization.
> L' The /
> T   / The imputed conceptualization of a reified "true" essence,
>   one who refutes the mode of asserting an imputed conceptualiza-
>   tion of a reified, "true" essence can be one who has a realization of
>   emptiness, can he not?
> :15 L' That's right.
> T   And one who refutes a mode of asserting an imputed conceptuali-
>   zation of a reified, "true" essence can be one who has not realized
>   emptiness, isn't it?
> L' That's right.

---

19. See also 181-83.

The conclusion here is that a formal refutation of imputed essences may or may not entail a realization of emptiness, depending upon the depth of the reflections of the person concerned. In addition to being an effective and collaborative summary of this portion of their discussion, it also demonstrates that T has been listening to L' well. The practical interest of the debaters is always to work their reflections into public formulations, to make their collaborative utterances into a congregational affair.

> T   Oh, now HOW DOES ONE FORMULATE THIS?
> L'   According to the analysis of the Syllogism-based Reasoning School /

6:08:21 T   / >~

> L'   According to the analysis of the Syllogism-based Reasoning School there is an imputed *conceptualization* of a reified "true" essence, isn't there?
> T   Oh.

At last L' gets to T's point, as the competitive dialectics succeeds in pressing him to some serious philosophizing, and the parties engage in some dialectical thinking:

> L'   There is also an *innate* proclivity to objectify an entity, but here there is no apprehension that considers well the essentialist reification of an entity's being that is produced by this innate proclivity to objectify. And such a subtle realization in terms of an awareness of the essentialist reification of an entity's identity / by the innate proclivity to objectify is required. //

Although the account L' offers is a little weak, he provides in his account an element—the innate proclivity to essentialist reification—that T quickly utilizes to ask a question of considerable probity: if removing the innate proclivity to essentialist reification is the critical task, then why do scholars devote any of their attention to the essentialist reifications that are created by conceptual projections (6:08:30)? This is an example of Tibetan dialectics successfully leading to an interesting question.

6:08:30 T   /   Oh,   TAKE
         THE TOPIC the analysis of the Syllogism-based Reasoning School // regarding the customary mode of reifying an essential nature. When one negates an *innate*, spontaneously arising object of attachment, right, in this system why then must one refute the object of attachment that is a *conceptually* imputed reification of a truly
  :39   existing essence? >~

L' IT FOLLOWS THAT one must BECAUSE according to their system, there is a reified apprehension of a "true" essence that is a
habit of conceptual imputation.

Unfortunately, L''s response is drawn too narrowly within the confines of the
formal logistics of the problem. Instead of contributing to their developing account of the problem, he retreats into a technical explanation, the formal truth of
which cannot be denied but one that lends little insight to the reflection.

T rehearses L''s point, making the problem clearer to all, and introduces another textual citation. And by doing so, he is able to *accelerate the pace of the
debate*:

6:08:54 T It would be good to present the textual citation, right? "*Subsequent
to being subjected to the three—the basis, its appearance to
awareness, and the path of analyzing and meditating upon it,*" IT
FOLLOWS THAT one refutes the object of attachment produced
by the imputed conceptualizations of the customary mode of
6:09:02 imputing an essential nature. >~
L' I ACCEPT. I ACCEPT.

T summons a repeat of L''s acceptance and then revisits L''s earlier commitment in his turn just prior to 6:06 (see 224), and L' begins to get confused
and contradicts his earlier reasoning:

T We say that it is refuted, don't we?
L' THAT IS ACCEPTABLE. THAT IS ACCEPTABLE. It is refuted.
T Uhh, when the object of attachment produced by an imputed reification is refuted, in actual fact IT FOLLOWS THAT one does not
6:09:09 necessarily realize emptiness. >~
L' I ACC- WHAT IS THE REASON that it follows that one does not
necessarily realize emptiness? There must be a realization of emptiness.

This matter begins a series of entanglements for L', commencing with T's
proposition at 6:09:09, which is a negative formulation that L' rejects. As we
have already observed, Tibetans are so accustomed to negative dialectics that
they frequently prefer that the first formulation of a matter be presented in an
incorrect and negative form. So here L' is lulled into a rote rejection, which will
cause problems for him later in the debate. It is quite noteworthy, ethnomethodologically, that this rejection is due more to the in-the-course structure and local
demands of the debate practice than it a result of deliberate logical deduction. L'
adds to his rejection (i.e., "WHAT IS THE REASON") the assertion that there
must be a realization of emptiness when an object of attachment produced by an
imputed reification is refuted. **The reader should take careful note of this**, due
to the strategic role this commitment will play in the debating that is to follow.

For his part, T PICKS UP L''s commitment and formulates it clearly, *even though he disagrees with it*, and gains L''s *authorization* for it (the "yes" at 6:09:12), thereby objectivating it. This is proper debate protocol.

      T   There must be a realization of emptiness.
6:09:12 L' Yes.

T's repeat of L''s assertion offers no additional information—it is only the practical work of exhibiting the interactional order. And the order here is logic: part of the formal grammar of logic is used not because it has a logical role but because it *orders* the talk-in-debate. That is, *logic is being used as an organizational device.* Whatever else logic may be, logic here is a social practice with which the parties can make of their thinking a public activity. The parties here are engaged in the practical, formal, exhibitable work of being philosophers.

T proceeds with his work of clarifying the reasoning, L' takes refuge in a recitation of the citation, and he uses it to deflect T's probe; nevertheless they use the occasion to engage in a dance about the citation:

  :13 T   There is what we speak of as the refutation of an object of attachment that is created by an imputed conceptualization of an habitually reified "true" essence, isn't there?

       L' *"Subsequent to being subjected to the three—the basis, its appearance to awareness, and the path of analyzing and meditating upon it."*

  :15 T   Oh, in accord with *"Subsequent to being subjected to the three—the basis, its appearance to awareness, and the path of analyzing and meditating upon it,"* there is a type of refutation of an object of attachment produced by an imputed conceptualization of a reified "true" essence. It's the same.

  :18 L' Exactly, exactly, exactly.

Once again T objectivates-by-repeating the assertion at 6:09:19, making it an abiding acquisition of the debate.

6:09:19 T   And there must be a realization of emptiness. >~
       L' I ACCEPT that there must be.

It is here that T offers the first of what will be four instances of what I term "PULLING THE RUG OUT FROM UNDERNEATH THE DEFENDER."[20] In the breath that follows his mocking of L's certainty ("Oh, because 'There must have been'?" [" *'O dgos par song tsang*"]), T declares *just the reverse* ("IT FOLLOWS THAT there must not be! ["*mi dgos pa yin par thal*]"). This is done

---

    20. Compare Socrates: "tripping them up and turning them upside down, just as someone pulls a stool away when someone else is going to sit down" (Plato 1961, 392).

so *swiftly* that it may be likened to a move in aikido during which a party deftly uses an opponent's own momentum to lay him flat on the floor:

> T   Oh, because "There must be?" IT FOLLOWS THAT there must not be! Right? BECAUSE *"Subsequent to being subjected to the three—the basis, its appearance to awareness, and the path of analyzing and meditating upon it,"* that is how the analyses of the *lower* tenets establish that entities are apprehended to truly exist by virtue of their own defining characteristics. This system addresses
>
> :29   such conceptual fixations. >~
>
> L'   Yes, sure.

T is suggesting that the methodology of these lower schools is not sophisticated enough to realize emptiness truly. At this point, L' is looking for any safe train to board, so he concurs. But now T, perhaps still irritated with L''s lack of cooperation earlier in the debate, or for the benefit of the examiners, is relentless. He moves in with another first-negatively-formed-then-positively-formed sequence, but this time L accepts the very reasonable initially negatively formed proposition, perhaps in hopes of arriving at some happy accord—one can witness gratuitous head-nodding of L' (cf. CD-ROM) during this passage:

> T   When one refutes that sort of reified fixation, *"Subsequent to being subjected to the three—/*
>
> L'   / That's right. // [L' nods his head assuringly]
>
> T   // *the basis, its appearance to awareness, and the path of analyzing and meditating upon it,"* IT DOES NOT FOLLOW THAT it is a refutation of the object of attachment produced by an imputed conceptualization of a reified
>
> 6:09:32   "true" essence. >~
>
> L'   I ACCEPT.

But just as it appears that *at last* T and L' are coming together, and with L' still nodding hopefully, T pulls the rug out again, being contentious with his positively formatted version. In order to remain consistent and to preserve some of his dignity, L' rejects this positive version (at 6:09:36). T performs more of his work as the clarifier of the reasoning and objectivates L''s position (at 6:09: 37), secures L''s authorization ("I ACCEPT"), and then PULLS THE RUG OUT once more, contending just *the opposite* of what T and L have just authorized:

> T   [Quickly spoken] IT DOES FOLLOW, BECAUSE it is a refutation of the object of attachment generated by the habitual, imputed
>
> 6:09:35   conceptualization of a reified, "true" essence. >~
>
> L'   THE REASON IS NOT ESTABLISHED.
>
> T   IT FOLLOWS THAT for such a person as this, the object of attachment produced by an imputed conceptualization of a reified,

:37   "true" essence is not refuted. >~
L'   I ACCEPT.

The pacing is extremely quick, and the formal analytic apparatus of the debate has reached its full flowering:

T   IT FOLLOWS THAT there is a refutation BECAUSE according to
     the lower schools of tenets' analyses, methods, and commentaries
     regarding the establishment of true existence, the true existence,
:44 uh, a type of reified apprehension is refuted. >~
L'   Yes.

The rapidity of the turn-taking here is a feature that is characteristic of Tibetan debates when the formal analysis is well in play. The debaters seem to enjoy the very speed their dialectics can gain. T begins to set a trap for L', who (at :44) goes along with the compromise notion that "a type" of reification is refuted, but in his succeeding turn (after :46) L' persists almost blindly with his position that the object of attachment is not refuted. T closely approaches the defendant and does a little dance (see the CD-ROM).

T   [Very quickly spoken] When one refutes this, IT DOES NOT
     FOLLOW that one has refuted the object of attachment generated
:46 by the imputed conceptualization of a reified "true" essence. >~
L'   I ACCEPT.

The argument amounts to the suggestion that when one has refuted "a type" of reification (*'dzin tshul gcig khegs*) one has not necessarily refuted the imputed conceptualization of reified "true" essences (*bden 'dzin kun brtags khegs*). Still moving quickly, T revisits L''s commitment immediately prior to 6:06 (224). In the face of the speed of the dialectics at this point L' is so engaged with the logical issues that are most proximal that he loses track of his objectivated commitment noted above (at 6:09:10-12, 229-30) and responds that a realization of emptiness "is not logically entailed," but that response **contradicts** his commitment that we noted there (230), that is, that "There must be a realization of emptiness" when an object of attachment produced by an imputed reification is refuted:

:47 T   [Quickly spoken] Now, when one refutes the object of attachment
          generated by the imputed conceptualization of a reified "true" es-
          sence, is it necessary to have a realization of emptiness?
:48 L'   If you're speaking of the imputed conceptualization of a reified
          "true" essence, then that is not logically entailed, is it?

At 6:09:50, T objectivates this latest view of L, making a public exhibit of it, and by doing so he is able to ridicule L'. T points out L''s inconsistency, and L' implodes (see photo for 6:10:00 in the CD-ROM's Appendix):

:50 T   Oh this, he asserts that there is no logical entailment. Here one has refuted the imputed conceptualization/ of a reified, "true" essence,//

    L'   / Now here, (unclear) //

    T   Now above we have already accepted such an entailment. But nevertheless here it is not necessary, is it?

    L'   Mm.

T's ridicule and his pointing out the inconsistency succeeds in getting L' to reverse his position, and at this point T could well get L' to say yes to anything.

    T   When one has refuted the imputed conceptualization of a reified

6:09:58   "true" essence, we say one must have a cognition of emptiness. >~

    L'   I ACCEPT.

Once the clarifier of the reasoning publicly recalls the respondent's earlier commitment, L' is obliged to fall into line. At last, it seems that the labored dialectics of these debaters has painfully reached some consensus. It might now be supposed that the matter can be settled once and for all. But in dialectics nothing is settled once and for all. T knows that L''s answer is incorrect and was affirmed only because of T's skillful exploitation of the immanent structure of the dialectics. *Just then* T diabolically PULLS THE RUG OUT from under L' one final time, declaring in a single breath,

6:10   T   Oh, it is necessary, isn't it? IT FOLLOWS THAT it is not necessary.

At this point L' seems to be dangling in the wind, practically ready to say "yes" to no and "no" to yes. T observes that the most profound school of philosophical tenets would not concur with L''s contention, but L' meekly tries to hold his ground:

    T   In this system, right? In the mental continuum of the Dialectical Middle Way School, the imputed *conceptualization* of a reified,

:05   "true" essence is not an object of concern. >~

    L'   If you say because there is no room for the imputed conceptualization of a reified essence for the Dialectical Middle Way School, THE REASON IS NOT ESTABLISHED.

It is noteworthy that a nervous flicker moves across the face of L' at this point (see the video on the CD-ROM, debate I.9, 6:10:00-04[21]). It is unclear what are the benefits to philosophical insight of such nervous flickers or, more generally, what the hermeneutic benefits of public ridicule may be, but L' seems

---

21. The viewer of the CD-ROM can use the hand control bar along the virtual bottom of the video screen to scroll slowly through these few seconds of video record.

to retreat into a sort of meditation with his eyes closed, which in itself may be a recognition (or L''s hope) that there is a truth that resides beyond the truth for formal analytic dialectics.[22] Faced with L''s valiance, T formats L''s position in another ARGUMENT BY ABSURD CONSEQUENCE. L' is ready to be persistent, but he recognizes the absurdity and reverses himself:

	T	Oh yes. IT FOLLOWS THAT in the mental continuum of a proponent of the Dialectical Middle Way School there is an imputed
6:10:18		conceptualization of a reified, "true" essence. >~
	L'	I ACCEP- Oh, an imputed conceptualization of a reified "true" essence. CHEE-CHEER!
	T	Oh so there is not, is there?
	L'	There is not.

T summarizes the conclusion, and by so doing emphasizes his victory:

6:10:28 T   In the Dialectical Middle Way System in the Dialectical Middle Way System, in their mental continuum there is *no* imputed conceptualization of a reified, "true" essence!

What is important for those of us wanting to assess formal analytic reasoning is that we witness the looks of things from the perspective of L' and that our appreciation and understanding of Tibetan debate is not merely that of a remote analyst who works with docile texts at a distance from the real world action. Rather, the horizons of meaning that operate for the parties can be retrieved by means of an ethnomethodologically specified description of the details of the dialectics. That is, what the parties are doing in assembling the orderliness of their inquiry, step by step, must be described from the perspective of the parties, and the public life of the thinking that takes place should be captured in a phenomenologically adequate way. Only from the perspective of these Tibetan philosophers, engaged closely with the local details of their dialectical practices, will Western scholars be able to assess fairly what is original or mundane about Tibetan philosophical culture and what are the tangible benefits and limitations of the formal reasoning there.

---

22. Yongdzin (1979) writes in his classical manual on debate, "Should a challenger make an effective refutation, the defender should not become upset but should remain undisturbed, in the way a great mountain receives the wind." See CD-ROM, Appendix, chapter 7 illustrations: photo I.9 6.09:55.

Part III

A Sociology of Reasoning

Chapter 8

Using Reasons:
Capabilities of Formal Analysis

> What is at issue here is not the "results" of their philosophy but the very character of their thinking, their way of questioning, the direction from which they pursued an answer to their questioning.
>
> —Martin Heidegger (1994, 112)

Most readers who consider the debate just presented (subsection "Dangling in the Wind") will have developed at some point a few sober questions about the benefits of taking formal analytic strategizing to such extremes. Granted that it may be possible for a skillful debater to tangle up an opponent into irresolvable philosophical knots, just what is the benefit of doing so? This is a question that may be addressed to philosophical dialectics everywhere, but here we raise it about the Tibetans' practices of reasoning in particular.

Those who have viewed the CD-ROM of this debate (Illustrative Debate I.9, included with this volume) cannot have failed to notice that as the defender attempted to navigate the rocky shoals of four occasions of the challenger pulling the rug out from under him, his efforts to remain stoic (6:09:20-23) were unsuccessful. The nervous flicker that rolls across the defender's face at 6:10:00-04 reveals the deep mental disturbance he is experiencing. What possibly can be the benefit of such a nervous flicker, which strikes so deeply at his practice of thinking? Each time the parties seem to come to a consensus, such as at 6:07:00 (226) and 6:09:37 (231-32), the challenger switches his position, confounding the defender. At 6:05:55, the respondent commits to the proposition that when one negates the habitual reification of true existence that is conceptually imputed upon a referent object, that does not necessarily mean that one has achieved a realization of emptiness, but then at 6:09:(10) he commits to the opposite position that when the object of attachment produced by an imputed reification is refuted, "There must be a realization of emptiness." But here it is more than a mere contradiction, for the challenger is able to turn the respondent at will, and he easily induces the respondent to reaffirm the first position at 6:09:48 (that when one refutes the object of attachment generated by the imputed conceptualization of a reified "true" essence, it does not entail that one has a realization of emptiness), only to force him to reverse his position yet again at 6:09:58 and reaffirm that one must have a cognition of emptiness. Although the respondent struggles to retain his philosophical integrity, it seems he is just "dangling" at the hands of the skillful challenger who is holding the strings. What, if anything, is philosophical about this?

The answer to this question is direct and simple if one acknowledges that by "philosophy" one must include those apophantic aspects that lend themselves to a formalization that creates its own economy which always risks separating itself from experience. As Husserl (1969, 153) described it,

> Our chief purpose is to show that a logic directed straightforwardly to its proper thematic sphere, and active exclusively in cognizing that, remains stuck fast in a naiveté which shuts it off from the philosophical merit of radical self-understanding and fundamental self-justification, or, what amounts to the same thing, the merit of being most perfectly scientific.

Tibetan scholars are well versed in the merit of "radical self-understanding," which is an understanding that recognizes that it itself is producing the very objects of reflection that occupy its attention. The doctrine of emptiness that this most recent debate is exploring consists of this very realization. But even in its fullness, there is no guarantee that *any* philosophical effort to reflect upon such a nature of things will not develop a formal economy of notions that can become so preoccupied with the local work of that economy that the phenomenon being addressed by its "proper thematic" reflection is lost to experience. That is to say, sophistry is sufficiently endemic to philosophizing that to hold seriously to the notion that "pure" philosophy can be separated out from sophistry may itself be nothing more than a naive idealism.

However, if one means by philosophy a more sustained engagement with the experiences from which one's concerns about truth have emerged, that is, a practice of thinking that employs formal analysis into its service but remains self-reflexively in control of what is being thought, then the answer to our question requires considerably more investigation into the formal practices of the thinking that these Tibetan scholars are doing. In this chapter we inspect a variety of reasoning practices in an effort to determine what about them is productive philosophically, and in the chapter that follows we will describe some occasions in which these formal analytic practices have limited the fruitful exploration of philosophical interests.

Communicating Clearly

Some Western admirers of Tibetan Buddhism seem to think that geshes (i.e., monks who have received higher academic degrees) and lamas (monks with disciples) obtain their intellectual sharpness through some sort of meditative osmosis. No doubt meditation contributes some clarity to mental functions; however, most Tibetan clergy derive their keenness of intellect by means of extensive study and debate. Among members of the Gelug sect, the emphasis upon debating produces scholars with considerable subtlety of mind, quick and readily able to identify philosophical weaknesses. Not only can they argue well; more importantly, they also learn how to listen well. In this volume I have been contending that for the most part thinking is a public activity, and I have been attempting to describe the contributions that dialectics provide to philosophical reflection. But for dialectics to function successfully, there must be some genuine communication between the two thinkers whose reflections are engaged with each other. Philosophers can collaborate with each other only when they can adequately hear what the other means to say. Even when their intentions are to negate the other, such negation will only be productive philosophically when the thinking of one has actually met the thinking of the other.

It is a principal argument of this volume that one of the important functions of any formal apophansis is to provide a public structuring of thinking to the extent that the reflection can be shared, so that the perspectives of two or more thinkers can actually "meet" and contend with each other. Only when one listens to another, and is listened to in turn, can there be any genuine dialectics. The Tibetans' practice of dialectics in formal public debates succeeds well in providing for adequate communication among collaborating thinkers, and it is their praxis of reformatting each of their reflections in formal analytic terms, and then seeking authorization for such objectivations, that insures that for the most part their dialectics will operate in an environment of clear communication. Dreyfus (2002, 227) emphasizes the importance of this clarity for Tibetan debating: "I managed to score a few points; but most important, I offered the kind of clear debate that comes from getting the path of reasoning." *This "path of reasoning" is the social praxis I am attempting to describe ethnomethodologically.* When the debaters are able not only to employ their practice of conveying each of their notions to the developing formal structure but also are able to use that praxis to reach the principal philosophical content that motivates their inquiries, their philosophizing attains its fullest potential.

Dialogic intercourse is prone to miscommunication far more frequently than most people suspect. Alfred Schutz (1971) has observed that interacting parties usually presume that no major incongruities exist between the perspectives of the parties; rather, they customarily put out of action doubts about any variance in perspectives and presume there is a reciprocity of perspectives. In the real and actual world, this presumptive adequacy in communication is not well founded, although social niceties may prevent the resolution of fundamental differences in the horizons of meaning that parties bring to an interaction. In several studies of intercultural communication (Liberman 1981, 1984, 1985, and 1994), I have shown that much of the time parties fail to understand each other adequately, but people are nevertheless highly skilled in employing gratuitous concurrence and exploiting ambiguities to disguise such failures. How can people know when they are communicating adequately? When people are able to interlace their speech, each speaking the words of the other in a context that is shared, they can achieve an adequacy of communication. That is, when the other has the opportunity to talk back and learn to use the same words in similar ways, meaning can come to be shared; but it doesn't happen on its own. It happens when there are social practices undertaken to accomplish such a state of affairs. We have here, then, an ethnomethodological specification of *just-what* adequate communication can consist of, that is, the specification of one such system of local practices that provides for the competent interlacing of terms and utterances, thereby furnishing vital opportunities for establishing adequate communication—the system of the give and take of utterances within the rhythmic flow of a typical Tibetan debate. This routine system requires more than merely intellectual understanding; it facilitates having some practical experience with the other's terms and horizon of meaning.

Foremost among these practices is the terrific faculty that the clarifier of the reasoning has for picking up the wording of a defender. This volume has been replete with such instances, and I have tried to point them out each time they have occurred. But these practices consist of more than the clarifier's mere formulation of the positions of the respondent; what is more significant is the promotion of those perspectives into the formal analytic structure with which the debaters are working. If the respondent adheres to the use of the proper forms of reasoning, each of the notions he cares to put forward will survive the tumult of the debating, and be heard. This is true even for notions that are patently idiosyncratic. Even when the challenger is highly skeptical, the respondent's ideas are usually fully and systematically explored.

Similarly, in an illustrative debate we will take up further at the end of this chapter (I.1, "The Customary Truth of Common Sense Practices") although the clarifier would prefer to ignore the tangential contribution of L" at 3:05:(16), the structure of their formal analytic praxis in debate compels the clarifier *to listen* to the respondent's point regarding a lack of realization. His listening improves the chances that his opponent will listen as well. Although the debate has grown heated and contentious, both parties are able to hear each other:

3:05:(16) L" Kind sir, you seem to be saying that "to establish" means only "to realize."

T Uhh, it says, *"Such a valid customary terminological cognition is incapable of establishing the falsity of ignorant habits of routine conceptualization that contaminate our awareness."* That "valid customary terminological cognition" is not what is generally considered to be a valid cognition, it must be considered to be a

3:05:22   mundane, everyday kind of valid cognition. >~ If it is not reckoned to be a mundane, everyday kind of cognition, right, then it would become an incorrect statement, wouldn't it?

The clarifier here informed me that he was irritated by the respondent's failure to take up the principal lines of inquiry he was attempting to present, and so he tried to ignore the respondent's comment at 3:05:(16). When reviewing the tape of the debate, he told me, "I'm not listening to him. I am going for the debate." He attempts to shut the respondent off with a respectable citation. But the respondent is not having any of it and perseveres with his concern:

:24 L" Kind sir, kind sir, you must distinguish an "establishing" from a "realization," do you not?

:28 T   No, not that one. That's not it at all.

T again tries to move past the distraction to his own point, but L" is persistent, so T interrupts with another recitation of the authoritative citation:

3:05:30 L" The mind that establishes and the one that realizes are two different ones.

T   Oh yes. These are different, but even though this is so, it doesn't affect the matter here.

L" Oh! Because it is that way, Rinpoche,[1] here you have—

T   He wrote, "*Such a valid conceptual cognition is incapable of establishing the falsity of ignorant habits of routine conceptualization that contaminate our awareness*," did he not?

:37 L" Oh yes.

Finally T addresses the respondent's specific point, and then L" begins to pay better attention.

T   When he says, "incapable of establishing," he is speaking about a lack of realization.

:39 L" Oh, when he says, "incapable of establishing."

T   Why does he say it like that? A consciousness that is contaminated by an ignorant habit of routine conceptualization is said to be something like a reification of an entity as having inherently true existence. There is a mistaken consciousness like that. It says that the valid customary terminological cognition is incapable of real-

:45   izing its falsity. >~

L' Oh, this is right.

L" Oh, this is exactly right.

---

1. "Rinpoche" is a term of address for reincarnated lamas, such as T of Debate I.1 is.

Brought more closely together by means of the dialectics, the respondents are able to listen to the clarifier's reasoning, and they can come to some agreement. The structure of the debating and its rapid give and take are oriented to keeping the debaters focused upon mutual concerns.

Many of the other features of Tibetan debating that we have examined contribute to the adequacy of communication. Persons who are only casually familiar with Tibetan debate sometimes remark upon how much "rote" repetition it seems to contain; however, the continual repeating of phrases is essential to the successful objectivation of notions that provides the clarity for the communication. The longer REHEARSALS of ground already covered in a debate are not mere dumb, mindless repetitions but a carefully orchestrated effort to erect a common ground (see 124-125) and to establish a rhythm. Those REVERSALS in which the negative form of a proposition precedes its rejection, to be followed by the (usually correct) positive form which is accepted, can lend elegance to a debate's *choreography*, a phenomenon that is missed almost entirely by Tibetologists. These are collaborative efforts that serve to energize a debate by producing a rhythm that is vital to Tibetan dialectical practice and which identifies its uniqueness as a philosophical enterprise. If one wishes to capture Tibetan Buddhist philosophy in a scientific and phenomenologically adequate way, one must capture it *as* dialectics and resist any temptation to reduce it to abridged summaries of theses abstracted from the real-world relations that engendered them (but afford ready comparison with corresponding European notions). In Tibetan philosophical culture formal reasoning is always materially embodied in the rhythmic forms of their dialectical practice. The intellectual dance that this practice can become when it is properly choreographed assists the readiness of each party to listen to the other.

It has been my experience that philosophical discussion among Western academics only seldom affords genuine opportunities for scholars to influence their colleagues, especially when those colleagues hold differing tenets. It is the rare "conference" that succeeds in getting each of the participants to listen to each other well, and I have attended many panel sessions, consisting of scholars who supposedly share the same subdiscipline, in which the proponents of competing perspectives carry on like two ships passing in the night, hardly sharing even the same language. During one of my extended stays in a Tibetan monastery in India, I was invited by the lay Tibetan community that surrounded the monastery to be one of the judges for a contemporary-styled forensic debate among Tibetan high school students. The debates were held on the stage of the community's auditorium, and there were several hundred people in attendance. The students were as competent as bright high school students are anywhere. But having just come from the monastery's debating courtyard the previous evening, I could not help but be impressed by how the forensic debating consisted principally of alternating monologues. Occasionally there was an occasion to negate directly the opposing analysis, giving thinkers the opportunity to learn what they may not have considered or anticipated, and there were moments where the participants listened to each other; however, such opportunities were considerably fewer in number than those provided by the classical Tibetan Buddhist system of public disputations. Gary Alan Fine (2001, 116) comments upon the limited role of dialogue in American forensic debate: "Debaters are talking *at* each other, not *with* each other." It is noteworthy that while Fine (23) mentions at the outset of his book-length monograph that "to be a debater is to be a talker—and a listener," the study, titled *Gifted Tongues*, is mostly a presentation about talking, and listening does not receive so much as a subsection worth of attention. This is not Fine's oversight, since he is being entirely faithful to his phenomenon. The brevity of turns at argumentation in Tibetan debating leads more readily to dialogue, and there is a greater arsenal of tools at hand with which Tibetan debaters are able to force the other to pay attention to the intricacies of one's thinking. These tools, such as the hand-clap, the TS'A, "PUT-UP OR SHUT-UP" (i.e., the *ste*—), etc., comprise what Tibetan scholars speak of as the *phul ba* or "forcing," which refers to the intensity with which a Tibetan debater is required to keep his nose to grindstone of contending argumentation. When the dialectics proceeds within the regimen of working under the critical eye of the TS'A, one is apt to pay close attention, thereby improving the prospects for communication.

Exposing a Lack of Clarity (the *phul ba*)

The hand-clap, which indicates that an utterance is intended to have some formal analytic status, is the most elementary of interactional tools in Tibetan debating; however, it has the capacity to bear considerable rhetorical force. When one perceives that the clap consists of a wind-up during which the challenger raises his right hand high above his head, often with his left foot raised in the air to waist level, and the right hand terminating on the open palm of the left hand, which is resting only a few inches from the respondent's nose (see the video illustrations on the CD-ROM, in the section, "The Grammar of a Tibetan Debate"), one can appreciate how effective it can be for securing a respondent's attention. Although it may seem unnecessarily physical, even violent, for philosophical discourse, it is efficacious for establishing the conditions for philosophical dialogue. In this short excerpt from III.1, the challenger is running a tight ship and is trying to force the defenders to listen to his point:

-084- T Professor, you need to address the way the mind can visualize the object corresponding to the coarse and subtle four noble truths. [L' laughs.] Except for the explanation required for the way one cultivates the capacity to visualize the subtle and coarse aspects of the four truths / there should be no explanation regarding whether or not one has abandoned the obstructions to meditation.

L'   / What?
L"   [to L'] (unclear). If one abandons the obscurations appropriate for
     this level, the mind will become transformed, right? //

The defenders are so preoccupied with their own reflections that they are
unable to hear well what the challenger is attempting to put forward. Therefore,
T presents a simple hand-clap that is unaccompanied by any words. This is so
effective that it forces the defenders to snap out of their self-absorption and attend to his argument:

9:34:09 T   // >~
L'   The mind will become transformed (*blo 'gyur*), the mind will be-
     come transformed. What is called mentally transformative activity
     is able to transform the mind. [L' and L" yell together.] One will
     be able to transform the mind and develop a thoroughly accom-
     plished capacity.
L"   This [referring to T's contention] is not right.

Together, these devices, including the hand-clap, the call to PUT-UP OR
SHUT-UP by a challenger, and the "CHEE-CHEER" [WHAT IS THE REA-
SON?] response by a defender, etc., serve as a vigil over the attentiveness of the
participants. As Dreyfus (n.d., XIV.14) observes, "Attention and concentration
. . . are important in debate where both parties need to keep track of the chain of
consequences," and these vigorous devices help to maintain that attention. The
pain on the expression of the defender (cf. photo I.6 4:50:15 on the separately
issued CD-ROM) reveals his discomfort when the challenger calls upon the him
to explain what he has just then agreed to accept. It can require considerable
intellectual courage to face such persistent forcing without losing one's concentration. Prior to this (at 4:48) the defender had been gaily participating in the
debate's synchronized rhythm of utterances, almost inattentive to his own
words; but the challenger insists that the defender put some meat behind his
empty slogans, and the challenger does this by teasing the defender (at 4:48:05):

4:48   L"   In the main, the Syllogism-based Reasoning School speaks of the
            conceptually acquired view of an ego reified as a self-sufficiently
            existent, independent person. In this sense, a self-sufficiently exis-
            tent, independent person and a permanent, partless, and autono-
            mous person are the same; so we speak of it like this.
:05   T   [to audience] What did he say? [to L"] You're speaking too fast.
            [Laughter]

At this point, the abbot of the monastery, who was in attendance at the debate, smiles in appreciation of the humor of the challenger's move (see photo
I.6, 4:48:08). The stratagem successfully forces L" into developing a formulation that is more articulate.

L" I said this, right? Our lower schools discern the emptiness of being a self-sufficiently existent, independent person and the emptiness of being a permanent, partless, and autonomous person as having a difference in their subtlety; however, in our view [i.e., the view of the Dialectical Reasoning School] there is no great difference. The lower schools speak of an ego as something that is self-sufficiently existent and independently established. The Dialectical Reasoning Middle Way School speaks of this as only a conceptually acquired view of an ego.

If one does not push one's logic (*rigs pas phul ba*[2]), it may be that a meaningful debate will never take place because the debate will lack the sharpness and acuity necessary for deep reflection. As I have observed, when the respondent is only moving along with the surface structure of the debate, agreeing without really knowing the issues at stake, pushing is justifiable. In our next excerpt (I.4), T scolds L", who merely insults T's proposal (T is deliberately formulating what he knows to be the opposite of L"'s position) without offering any argumentation, pressuring L" into making a substantive contribution:

T In our system, if there is a mental positing there must be an object. And if there is a conceptual projection, an object does not necessarily exist. It's like this, right?

L" You can take this notion and depart! [Audience laughter.]

3:43:48 T Now you PRESENT. >~ You PRESENT how it is.

The intensity of a challenger's ridicule has the capacity to prompt a respondent into an insightful exegesis of his views.

Ridicule, argument by absurd consequences, deliberate obfuscation, etc.— what are the benefits of such practices? Making matters difficult for a partner requires that he display some excellence. One must know what one thinks and why one thinks it. If dialectics is to be effective, real philosophy must somehow transcend the talk. One has to be qualified to do philosophy because it is more than just talk—it is thinking. By eliciting contradictions in a debater's thinking, shortcomings in his studies or understanding may be exposed and remedied. It is indeed exegesis by push and shove, but it bears some philosophical vitality. The more control one can gain in concentration, self-reflection, attentiveness, etc., the better will one be able to think, and to communicate that thinking.

In Tibetan debating the challenger is trying to influence the thinking of the defender, and the defender is trying to influence the thinking of the challenger. How can both be effective at once? It is the role of rhetoric to gain the attention

---

2. *Phul ba* literally means "to put" or "to present," but its meaning for Tibetan scholars implies a degree of force, as in *dpung phul* (Tsong Khapa 1997, 756), which means "forceful putting." Following the sense of my Tibetan teacher Khensur Lobsang Tsering, I have translated this key figure, so descriptive of Tibetan debate, as "pushing."

of the other party, and rhetoric is part of the communicative competence of their system of philosophical reflection. Rhetoric involves the art of understanding and of making oneself understood, and so the persuasive ability to convince others is part of the expertise. As one of my Tibetan colleagues reminded me on the debating grounds, "You have to push!" The success of this facility is to be measured by how well it serves for gaining the attention of one's partner and for facilitating becoming engaged with the thinking of the other. When it is working well, the moments of dialogue in Tibetan debating will outnumber the moments of monologue.

The "*ste*—": "Put-Up or Shut-Up"

The very formality of formal analytic reasoning permits debaters to communicate with each other well and allows philosophical questions to become public matters. And as a debater gains fluency with the philosophical forms, he is able to prance through his arguments with some confidence. While such confidence can add energy and rhythmic pacing to a debate, it can also close a thinker off to further exploration of pertinent issues. When such a debater is challenged face-to-face with the perspective and criticism of another, he can be halted in his tracks and forced to reflect upon his positions in a more original way. One may know how to argue lucidly, but does one also know how to hear, how to alter one's view when it becomes necessary, and how to open oneself up for being transformed by the dialectics at work? The relentless questioning of notions in Tibetan debates helps to mitigate the myopia of self-confidence that expertise with formal analytics so easily produces, and it can compel Tibetan scholars to reassess their thinking.

Whereas in most conversations it is easy to "pass" as a competent listener, the intensive dialectical format of Tibetan debate requires the continual monitoring and display of communicative competence. One cannot just "get by" with a smile and a nod—all too frequently one must put-up or shut-up. What may be grasped initially only as a slogan, a vague received notion, or a serendipitous piece of sophistry can under dialectical challenge acquire some philosophical specificity. Any lack of clarity in one's understanding may become exposed, whereas without dialectical challenge one's own lack of clarity can more easily pass unrecognized. Husserl (1970a, 615) contrasts facile assent with an internalized understanding of a judgment:

> Straightforward agreement often is thought of as assent, while true assent consists in the complex experience where a perceived or presented judgment leads to a phase of questioning, which in its turn finds fulfillment in the corresponding actual judgment.

True assent, then, involves more than logistics; it consists of more than just getting the wording correct. It involves understanding the philosophical significance of what the words describe, and so ultimately it relates to an experience. A question for a philosophical anthropology is how can engaging with the words lead to such an experience, or, how is experience to be integrated with the logical structure of formal thinking so as to guarantee the originality of its thought?

The facilities in Tibetan debate for pulling a partner up short and forcing him to move beyond the words provides some opportunities for experience to be introduced into their philosophizing. In this short dialogue, T forces the defender out of any complacent, straightforward assent:

> T TAKE THE CASE OF a cloud, IT FOLLOWS THAT it lacks an intrinsic identity. >~
>
> L I ACCEPT.
>
> T PRESENT [*yin ste*] why it lacks an intrinsic identity.

The *yin ste*[3] forces one to add some insight to one's positions and to know why one thinks what one does. When a defender offers a gratuitous assent, such as the "Exactly, exactly, exactly" in I.9 6:09:18, a challenger can force him out of his facile sureness with a *ste*— or with a skillful use of reversals.[4] When a defender tries to waffle his way through the reply to a query, the challenger can cry out, "So DECIDE!" (*thag chod zhog*). As Dreyfus (n.d., VI.1) observes, "The kind of full internalization that [Tibetan debaters] seek cannot be achieved solely through retrieval [of received notions]. A moment of suspicion must intervene in order for the understanding of the text's content to be brought to fruition." The negation provided here is a challenge to explain one's understanding more fully, and it compels Tibetan debaters to reflect philosophically.

A good deal of the effectiveness of the social organizational item that is the "*ste*—" is that it comes extremely quickly, and the exegesis that it calls for must be delivered without any hesitation. A delay of even a few seconds will leave a debater open for ridicule by the audience as well as the opponent. In this illustration from II.6, the respondent formally rejects the position put forward by the clarifier of the reasoning, and the clarifier retorts by calling for the respondent to provide an immediate exegesis:

> T Oh yes, oh yes. But please listen! We say, for example, the path of liberation at the first level—
>
> L' Yes.
>
> -058.5- T —is capable of invoking the direct antidote to the grossest innate
> 9:52:12 habits. >~

---

3. Note that in Tibetan grammar the verb, here the "*yin ste*," is placed at the *end* of the sentence, just prior to the defender's reply. I frequently prefer to spell *ste*— with a hyphen, in order to indicate its proximate connection with the defender's reply, which must follow immediately. "*Ste*—" is pronounced sharply, "tey!"

4. For the strategic use of reversals, see 169-170.

L' Oh it can? THE REASON—it is capable of invoking that—IS NOT ESTABLISHED.
T   Oh yah?!
L' THE REASON—it is capable of invoking that—IS NOT ESTAB-LISHED.
T   And why is it not capable? [*ma yin ste*— ?]

The "*ste*—" shoves the defender out of his complacency in II.3, where the debaters are dealing with the issues of faith in ultimate freedom and an understanding of what ultimate freedom means, L' cycles through a number of widely accepted slogans about the matter, mostly with T's complicity, until T abruptly demands, "Why is it necessary that a mind that is intent upon achieving freedom fully understand it? [*yin ste*—] >~" T's hand-clap reinforces the inescapable immediacy of his demand for an explanation.

What is useful about the PUT-UP OR SHUT-UP, that is, the "*ste*—", is that a respondent cannot rely upon the terms alone. He must be capable of providing in public an understanding for any term he uses, on call. Similarly, when the respondent replies to a challenger's assertion with "CHEE-CHEER" [*ci phyir*] or "WHAT IS THE REASON?" the challenger must be capable of publicly displaying an understanding of his own argument. One sure benefit of these facilities is to expose false reasoning to the light of public scrutiny and to provide opportunities for correcting and deepening the debaters' understanding. This leads to thinking that is less muddled and to interpretations that are less riddled with idiosyncrasy since the analyses are developed collaboratively. It is the function of dialectics to get thinkers out of their being locked within their own reasoning. When it is practiced regularly it can develop a thinker's flexibility and dexterity in handling concepts. Merely fitting one's formulations into the logic being celebrated may be a practice that is insufficient for real philosophical reflection.

But what benefit is there to deliberately confusing a debate partner, when he need not have been confused at all? In II.1 while discussing the difference between appearance and reality and contrasting the cases of an image in a mirror and the inherent self-existence of a pot, T works the defender into a resolution of the dissimilarities in these two cases that is incompatible with a citation from a well-known textbook. It seems as though the mistake in the defendant's reasoning was set with the challenger's own cement, a successful effort at deliberate obfuscation. But the perpetual risk of such diabolical tactics requires respondents to actually know why they believe what they affirm. In chapter 3, I discussed the case where the entire audience ganged up on a respondent who was advocating a correct view, and the respondent eventually came to reverse his position and adopt the incorrect thesis. When a challenger solicits a wrong commitment and begins to confuse a defendant, it is best to stick with one's own insight and not be too pliable in the face of a challenger's onslaught. Thereby one may develop the capacity to think for oneself, and a certain resoluteness in one's reflections may be fostered.

When the possibility always exists for the challenger to deliberately fool the respondent, a defender may be nudged into a more objective orientation to the questions because he cannot rely upon the durability of any emerging dichotomy in the contending views, a situation that necessitates that each reply must be evaluated on its own merits. If only by compulsion, one learns to treat each new reflection in a fresh way. Dreyfus (2002, 262) describes how he coped with the instability and sometimes suffocating pressure of Tibetan dialectics: "The trick in answering is to be open, unconcerned by the final outcome, just focused on the topic." And Dreyfus (2002, 268) reports that there is "an exhilarating sense of openness that comes from the inquiry that debate supports."

Further, when one knows that any reply can be challenged and that a call for a fuller explanation can come at any time, a respondent is forced to consider each one of his answers carefully, even those that never face any challenge. And one cannot quit thinking further when one answers correctly, for one can never be entirely certain about one's correctness since the dynamics of these dialectics keep many matters in suspension for a considerable time. This obligates a respondent to examine the nature of a philosophical problem more carefully than if he facilely discovered that his answer was the correct one, and allowed his attention to relax.

Throughout Tibetan debating the clarity of the argumentation is related to the tightness of its apophantics, and this tightness in turn is allied with the speed of the utterances. Why is speed such a virtue? Are there not occasions where one might benefit from an opportunity to reflect quietly without being suffocated by the immanent demand to respond? It seems counterintuitive that a tradition like the Tibetans, which places such a premium upon the clarity that is provided by meditation, should race through their dialectics at such a gallop. It may be that a sharp mind, one that has been cultivated in part by a meditative contemplation of epistemological issues, ought to be able to respond lucidly without procrastination. In any event, the Tibetan method has the benefit that any lack of clarity in one's thinking will become apparent when one is shoved by the *ste—* into unforeseen uncertainties.

Negative Dialectics (*thal gzhag*)

Theodor Adorno (2000, 137) observed, "Ideas gain their depth by chafing against each other." The founder of the Gelug order Tsong Khapa endorsed a similar sentiment, "We subject whatever system of reasoning we face to objections and rebuttals (*brgal len*)," and the Gelug scholars I studied with follow this advice. In reply to my question regarding how difficult it is in everyday life to

retain the emptiness view, my teacher Lobsang Tsering, who at the time was
abbot of the monastic university, replied,

> We Buddhists do it like this [claps his hands as in a debate]—we do negative
> dialectics.[5] We spend many years debating philosophical matters in this way.
> You haven't done so; therefore, you're not going to be able to understand eve-
> rything right away.

Here it is evident that the abbot associates negative dialectics with a capacity for penetrative understanding, and his suggestion is that when one carries
into one's everyday life a praxis of negative dialectics that has been internalized
one will be capable of sustaining profound philosophical insights, including the
recognition that phenomena lack the inherent essences that we project upon
them. The course of study for such a method, which is a way of being as much
as it is a way of understanding, involves many years not only of textual studies
but of exposing one's thinking to the negations repeatedly offered by one's colleagues while engaging in philosophical debates.

During his daily classes, Lobsang Tsering would prefer to debate with his
students rather than lecture them about the issues that arose during the textual
portions to be discussed on a given day, and he would challenge their thinking
with astute arguments punctuated by formal hand-claps. His purpose seemed to
be two-fold—first, he wanted to prepare them for the arguments they would
likely face later in the day during the courtyard debating and offer them some
practice in formulating their retorts; secondly, he wanted to stir their thinking
out of any complacency. Dreyfus (2002, 288) makes a similar observation about
his teacher at another monastic university: "In Gen Nyi-ma's teaching, no answer was allowed to stand as final. . . . He would use debate as a way to undermine students' attempt to stop the investigation and lock their mind on any answer, [including] the right one." Another Gelug scholar, Geshe Lhundrup Sopa,
who was an examiner of the current Dalai Lama when they resided in Lhasa and
who later came to the University of Wisconsin where he was a professor for
more than thirty years, punctuates his discourses with challenges to his students,
tempting them with clever arguments that are deliberately flawed. Even when
his students (myself among them) propose a correct philosophical view, he will
undermine them with diabolical reasoning that will expose whatever inconsistencies exist in their positions. *The function of such practices is to drive scholars
into more original thinking.*

This tendency to find some way to confuse the thinker is very local work,
and I have attempted to display the details of that work in previous chapters: one
forces a defender into one commitment and then seeks to push him into a contradictory commitment by means of negative dialectics, such as arguments by

---

5. "*Nang pa la 'dug zer* [hand-clap] *byad ba 'di. Thal gzhag byad yag.*" I have translated *thal gzhag* as "negative dialectics"; more literally, it means "to force the consequences."

absurd consequences and the like. As we have observed, there are occasions when no matter what answer one gives, it will be declared erroneous. When a challenger has confidently prepared a line of correct argumentation, a defender—as well as the attending audience—may yell "NOT ESTABLISHED" no matter how well it has been argued, in an attempt to spill the protagonist off of any unsteady pedestal. If the platform is truly solid then the challenger will be steadfast and he will win his point; but if he has any hesitation the tactics will lead him to dream his worst fears about his own arguments. In this fashion, negative dialectics play with scholars' minds; however, it does not do so only out of sophistry but with the intention of training them in thinking logically. Tsong Khapa (n.d. b, 263) cites Chandrakirti's *Madhyamakavara*[6] approvingly: "Our analyses of philosophical treatises are not performed out of a love of analytic disputation but to explicate the nature of reality so that people will be liberated." That said, it should be noted that the actual use of negative dialectics in the Tibetans' daily debating sessions is frequently more combative than this recommendation would lead one to surmise.

These practices demonstrate that Tibetan philosophical debate consists of more than the routine articulation of formal reasonings memorized by rote. Faced with negative dialectics, Dreyfus (2002, 268) concludes, "They wanted to know whether I was able to go beyond what the text was saying, whether I was able to question the concepts of the text rather than accept them as self-evident." The highly original way in which teachers and colleagues explore reasoning is praised by Dreyfus (n.d., X.15): "There is another kind of questioning that refuses to remain prisoner of the text and seeks to open the text by reading it against itself and questioning its authority. It is this critical and at times deconstructive strategy that I find present in Tibetan debate."[7]

One such instance of reading a text against itself was presented in the excerpt presented on 138, where in I.1 the clarifier of the reasoning forces the respondent to accept something that turns out to be inconsonant with an authoritative text, a textual passage that the clairifer himself wishes to call into question:

T	TAKE AS THE SUBJECT the reification of an entity as having inherently true existence. IT FOLLOWS THAT it is distorted
3:08:44	common sense. >~
L'	/ IT IS ACCEPTABLE!
L"	/ IT IS ACCEPTABLE!

Having secured their agreement, T pulls the rug out from under them:

---

6. Chapter 6, stanza 118.

7. In his 2002 book, Dreyfus comments, "This interpretive strategy follows some of the same principles found in Derrida's deconstructive supplementation."

> T   IT DOES NOT FOLLOW THAT it is distorted common sense. IT
>   FOLLOWS THAT a person whose thinking does not understand
>   emptiness does not necessarily realize that it is a distorted con-
> 3:08:49   sciousness. >~
> 3:08:50 L' IT IS ACCEPTABLE.
>   L"   IT IS ACCEPTABLE.

Now that their thinking has been opened by having to confront contradictory positions, T points out that their latter position is in contradiction with the
text, and he leaves them to sort it out for a time:

> T   The text says that it is necessary,[8] and you have contradicted the
>   text, whose contents seems to have slipped from your memory.
> L'   The citation refers only to what appears to mundane consciousness.
> T   Yah. This is a contradiction due to memory lapse, is it not?
> L"   What?
> T   If it is common sense and it pervades that it is distorted common
>   sense, TAKE AS THE SUBJECT *"the reification of an entity as
>   having inherently true existence."* Now, yahh, *"That FOLLOWS
> 3:09   BECAUSE of this reason."*
> L'   There is a statement like that.
> L"   Oh. Oh. This is right.

Now the way is prepared for the respondents to consider T's criticism of the
text itself. The monastic textbook *General Explanation of the Meaning of the
Middle Way* contends that understanding that noema[9] do not exist in the way
that they appear does not entail an understanding of emptiness, whereas the understanding that the phenomena intended by noema do not exist in the way that
they appear does entail an understanding of emptiness, and the clarifier of the
reasoning here wishes to challenge this authoritative contention. First T reviews
what the debate has achieved:

> T   When pot appears to the thought that apprehends a pot, and one
>   realizes that it does not exist in the way that it appears—
> L'   Mm.

---

8. Cf. Jetsun Chogyi Gyaltsen (1997, 286).

9. *don spyi.* Although some translators prefer to use the term "meaning generality"
to translate *don spyi*, it is less germane (an instance of a correct literal translation that
communicates its sense poorly) than the phenomenological term "noema" as it is used by
Husserl and contemporary Continental philosophers. A noema, like a *don spyi*, is not a
consciousness though it is an ideality produced by a consciousness and facilitates the
intentional relationship between a consciousness and the object that the consciousness
apprehends. That is, a noema coordinates and stabilizes the sense that is projected upon
an object.

3:10:19 T   —yeahh, one must realize the suchness that is based upon the pot.
              >~

       L'   /Yes.

       L"   /Yes.

       T   Ohhh. Why is that necessary, huh?

   :21 L'   The pot does not exist in the way that it appears.

   :54 T   ... For the thought of a pot, when one realizes that a pot does not
              exist in the way that it appears, IT FOLLOWS THAT one neces-

   :58   sarily realizes emptiness. >~

       L'   I ACCEPT.

Now T introduces his own position regarding the relation of an understanding of
noema to an understanding of emptiness, but the defenders prefer to remain with
the orthodox interpretation about noema and they reject his proposal:

       T   If that is so, when one realizes that the noema of a pot does not
              exist in the way that it appears IT FOLLOWS THAT one neces-

3:11:02   sarily realizes emptiness. >~

       L'   The noema of a pot for the thought that apprehends a pot—CHEE-
              CHEER, indeed.

       L"   CHEE-CHEER. It's not necessary. It's not necessary.

   :04 T   TAKE AS THE SUBJECT the noema of a pot. It also appears to
              the thought apprehending a pot as if it was established as truly

   :08   existing. >~

       L'   /Yes.

       L"   /Yes. That's correct.

T finally offers a summary formulation of the defenders' position:

3:11:09 T   Now, although it is like that, for the thought that apprehends a pot,
              yahh. When one realizes that the pot, for example, that appears to a
              thought that apprehends a pot does not exist in the way that it ap-
              pears, one necessarily realizes emptiness. When one realizes that
              the noema of a pot that appears to a thought that apprehends a pot
              does not exist   in the way that it appears, one does not necessarily
              realize emptiness.

3:11:19   What is the reason for this? >~

To review this difficult but philosophically rewarding excerpt, having already opened up the defenders' thinking by confronting them with their contradictory positions (cf. 3:08:49-3:09), T then uses the logic implicit in the reasoning that the noema of a pot, being a conceptual event and not a sense-
consciousness, should entail a hermeneutics of emptiness similar to that of the
conceptual misunderstanding of the being of the pot. In this way T has employed

the logic of the text against itself and used negative dialectics to find his way to a reflection that is original.

Some of my Tibetan colleagues have reported to me that when they are debating in the position of a defender, they may deliberately commit to a thesis that they know is incorrect just for the challenge of defending it. Is this a healthy philosophical practice or mere sophistry? One Tibetan scholar described to me, "When I find that I have given a wrong answer, sometimes I keep going as far as I can go with even the wrong answer to try to prove it is correct. In this way the benefit is to get new ideas, and also to train the mind in analysis." Not only can such a challenge develop scholars' dexterity with concepts, it can assist debaters in locating and overcoming weaknesses in their thinking, which is part of the purpose of dialectics. It has some affinity with a scientific perspective, in that one knows that the currently held thesis is flawed in some way, and that there is benefit in exposing those flaws. As one informant put it enthusiastically, it is a way of discovering "new information." Also, older students will answer incorrectly in order to give to younger clarifiers of reasoning some practice at working things out or "getting new *rigs pa* [formal understanding]," as it was put to me.

Another common practice is to use irony to highlight a good idea. Such use of irony assists debaters to deepen their understanding of vital matters (II.4):

	T	If one understands the way of positing how all phenomena are conceived according to imputations—right?—must one recognize
9:30:33		that concepts are merely imputations? >~
-033-	L	Yes.
	T	One must, right?
	L'	Yes.
	T	Now —
:40	L"	—If one understands the way of positing it. /
-035-	L'	/ If one understands the way of positing it, must one come to realize it?
	L"	It's a little bit (unclear) when one knows how to posit it.
	L'	Understanding how to posit it is a little easier than realizing it.
:49	L"	When it is said that concepts are mere imputations, then we can develop a formulation for that. There is a way of formulating the notion isn't there?
	L'	We know how to formulate it, right? If it is accomplished, then it is really grasped; however, if we say, "It is realized," it is not necessarily a realization, right?
9:31	T	So, if one understands how to posit that concepts are merely imputations, IT FOLLOWS THAT one does not necessarily realize
:02		that concepts are merely imputations. >~

:04 L' What did you say? If one understands how to posit it, huh? It is not necessary.

By formulating the irony, T permits the debaters to savor the quandary.

In Tibetan debating the productivity of the formal apophansis does not depend so much upon the resolution of the truth of a matter as it does upon an apposite display of the philosophical dilemma being addressed. The objective is not always to solve a quandary but to sustain it before the gaze of the scholars. During the annual examinations a panel of senior teachers evaluates each debater. What the evaluators are rating is not the correctness of the propositions, nor even the rectitude of the argumentation, but the extent to which an examination of a philosophical issue has been fecund.[10] As Cabezón (1994, 85) has observed, "What determines someone's ability as a debater? Strangely enough, it has little to do with winning. In Tibetan formal disputations there is rarely any talk of victory or defeat." At its best, the goal of Tibetan debating is to bring a philosophical dilemma or contradiction to life, so that it may be experienced in an intimate way, or even better, so that the way that the mind works can be made visible. There is hidden here, perhaps, a notion of truth that may be at some variance with the more static and certain truth of European scholarship, one that is more attuned to the necessarily dynamic context in which, and as which, any truth worthy of the name operates. Dreyfus (2002, 200) comments,

> In both [modernist and logicist] approaches, reasoning is evaluated from the point of view of its providing deductive certainty. This assumption goes back to the beginnings of Western modernity. . . . Logical argumentation is seen by most European thinkers as limited to deduction, which is based on and aims at certainty. . . . Tibetan debates are *dialectical practices* aimed at reaching greater understanding and developing virtues such as a spirit of inquiry and critical acumen.

A *compulsion* for deductive certainty may not be in force as strongly in Tibetan dialectics, since the aim frequently is to simply open up the movement of a course of thinking so that its work and nature may be scrutinized. There are numerous occasions during which the project of settling upon the single correct philosophical position is eclipsed by the task of developing an inquiry that facilitates the parties coming to witness the activity of some conceptualization *in its flow*. For this to succeed, the in-the-course complexion of conceptualizing must be captured *in vivo*, and displayed as such without losing its character as an actual event of the life-world. Since this is a task for Tibetan debaters, social researchers have an obligation not to lose this phenomenon when representing Tibetan philosophical problems.

---

10. This is a generalization—some Tibetans complain of a few evaluators who are overly swayed by ruffles and flourishes that are irrelevant to the fecundity of the reflections.

During our examination of logical strategies in debate, we reviewed a classic case of suckering a defender into accepting an absurd consequence (see III.2, 179-183). The clarifier of the reasoning here was rated second out of fifty-three debaters examined in his class because of the deftness with which he sustained a vital philosophical quandary before the gaze of the debaters. Let us examine this debate further, not as a docile text (which as a readily tameable phenomenon lends itself more readily to the European preference for stasis in matters of truth) but with an eye for following the dialectics as a course of developing reflection. The debate involves another attempt to sort out what must be rejected about notions that are reified by a praxis of understanding that concretizes its conceptualizations and what must be accepted about the objects that are being understood, in order to avoid a nihilistic solipsism. Each school of Buddhist philosophy draws the line between what does exist (the world) and what does not exist (what is produced by our projections) at a different location. Here the clarifier begins by inquiring whether the object that is apprehended appears in an identical way to each of the philosophical schools, with the differences among them lying only in the degree to which their methods deconstruct or refute what has been imputed. T commences the debate by exploring the refutations of two philosophical schools, suggesting that the objects that appear to them are grasped initially in the same way.

III.2 "Does Wisdom Formulate Emptiness As Existing?"

-000-   T   DHII![11] TAKE SUCH A SUBJECT. The two Middle Way objects of refutation do not appear differently to the mind. NOW IT FOLLOWS THAT one cannot say that the actual appearance of the object to be refuted appears differently to the mind. >~

-004.5- L"   Generally, its establishment from the side of the basis for any conceptual designation must be presented, isn't it? One must present the object to be refuted.

        T   First the objects to be refuted for the two Middle Way Schools must be presented.

With the topic of the debate organized, the debaters now turn to the first object to be refuted:

        L"   How is it said? Hence, generally how is it said? An object that is not present merely through the force of appearing to the mind is posited as existing in its own uncommon mode of abiding from the side of the basis for any conceptual distinction, right?

Audience   That's one.

---

11. "DHII!" is an invocation from the mantra associated with the god of wisdom, Manjushri. It is used frequently for commencing debates.

    L" One is to be established as existing on the side of only the basis for any conceptual designation; one must present this object of refutation, mustn't one?

-007- T That is correct . . .

-009-   Now for example, according to the Syllogistic-based Reasoning School, when one speaks of how the object to be refuted must be presented—

    L" One can present an object that is not present merely through the force of appearing to the mind but whose uncommon mode of abiding is to exist from the side of the basis for any conceptual designation.

The phenomena articulated by the Syllogistic-based Reasoning School have a bit more real substantive existence left after refutation than do phenomena for the Dialectical Reasoning School. T summarizes briefly what they have considered and poses a difference between the two schools:

    T "Present through the force of appearing to the mind," and the mind spoken of when we say, "posited by the mind" are two different ones, aren't they?

And L' and L" reply,

    L" The Dialectical School's way is to say "posited by the mind," is it not?

-015- L' There is a difference between the two—"present through the force of appearing to the mind" and "posited by the mind." There is, isn't there?

It seemed to be T's intention to turn the idea that the perceived objects in fact appear to the mind in identical ways, since their appearance takes place *before* the application of any methods of philosophical refutation. This would be somewhat ironic since the two schools' objects of refutation differ substantially; however, L' and L" (tipped off by a member of the audience) are astute enough to accurately anticipate the direction of T's thinking:

Audience Here maybe they're the same.
    L" They're the same here.
    L' Are they the same?
    L" Yes yes.
    L' Are they the same?
    L" Yes yes.

Since this leaves T without anything to debate, he takes up another issue, the fascinating matter of what is the nature of an understanding of emptiness and the extent to which that understanding also involves conceptual formulations about the existence of emptiness. This topic develops somewhat serendipitously as T follows up the defenders' replies dialectically in the dialogue presented on 179-180 (see Illustrative Debate III.2 on the CD-ROM). The series of consequences posed by T acquires its own logic and rhythm, and the quandary to which the debaters find their way to a considerable degree fortuitous, an example of how Tibetan dialectics can occasionally lead to novel and fruitful topics In brief, T gains the defenders' assent to the notion that a pot is "posited" by an eye-consciousness (-021-, 171). Retaining a parallel structure in the formulations of his propositions, T then secures the defenders' assent to the notion that "the nature of things" (*chos nyid*) is "posited" by the wisdom of an Arya's meditative equipoise (-022.5-). T then extends the list of formal commitments to "the nature of things" being "posited" by the wisdom that realizes just how it is (*ji ltar ba*) ((024)). Finally, T extends the commitments of the defenders to an absurd consequence, that "the nature of things" is "formulated" (*'jog*) by the wisdom that realizes just how it is (-024.5-). This is incorrect since any such formulating would tend to reify the existence of things whose empty nature it is to lack the reification we ascribe to it. Formal conceptualization could only interfere with and disturb the sight of a wisdom that realizes just how it is. Once the defenders' commitments extend this far, T is able to bring them up short with a TS'A accompanied by a backward hand-clap:

	T	Well then, TAKE AS THE SUBJECT something like the nature of things, IT FOLLOWS THAT it is formulated by the wisdom that
-024.5-		realizes just how it is. >~
	L'	I ACCEPT.
	L"	I ACCEPT.
-025-	T	Positively, TS'A! =v= You are contradictory! IT FOLLOWS THAT there is no such formulation.

What is important to observe here is that the philosophical issue is not being presented merely in theoretical terms; rather, the thinkers are brought into a direct and immediate confrontation with the inconsistencies that arise naturally in the analysis of emptiness. One is inaccurate whether one says that the existence of emptiness is formulated or is not formulated. And it is this quandary that carries the debaters *closer* to how an understanding of emptiness is to be applied. As I remarked previously, how does one deliberately resolve not to deliberate? It would not be quite as revealing if the dilemma was straightforwardly resolved by a logical calculus; instead, the quandary must be made to live and to stir the debaters out of any complacency. It must be recognized here that the rhythm of the debating greases the wheels with which T has carried the defenders through a chain of consequences that culminates in their accepting this absurd consequence. The success of Tibetan dialectics can never be assessed fairly without respecting how the reasoning is embodied in the aesthetics of skillful logical formatting.

Now T formulates the quandary in a way that calls attention to its irony:

-027- T Although there the nature of things may be formulated as arising through the force of appearing to the mind, it is not formulated so (*'jog kyang mi 'jog*). It's this way is it not?

In fact, the defenders attempt to resolve the quandary by reference to the account of an authoritative text, but the challenger does not wish to reduce the fecundity of the problem here, and he maintains a tight ship by preventing the defenders from distracting themselves from anything except a face-forward confrontation with the crux of the irony:

-031- L' It is said that there is no such formulation that formulates emptiness as existing concretely in the face of the realization that cognizes the nature of things. Do you follow? According to the *Great Digest* —/

        T   /(In the face of the realization...)

-031.5- L" No no.

        L' Now we discuss it, do we?

        T Now we don't need too much talk!

        L" This is said—one does not formulate it as existing concretely; it's the same. It is formulated, but it is not formulated as existing concretely.

        T IT FOLLOWS THAT the wisdom that realizes just how it is,

-033- yah, does not formulate emptiness as existing concretely. >~

T has brought them back to the irony, and they then accept his formulation, but T challenges them to reflect *even more deeply* by offering another backward hand-clap and a TS'A, and in this case the fact that the backward hand-clap *precedes* the utterance of "TS'A" adds to its rhetorical force:

        L" I ACCEPT.

        L' It does not formulate that.

        T =v= TS'A!

If the wisdom does not think anything, how can it realize emptiness? The TS'A brings the quandary to life, conveying the contradiction to the defenders' immediate experience; the defenders learn about the topic by means of a live exploration of it, and with it. Further, T's presentation of the quandary is koan-like, in that the philosophical problems are not resolvable without developing a penetrating insight into the nature of being and emptiness.

L' insists that his answer is correct:

        L' The realization that cognizes such does not formulate that.

And so T objectivates L''s position into an absurdity:

T   IT FOLLOWS THAT the wisdom that realizes just-how-it-is, yah,
-034-   does not formulate emptiness. >~

But L' and L" cannot abide such an absurdity and the condemnation that it implies, for wisdom does depend upon logical reasoning, so they reject T's proposition, but T snaps back with a *ste* (i.e., PUT-UP OR SHUT-UP):

L"   CHEE-CHEER.
L'   CHEE-CHEER!
T   How then is emptiness formulated? [*stong snyid 'jog ste—*]

L' and L" then stumble about, for which they are rewarded with another backward hand-clap and TS'A, and T then formulates a proposition that is just the opposite absurdity of what he proposed at -033-. In this fashion, the debaters hover between two absurdities:

L"   The mind formulates it.
L'   What?
L"   There is a realization of emptiness.
-034.5- T   =v= TS'A indeed! IT FOLLOWS THAT the wisdom that realizes
           just how it is, yah, formulates emptiness as existing concretely. >~

The defenders reply with another chorus of CHEE-CHEER, which is the defender's equivalent of a TS'A, as they are eager to stay away from trouble, but do not mind giving trouble. But T just keeps hammering them with the absurd proposition, repeating it for the sheer joy of it as well as to sustain the quandary, substituting (at -036.5-) "realizes" for "formulates":

-035- L"   CHEE-CHEER.
       L'   CHEE-CHEER. For the system of the *Great Digest*? For the sys-
            tem of the *Great Digest*? You're—
       T   IT FOLLOWS THAT the wisdom that realizes just how it is, yah,
-036-   formulates emptiness as existing concretely. >~
       L'   /CHEE-CHEER.
       L"   /CHEE-CHEER.
       T   IT FOLLOWS THAT emptiness is formulated as existing con-
            cretely—
       L'   What?
       T   —BECAUSE the wisdom that realizes just how it is, yah, realizes
-036.5-   emptiness as existing. >~

In the succeeding line L' rejects the proposition; however, L" elucidates the rejection by observing that there is no logical pervasion (i.e., since the reason itself is a matter not to be directly contradicted, the flaw lies instead with the application of the valid reason to the thesis):

L' "IT FOLLOWS THAT such a realization so cognizes," THE REASON IS NOT ESTABLISHED. Does such a realization pose it so? You were just saying so, were you?

L" What? It must be said that THERE IS NO PERVASION. Now what?

T keeps sustaining the quandary:

-038- T IT FOLLOWS THAT the wisdom that realizes just how it is, formulates emptiness as existing.

L" Mm.

-038.5- T BECAUSE the wisdom that realizes just how it is cognizes emptiness. >~

L' THE REASON IS NOT ESTABLISHED.

T CONFOUNDED BY ALL THREE!!

So we have had here a full display of the principal tools by which Tibetan dialectical reasoning is organized, including the TS'A and CONFOUNDED BY ALL THREE! of the challenger and the CHEE-CHEER, THE REASON IS NOT ESTABLISHED, and the THERE IS NO PERVASION of the defenders. These tools enliven what might otherwise be dry, scholastic inquiry, and they keep the logical discussion well organized. T pursues the core irony further, observing that any cognition must have subtle flaws, rendering suspect the completeness of even wisdom's realization of emptiness:

-042- T When the wisdom that realizes just how it is realizes emptiness as existing, IT MUST FOLLOW THAT the wisdom that realizes just how it is, yah, is a subtle cognition that conceals as a customary practice. IT FOLLOWS THAT there is this flaw. >~

-043-

But L' is not buying into any such heterodox view, and he rejects the idea, only to be faced with T's *ste*:

L' It is not said to be this way. It's not said. This reason is not posited, is it?

T EXPLAIN HOW is it that the wisdom that realizes just how it is

-043.5- does not cognize emptiness as existing? [*ma rtogs ste—*] >~

L' Emptiness is a nonaffirming negation. Emptiness is a nonaffirming negation.

But T presses close dialectically, appropriating L"'s observation into the quandary:

-044- T If emptiness is a nonaffirming negation, does the wisdom that

-044.5- cognizes just how it is, not cognize emptiness as existing? >~

L' then ruminates on a resolution to the quandary,

> L' Oh. That emptiness is an affirming negation. They are the beliefs of an analytic mind (*mos pa rnam dpyod kyi blo yin*). Then how must it be said? It pervades that an established subjectivity is not entailed.
> T (unclear) What?

In order to keep up the dialectics, T must pull L' out of his momentary absorption in his thoughts and back into reciprocal communication, and T does so with a contradictory position and a TS'A:

> L' Oh now. That's exactly right. That's exactly right.
> -046.5- T (unclear), yah, IT FOLLOWS THAT it is established (*sgrub*). >~
> L' CHEE-CHEER!!
> -047- T =v= TSS'A! The established subject (is implied).

T cultivates further ironies that accent the difficulty of the dilemma. The defenders seem willing to go along with T for a while, and T uses the opportunity to take them to *as extreme a view as he can manage*; but when he attempts to objectivate the position that emptiness does not exist (line -058-), the defenders refuse to follow, uttering "CHEE-CHEER!":

> T IT FOLLOWS THAT the wisdom that realizes just how it is does
> 056.5- not cognize emptiness as existing concretely. >~
> L' I ACCEPT.
> T IT FOLLOWS THAT for the wisdom that realizes just how it is, in the face of the realization of just how it is, emptiness does not
> -057- exist. >~
> L' It doesn't, it doesn't, it doesn't.
> L" It does not exist.
> T Oh, IT FOLLOWS THAT the wisdom that realizes just how it is, in the face of the realization of just how it is, emptiness does not
> -058- exist. >~
> L' According to who? "IT FOLLOWS THAT emptiness is non-existent"—CHEE-CHEER!

By skillfully keeping the defenders hovering between acceptance and rejection, T sustains the koan-like character of the inquiry and L' and L" are placed directly in the center of two mutually exclusive possibilities, a condition to which the hermeneutics of emptiness is naturally prone. The very instability of their reflections is the achievement in this debate; that is, the philosophical merit rests precisely in what is not resolved:

> -058.5- T =v= TSS'A! IT FOLLOWS THAT for the wisdom that realizes just how it is, in the face of the realization of just how it is, there
> -059.5- is no cognizer of emptiness as existing concretely. >~

The Productivity of Tibetan Debate

John Dewey (1916, 349) has argued that formal logic has a limited compass, and that the originality of thought is to be derived from sources that are extrinsic to the apophantic work: "Bare logic, however important in arranging and criticizing existing subject matter, cannot spin new subject matter out of itself." However, this may be too harsh of a judgment, since from its abstract vantage point it seems to ignore the serendipitous creativity of the *in vivo* work of thinkers who work with the logic. The formal apophansis can open up new avenues of reflection *when thinkers follow up various structural relations* of its elements and reflect upon the meaning of the unforeseen internal relations of notions.[12] By being confronted with strictly formal relations, structural inconsistencies and the like, thinkers may be driven to gain new insight by contending with these fresh avenues of reflection opened up by the logical apophantics, sometimes intentionally and sometimes blindly. Dewey seems to bifurcate the formal aspects of reasoning and its intuitive aspects, when in fact the two aspects are interdependent, and thinkers work creatively with whatever structure they are confronted. A social phenomenological methodology like ethnomethodology can capture this real world creativity of thinkers working with, through and "beyond"[13] the forms. As Harold Garfinkel has recommended, "Every topic that the Greeks promised us is to be respecified as the work of the ordinary society," that is, as the orderliness of local work.

Husserl (1970) similarly criticizes the formal aspects of thinking, whose methodic routinization can rob reflection of its originality. Husserl worries about the extent to which the categories of reason direct our experience of the world, instead of our experiencing leading the categorization. Formal reasoning may introduce alienation into our own reflective life, and we can become prisoners of our own categorial constructs. Certainly, Buddhist hermeneutics is exploring some related concerns. But postmodern thought is skeptical about the possibility of there being such a "pure" realm of mental life that has overcome all alienation, in which the apophantic elements of reflection are purified (Husserl's term) and all of the naively accepted received notions made fully original.[14] A

---

12. This falls within the scope of what Husserl terms "judgment fulfillment."

13. See Gendlin (1992).

14. Tibetan Buddhist scholars speak of purifying consciousness, but they vary considerably in what they mean by the phrase. Some sects emphasize the idea of "Buddha nature" (*de bzhin gshegs pa snying po;* Skt. *tathagatagarbha*), although in the Gelug monastery I lived in, it was hardly ever discussed. Even in the Gelug world, it is treated with varying attention and meaning. I am especially impressed with a subset of Gelug philosophers who maintain that the "purity" of the Buddha nature is not at all because it is originally or fundamentally pure but because the flaws of our consciousness can be removed., that is, like anything else, they are not part of a fundamental essence. That is, they steadfastly refuse to turn sound epistemological insight about emptiness, ultimate truth, and Buddha nature into an essentialist metaphysics. Incidentally, Ruegg (1989, 7)

certain structuration of our thinking is inevitable and a moment of thematization may separate out from our thinking, quickly become reified, and confront us as an alien force. But there is no pessimism in this view, since thinkers are always able to *subvert* the categories they are saddled with, and they learn to exploit the economy of semiotic relations which the developing apophansis presents to them. That is, they are able to productively mine the semiotic and apophantic resources of the formal position to which the logic has carried them. And most importantly, formal analysis has the capacity to carry them to a semiotic environment in which they can gain new insight by being compelled to contend with and make meaningful unanticipated relations. In such a fashion, the formal aspects can convey thinkers' original reflection to novel places. Marc Richir (1993, 75) may be more to the point when he observes, "Alongside a 'bad' use of reflection, that which disentangles the threads of the tissue to reduce them to threads of reasons, there is a 'good' use. The latter, instead of proceeding to abstraction which isolates, . . . allows a new *field* of phenomena to come into view."

To illustrate this serendipitous productivity of formal reasoning, let us examine debate I.9, in which the defender has first committed to the proposition that some realization of emptiness can occur *without* realizing that an entity lacks a true identity and then committed to the related thesis that a realization of the emptiness of a pot does *not* necessarily entail that one understands the way in which the pot nevertheless exists with some functional efficacy. Following these commitments, the challenger then confronts the defender with a comprehensive summary of what it means to understand emptiness:

> T
>
> 6:03:50
>
> :59
When undertaking an analysis of the emptiness of the way one customarily apprehends and reifies a referent object. Oh. Yes. When one refutes, uh, a referent object's inherently true existence, then one posits its emptiness, doesn't one? >~ Depending upon whether one does or does not realize the correct limits of emptiness [i.e., what is to be negated and what is not], right, when one considers and reflects upon what is an acceptable way of formulating the functional conventional existence of the entity, which does have efficacy, without forgetting having negated the previous habit of reifying the entity's being, there *is* what we call a realization of emptiness. >~

Despite the fact that the summary is correct, the defender cannot accept it since he has already committed to the two previous contradictory theses. Ac-

---

has commented, "The *tathagatagarbha* theory was a syncretism, or a symbolic accommodation, with the *atman*-doctrine of Brahmanic thought—that is, in effect, a crypto-Brahmanic 'soul' theory in Buddhism." The issue is still debated among contemporary Tibetan sects.

cordingly, when he is asked whether there is a realization of emptiness when one posits an object's emptiness, the defender is compelled—by the way they have structured the argumentation—to say no:

6:04   L'   YOUR REASON IS NOT ESTABLISHED.

But forced into this idiosyncratic position, the defender *makes the best of it* and finds his way to a genuinely original insight:

> L'   There may or may not be a realization of emptiness. One who un-
> derstands only the assertion of emptiness merely posits an empti-
> ness, yes.

That is, L' avoids the extremity of denying that an understanding of emptiness may be involved and observes cogently that the formal positing of emptiness, however correct in terminology, may not entail that the thinker actually understands emptiness. In other words, one can be technically correct without having any meaningful experience. Only by being brought to face a potential formal error directly did L' have the opportunity to extend his philosophical imagination to a realm he in no way was anticipating. In this fashion the formal aspects of logical reasoning can become philosophically productive, especially under the discipline of a successful social practice of dialectical reflection, as we have been describing.

The success of dialectics is to be judged not only by whether scholars have listened to each other, it depends also upon the extent to which they have been able to learn something together. It is this second feature that most critics of Tibetan debating raise. There is the suggestion that Mahayana Buddhism is a closed system that is not open to any transformation. The Tibetologist Giuseppe Tucci (1987, 33) has characterized Tibetan intellectual practice in a frankly demeaning way: "Hardening of the arteries set in with the double threat of formulas replacing the mind's independent striving after truth. . . . A tendency to formalism and worship of the letter gained ground on spiritual research." That Tibetans make heavy use of the memorization of texts as a study strategy makes them especially vulnerable to this charge.

It has been suggested that under conditions of a philosophical monopoly, the opportunities for creative scholarship are scarce. As Randall Collins (1998, 380) contends in his sociological investigation of the world's philosophical traditions, "When external conditions enforce a single orthodoxy, creativity dries up." It is the prejudice of much Indocentric (which is, ultimately, Eurocentric) scholarship that the creative period of Buddhist philosophical development occurred only in India, and that the highly conservative and traditionalist Tibetans have contributed little, being hardly more than a medieval cultural icebox that retained the philosophical achievements of classical India intact, with little progress, for the last eight centuries or so.

Tibetological scholarship has contributed to the identification of an innovation developed by the Tibetans—the formal organization of the seminal texts of
Mahayana Buddhism by means of elaborate topic outlines. But this is praise that
implicitly supports the notion that Tibetans are given over to scholastic minutiae
and lack the philosophical depth necessary for truly innovative philosophical
contributions. The suggestion is that philosophy involves something more than
the rote memorization of logical routines, and that Tibetans may lack a fulfilled
understanding of the presented judgments, which Husserl described as being the
heart of philosophy.[15] As already mentioned,[16] Gene Smith, who has contributed
as much as any Westerner to the preservation of Tibetan Buddhist texts, has
denigrated Tibetan dialectics as the mere parroting of memorized sequences
without really probing the underlying meanings (Smith 1969, 10); he has also
suggested (2002), "The rank and file Dge lugs pa monks concentrated upon the
slavish pursuit of formalistic argumentation according to the scripts set forth in
the *yig cha*." Another Tibetologist, Shunzo Onoda (1992, 45), who has special-
ized in studying Tibetan debate but has done so only by means of texts and not
live, empirical debates, has observed, "The answerer can provide an answer
without much individual imagination." Comments such as these are not atypical.
In the next chapter we will consider some of the limitations that scholasticism
and, indeed, any use of formal apophantics places upon philosophical reasoning,
but it must be acknowledged that any scholastic tradition, Eastern or Western, is
vulnerable to this criticism. Nowhere is there a "pure" philosophizing that is
divorced from routine formalization. As Wittgenstein (1972, 85) described,
"Remember we sometimes demand definitions not for the sake of their content,
but of their form. Our requirement is an architectural one; the definition a kind
of ornamental coping that supports nothing." All philosophical cultures confront
problems of sophistry and develop strategies for carrying through their inquiries
despite the necessary limitations that accompany having to organize those inquiries into formal structures.

But can the Tibetans really admit anything new? The answer is certainly
positive, but first it occurs to me to ask why something must be new in order to
be profound? Why cannot an old piece of wisdom be allowed to endure? It
seems that in some of the criticisms of Buddhist philosophy that I hear from my
colleagues there is almost a fetish about what is "new." As Anne Klein (1994,
27) has cogently remarked, "The production of a 'novelty' that expresses one's
new and unique interpretation is not the goal." The critical question is whether
there exists an openness within Tibetan rationality, and we have learned enough
to be able to reply that there is. We have witnessed the creative force of their
negative dialectics and have observed that Tibetan scholars appreciate the shortcomings that can always be identified in any formal argumentation. Whether in

15. See 238.
16. See 38.

their classes (*dpe 'khrid*) with their teachers or in their debating sessions, Tibetan scholars are trained to have their thinking uprooted continually. Their practice of dialectics leads not to rigidity of thought but to flexibility of mind.

We have witnessed in our exposition of debate I.1 in this chapter how the challenger has called into question a text's exegesis of noema. In another debate (II.4), the defender remarked, "That's why I don't accept it just according to holding onto words in a literal way." It is misconstruing Tibetan philosophical practice to conclude that Tibetans are frozen within a blind conformity that has no capacity for transformation. In his volume of meditative songs, Geshe Rabten (1989, 75) expresses doubt about the efficacy of liturgical ritual: "I became convinced that rather than just making vast offerings in the temple it was better to give a bowlful of food to an unfortunate dog." Occasionally my own teacher, Lobsang Tsering, who was abbot of the monastery, would reject the position of Tsong Khapa, the founder of the Gelug order, and he frequently commented, "You must have reasoning before you can have faith"; however, when I queried another teacher of mine about this, he replied that faith comes before reasoning. On occasion even the monastic textbooks criticize Tsong Khapa's arguments, such as his view that the "independent, self-sufficiently existing self" of the Syllogistic Reasoning Middle Way School is only a conceptual imputation and not at all a notion that is innate. In one short text, another teacher of mine, Ngawang Dhargyey, questions the Buddha himself, echoing the topic of the debate (III.4) we have just considered. Citing words of the Buddha from a sutra—"I, through abiding in emptiness, am now abiding in the fullness thereof"— Dhargyey (1990, 81) asks, "In what fullness does the Buddha reside, when all phenomena are recognized as empty?"

Strong disagreements flourish among the theorists and monastic textbooks of the various colleges, and even in the interpretations of them by the regional institutes (*khang tshen*) within a college. For example, according to Jetsunpa, a realization that directly perceives (*dngon sum du stogs pa*) can perceive itself, while a conceptual mind cannot; however, Khedrup and Panchen Sonam Drakpa assert that neither can perceive itself. Similarly, some teachers at Sera Je Monastic University say that at the grossest level of innate truth habits (i.e., at the second bodhisattva level) there is no relevant distinction between a rough and subtle understanding. Other teachers claim there is a relevant difference. There is one debate regarding whether or not a Buddhist Middle Way scholar and a Hindu Samkhya scholar are able to share a common perspective (*mthun snangs*). According to some teachers at Sera they can, but according to others there it is impossible. This has important consequences for how communication in debate itself can take place, as well as for the methodology of refutation. The students of these teachers who receive different instructions battle it out on the debating grounds. It may be complained that these battles, too, are predictable, with each side adopting the orthodoxy of their own house, and that they merely repeat in more or less an identical form the same arguments that have been rehearsed for several generations, so they do not entail very much original reflection; however, I have found that it is not uncommon for students to fail to follow the direction of their regional institutes and to think for themselves. The most that may be said is that students (and teachers) who hold heterodox views are reluctant to advertise their dissension publicly, but in private they display a critical acumen that is quite ready to think originally. It is pertinent to observe that many Western scholars adopt unorthodox ideas out of a sort of fashionable dissension, but this is only a conformist lack of originality at another level. On occasion, it seemed that meeting me afforded some young Tibetan scholars an occasion to pour out a good deal of their pent up doubts about the philosophical notions they have been examining. These scholars demonstrated that they were not just engaging in meaningless calculations but were fully engaged with the internal relations of the notions they were debating.

From time to time young scholar-monks would invite me to the debating grounds so that they could test their minds against "new ideas and opinions" (*blob skyed gsar pa*), as they put it. They would tell me that just following the traditional lines of analysis was too limiting, and they appreciated opportunities to broaden their knowledge.[17] The first Western scholar to live in a Tibetan monastic university, in 1730, reported similarly about how curious Tibetans were about ideas that were different from their own: "My house suddenly became the scene of incessant comings and goings by all sorts of people, chiefly learned men and professors, who came from the monasteries and universities, especially those of Sera and Brebung [Drepung], the principal ones, to apply for permission to see and read the book." That does not describe a philosophical imagination that has stagnated. In 1997, six geshes living in Australia met in Melbourne and spent several days discussing and debating such contemporary matters as cloning. The same praxis of debate was used to explore vital issues, using Vasubandhu's *Abhidharmakosa* (which analyzes karma) as their starting point.[18] Their capacity and readiness to apply their philosophical praxis to new and unfamiliar topics reveals the creative resources that it bears.

Finally, let us take up the concluding discussion from debate I.1, which we have been considering. Although the challenger displays considerable originality in analyzing noema, the respondents are unwilling or unable to match him. Throughout this debate T has been running a tight ship, steering hard by means of authoritative citations, TS'As and not permitting digressions. At 3:06:(36), T turns his back to the defenders (see 186) in an effort to subdue them into stick-

---

17. This is an important aspect of a genuinely philosophical culture: important friendships are cemented only when the parties are able to interact in a dialectical way and share some philosophical life together in the appropriate manner (although on occasion it may have been simply that the idea of defeating an American "professor" in a debate was just too tempting an opportunity for them to pass up).

18. "Geshes Discuss Cloning in 'Vigorous Debate,'" *Mandala,* July/August 1997: 12.

ing with the formal apophantics. When one of the defenders attempts to raise his own authoritative citation, T shuts him down in order to drive him to the point of his challenge. Ridicule was also applied (see 3:08:(55), 217) in order to assist the effort to keep the defenders on task. Even when it is hardly more than sophistry, such adherence to strict analytic forms is justified when the defenders lapse into thinking by rote and fail to engage what is original about T's inquiry. That is, in this case the formality of the analytics is not a pedantic logistics but is used to provoke the defenders to move beyond their routine understanding.

To continue from the assertion where we left off the debating on page 243, wherein T inquires about the sensibility of the textbook's position:

T   When one realizes that the noema of a pot that appears to a thought that apprehends a pot does not exist in the way that it appears, one does not necessarily realize emptiness. What is the reason for

3:11:19   this? >~

L'   /It is said that the way to realize that the noema of a pot does not exist in the way that it appears to the thought that apprehends a pot is that the noema of the pot is not the pot.

L"   /(   ) that pot's noema, right? [L" and L' discuss the matter with each other.]

The defenders' reply is correct, but it does not explain anything or reveal any helpful understanding of T's inquiry, as it offers little more than a mundane slogan. T promptly brings the defender up short, calling for him to conform better with the formal apophansis, and they struggle for a time:

:22 T   Not that—if I asked you what is the way to realize that it [the noema of a pot] does not exist in the way that it appears // then you could give that answer.[19]

L"   // This *is* the way to realize it because it's a thought.

:26 T   You still need to prove your point properly from the beginning.

:28 L" One realizes that the noema of a pot is not a pot.

T   No, not that! The way to realize that a pot does not exist in the way that it appears to the thought apprehending a pot—yahh, the way a noema of a pot appears is not the way to realize that it does not exist in the way that it appears as the noema of a pot. >~

Even though the defenders' thinking is shallow and T is attempting to coax them into a more profound engagement with the question, T here displays that

---

19. That is, that the noema of a pot is not a pot; rather, T is asking not about its appearance but why it is that when one understands that a noema does not exist in the way that it appears, it is not necessary to realize emptiness.

nevertheless he *does hear* what L' and L" are saying. In this way some solidarity is built up, and T can use that to direct them to what is his question:

> L" It's not, right.
>
> L' It's not.
>
> T It's not, right? Now, what is the reason why it is necessary that the way to realize that the noema of the pot does not exist in the way that it appears to a thought apprehending the pot is to realize that
>
> 3:11:41 the noema does not exist as a pot in the way that it appears. >~

But the defenders are not up to the task, and so T scolds them again, forcing them into proper formal argumentation:

> L" If you want to know why this is—this one.
>
> T You don't answer, "If you want to know why this is."
>
> L" You don't answer by speaking in such a manner.
>
> :42 T (Laughs). You're not obligated to answer anything.

Placed in this position, the defender is compelled—if only by the claustro-phobia of the immediate forms—to say something in a formal way, and L" man-ages to present a reasonable answer; however, it is still one that fails to grasp the purport of T's inquiry:

> L" There are many such things whose realization is subtle and many other things whose realization is obvious, right?
>
> :46 T So?
>
> L" There are many things whose ways of appearing are subtle, and there are other things whose way of appearing is obviously false, right? [I.e., a noema is subtle and a thought is more obvious.] That's why this happens.
>
> :50 L' There is only a mere appearance [of the noema] to that [the thought of the pot]. There is no object corresponding to the apprehension of the noema of a pot.

Since they still miss the import of the matter (see footnote 17), T continues to press further. He wants to ignore these extraneous matters, but he also has an obligation to be respectful of the defenders' topics:

> 3:11:53 T The object as it may or may not be apprehended / is a topic that does not need to be raised.
>
> L'   / Hence this is the explanation from this perspective.
>
> :56 T Now.
>
> L' Mm.
>
> T If we do take up the apprehended object, then it is necessary to / provide some proper reasoning, with a proof, etc., even for that.

L'

/

A pot—Ohh, mm-hm.

T The matter of the apprehended object, yah, is not capable of

3:12   proving the issue. >~[20]

L" What? [Silence 2.0]

Note how at 3:11:(57) T is still able to hear the defenders, even as he pushes them. In this case, the silence at 3:12:(02) is probably a good sign. T uses the opportunity to present an excellent summary:

T Right? Your reason about the apprehended object "pot" tells us absolutely nothing about why it is that when one realizes that the pot does not exist in the way that it appears, it is necessary to realize *emptiness*; whereas, when one realizes that the noema of a pot does not exist in the way that it appears, it is not necessary to

:11   realize *emptiness*. >~

The video (see also the photos at 3:12:03 and 3:12:13) depicts the fashion in which T uses his hands to orchestrate, like a conductor, the reply that follows, holding open or closing his hands to indicate to L' how long his answer should proceed and how its contours can evolve:

L' That's why to say that one realizes that the noema of a pot does not exist in the way that it appears is to say that the noema of a pot does not exist in the way that it appears to a thought. To a thought, that is, it is the way that the noema of a pot appears as a pot to a thought, that's all [i.e., it doesn't have to do with emptiness].

Despite the clarifier's work, L' still has not fully grasped the philosophical import, so T makes the connections for him:

3:12:17 T No, not that. When one realizes that a noema of a pot does not exist in the way that it appears to a thought *generally speaking*, it is necessary to realize what is considered to be emptiness.

L' Mm.

T Now, when one realizes that it [the noema] does not exist [in the way it appears] to a specific thought apprehending the pot, it is said [L' says, the text says] to not necessarily be a realization of emptiness. >~

L' Yes.

---

20. That is, T's principal topic—the question of why a realization of the noema's not existing in the way that it appears—would not necessarily entail a realization of emptiness.

Finally having secured L''s willingness to engage the question of emptiness here, T can bring home the question he has been trying to compel L' to address all along:

T   Now, why is this?

Unfortunately, the bell ends the debate here after fourteen minutes of discussion. In fact, the debate ends right where it finally commences. However, the principal concern of debaters is to build cooperatively an analytic apparatus, based upon formal reasoning, that is actively engaged in an inquiry about truth, and this has been achieved.[21] The products of this reasoning may be disappointing philosophically, but the debate does display that the dialectical structure is inclined to be intolerant of rote answers or mere repetition of memorized philosophical slogans. That is, Tibetan debating is more than logical exercise and does indeed contain some resources to provoke Tibetan philosophers to reflect in philosophically consequential ways.

---

21. As Nietzsche (1969, 95) has remarked, "It is not through the possession but through the inquiry after truth that his powers expand."

Chapter 9

Some Betrayals of Formal Analysis

Thematization is then inevitable, so that signification can show itself, but does so in the sophism with which philosophy begins, in the betrayal which philosophy is called upon to reduce. This reduction always has to be attempted, because of the trace of the sincerity which the words themselves bear and which they owe to saying as a witness, even when the said dissimulates the saying in the correlation set up between the saying and the said.

—Emmanuel Levinas (1981, 151-52)

We have been investigating the benefits that formal analytic reasoning provides to thinking, and we have concluded that the formalization of thinking permits thinkers to communicate clearly and can assist their collaboration regarding what thinking is most appropriate. Such "thematization," in Levinas's words, permits signification to "show itself"; that is, it permits thinkers to retain their thoughts so that they can examine them and extend them. This "showing" of signification is a *social* event as well as an individual one; in fact, the primary benefit of thematization is that it permits thinking to proceed as a public activity. Indeed, "thematization" as a human phenomenon must have evolved along with language and rationality, whose impulses and motives were entirely social. But thematization also induces sophistries and betrayals that may obscure the insight or truth concerns that motivate thinkers' inquiries in the first place. Accordingly, sincerity and sophism exist alongside each other. Tina Chanter (1997, 72) concisely summarizes the irony that Levinas is describing: "Philosophy's very strength—its systematic thematization—is also its weakness." The present study is in large degree an ethnomethodological exploration of the problem.

This irony was described in more empirical terms by a Sera monk and friend of mine: "The purpose of debate is to clear the mind of doubts, but it ends up creating more doubts and complications than it clarifies." Such is the dilemma that human reflection faces everywhere. Almost universally, rigor in thinking is associated with clarity and precision, but is what is more precise and more clear always deeper and more insightful, especially when it narrows what is thought and closes off access that reflection might otherwise have to domains of reality which, while indeterminate, may yet be true? Social demands for clarity can trump the philosophical demand to witness the truth in just the way it shows itself. We have reviewed occasions where one may be right about an issue but still become so absorbed in the local complications of the contingent logic that one will have to surrender formal access to one's own best insight. At the same time, it is possible to satisfy the local demands of a formal analysis without understanding anything philosophical about it. Resolving thematic, structural problems may not necessarily resolve deeper, intuitive issues.

In the debates we have been examining, time and again defenders have been artificially pressured—by the aggressiveness of the interrogator, by the flow of the debate's rhythm, and by their own misplaced enthusiasm—to answer before they have considered an issue deeply; and later they were required by the rule of consistency to adhere to that commitment long after they had recognized its inaccuracy. The pace may become so quick that the respondent has no time to do anything *but* remain consistent. In many debates we have observed parties agree without knowing just what they were agreeing to; indeed, it can become the principal agenda of the debaters to learn from the ensuing dialogue what it is they have decided. On occasion, we witness on the video record the heads of all the debaters nodding with far more assurance than understanding; and however unknowingly, they nod comfortably. That comfort is more of a social achievement than it is a philosophical one; and yet they ready themselves to take up the philosophical work, too, but only subsequently. In so many situations, the interest in protecting oneself seems to eclipse the interest in pursuing the truth. How many times have we heard the reply, "In which system?" at the moment of a defender's aporia? How many unjustified and unjustifiable TS'As have we observed? The contingencies of the local order can serve the truth interests and they can betray it, and even do both at once. In fact, it is unclear just where sophistry leaves off and philosophy begins. The same technical skills with words and judgments that succeed in securing the sober attention of one's partner also serve well to obfuscate vital philosophical issues.

The forms of an emerging apophansis are needed to organize the debating, but these forms can get in the way of the debating. It is not that the logical forms or any other organizational interests are a problem to be remedied—they are necessary if philosophers are going to think together. Unless thinkers can learn to reason by telepathy, they are stuck with the formal thematization of their best insights, thematization that is fully able—indeed bears within itself the tendency—to betray those insights. In taking up what he terms "the correlation between the saying and the said" (see epigraph), Levinas turns to the practical work of reducing this betrayal, knowing that its complete removal is not consistent with the human condition. The "said" are the ideas that follow from "saying as witness" and become reified: "the apophansis, the said, . . . the source of a subreption that limits what is thought to essence and reminiscence" (Levinas 1981, 155). And yet it is within the power and originality of thinkers to divert the said toward what their intuition is driving them. Levinas (1981, 7) sets up the philosophical anthropological investigation of problems introduced by the necessary reification of ideas within an analytic practice:

> A methodological problem arises here, whether the pre-original element of saying (the anarchical, the non-original, as we designate it) can be led to betray itself by showing itself in a theme, and whether this betrayal can be reduced.

The reduction of this betrayal has been the task of thinkers everywhere.

Philosophical work, for Tibetans and for other philosophical cultures, entails the public objectivation or thematization of thinking to an extent that will permit thinkers to correlate their interpretations. The semiotic matrix they find their way to, which is part deliberate and part serendipitous[1], leads them to an itinerary of local organizational work that may either assist or distract their efforts, *and usually both*. The philosophers' success rests as much in what they do with the logical forms they develop as it lies within the capacity of those forms themselves. That is, what is "philosophical" has to do with philosophical aptitude as much as it does with philosophical structures. The history of Western philosophy has been populated with efforts to abolish sophistry from its practice, but there can be no question of abolishing it (as Levinas makes clear) because it always accompanies the very thematization that permits us to sustain philosophical practice itself. They are not extricable from each other. If one were to abolish sophistry, then no thinking of any sort could develop; instead, one must maturely accept the limitations that are natural to reflection, which does not rule out efforts to "reduce" sophistry. In the words of another of my Tibetan teachers, Geshe Lhundrup Sopa: "Of course you need argument, for improving understanding and for sharpening the mind. But *merely* arguing is a counterproductive practice." However, there is no method for reducing sophistry that one can rely upon routinely, for any such method would only institute another "subreption" from the "saying as witness." So what is genuine philosophical practice? To invoke a common Tibetan metaphor, how does one separate milk from water?

The Vertigo of Eloquence

What we have learned in these investigations enables us to appreciate that a part of the genius of dialectics lies in its capacity for exposing inconsistencies and inadequacies. But this genius sets its own trap when it operates without control, uninterruptedly—because it must listen in order to understand. With amazing precision, Heidegger has described the perspective that truth lies in the disclosedness or unconcealment of what seems to be self-concealing; and the apophansis may be part of the concealing. In place of, or alongside of, the relentless

---

1. See Liberman (1999a).

questioning of negative dialectics must be "a thinking that engages in, and lingers with, what is worth questioning" (Heidegger 1991, 9). Why is it necessary to always push the other's thinking, as Tibetan debaters do? What is the benefit of continually interrogating everything? As a dialectical moment, it can certainly be salutary for reflection, but when it is performed like an addiction and never leaves off its work, it seems to be an impediment to reflection. As Jeffrey Hopkins (1987, 41) has commented about Tibetan philosophical practice, "It is possible to become so addicted to reasoning that when you arrive at the point where you are about to cognize emptiness, you leave it and return to the reasoning." And why is it a good thing to answer quickly? What is wrong with answering slowly? The speed of debate I.9, presented under the section "Dangling in the Wind" in chapter 7, was impressive, but it left the defender time enough only to try to remain consistent and not really time for thinking.

There have been many debates where we have marveled at the efficiency and decorum, and occasionally even the productivity, of a smoothly functioning, tight formal analytic practice, one that seemed to sift through pertinent notions like a logical machine. The production of such a "logical machine" is a principal objective of Tibetan debaters, valued for its own sake for its aesthetic as well as philosophical virtues. The Tibetan debaters in our video records seem to relish being "in the zone" of a crisply functioning, syncopated debate of vital issues. Part of the praxis of Tibetan debate is to stay in this zone as much as possible, and it may even be that potential philosophical accomplishments are abandoned for the sake of the flow of a debate. Every assertion is made to follow clearly from a previous item, in a decisive procedure that is deducible from the formal calculus. The "logical machine" is made to run by itself,[2] in what may be called, following Claude Lefort (in Merleau-Ponty 1968, xxix), a "vertigo of eloquence."

Tsong Khapa (1997, 702) once observed of a scholar, "Although you pontificate, you don't understand;"[3] that is, the worth of an idea cannot necessarily be measured by the formalities with which it is packaged. We have witnessed debates where the participants seemed caricatures of logicians, and kept saying things like "It pervades that it pervades," that is, in dry forms about which Heidegger's description (1994, 9)—"scholastically degenerated philosophical learnedness"—is apt. In one such debate (I.4) the defender was frequently denied the right to make an exegesis, and it was proper apophantic form that performed the silencing:

> L″   Here, when we speak about the system that discusses the mere projection of a notion, there are a great many things to say about the mode of establishing objects.

---

2. See 58, 132, 143, and 168.
3. *Brdzod kyang mi shes.*

T   We're talking about the mere projection of a notion. There is no talking about other things. IT FOLLOWS THAT it is merely the
3:38:30   projection of a notion. >~

We have also observed the use of CONFOUNDED BY ALL THREE! (KOR SOOM!) to keep a respondent unstable and to squelch clarification. Also from I.4:

3:35:59 T   Mere establishment by awareness—
3:36   L" Now you (unclear).
      T   Hold on, TUT-TUT-TUT-TUT-TUT.
      L" I'm citing from the textbook!
      T   Mm-mm-mm-hm! Oh, where is such a citation in the textbook?
  :07 L" How do we say it (unclear). During the explanation about the definition of false imputations, the apprehension of reifications is one type. The mere projection of notions is another. Do you understand? Here / if it's established by the projection of a notion—
3:36:15 T   / CONFOUNDED BY ALL THREE! Quiet, quiet, quiet, quiet, quiet. I'll speak. Now. Hold on! Right, regarding the positing by the mind, it follows that the existence of an object is
  :25 not necessary. >~
      L' I ACCEPT.
  :26 T   Whooo-ee! CONFOUNDED BY ALL THREE [KOR SOOM] indeed! [falsetto scream]

This passage might well be subtitled, "*Kor soom* in your face." Nowhere is L" given the chance to reply to the very question put to him by T (at 3:36:(06)). While CONFOUNDED BY ALL THREE! has value in constraining waffling, its unrestricted use will not afford a respondent the opportunity to offer a full response. Order in debate demands firmness, but firmness itself is no guarantor of being right. "Hold on, TUT-TUT-TUT-TUT-TUT" may have limitations as a dialectical strategy. Later in this debate, L" is desperate for a chance to get a word in edgewise, but the clarifier of the reasoning shuts him down, again by means of a correct use of proper analytic form:

      L" Oh. There must be.
      T   Well then, here there must be!? Ohh, like this?
      L" There are some things to be said about this. You, you don't see.
3:41:33 T   Oh, are there? This is completely wrong isn't it?
      L" Just because you don't see it doesn't mean that it isn't so.
  :35 T   Except in the case where a mind posits, for which we say there must be an object, there is no speaking about an object existing when there is mental projection, right? But when it is posited by the mind, we say that it must exist. So, it's like this, right?
  :41 L" Oh, now. TAKE THE CASE OF the horns of a rabbit.

T   If it's like that, quiet.

L" If the mind posits it, / the horns of a rabbit are apprehended by a concept.//

T   If it's like this, quiet. / If it's like this, yaaa, TAKE THE CASE OF the reflection of an image // in the mirror. IT FOLLOWS THAT it

:48 is merely posited by the mind. >~

We have also examined in some detail the diabolical way in which CON-FOUNDED BY ALL THREE! can be thrown to an opponent just when it seems that an issue has finally been resolved (cf. the phenomenon of "pulling the rug out"). It cannot be said *a priori* that such a move (or that of the TS'A a few lines later) is sophistic, for it all depends upon the quality of thinking and communicating that is entailed. But when the respondent pleads, "Please listen!" (III.4 (127)) as much to gain some space to think as to reply, the practice can be questioned. There are even moments when a challenger himself will implore, "Now let's slow down a moment," as T says just before he offers a very profound insight.[4] The best thinking is not always that which is performed under pressure but may be better accomplished while "lingering," as Heidegger recommends. The "witness" of which Levinas speaks (cf. epigraph, 273) can be a silent one. A dialectics that doesn't stop to listen is not a dialectics in any pregnant philosophical sense, and this is not even to mention the worth of remaining silent when one doesn't know.

Within a discipline under which silence is no option, the expansion of evasions and obfuscations may only be encouraged. When even the best attempt of an opponent is rubbished indiscriminately, in order to keep stirring up the pot of notions until a weakness rises visible on the surface, sound philosophical practice can become sophistry. But are not philosophical practice and sophistry brethren? James Crosswhite (1998) has questioned, "Does philosophy explain rhetoric, or does rhetoric explain philosophy? Neither can have the upper hand, but they are interdependent. Are there philosophical moments that can be distinguished from rhetorical moments?"

The reader should not imagine that Tibetan philosophical practice is limited to the reflection that occurs during these scholastic debates, for there are many other occasions and contexts for Tibetan Buddhist philosophical reflection. Anne Klein (1994, xv) describes one of her teachers, "Kensur's physical posture and personal ambience was always relaxed, with no sign of the breathy or obsessive air one often sees associated with rigorous thinking . . . his manner was always the same: kindly, patient, with a quiet enjoyment in what he was doing." But even her subject's mind was formed in earlier years under the discipline of Tibetan formal analytics within their scholastic disputations. Philosophical de-

---

4. "When one understands formally the way of positing how concepts are merely imputations, IT FOLLOWS THAT one does not necessarily realize that concepts are merely imputations." >~ (II.4 9:31:23)

bating is the signal practice that characterizes the uniqueness of Tibetan philosophical culture; however, each monastery offers a different ratio of debate to meditation. Not all philosophers are warriors, and not all of Tibetan scholarship consists of philosophical martial arts.

Norah Martin (1997) offers some cogent criticism of philosophy as intellectual struggle, a regime she terms "masculinist"—

> The model that "masculine" philosophers seem to be advocating is that one presents an argument and then defends it, as it were, to the death, while one's audience attacks it as viciously as possible. One defends one's arguments against others no matter what. This seems to preclude actually listening to others and further developing ideas in conversation with them.

She also observes that the most interesting ideas may never be presented since they may be the most difficult to defend. Just as the obligation to fit one's ideas into correct logical formulations can reveal inconsistencies, promote clear communication, and lead (as we have seen) to productive and novel insights, it can also distract thinkers from their most serious work, which includes developing profound insights, however hesitant, into the nature of things.

We observed in I.9 ("Dangling in the Wind") that several questions of considerable probity went unengaged by the defenders who were more concerned to stay away from trouble than to increase their understanding. At one point the course of the debating leads the clarifier of the reasoning serendipitously to an intriguing and compelling problem—since the refutation of a *conceptually imputed* reification of an essential nature is easier than, and preliminary to, the refutation of an *innately* experienced reification of an essential nature, and the latter is what is critical for achieving freedom from one's own obsessive mental habits, then when one has accomplished the latter refutation why is it at all necessary to labor to accomplish the former refutation? It would seem that the answer to this question might shed some light upon what is unique about conceptual imputations. But the defender fails to rise to the occasion, and instead of serious philosophical reflection, he offers a safe but pedantic slogan that falls short of addressing the deeper irony that the clarifier's question is pursuing:

6:08:30 T When one negates an innate, spontaneously arising object of attachment, right, in this system why then must one refute the object of attachment that is a conceptually imputed reification of a truly
   :39 existing essence? >~.
     L' IT FOLLOWS THAT one must BECAUSE according to their system, there is a reified apprehension of a "true" essence that is a habit of conceptual imputation.

This is a failure to engage what is most serious in the dialectics. There are failures on the side of challengers, too. Should a defender take the time necessary to think, or offer a hesitant first reply, the likelihood is that a challenger will pounce on the respondent like a cat on a mouse. Earlier in the same debate when the clarifier inquires about the durability of an understanding of the emptiness of inherent existence, the respondent pauses for an instant to consider the problem. The challenger relentlessly insists that the respondent finalize his thinking at once:

> T　　If due to a previous realization of the emptiness, one has destroyed the habitual mode of reifying the ascertained object, DOES IT
> 6:04:25　　NOT FOLLOW THAT one has realized emptiness? >~
> L'　　A realization of emptiness—?
> T　　—[very rapidly] In this case are you saying that there is a realization of emptiness, or not? When one is confident that . . . .

Learning to think on one's feet, in the face of contention, has its benefits, but when the contentiousness magnifies mistakes in speaking and thinking, those benefits are compromised. In the same way, formulating the most absurd version of the issue at hand may not always be what is most helpful for reflection. There are many times when it is constructive for the fecundity of the thinking, but on other occasions it can be detrimental to the productivity of their philosophical work.

It seems that when the debaters have little understanding of the meaning of the notions they are considering, they are more inclined to find refuge in the accepted protocols of the formal apophansis. The subject of the last illustration, the levels of a bodhisattva's advancement in spiritual understanding, is a frequent topic of debates, but it is a subject with which these young scholars have had zero personal experience. Their talk is based upon the texts of people who themselves are writing about other people who have had such noble accomplishments. This means that they are at least two stages removed from any original experience, yet they speak authoritatively about these matters. Even some of the great sages confess in their writings that they lack the requisite experience with the states of being they discuss, for example, Shantipa (Jackson 1994, 146): "I have not myself directly experienced the ultimate reality that I teach." Western scholars are one additional stage removed from an original experience, since they are reading texts prepared by translators who, for the most part, are similarly deficient. By that time it could be a text prepared about a text written about a text by a scholar whose own admission is that there is not any accomplishment of the sort the literature is referencing.[5] Such discourse, even when it is dressed in an attractive dialectics, could well be the poster child for a widely held image of scholasticism, one in which eloquence and erudition have so displaced reflection that it is forgotten that any concealment has occurred.

---

5. This strikes me as a classic case of what Derrida has described as the endless deferral of an origin.

Ridicule and Mockery (*zur za*)

The humor that enlivens so much Tibetan debating extends to ridicule and mockery by hyperbole. Among the standard phrases of ridicule that I have collected are "Your wrong answer is famous," "Your reply doesn't come within eighteen handspans of being relevant," and "Your reason could not be established within nine dark years." Although such ridicule is probably not a feature that one would wish to abolish altogether, since it can become quite sporting, it is proscribed by the authoritative texts. Prancing about, shrieking, and "mudslinging disputations" (Guenther 1994, 125) are considered flaws of character. For example, declaring, "This is extremely wrong-headed!" (1.9, 6:05:24), is not the approved method of rejecting a thesis. Sakya Pandita complains (Jackson 1985, 98), "In debate it is going too far if one party cries out 'I have won' merely because the opponent is sitting quietly." One does not need to be abstemious to find it offensive for a challenger to get worked up each time he catches an opponent out (especially when he used confusion or sophistry to do so) or grow weary of hearing the cry, CONFOUNDED BY ALL THREE!, at every slip of the tongue.

Let us consider this illustration from I.6:

	T	If one apprehends an inherently existing person, IT DOES NOT PERVADE THAT that is a view of an ego.
4:43:08	L"	Oh, IT DOES NOT PERVADE.
	T	Oh so. Therefore—so, when is an ego is reified as a person? Why
:18		don't you give the text's definition for an ego this time? >~ [Laughter]

This teasing may be justified by assisting T to elicit a well-considered reply from the respondents, but T does not give them a great deal of scope for developing a definition:

:19	L'	In the text.
	L"	The text speaks of "you" and "me."
	T	Wait. Wait. Wait.
4:43:24	L'	What? The definition of one's own ego?
	L"	"I" and "mine" are perceived, "I" and "mine."
:29	T	TAKE THIS AS THE SUBJECT. Those apprehended objects, how
:33		do they arise? Knowing sir, now explain properly, please. >~

T is patronizing the defender, who attempts to offer his best understanding of the matter, but T does not tolerate anything less than compliance with the formal apophantic language. At 4:43:42, T employs strict analytic form to develop the public assertion that L" is clueless:

> L" I won't give you the exact wording, but I'll present an account from my understanding. But it will be the same.

4:43:42 T   In giving your understanding of the definition of one's ego, IT
    :46   FOLLOWS THAT you don't know the precise wording. >~ [Audi-
            ence laughter] No, no, no.
    L"   I have some wording. Really.
    L'   When one perceives either the "I" or "mine" that has become one's
            object of observation, it is explained that the afflicted conscious-
            ness that reifies an "I" that exists according to its own characteris-
            tics reckons that there is an ego [much talking over each other and
            by the audience, for thirty seconds].
4:44:29 T   Now you are going to be a professor, but you are speaking non-
            sense! [Laughter] Now listen. One's ego, right? Yah, IT PER-
            VADES THAT . . .

It is difficult to find any redeeming characteristics in such wholesale ridicule.

Let us take up another extensive illustration, from II. 6, during which T
suckers L' into accepting the incorrect assertion that when one realizes the
grossest level of rough abandonment of obscurations one does not realize the
abandonment of the grossest innate truth habits. This is incorrect because the
notion of there being "rough" and "subtle" levels of abandoning truth habits
applies only to innate truth habits and not to the more easily abandoned conceptually acquired truth habits; hence, any mention of "grossest truth habits" implies "grossest innate truth habits." However, T leads L' up a rosy path to the
wrong assertion, and then upon successfully duping him, T jumps all over him:

9:51:14 T   If it's not so realized, DHII! CONFOUNDED BY ALL THREE!
            [Circles L"s head with rosary beads.] IT FOLLOWS THAT it is
            realized. IT FOLLOWS THAT it is realized. It is Jetsun Chokyi
            Gyaltsen's human embodiment of Manjugosha who presents the
            splendid thought—
    L'   Oh yes.

L' is unnerved by this and becomes unable to think clearly, in part because
T keeps hold of him by the short hairs:

        T   It is said that a person on the path of liberation directly witnesses
            the suchness of his mental continuum without the roughest sort of
9:51:40   innate truth habits. >~
    L'   For the object to be abandoned corresponding to that point.
    T   Oh yah. We don't speak of "corresponding" do we?
    L'   [speaking excitedly] We must say this! We must say this! *This is
            the import of the objects to be abandoned from the second to the
            seventh bodhisattva levels' objects of abandonment.*[6] We say it,
            don't we!

---

6. From Tsong Khapa (n.d.) *Dbu ma gongs pa rab gsal.*

9:51:47 T   But, DHII! CONFOUNDED BY ALL THREE.

Contentiousness has smothered listening, and the competition becomes so keen that T grows excited enough to misspeak himself in his next turn:

L' *"This is the import of the objects to be abandoned / from the second to the seventh bodhisattva."* We say this, don't we!

T   / Please listen.

Please listen. However, uhh, at the first level—at the *second* level—

[101] L' Yes.

9:52 T   IT FOLLOWS THAT the grossest innate truth habits are abandoned.

It seems that shrieking and ridicule are counterproductive. At about 9:52:(31) L' is trying his best to consider when it is that a Buddhist practitioner first begins to abandon the innate obscurations to wisdom, but each time he stumbles even slightly T gives him a further shove, which seems not to be productive for anything other than forcing L' to misspeak (at 9:52:(42)), giving T another opportunity to shriek, "CONFOUNDED BY ALL THREE!":

T   . . . Then what are you saying?

L'   Uh, how do we speak of the gross level, the way of speaking about that is that that is when we first begin / to abandon the obscurations to wisdom. //

T   / Explain yourself. Explain yourself. //

L'   One first begins to abandon the obscurations to wisdom.

9:52:39 T   Which one?

L   The obscurations to wisdom, we say. Or how do we say? The truth habits of reification. One begins to abandon the innate truth habits.

:43 T   DHII! CONFOUNDED BY ALL THREE. When we begin to abandon the afflictive obscurations.

It seems that T is affording L' no opportunity to contribute to the discourse in a meaningful way. He continues to press him by presenting an absurd consequence:

9:52:55 T   . . . IT DOES NOT FOLLOW THAT we must distinguish between the rough and subtle? >~

L'   What are you saying? The afflictive obscurations?

It seems that L' is too affected by the claustrophobia, which the contentiousness has produced, to think clearly:

T   Oh yes.

L'   The afflictive obscurations?

T   When one first begins to abandon the afflictive obscurations.

9:53   L'   It's not necessary. How do we say it?
        T   Oh, TS'A!

The TS'A here seems unjustified, except for the fact that L' is having difficulty finding the precise wording, so L' becomes angry:

9:53   L'   [shrieks] The innate delusions!
 :06   T   When one first begins to address the innate delusions, then must one distinguish between the rough and the subtle? >~
        L'   One must because / IT PERVADES THAT // one must because if there is subtle///
        T   /   Oh Yah!   //   Why must there be?   ///   Why must there be?
        L'   One's progress is slow at first, and one is unable to abandon the most difficult truth habits right at the start.

T persists with pushing L', even though it seems that T is not listening carefully:

 :11   T   Why must one? Why must one?
        L'   At first one works on the smallest, it has to be just like that. If you have not accomplished the first part of the path—
        T   —Which? Which?
 :16   L'   [yelling] One learns gradually, and on that basis one becomes capable of abandoning—
        T   —That's why—
 :20   L'   [shrieks] Gradually one begins to abandon and on that basis one comes to stabilize one's abandonments.

It seems that in spite of the impediments, L' has at last offered some constructive explication of the issue. Nevertheless—

        T   DHII! [shrieks] CONFOUNDED BY ALL THREE! When one begins to abandon the conceptually acquired truth habits, uh, yes,
 :28   yes, uh, one has begun to abandon the innate obscurations. >~

This is deliberately phrased incorrectly, and L' rejects it but receives only another unwarranted TS'A for his troubles, followed by another deliberately false absurd proposition:

        L'   CHEE-CHEER! [BECAUSE OF WHAT?]
9:53:29 T   =v= TS'A! When one has begun to abandon the afflictive obscurations, IT FOLLOWS THAT one needs to distinguish between the roughness and the subtlety of the afflictive obscurations at the
 :35   first. >~
        L'   CHEE-CHEER!
        T   TS'A! IT FOLLOWS THAT one must . . .
        L   There is innate and there is conceptually acquired.

:46 T   DHII! CONFOUNDED BY ALL THREE!

T returns to his absurd consequence, which is wrong because it is stated too generally, but this time L' agrees, which elicits another shriek—even though L' makes a feeble attempt to specify the over-generalized assertion:

:51 T   . . . IT FOLLOWS THAT one must distinguish between the roughness and the subtlety of what is to be abandoned. >~

    L'   Whose? Yes, yes.

:53 T   If it must, DHII! [very loud shriek] CONFOUNDED BY ALL THREE.

    L'   That is for an innate truth habit, is it not?

T comes to repeat his absurd consequence, L' rejects it again, and L" feels inspired to contribute his own ridicule to the scene:

9:54:04 T   IT FOLLOWS THAT there is a distinction between roughness and subtlety. >~

    L'   At the very commencement of an attempt to abandon?

    T   Oh, yes.

    L'   Then, CHEE-CHEER.

    L"   Right.

:08 T   =v= TS'A! IT FOLLOWS THAT there must be. Yah, BECAUSE it is an innate truth habit. >~

    L"   Now you are full of consequences!

L"'s ridicule does seem apt, for T's sophistry has come to eclipse the debate. There is no need to deliberately obfuscate an argument just to elicit a formally incorrect commitment that does not reflect any failure in understanding. When one does poorly in a debate because of flaws in one's understanding, it might be said in defense of ridicule that it can compel one to study with more vigor than one might have done otherwise. More importantly, when a course of intensive ridicule activates a debater's instinct to protect himself, this newly active egoism can interfere with the clarity of the debater's thought processes. While this can inflict damage upon the philosophical productivity of a debate, it can also provide training in maintaining one's mental stability in the face of intensive scrutiny. When one can weather insult without becoming defensive, one has taken an important step toward taming one's ego, a step that will make it more likely that one will be able to engage in thinking that gives priority to the philosophical motives at hand. But when the intensity of ridicule itself generates minor errors or when public declarations of contradiction and failure are made gratuitously, without grounds or any deficiencies in an opponent's philosophical comprehension, the practice of a debater does not rise above sophistry.

Sophistry

It is told that the Hindu Brahmin Matrceta once came to the great Nalanda University in northern India to challenge the Madhyamaka master Aryadeva in a philosophical debate (Rinchen 1994, 14). At one point during the debating that ensued, Matrceta produced a debating parrot who was capable of giving the right answers. This story reveals that Buddhist scholarship is well aware of the tendency of their own scholastic practice to devolve into a shallow and meaningless recitation of words. The term *tshig skam po*, "dry words," is a common complaint heard throughout Tibetan philosophical culture when reasoning has reduced itself to what Hegel (1989, 279) described as "the routine of method." It is beyond the scope of this study, but Tibetans employ a variety of hermeneutic strategies and mind trainings (*blo sbyong*) designed to repair these shortcomings of philosophical practice and to infuse philosophical reflection with meaning and social responsibility.[7] Every single human practice that is exercised falls prey to becoming routinized, and even those methodologies designed to remedy such routinization can themselves become routinized.[8] Ultimately, the problem may be without remedy, simply part of the human condition, and the best one can achieve may be to be frank about acknowledging those occasions when one has lost reflexive oversight of one's philosophical practice, as is the respondent in this excerpt:

7:17:16 T   IT FOLLOWS THAT no such appearance of true existence is cognized. >~

       L   I ACCEPT.

       T   There is an appearance that seems to be truly established. It is said that there is no such appearance of true existence, is it?

       L   I'm saying it like that. Actually, I don't really understand it.

Sophistry appears whenever philosophical understanding is lacking; however, it cannot be said that the practice of parroting routines and following up dry words wherever they may lead is *always* unproductive philosophically, because considering the words one is using—that is, learning by using words—is one way that thinkers can come to new understanding. Ethnomethodologically speaking,[9] in this way philosophical insight can come to ride on the back of sophistry. The notion that the pure and the corrupt in reflection can be cleanly isolated from each other is too ideal of a sentiment. As a matter for empirical

---

7. This topic will be addressed in a sequel to this study, to be entitled, *Reason and Wisdom*.

8. Ethnomethodological research has paid particular care to describing just such mundane eventualities (see especially, Garfinkel 2002).

9. By "ethnomethodological," I refer to an analysis that proceeds from the perspective of the actors' preoccupation with the methods they use to provide for the orderliness and sensibility of their social interaction.

sociological investigation and not philosophical inquiry, it seems that sophistry and "serious" reflection are too inextricable from each other to imagine that one could exist without the other. That does not mean that sophistic practice cannot furnish to reflection a staleness that repels any serious thinker. Upon viewing my video tape of the defender in I.9 (3:08:39), in which the defender competently responded with a narrow assertion that missed the philosophical import of the challenger's inquiry, an Indian colleague of mine remarked, "He has all the terminology right, but he hasn't got a clue!" What he meant is that the social practice of learning how to use words correctly and how to converse in an appropriate manner are competencies that may be learned *independently* of having philosophical vision. But the task that philosophy faces is not that of practicing philosophy while banishing sophistry—it is to learn to practice philosophy amidst and alongside the inevitable presence of sophistry.

There is a common distinction that Tibetan monks employ when they discuss the evening's debates. They divide the debates they had between "meaning debates" (*don gi rtsod pa*) and "word debates" (*tshig gi rtsod pa*). When during a particular debate a party employs some strategy that involves an exclusive concern with words without real consideration given to their meaning, the other party may accuse the former of using a "word trick" (*tshig tsha*), and the very availability of this criticism may help to mitigate its use (frequently there is an audience to help arbitrate such a complaint). Similarly, a finely worded argument that is not devoid of meaning but borders on the sophistic will be called "a tricky thing" (*zhib bya*), and its philosophical probity will be distrusted. Throughout Buddhist logical literature there is the distinction between logical inference and "fascimiles of inference,"[10] so these hermeneuts are in no way naive pedants as some of their worst critics, Tibetan and European, have suggested. There are indeed arguments by *petitio principii* and other specious logicism, and the sporting character of such practices sometimes encourages their production. One fellow student once leaned over and excitedly whispered into my ear while we were attentively sitting nearby a debate; he told me, "Now he needs to debate!" By "debate" my Tibetan friend meant "confuse," or at least "challenge hard" (*ngar shog*). This would include the use of "CONFOUNDED BY ALL THREE! " to keep a defender unstable.

While offering advice about debating, one accomplished debater in the monastery emphasized that one must learn how to set up one's thinking in a logical sequence. Then he offered this curious suggestion: a debater can pursue a word debate or go for the meaning. He compared the meaning to food, and the employment of clever wording (which would not exclude sophistic uses of language) to the spices. He suggested, "If you totally disregard words, it is like food without spices. And you need both food and spices."

---

10. Cf, Tsong Khapa (1997, 618), *rjes su dpag pa ltar snang.*

A broader question that a philosophical anthropology must consider is whether the formal obligation to fit one's thinking and responses into a developing logical order has a natural course that is likely to carry thinkers to sophistry. That is, far from being philosophy's adversary, is sophistry part of its very nature? Let us revisit a lengthy excerpt from "The Samkhya View of Production From Self" (III.4)[11], which culminates in a bit of sophistry during its final moments. In order to appreciate the character of the sophistry, we must examine as well the debating that precedes these moments:

	T	TAKE AS THE SUBJECT an already manifested sprout . . . If it has phenomenal existence at the time of its production, IT PERVADES THAT the Samkhya accept that it is established by
-064.5-		way of its own intrinsic essence. >~
	L"	IT PERVADES. IT PERVADES.
2:16:21	L'	IT PERVADES. IT PERVADES. IT PERVADES. IT PERVADES.
	T	CONFOUNDED BY ALL THREE.

The challenger is attempting a classical Madhyamaka refutation of the Hindu Samkhya essentialist view that the being of a sprout rests inherently in the cause of the sprout, that is, the seed. Tsong Khapa elaborates this refutation at great length, arguing that if such being was inherent in the seed, there would be no need for soil, moisture, planting, farmers, etc.[12] The Samkhya are forced to accept that in the seed, that is, "at the time of the cause," the sprout has some existence in an unmanifested way, but they do not accept that such existence entails actual "production" of the sprout. The Madhyamaka argument is that they must accept that any such existence of a sprout would entail production, and that would imply that any subsequent appearance of the sprout would be production for a second time, which is logically absurd. The key term at -064.5- is "establish" (it can also mean "exist"—*grub*), which is not the same as "production" (*skye ba*). The defenders reply accurately about the Samkhya position, but T merely abuses their answer. T proceeds to rehearse their commitment:

	T	IT FOLLOWS THAT they accept that such an already manifested sprout is established at the time of its cause by its own intrinsic
-066.5-		essence. >~
	L'	What is he saying?
Audience		ACCEPTABLE ACCEPTABLE ACCEPTABLE.
	L"	IT IS ACCEPTABLE.
	L'	IT IS ACCEPTABLE.
	T	IT FOLLOWS THAT they accept that it is established by way of

---

11. See 151-53, where the debate was examined from the standpoint of the debaters producing its rhythm.

12. Cf. Tsong Khapa (1985b, chapter 2).

:27   its own intrinsic essence. >~

       L"   / I ACCEPT, indeed.

       L'   / I ACCEPT, indeed.

This repetition objectivates the defenders' position and sets the tempo for the debating.

       T   If you accept, IT FOLLOWS THAT they accept that an already

-069-   manifested sprout is established at the time of its cause. >~

       L"   CHE-/   // They can accept that.

       L'   / I ACCEPT, indeed. //

Audience   They accept that. They accept that.

T now tries to extend the defenders' commitment to a logical absurdity:

2:16:32 T   At the time of its cause they accept that it is produced. >~

       L'   CHEE-CHEER!

       L"   They do not accept that it is produced!

       T   What?

       L"   It exists in an unmanifested state. Sure. It exists in an unmanifested state, right?

       L'   If it is produced, it must be an object for an eye-consciousness.

The defenders have done a decent job of clarifying the Samkhya position, explaining that "production" requires the existence of a physical object that is visible to the eye. T picks up their clarification and reproduces it in formal terms:

       T   Therefore, if it is then an object for an eye-consciousness, yah, IT

-074-   PERVADES THAT it is not produced at the time of its cause. >~

       L'   IT PERVADES THAT it is not produced.

And T attempts to use that to refute the Samkhya position; but the defenders disagree, holding to the Samkhya view that the sprout exists but cannot be seen, so is not "produced":

-074.5- T   Then IT PERVADES THAT it does not exist at the time of its cause.

       L'   [According to Samkhya proponents,] IT DOES NOT PERVADE.

       L"   No. No.

Audience   / Oh yes.

       T   TAKE AS THE SUBJECT a sprout that / has already manifested. They do not accept that such an already manifested sprout, yah, is

-077-   produced at the time of its cause. >~

       L'   Yes.

:51 T   Then IT FOLLOWS THAT they accept that that already mani-

-078-   fested sprout, which exists at the time of its cause, is produced that way. >~

With the introduction of the phrase "that way" the debaters enter a slippery slope, for the semantic content that fulfills that gloss is highly indexical, and each party is able to agree to the statement while attributing to it differing content. The defenders acknowledge the potential confusion between "exists" and "produced," and so they are careful to define the context of their acceptance. They rehearse the phrase "that way," and at 2:17, T engages in some fine wordsmanship with his phrasing:

L'   What is he saying? They accept that it exists at the time of its cause. "IT FOLLOWS THAT they accept that it is produced?"
L"   They do accept that it is produced in that way, existing in an un-manifested state / at the time of its cause!

2:17   T   / It exists at the time of its cause. And they accept
-081-   that it is produced that way. >~
L"   // THAT IS ACCEPTABLE.
L'   // They accept that it is produced that way. /// They accept that it is produced that way.
T   /// IT FOLLOWS THAT
-082-   they accept that it is produced.

It is here that the sophistic move is made. T drops the qualification "that way," which leaves him with an occasion to extend the meaning of the form of this accepted assertion beyond anything the respondents intend to mean:

L'   / THAT IS ACCEPTABLE.
L"   THAT IS ACCEPTABLE.
-082.5-   T   Then IT FOLLOWS THAT it is produced again. >~
L'   CHEE-CHEER.

T's "wordsmanship" is technically correct, but in obfuscating the meaning of the dialogue he has carried reflection away from a constructive interrogation of the matter. Following the words literally, paring them down, and then lifting them out of context is not philosophy.

Rebutting an opponent's thesis by exploiting an alternative meaning of a term, one that is never intended by the opponent, is called a "quibble." The Tibetan term for quibble is *tsig skyon* (I.1 3:04:33), and it is a strategy that younger debaters rely upon during those stages where they cannot tell sophistry apart from philosophy. The proliferation of terminology in Tibetan about sophistic acts implies that the practice is a major concern in Tibetan philosophical culture, and it must be acknowledged that both their literature and their everyday tutorials warn repeatedly against engaging in the practice, though it may be not much more than lip-service. Tsong Khapa (n.d., circa 1996, 195) has advised,

"Having identified just how wrong knowledge arises spontaneously in one's mental continuum and takes a hold of it, we should make efforts to combat it. And no wise person will ever take any pleasure in mere squabbling (*gshags 'gyed*) with one's philosophical colleagues!"

It seems that there are no such wise persons in this next excerpt (from II.1, "The Reflection of a Face in the Mirror"):

	T	A person who has not cognized emptiness sees an image reflected
9:04:06		in the mirror. >~
-067.5-	L	I ACCEPT. He does so posit.
	T	A person who has not cognized emptiness posits that an image reflected in the mirror is erroneous, and that way of positing what is erroneous about an image reflected in the mirror posits is errone-
:12		ous in the full sense of what is erroneous, in just the right way. >~
-069-	L	Oh, in just the right way [tone of irony]. When one comes to posit what is erroneous, it is not necessarily how the Middle Way tenets formulate what is erroneous. That is because it may be just the right way of cognizing that there is not a real image in the mirror.

T is raising the case of an ordinary person who is able to recognize that the image in the mirror doesn't exist there. As in our previous illustration, the gloss "in just the right way" is vulnerable to multiple interpretations that can be exploited sophistically, so L attempts to provide a context for his answer, specifying at -069- that the understanding of an ordinary person has nothing to do with a Middle Way understanding. Nevertheless, T proceeds to build his argument by twisting L''s reply in such a way that an appreciation of the Middle Way School's notion of "what is erroneous" and a Middle Way interpretation of "lack of accord" *could* be inferred:

	T	IT FOLLOWS THAT one must posit what is erroneous BE-CAUSE one must posit the lack of accord between the appearance
9:04:35		of an image reflected in the mirror and its mode of being. >~
-073.5-	L'	(One posits it. [unclear, a member of audience is also speaking])
	L"	IT DOES NOT PERVADE.

L" is anticipating the coming trouble and tries to evade it by not accepting T's proposition. So, instead, T reverses his field and blasts L" with a TS'A, presumably for rejecting the assertion *when it is taken as affiliated with* the interpretation that the "erroneous" here is only *the ordinary sense of a common sense denial* of the existence of what appears in the mirror.[13] L" would have received

---

13. Note that the parties are continuously addressing their attention to the multiple meanings of their utterances that exist at the horizon of their reflections. As in all regions of everyday life, one must keep in view these horizonal phenomena—which are collaboratively hewed—if one's analysis is ,to be a phenomenologically adequate one. Eth-

the TS'A *whichever* way he replied, for a suitably damaging semantic content would have been affiliated to his utterance. This is what renders the argumentation sophistic.

> T   TS'A indeed! Since one has come to posit the lack of accord of its appearance and its mode of being—
>
> L"   That lack of accord between "appearance" and "mode of being" is not necessarily the cognition of the lack of accord with its appearance as having an inherently true essence.

Although it is apparent to everyone present what the defenders mean, a sophistic use of the surface structure of the reasoning has permitted T to condemn their replies. This is an instance of what was condemned by Tsong Khapa (n.d. *dGongs pa rab gsal*, 129), when he cautioned, "If one only establishes refutation via outward relations, then it will be of very little benefit."

It is said that some clever people can never be defeated. Although such defenders may know that their position is incorrect, they are too skilled at obfuscating the terms of a debate to be touched by sound logical reasoning. It is said that the early twentieth century scholar Gendun Chophel, for example, would visit the debating courtyard "to confound his fellow students, sometimes disguised as a *ldap ldop*" (Lopez 1992, 491). A *ldap ldop* is a clown or a fool, and what is being described here is that Gendun Chophel would deliberately sucker his opponents by disguising himself as an easy-to-defeat ignoramus, whose ignorance would nevertheless prove too tenacious to overcome. Dreyfus (2002, 233) comments insightfully, "Debate tend to favor analytic rigor over richness in understanding. . . . Some are almost exclusively preoccupied with winning arguments and exposing contradictions . . . They tend to overuse allowable tricks at the expense of more meaningful inquiry. Their answers are consistent but uninteresting." While a certain sport and playfulness sometimes accompanies the sophistry, these may not provide the best resources for philosophical reflection. As Heidegger (1991, 46) has described,

> When thinking does not bring into view what is most proper to what is seen, then thinking looks past what lies present before it. The danger that thinking may overlook things is often exacerbated by thinking itself, namely by the fact that thinking too hastily presses forward to a false rationale.

We have witnessed a great deal of this "pressing forward" in our Tibetan debates, but we are forced to recognize the reality that a philosophical "pressing forward" has resources as well as limitations.

---

nomethodological rigor requires that close attention be directed to the fine detail of face-to-face interaction, and sustaining such rigor can be challenging (even to readers). T is playing with potential projected interpretations of L"'s replies, shifting the semantic domains at his convenience.

Before Heidegger, Hegel (1989, 682-83) acknowledged frankly that the formal structure of logical reasoning was both necessary and limited:

> Though contempt for the knowledge of the forms of reason must be regarded as sheer barbarism, equally we must admit that the ordinary presentation of the syllogism and its particular formations is not a *rational* cognition, not an exposition of them as *forms of reason*, and that syllogistic wisdom by its own worthlessness has brought upon itself the contempt which has been its lot. Its defect consists in its simply stopping short at the *understanding's form* of the syllogism in which the Notion determinations are taken as *abstract*, formal terms. It is all the more inconsequent to cling to these determinations as abstract qualities, since in the syllogism it is their *relations* that constitute the essential feature.

As we described carefully in chapter 7, each party to a debate is attempting to normalize their rhetorical practice and construct truths that are made to appear to follow mechanically from logical validities. Each invokes a logical order against the other, and the dialogue is in part an effort to sort out whose formal order is to be followed. But what is a *logical* order? And how is it related to an *understanding* of the relations of the forms that compose it? In order to obtain a closer look at the association of philosophy and sophistry, let us analyze the internal dialectics of portions of several debates that employ sophistic methods.

An Ethnomethodology of Sophistry

The problems that sophistry poses to reflection are endemic to philosophical practice. Some Tibetologists and not a few European philosophers claim that Tibetans have no notion that corresponds precisely with the European idea of "philosophy." The term *mtshan nyid* has been translated as "philosophy," and it is a term that is commonly found in English-Tibetan dictionaries; but more precisely, it refers to the study of the formal characteristics, or even definitions, of things. Perhaps this formal element renders it apt for philosophy in a positivist sense, but it lacks the full, reflexive range of much philosophical scholarship. The Tibetans also have terms for "formal analysis" (*tshad mas grub par rtags*),[14] "reasoned analysis" (*rigs pas rnam par dbyad pa*[15] or *rigs pas dpyad*[16]), rational investigation (*rigs pa'i dpyad bzod*),[17] and "logical formulation" (*rtags su bkod*[18] and *bkod pa'i sgrub byed*[19]). But the most general term for formal reasoning is *rigs pa* (as in *rigs pa nyid*)[20] and "analytic reason" (*dpyod pa'i rigs pa*[21]). *Rigs*

---

14. Tsong Khapa (n.d., circa 1996, 211).
15. Tsong Khapa (1997, 675, 705, and 774).
16. Tsong Khapa (n.d., circa 1996, 213).
17. Tsong Khapa (1997, 757).
18. Tsong Khapa (1997, 680).
19. Tsong Khapa (1997, 708).
20. Tsong Khapa (1997, 757).

pa is employed as a sort of mental discipline or rigor, and it is considered to have great utility for the wider truth concerns of valid knowledge (*tshad ma*) and "thinking"[22] more generally.

Rigs pa implies a methodic character on the part of reflection, but even when it is routinized in one or another well-accepted form, ethnomethodological scrutiny reveals that *rigs pa* cannot operate independently of the social praxis that formulated it, authorized it, and sustains its credibility. Formal reasoning does not work alone—nowhere is there a pure "truth" that can stand in its full-ness on its own valid grounds apart from the practices of thinkers who, as their social practice, organize those grounds, assess issues of the adequacy of criteria, reliability of methods, and validity of the results of philosophical procedures. The propriety of the logical structures is itself a social achievement, and it is obvious to the most cursory *in situ* inquiry that logical structures are always in development and their evolution is never finished.

The *propriety* of formal analytic procedures and the *obligation* to fit one's thinking and responses into the developing logical order, which we have been examining, are social as well as logical events. A logical order is a social fact in Durkheim's (1964) pregnant sense. That is, it is a massive presence whose valid-ity is believed to have originated from somewhere outside of a collection of social practitioners and to have application beyond them. Durkheim had his eye keenly set on the right order of social phenomenon, only he misinterpreted it,[23] and its supposedly metaphysical facticity is exclusively a social production. Durkheim (1915) also correctly described the moral force of social facts. Though his study of religious behavior practiced sociologism by reducing spiri-tuality to only its social dimensions, as Bellah and as Preston have observed (Preston 1988, 2), he was absolutely right that the products of public social par-ticipation collect a moral force that renders them compelling for all social actors. In his classic study, Durkheim (1915) failed to recognize that this moral flavor of collective products was not exclusive to the religious domain of Aboriginal social life but could be found in most regions of their everyday life as well (Liberman 1985, 26-27). Whatever else they may be, the propriety of formal analytic procedures and the obligations they elicit from philosophers are social accomplishments. Especially when Tibetan debaters have provided an account-able structure of reason and it has been ratified by means of the formal methods of authorization that we have described, the demand to conform with the emerg-ing local order, *which here is a logical order*, is a moral obligation.

---

21. Jnanagarbha (1987, 173).

22. In his later career, Heidegger used the term "philosophy" infrequently, preferring the term "thinking" to describe his aim. By "thinking," he meant a reflexive contempla-tion that lingers with things, without dominating their being.

23. Cf. Garfinkel (2002, 65-68).

These matters are ever-present practical matters for any cohort of philosophers reasoning anywhere. And the sophistry that may accompany these matters cannot simply be expelled by the application of some correct methods; that is because the social practices that produce and validate such methods are themselves another natural medium for sophistry. That is, the very practices for eliminating sophistry from philosophy are vulnerable to sophistic treatment, so the presence of sophistry is, ultimately, without remedy, which is different than asserting that sophistry cannot be reduced. All reasoning involves betrayal. The originality of the first insight—"the saying"—preserves itself by losing its creativity in "the said" (see the epigraph to this chapter, 273). But the dialectic that takes place between the saying and the said is not without creative resources for exploring truth. For philosophy, and for *rigs pa*, both the saying and the said are necessary, and rhetoric and original intuition work philosophically only when they work in tandem.

Rhetorical processes do not "contaminate" reason but operate at its core and are part of its very nature, its "suchness" as it were. The best and worst of sophistry and rhetoric—devices for interrogating the depth of the other's thinking, getting one's partner to listen, confusing the other, forcing the other into making contradictory commitments, etc.—are not separable from the praxis of producing a truth. And the worst always accompanies the best. We require formal reasoning to organize things, to assist communication, to promote clear thinking and consistency, and to maintain a reason-*able* social order, that is, to think better. But the most vital insights sometimes ride piggyback on the more mundane forms of rationality. That one cannot do it *without* the mundane, even sophistic, forms, doesn't mean that it is not possible to *fail* to do it *with* the mundane forms.

But it is too simple although true to claim, along with Husserl and Levinas, that these mundane forms coerce and distract truth inquiries; rather, we need to understand ethnomethodologically *just how* this coercion and distraction occurs and just how reasoning is done. The phenomenologists may have overstated the incapacitation of humans in the face of rational forms. In their zeal to undo the illusion that all philosophical considerations can be exhausted by deriving truth deductively from a universally valid method, they adhered too strongly to the belief that the application of formal analytic methods entails flaws that are terminal for philosophy. Gendlin (1992, 124) contests this view and argues that we need to take a closer look at what thinkers are actually capable of doing *with* those mundane forms: "The forms close and do not enclose. They work alone and do not work alone. They are themselves but they are always something else . . . . Their working is always other and *more than* they are as patterns alone." We require an ethnomethodological respecification of the problem, with the assistance of detailed studies of some formal analytic betrayals of philosophy, studies that capture in their local details the local organizational concerns of serious philosophizing, concerns that not only respect their interests in the truth but also respect the logical order, which bears a moral force that is derived from the sanctity of the emerging social structure. As a philosophical anthropology, our investigation is concerned to describe *in situ* the real worldly work of *rigs pa*. And once we embark upon such inquiries we notice immediately that Tibetans learn how to use whatever rational forms there are to do original and probative things. To say that people are constrained by forms is to tell only half of the story, and it is not an observation that can be sustained without amendment once one begins to investigate the *in situ* work of reasoning. The other half—that people innovate and not infrequently end up satisfying their own intuitions—becomes evident once we address our inquiries to real world materials.

We have seen during these investigations how the confusion, uncertainties, pushing, etc., can provide training in maintaining one's focus on one's own thinking amidst the distraction of the rhetoric. An Indian colleague once asked me skeptically, "It may help them in character building, but does it help them get at truth?" We have examined some occasions where the obligation to fit into the proper logical forms was made a productive practice by the ingenuity of the debaters.[24] But is not every truth of assertion embedded in a local order? The local contingencies of that order are not extraneous considerations, for *every* philosophical insight keeps such company: there are always local contingencies. The desire for a context-free "truth," absolute and all-pervading, is a truth-habit that is obsession, not philosophy. It is nowhere to be found; social factors are always part of its context.

There are, however, some unique problems with the Tibetan practice of philosophical debate. In debate after debate, Tibetan scholars endeavor to work collaboratively in building a smoothly functioning logical order. Their success at this may be assessed in part by the rhythm of their synchronized utterances, which itself lends a mechanical energy to the dialectics. Debating is achieved, and it may be said that the Tibetan scholars become intoxicated by their formal analytic structures; that is, it is a practice that provides to the parties a physical as well as mental catharsis. On such occasions, are Tibetan debaters being formulaic or are they being philosophically productive? As in the case of prayer or davining (in the Jewish tradition), the experience can be *either* a trivial parody of itself or profound. It is possible for the Tibetan practice we are investigating to be part of serious philosophizing. By that sanctimonious phrase, I mean that the formalization of their reflections may be placed skillfully in the service of questioning what is most worthy of being questioned. When that is achieved it may be said that real *rigs pa*, the zenith of Tibetan philosophical practice, has been attained.

There is some discussion, even among Gelug practitioners, that there are too many complications contrived during some debates. Some things are complicated, so they require complications; other things are simple, and there is no

---

24. See 199.

need to complicate them unnecessarily. One difficulty with Tibetan philosophical debate is that the embodied aesthetics of their dialectical practice encourages complications, even when they are not necessary. In order for scholars to enter into the debate forms and flow with them, in order to exercise their intellects in the dialectical ways of which they are so fond—they may contrive complications that afford them an occasion for serializing the give and take of their utterances and carrying them to some desired synchronization. When their system flows it seems to run itself, and it becomes an excellent illustration of a Durkheimian social fact, since in its self-flowing it displays its purported cohort-free objectivity. As a philosophical event, this is the local achievement of Tibetan scholars. A danger is always that the debating can withdraw into a hollow shell of sophistic formalities. But it is not merely that. Or, rather, it *is* that, but may also be made something more.

Although *rigs pa* is thought to proceed by means of rational procedures, like any good Durkheimian object it can acquire a life of its own. The philosophical work of Tibetan debaters provides for order, but eventually that order may not be knowable in any complete sense. It just goes on, and it derives its justification as much from mimesis as from any formal rationality. Indeed, like any social order, the order "knows" more than the participants. The Sartrian notion that every knowing must be made an authentic experience is naive, however salutary may be his advice for reducing the betrayals of philosophy. The idealization of a "pure" thinking free of all contamination can too easily become self-delusion, especially when a corrective practice of negative dialectics is absent. But any practice of negative dialectics comes with an increased risk of sophism. Let us turn away from these abstract speculations and take up some ethnomethodological examination of instances of sophistry in actual debates.

Early in debate I.1 (see Illustrative Debate section on the CD-ROM), T is able to secure the commitment of L' that the appearance of an image in a mirror is an erroneous perception. Because L' recognizes that the perception of this appearance is a matter of sense-consciousness, he slips inadvertently into an additional commitment that the understanding of its erroneous nature is a capability of "sense-consciousness."

	L'	The truth is not recognized. In general—
	T	Yes?
2:59	L	For the example of the reflection of an image in the mirror, what appears to sense-consciousness and the way it actually exists are not in accord with each other.
	T	When "is not the customary truth" is written, it refers to sense-consciousness, is it?

The notion "is not the customary truth"[25] refers to an act of mere mundane reasoning about mirrors—reasoning that, presumably, still involves conceptualization; yet L' clings to the idea it is sense-consciousness:

> L' Oh, it is reckoned to be sense-consciousness.

This is hardly more than a blind repeat, an instance where the defender is just following the words, without a good deal of reflection. T then objectivates this, in order to formalize the commitment:

> T Oh is it?
> L' It is said that what appears to sense-consciousness is not true.
> :10 T IT DOES NOT FOLLOW. Now, it's this way, it is?
> L' It's this way, it's this way.

Note especially the photo of L' at 2:59:04. It shows L' earnestly searching in T's response for the significance of what he has just said, for which he may come to be made responsible. The gaze of L' displays the veracity of Merleau-Ponty's (1964b: xv) keen observation that "The germ of universality . . . is to be found ahead of us in the dialogue into which our experience of other people throws us." T moves to clarify the situation:

> T For the regard of common sense, why is the image in the mirror
> 2:59:33 not true? BECAUSE it is said that it is, for example. >~
> L' Oh. This is so.
> T Is it?
> L' It's so.
> T NOW IT DOES NOT FOLLOW. A common sense thought like that is posited by the eye-consciousness, is it?

T has now moved to reaffirm L''s commitment. But L' has not yet clarified his thinking, *and he is trying to think the matter through at the same time that T is pressing him.* In order to gain an instant to reflect, he merely repeats T's utterance, offering a synonym instead of furthering the inquiry:

> L' The eye-consciousness. Sense-consciousness.

But this repetition, *which was uttered for the practical purpose of stalling,* only solidifies L''s commitment and his obligation to defend it:

> T NOW IT DOES NOT FOLLOW. Yah, isn't it necessary that a cognition reasoning validly establishes that a sense-consciousness is an incorrect consciousness?
> L' A sense-consciousness. Mm.

---

25. From Tsong Khapa (1988, 186): "Whatever common sense knowledge recognizes to be false is not what is meant by a customary truth." (*Gang zhig kun rdzob tu yang brdzun pa ni kun rdzob kyi bden pa ma yin no.*)

T works within the obligation to pick up the wording of L', so since L' has raised the term "sense-consciousness" again, T proceeds to use it as a tool in the ensuing development of the reasoning. In this way the term has won its life somewhat serendipitously; however, it can now play a vital role in the formal argumentation.

T begins to press harder, and L' is locked into his commitment, even though it is derived coincidentally from the contingencies of the local interaction. First raised as a tool to deflect T's press, he now has a logical obligation to defend it, a defense he attempts in vain:

T   Some conceptual cognition must establish that, or not?
L'   Not necessarily.
2:59:46 T   One does not require such a cognition reasoning validly to say that the reflection is untrue? . . . So for the sense-consciousness it is true. / It's not untrue.
L'   / It's not true. It's not true. If you want to know the reason why it's not true, it's because the sense-consciousness is capable of realizing that something is not true in the way it appears; there is a capacity to recognize that the mode of appearance and the way that what appears actually exists are not in accord with each other.

The local contingencies of the interaction have carried L' to an indefensible position. Ethnomethodologically speaking, the itinerary of the formal analysis here is to a considerable extent a product of the local social organization, and L' is now well and truly stuck in a corner. It cannot even be said that it is a corner of his own making, because it was the natural flow of the local orderliness of the debating that carried him into the corner, almost unwittingly. Whether this discussion amounts to anything philosophically depends upon what T and L' do with the tools the debating has provided to them. Unfortunately, L' becomes capable of doing little more than search for a way to get out of his corner:

T   NOW IT DOES NOT FOLLOW. For an ordinary, everyday person who is practiced in applying conventions, the reflection of an im-
3:01:12   age in the mirror is not said to be true, it is said to be false. >~
L'   I ACCEPT that it is, indeed.

L' at last surrenders his indefensible position:

:15 T   That sort of customary truth is necessarily determined by a
3:01:19   conceptual cognition that is valid. >~
L'   Yes.
T   That sort of customary truth, right?
L'   / If you present customary truth that way it's all right.
L"   / A common sense mind.
T   What?

L'   Yes yes.

But now T wants to assure himself that L''s agreement is in his understanding, as well as in form, so he requires him to develop some thinking with the
terms they have agreed to:

T   NOW IT DOES NOT FOLLOW. Yah, TAKE AS THE SUBJECT
:30 a common sense mind. Why must it be established by valid con-
     ceptual cognition? >~
L'   For that sort of common sense mind.
T   What about that common sense mind?
L'   It is the realization that the image does not exist in the way that it
     appears. Now that mind, huh?
:35 T   That common sense mind.
L'   Mm.
T   Earlier you answered that it was established by sense-
     consciousness.
:39 L'   Not just for any common sense mind, though—for the common
     sense mind which is definitely able to establish that such an ap-
     pearance is not in accord with the way it exists, and so is false.

It seems that L' is listening *only* for how to extract himself from his difficulties and is not capable of contributing to any serious dialectics. If "philosophy is
the free unfolding of a human capacity, that of thinking," as Heidegger (1994,
157) suggests, then the lack of freedom in this debate would disqualify it as philosophy. L''s reply here has the appearance of being some sort of defense, but it
is difficult to determine whether it means anything at all. When reviewing this
part of the video tape, the challenger commented aloud to me about the contribution of L' at 3:01:39, "This is no debate—it is no doubt to anybody."

Minutes later, the debate does proceed to some profound topics, with the
dialectical weight carried mostly by the challenger, including the interrogation
of the status of noema which we examined at pages 257-60. The dialectics discussed there demonstrate the best and the worst of Tibetan debating—T's original criticism of accepted philosophical tenets and L''s narrowly drawn replies
that are technically correct but reveal no philosophical understanding. If the dialectics presses too heavily upon a respondent, and he feels trapped within the
logical structures that have emerged, he may be rendered philosophically impotent by the claustrophobia of having to find not the best but *any* rhetorical solution to his problem. As Dreyfus (2002, 262) has commented, "Instead of trying
new answers, I became fixated on the two or three answers I could come up
with, my mind racing to find the gap that would allow me to escape."[26] Kensur

---

26. Sudnow (1979) describes the similar experience of jazz musicians caught deep
within the course of serious improvisation.

Lobsang Tsering once cautioned me against debating with such a narrow perspective, "You must not only have the right answers, 'Yes, yes. No, no' [*yin yin, med med*] you must also have the right reason. It's not all right to give answers without reasons."

In debate I.7, L" has become so contentious (see 5:46:07, 209) that it has spoiled the debate. L" ridicules T's argumentation and calls for him to debate properly, with greater logical formality. T responds, interestingly, with the comment, "Terminology is not absolutely necessary for there to be reasoning," which L" promptly rejects. T asks a pertinent question that the defenders should have no trouble in answering, but the defenders are left speechless:

> T   How do we establish a direct valid cognition?
>
> L"   How do we put it? Ohhh. I've forgotten. When asked, "What is the definition of a direct valid cognition?" Mmm. [3.0 seconds]
>
> 5:47:17   T   >~ [5.0 seconds]
>
> :23   L'   Oh like this.
>
> T   What?

Up against the embarrassment of this lengthy silence, L' provides a comprehensive demonstration of how the use of correct terminology can contribute nothing at all to reasoning. The defender's first utterance is news from nowhere:

> L'   If it is a valid cognition, we say that IT DOES NOT PERVADE THAT it is an inferential valid cognition.
>
> T   Oh, if it is a direct valid cognition IT DOES NOT PERVADE THAT it is an inferential valid cognition. We say it like that, right?

T has treated him charitably, and L' engages in a meaningless dance with petty forms, almost fetishizing Tibetan formal analytic praxis. It is the philosophical equivalent of the "rope-a-dope" of professional boxing, and nothing is accomplished philosophically:

> L'   Oh, CONSIDER a valid cognition.
>
> T   Oh.
>
> L'   IT DOES NOT PERVADE THAT it is an inferential valid cognition.
>
> T   What.
>
> L'   Oh, CONSIDER a valid cognition. IT DOES NOT PERVADE THAT it is an inferential cognition.
>
> T   CONSIDER a valid cognition. IT FOLLOWS THAT it pervades that it is not necessarily an inferential valid cognition.
>
> L'   Like this.
>
> :36   T   >~ So, said like this, IT FOLLOWS.
>
> L'   THAT IS ACCEPTABLE.
>
> T   IT FOLLOWS THAT it pervades.

L'   Yes.

When the dialectics leads one or both of the parties into a constraining logic, in order, as a hermeneutic practice, to show them an important contradiction or a new insight, to set up a rhythmic tempo for the debating, or even to explore reasoning itself by displaying the limits of formal analysis (as in III.2, 179-82), then such strategies may be said to be dialectical and not merely sophistic; however, when it closes off thinking and suffocates the debaters in the safety of proper forms, it does not rise above the level of sophistry.

For our final illustration we will revisit II.2 (discussed on 183-85). T is endeavoring to imprison the respondents within the shallow forms of their public commitments, and he deliberately manipulates them into the contradiction they find their way to. In fact, this is a fairly common event in Tibetan debating and is responsible for a good deal of the charge of sophistry laid against them. It may be said that such pedantic examination provides exercise for learning to think carefully, and it is probably adequate for a sophomoric level of studies; however, it is philosophically embarrassing when senior scholars or an otherwise potentially interesting debate degenerates into dialectical martial arts.

Even the exposure of this sophistic "contradiction" has the practical benefit of gaining the attention of the defenders, and by the time we again pick up the debate the parties are paying very close attention to each other. With this degree of alertness and communication something worthwhile philosophically could be pursued, though this has not yet taken place. T rehearses his proposal, and L' attempts to provide the relevant context for their replies.

T   TAKE AS THE SUBJECT Bhavaviveka, IT FOLLOWS THAT
9:12:11   he is not a Middle Way scholar. >∼
L'   Who? He is not a Middle Way scholar?
L"   Bhavaviveka is not a Middle Way scholar.
L'   He is not a Middle Way scholar who adheres to this system's explanation.
T   CONFOUNDED BY ALL THREE!

It is a scholars' illusion to contend that the formal apophansis can handle all of the philosophical content of the utterances independently of the philosophers' interactional work in coordinating the sharing of the horizon of meaning within which the utterances find their sense. Accordingly, there is a good deal of "context talk" in Tibetan debating, that is, brief intimate discussion during which the strict apophantics is momentarily suspended and a more direct discourse is used. Without directing their colleague to the correct sense of a response, the formalities would take them forever, and so the formal and informal elements are frequently woven together. The coordination of understanding cannot be done without the formalities, but the formalities by themselves would be impotent.

Unfortunately, in this case the challenger is deaf to L''s attempt to provide a context for their commitment.

But a good consequence move is like a shot of adrenaline. Not only are the debaters now excited, but most of the audience is keenly involved as well, and L" is smiling deeply. The contradiction has the potential to address something interesting, even though it is based upon a dialectical move that is pedestrian. Here again, an ethnomethodological study affords an opportunity to observe a phenomenon that is easily missed when one investigates only a docile text: what is sophistry does not depend exclusively upon the *apophantic form* of the reasoning under consideration, it depends very much upon *what members do* with those forms. The philosophical productivity or lack of it will depend upon the originality and resourcefulness, or shortcomings, of the debaters.

In the short run, the debaters adhere to a technical compliance with the forms, and it seems that the locally produced consistency is limiting their capacity for reflection. T's narrow interest in confining the defenders to their formal commitments renders him blind to the defenders' attempt to communicate the wider sense of their utterance. One of the founders of the Gelug order Khedrup (*sTong thun chen mo*, 379) describes such a practice as "Shooting the arrow that refutes the argument without paying any attention to the target."

	T	TAKE AS THE SUBJECT Bhavaviveka.
	L'	Yes.
	T	Uh, IT FOLLOWS THAT he is not a Middle Way scholar! [heat-
:17		edly presented] >~
-098	L'	/ I ACCEPT // He is not a Middle Way scholar.///
	L"	/ I ACCEPT // /// He is not a Mid-
		dle Way scholar.
	L'	[Yelling at T] If you are referring to the Dialectical Reasoning-
		based Middle Way School, he is not a Middle Way scholar.
:20	T	IT FOLLOWS THAT he is not a Middle Way Scholar. >~
-100-	L'	I ACCEPT!
9:12:22	T	This contradicts the text! >~

Nearly a minute later, T finally introduces some interesting reasoning for why Bhavaviveka should be considered a Middle Way scholar (see 9:13:13). This reason offers the example of a monk who violates his vows (for instance by drinking or having sexual relations)—although he is in error, he is still a monk:

	T	Therefore, though the Master Bhavaviveka has accepted the exis-
		tence of falsely established objects—
	L'	Though he has.
9:13:09	T	—it is said that he is still a Middle Way scholar, uh, that must be
		the assertion. >~
	L'	No, no, no.

> T   That illustration of a monk who has vows contradicts them and
> :13   acts inappropriately [much audience discussion] is presented. >~
>   He is a Middle Way scholar. Is it said that according to our system
>   he is not a Middle Way scholar?
>
> -117- L'   Who?

The defender's attempt to make a clarification is again shut down:

> :15 L"   According to our system he is not a Middle Way scholar. Be-
>   fore,—
> :18 T   —TS'A! TAKE AS THE SUBJECT the Master Bhavaviveka,
>   is he a Middle Way scholar?!
>   L'   / According to our system he is not a Middle Way scholar.
>   L"   / According to our system he is not a Middle Way scholar.
> -118- T   Does our system explain that he is a Middle Way scholar or not?
>   Do you hold that he is a Middle Way scholar?!
>   L'   He is a Middle Way scholar.
> 9:13:25 T =v= TS'A here. Definitely TS'A!

T had finally trapped L' in a sophistic inconsistency. Finally out of patience, L' scolds T for his sophistry:

> L'   There is no "TS'A." There is no "TS'A." According to this system
>   he is not a Middle Way scholar. [All speak at once.] According to
>   this system he is not a Middle Way scholar. But it has been said
>   that he is a Middle Way scholar, hasn't it?

Surprisingly, T responds to this last utterance by accusing L' of sophistry, which is certainly a case of the pot calling the kettle black. At least it demonstrates that these Tibetan debaters recognize that sophistry can be a problem. However, it is demagoguery to so accuse L' when he is conscientiously trying to solve the semantics of the dispute:

> -120- T   Now, does our professor quibble here over a technicality?
>   L' We've covered it already.
>   T   Yah-yah-yah-yah-yah, TS'A.

Conclusion

Geshe Lhundrup Sopa summarized both the risk and the promise of Tibetan dialectics when he advised, "Just reviewing the arguments as a dead inventory in insufficient. We need to place our minds within the living quandaries that each position faces." We have observed that Tibetan debating is inhabited by both living sophistries and living quandaries. The criticism that it is more inclined toward dry formalism than other philosophical cultures seems too severe, however. In fact, this criticism is made more likely when the critic her/himself is constricted to a logocentric view of Tibetan Buddhist tenets, a perspective that is deficient in having familiarity with lived reflection *in the course* of actual formal reasoning. What they see as dry formalism is dry in part because the Buddhologists employ a hypertextual dependency that regards words in a way that is dislocated and disembodied from any lived sense that they may have or come to have. What are assumed to be blindly accepted received notions may in fact be made vulnerable to a path of vigorous dialectics, depending upon the skills of the Tibetan debaters involved. Further, the endless rehearsing of commitments and truisms may be about organizing the local orderliness of the talk and preliminary to what will be philosophically germane.

The notion that European philosophy is self-reflective in a more original way is too chauvinist to be taken seriously, for Europeans also have their received notions, and these received notions provide for European thought much of its intelligibility. We have learned that what is logical is also social, and that is necessarily the case for European as well as Tibetan scholars. The determination of when grounds have been given and the dialectics can proceed to other things is in part a social determination. The idea that there can be a pure thinking without any sophistry is unsound, for any thinking requires some formalization, and any formal apophansis will support sophistry.

There are important differences between the two philosophical cultures. For one, among Tibetan scholars individualism is less valued as a personal creed or as a methodological practice. It is much like the difference between European and Tibetan painting—Europeans seek an individual style, sign their canvases, and paint self-portraits; whereas, Tibetan painters do not sign their canvases and seek to paint only just like any other expert painter. But is individualism really a necessary requirement for either artistic or philosophical sensibility? I think many European scholars, in a fit of self-aggrandizement, would insist that this is the case, but I doubt that it is. It seems to me that, as Rudy Visker (1997) once suggested, a philosopher should neither repeat the obvious nor soar above it. Given this characterization, both philosophical traditions have successes and failures that may be identified.

Another European criticism must be taken more seriously, and indeed it has been by most active contemporary Tibetan scholar-monks. This is the criticism, also formulated by Leibniz in his speaking of the balance of reason, that reason should not have any particular agenda. The complaint is that Buddhist dialectics is a journey the destinations of which are too well known; hence, it is not philosophy. Stephen Batchelor (1990, 12), who spent ten years as a Buddhist monk, has complained, "Reason was subordinate to faith. In other words, you only set out to prove what you have already decided to believe," and there is some truth to his charge. Two Tibetan colleagues of mine once confessed to me, "We admire you Westerners, you say whatever you think just on the basis of your own reasoning." But it seems excessive to assert that this portrait exhausts the capacity of Tibetan philosophical culture. This study has demonstrated that alongside reasoning with routine forms exists a capacity to sustain intriguing philosophical insights. Any philosophical culture includes this diversity.

Georges Dreyfus (2002, 306 and 311), a European who also spent a decade as a monk, offers the criticism that "the quasi-canonization of definitions in contemporary Ge-luk practices manifests an essentialist tendency" that contradicts the anti-essentialism that is at the heart of their philosophical tenets. However true in the deepest possible ways, this again is the living irony of any, and every, philosophical practice. In three of our debates, the debaters offered some truly penetrating insight into the shortcomings of essentialism and the limits of formal analysis, *yet* in their own philosophical practice each of them violated the spirit of their insight.

In debate II.3, the debaters ask whether logical theses are necessary for a realization of emptiness, and they conclude that such theses may be useful but do not guarantee a realization of emptiness. They draw a distinction between "nondual innate awareness" and formal analytics, but the distinction in itself is formal analytic, and they recognize that it is, and they continue to work formally to establish a universal truth about the matter. In debate II.4, the scholars collaborate in a dialectical examination of essentialism. The clarifier of the reasoning asserts, "When one understands the way of *positing* how concepts are merely imputations, IT FOLLOWS THAT one does not necessarily *realize* that concepts are merely imputations. >~" Conceptual understanding and an actual realization are not identical. The respondent concurs, "We speak of a general understanding of the formulation that concepts are merely imputations. . . . We *say* that concepts are merely imputations," and he goes on to argue, echoing Hegel,[27] that understanding a formulation is less than a fulfilled understanding of its meaning or, even more vital, its habitual integration within one's everyday praxis. This latter interest, being the real motive for their philosophical inquiry, ought to serve to reduce the vulnerability of Tibetan philosophical practice to sophistry. However, the practical work of the debaters remains developing a logical discussion about not needing logic. Debate III.2 sustains a brilliant philosophical quandary,[28] and gives no ground to sophistry, even at the price of irresolvable irony. These debaters acknowledge that realizing emptiness requires that one think the unthinkable. The clarifier of the reasoning summarizes,

> T: Although there the nature of things may be formulated as arising through the force of appearing to the mind, it is not formulated so (*'jog kyang mi 'jog*). It's this way is it not? It is not formulated so, and although the wisdom that realizes just-how-it-is formulates the nature of things through the force of the mind, yah, the wisdom

27. See 293.
28. See 179-82 and the Illustrative Debates section, Debate III, of the CD-ROM.

that realizes just-how-it-is does not formulate the nature of things as existing in that way.

Even philosophical insight into the meaning of nonessentialism is "a subtle notion that conceals as a customary practice." And despite such a splendid insight, the debaters themselves perform, by means of their apophansis, the work of concealing, in the form of the essentialism of trying to formulate the idea that an understanding of emptiness is not capable of formulation.

More simply put, these Tibetan scholars are philosophers, which entails a double helix of original insight and sophistry. The fact that Buddhist philosophy takes for its topic the ways that philosophy betrays itself offers not the slightest protection that it itself will not betray itself every bit as quickly as any other culture's practice of reasoning does. Even great profundities, if they are to be communicated, must be thematized; and thematization leads naturally to betrayals. The founder of the Gelug sect Tsong Khapa (n.d., *dGongs pa rab gsal*, 36) formulates this universal human dilemma in a question about the pedagogy for meditation on emptiness: "Although one travels across the sky-like suchness, that mode of traveling—the accomplished being's meditative experience—cannot be described by them. So how, by what witness, will a hearer ever be able to listen?" It seems to be that it is humankind's curse and blessing that once the talk begins, even sky-like insight may be dragged earthward.

Bibliography

Abram, David. 1996. *The Spell of the Sensuous*. New York: Vintage.

Adorno, Theodor. 1992. *Negative Dialectics*. New York: Continuum.

———. 2000. *Introduction to Sociology*. Stanford: Stanford University Press.

Agre Phil. 1998. Presentation to Ethnomethodology Panel, Annual Meeting of the American Sociological Association, San Francisco.

Bar-Hillel, Yehoshua. 1954. "Indexical Expressions." *Mind* 63.

———. 1964. "Bgidat Halogicanim" ["The Logician's Treason"] *Iyyun* 14: 120-125.

Batchelor, Stephen. 1990. *The Faith to Doubt*. Berkeley: Parallax Press.

———. 2000. *Verses from the Center*. New York: Riverhead Books.

Bernasconi, Robert. 1995. "On Heidegger's Other Sins of Omission: His Exclusion of Asian Thought." *American Catholic Philosophical Quarterly* 69, no. 2: 333-343.

Boeder, Heribert. 1997. *Seditions*. Albany, N.Y.: SUNY Press.

Cabezón, José. 1994. *Buddhism and Language*. Albany, N.Y.: SUNY Press.

———. 1995. "Buddhist Studies as a Discipline and the Role of Theory." *Journal of the International Association of Buddhist Studies* 18, no. 2: 231-268.

———. 1997. "The Regulations of a Monastery." In *Religions of Tibet in Practice*, ed. Donald S. Lopez, Jr., 335-351. Princeton, N.J.: Princeton University Press.

Chanter, Tina. 1997. "The Betrayal of Philosophy." *Philosophy and Social Criticism* 23, No. 6: 65-79.

Chattopadhayaya, Debiprasad. 1979. *Studies in the History of Indian Philosophy, Vol. III*. Calcutta: K. P. Bagchi.

Collins, Randall. 1998. *The Sociology of Philosophies*. Cambridge, Mass.: Harvard University Press.

Coward, Harold. 1990. *Derrida and Indian Philosophy*. Albany, N.Y.: SUNY Press.

Crosswhite, James. 1998. "What Is It over Which Philosophy and Rhetoric Are Divided?" Northwest Philosophical Association Meeting. Eugene, Ore.

Csikszentmihalyi, Mihaly. 1996. *Creativity*. New York: HarperCollins.

Dallmayr, Fred 1987. *Critical Encounters*. South Bend, Ind.: University of Notre Dame Press.

———. 1996. *Beyond Orientalism*. Albany, New York: SUNY Press.

Das, Veena. 1982. *Structure and Cognition: Aspects of Hindu Caste and Ritual.* Bombay: Oxford University Press.

Das, S. C. 1902. *A Tibetan-English Dictionary*. Calcutta: Bengal Secretariat.

Dascal, Marcelo. 1990. "La Arrogancia de la Razón." *Isegoría* 2: 75-103.

Derrida, Jacques. 1974. *Of Grammatology*. Baltimore: John Hopkins University Press.

———. 1978. *Writing and Difference*. Chicago: University of Chicago Press.

———. 1982. "Différance," in *Margins of Philosophy*. Chicago: University of Chicago Press.

———. 1994. *Spectres of Marx*. London: Routledge.

Desideri, Ippolito. 1931. *An Account of Tibet*. Edited by Filippo de Filippi. London: George Routledge and Sons.

Dewey, John. 1916. *Democracy in Education*. New York: Macmillan.

Dhargyey, Ngawang. 1990. "What Is Non-existent and What is Remaining in *Sunyata?*" *Journal of Indian Philosophy* 18: 81-91.

Dreyfus, Georges. 2002. *The Sound of Two Hands Clapping: Memory, Commentary, and Debate in Tibetan Monastic Education*. Berkeley: University of California Press.

———. n.d. *The Sound of Two Hands Clapping,* typescript.

Durkheim, Emile. 1915. *The Elementary Forms of Religious Life*. New York: Free Press.

———. 1964. *The Rules of Sociological Method*. New York: Free Press.

———. 1983. *Pragmatism and Sociology*. Cambridge: Cambridge University Press.

Embree, Lester, et al., eds. 1997. *Encyclopedia of Phenomenology*. Dordrecht: Kluwer.

Fine, Gary Alan. 2001. *Gifted Tongues: High School Debate and Adolescent Culture*. Princeton, N.J.: Princeton University Press.

Gadamer, Hans-Georg. 1975. *Truth and Method*. New York: Seabury.

Garfinkel, Harold. 1977a. "When Is Phenomenology Sociological?" In Myrtle Korenbaum, ed., *Annals of Phenomenological Sociology, Vol. 2*. Dayton, Ohio: Wright State University.

———. 1977b. "Lecture Notes." Los Angeles: UCLA Department of Sociology.

———. 1998. "Evidence for Locally Produced, Naturally Accountable Phenomena of Order,* Logic, Reason, Meaning, Method, Etc., In and As of the Essential Quiddity of Immortal Ordinary Society." *Sociological Theory* 6, no. 1: 103-109.

———. 1991. "Respecification: Evidence for Locally Produced, Naturally Accountable Phenomena of Order, Logic, Reason, Meaning, Method, Etc., In and As of the Essential Haecceity of the Immortal Ordinary Society." In Graham Button, ed., *Ethnomethodology and the Human Sciences*. Cambridge: Cambridge University Press.

———. 2001. "Plenary Talk" to the Conference on Orders of Ordinary Action, Manchester, England, July 10, 2001.

———. 2002. *Ethnomethodology's Program*. Lanham, Md.: Rowman & Littlefield.

Garfinkel, Harold, and D. Lawrence Wieder. 1992. "Two Incommensurable, Asymmetrically Alternate Technologies of Social Analysis." In *Text in Context*, ed. Graham Watson and R. M. Seiler. Newbury Park, Calif.: Sage Publications.

Gendlin, Eugene. 1992. "Thinking Beyond Patterns." In *The Presence of Feeling in Thought*, ed. B. denOuden and M. Moen. New York: Peter Lang.

Geertz, Clifford. 1973. *Interpretation of Cultures*. New York: Basic Books.

Giddens, Anthony. 1972. *Emile Durkheim: Selected Writings*. Cambridge: Cambridge University Press.

Goffman, Erving. 1967. *Interaction Ritual*. Chicago: Aldine.

Goldberg, Margaret. 1985. "Argumentation and Understanding: A Study of Tibetan Religious Debate." Ph.D. thesis, University of Illinois at Urbana-Champaign.

Guenther, Herbert V. 1989a. *A Visionary Journey*. Boston: Shambala.

———. 1989b. *From Reductionism to Creativity*. Boston: Shambala.

———. 1992. *Meditation Differently: Phenomenological and Psychological Aspects of Tibetan Buddhist Practices*. Delhi: Motilal Banarsidass.

———. 1994. *Wholeness Lost and Wholeness Regained*. New York: SUNY Press.

Haberman, David L.. 1999. "Religious Studies 2000." Denver: The Lester Lecture on the Study of Religion, Department of Religious Studies, University of Colorado.

Halbfass, Wilhelm. 1988. *India and Europe*. Albany, New York: SUNY Press.

Hegel, G. W. F. 1967. *A Phenomenology of Mind*. Trans. by J. B. Baillie. New York: Harper and Row.

———. 1977. *A Phenomenology of Spirit*. Trans. by A. V. Miller. Oxford: Clarendon Press.

———. 1989. *Hegel's Science of Logic*, Trans. by A. V. Miller. New York: Humanities Press.

Heidegger, Martin. 1957. *Holwege*, Frankfurt (Third Edition); cited in Halbfass, 1988: 168.

———. 1962. *Being and Time*. Trans. by John Macquarrie and Edward Robinson. New York: Harper and Row.

———. 1967. *What Is A Thing?* Chicago: Henry Regnery.

————. 1991. *The Principle of Reason*. Bloomington, Ind.: Indiana University Press.

————. 1994. *Basic Questions of Philosophy*. Bloomington, Ind.: Indiana University Press.

————. 1996. *Being and Time*. Trans. by Joan Stambaugh. Albany: SUNY Press.

Hengst, Julia. 2000. "A New Generation of Tibetan Lamas." *Mandala* (September-October). Pages 63-65.

Hopkins, Jeffrey. 1983. *Meditation on Emptiness*. London: Wisdom Publications.

————. 1987. *Emptiness Yoga*. Ithaca, N.Y.: Snow Lion.

————. 1992. *Tibetan-Sanskrit-English Dictionary*. Dyke, Vir.: Tibetan Studies Institute.

Huntington, Jr., Charles. 1989. *The Emptiness of Emptiness*. Honolulu: University of Hawaii Press.

Husserl, Edmund. 1964. *The Idea of Phenomenology*. The Hague: Martinus Nijhoff.

————. 1969. *Formal and Transcendental Logic*. The Hague: Martinus Nijhoff.

————. 1970a. *Logical Investigations*. New York: Routledge.

————. 1970b. *The Crisis of the European Sciences*. Evanston, IL: Northwestern University Press.

————. 1973. *Experience and Judgment*. Evanston, IL: Northwestern University Press.

Inden, Ronald. 1990. *Imagining India*. Oxford: Basil Blackwell.

Jackson, David P. 1985. "Sa-skya Pandita on Indian and Tibetan Traditions of Philosophical Debate." Ph.D. thesis, University of Washington.

————. 1994. *Enlightenment by a Single Means*. Vienna: Verlag, Der Osterreichischen Akademie Der Wissenschaften.

James, William. 1890. *Principles of Psychology, Vol. I*. New York: Henry Holt and Co.

Keith, A. Berriedale. 1923. "The Doctrine of Negativism." In *Buddhist Philosophy in India and Ceylon*. London: Oxford University Press

King, Richard. 1999. *Orientalism and Religion*. London and New York: Routledge.

Klein, Anne. 1994. *Path to the Middle: Oral Madhyamika Philosophy in Tibet*. Albany, N.Y.: SUNY Press.

Korenbaum, Myrtle, ed. 1977. *Annals of Phenomenological Sociology, Vol. 2*. Dayton, Ohio: Wright State University.

Labov, William, and D. Fanshel. 1977. *Therapeutic Discourse*. New York: Academic Press.

Lefort, Claude. 1968. "Editor's Foreword." In Merleau-Ponty 1968: xi-xxxiii.

Levin, David Michael. 1985. *The Body's Recollection of Being*. London: Routledge.

Levinas, Emmanuel. 1969. *Totality and Infinity*. Pittsburgh: Duquesne University Press.

———. 1981. *Otherwise Than Being, Or Beyond Essence*. The Hague: Martinus Nijhoff.

———. 1993. *Outside the Subject*. Stanford, Calif.: Stanford University Press.

Liberman, Kenneth. 1981. "Understanding Aborigines in Australian Courts of Law." *Human Organization* 40, no. 3: 247-55.

——— .1982. "The Economy of Central Australian Aboriginal Expression." *Semiotica* 40, no. 3/4: 81-160.

———. 1984. "The Hermeneutics of Intercultural Communication." *Anthropological Linguistics* 26, no. 1: 53-83.

———. 1985. *Understanding Interaction in Central Australia*. London: Routledge.

———. 1992. "Philosophical Debate in the Tibetan Academy." *Tibet Journal*, 17, no. 1: 36-67.

———. 1994. "A Natural History of Some Intercultural Collaboration." *Research on Language and Social Interaction* 28, no. 2: 117-46.

———. 1996. "Negative Dialectics in *Madhyamika* and the Continental Tradition." In *East-West Encounters in Philosophy and Religion*, ed. Ninian Smart and B. Srinivas Murthy, 185-202. Long Beach: Long Beach Publications.

———. 1998. "Can Emptiness Be Formulated?: A Debate from a Gelugpa Monastic University." *Tibet Journal*, 23, no. 2: 33-48.

———. 1999a. "The Social Praxis of Communicating Meanings." *Text* 19, no. 1: 57-72.

———. 1999b. "From Walkabout to Meditation: Craft and Ethics in Field Inquiry." *Qualitative Inquiry* 5, no. 1: 47-63.

———. 1999c. "The Dialectics of Oppression: a Phenomenological Perspective." *Philosophy Today* 43, no. 3/4: 272-82.

———. 2001. "The Digital Ethnography: Multimedia in Qualitative Analysis." *Glimpse* 3, no. 1: 63-67.

Lilla, Mark. 1998. "The Politics of Jacques Derrida." *The New York Review of Books* 45, no. 11: 36-41.

Lopez, Donald S., Jr. 1992. "dGen 'dun Chos 'phel's *Klu sgrub dgongs rgyan*: a Preliminary Study." In *Tibetan Studies, Vol. I.*, Per Kvaerne, ed. Oslo: Institute for Comparative Research in Human Culture.

———. 1995. *Curators of the Buddha: the Study of Buddhism Under Colonialism*. Chicago, Ill.: University of Chicago Press.

———. 1998. *Prisoners of Shangrila: Tibetan Buddhism and the West*. Chicago: University of Chicago Press.

Lynch, Michael. 1993. *Scientific Practice and Ordinary Action*. Cambridge, U.K. and New York: Cambridge University Press.

Maglioli, Robert. 1984. *Derrida on the Mend*. West Lafayette, Ind.: Purdue University Press.

Marcuse, Herbert. 1960. *Negations*, New York: Free Press.

Martin, Norah. 1997. "Philosophy—It Takes a Village," paper presented at the conference, *Engendering Rationalities*, University of Oregon.

Mead, George Herbert. 1962. *Mind, Self and Society*. Chicago: University of Chicago.

Merleau-Ponty, Maurice. 1962. *Phenomenology of Perception*. London: Routledge and Kegan-Paul.

———. 1964a. *Signs*. Evanston, Ill.: Northwestern University Press.

———. 1964b. *Sense and Non-Sense*. Evanston, Ill.: Northwestern University Press.

———. 1973. *Consciousness and the Acquisition of Language*. Evanston, Ill.: Northwestern University Press.

———. 1968. The *Visible and the Invisible*. Evanston, Ill.: Northwestern University Press.

Nagarjuna. 1995. *The Fundamental Wisdom of the Middle Way* (*Mulamadhyamakakarika*). Trans. by Jay Garfield. New York: Oxford University Press.

Nandy, Ashis. 1983. *The Intimate Enemy*. Delhi: Oxford University Press.

Nayak, G.C.. 1987. *Philosophical Reflections*. Delhi: Motilal Banarsidass.

Newland, Guy. 1996. "Debate Manuals (*Yig Cha*) in dGe lugs Monastic Colleges," In *Tibetan Literature*, ed. José Ignacio Cabezón and Roger R. Jackson. Ithaca, N.Y.: Snow Lion.

Nietzsche, Friedrich. 1969. *The Birth of Tragedy*. New York: Random House.

Omvedt, Gail. 1995. *Dalit Visions: the anti-caste movement and the construction of an Indian identity*. New Delhi: Orient Longman.

Onoda, Shunzo. 1992. *Monastic Debate in Tibet*. Vienna: University of Vienna (Arbeitskreis fur Tibetische und Buddhistische Studien).

Paz, Octavio. 1956. *The Bow and the Lyre*. New York: McGraw-Hill.

Perdue, Daniel. 1976. *Debate in Tibetan Education*. Dharamsala, India: Library of Tibetan Works and Archives.

———. 1992. *Debate in Tibetan Buddhism*. Ithaca, N.Y.: Snow Lion.

Plato. 1961. *Euthedymus*. In *The Collected Dialogues of Plato*, ed. Edith Hamilton and Huntington Cairns. Princeton, N.J.: Princeton University Press.

Pollner, Melvin. 1991. "Left of Ethnomethodology." *American Sociological Review* 56: 370-80.

Preston, David L. 1988. *The Social Organization of Zen Practice*. Cambridge: Cambridge University Press.

Rawls, Anne. 1996. "Durkheim and Pragmatism." *Sociological Theory* 15, no.1: 5-29.

Rato Khyongla Rinpoche. 1978. *My Life and Lives*. London: Rider.

Richir, Marc. 1993. "The Meaning of Phenomenology in *The Visible and the Invisible*." *Thesis Eleven* 36, no.1.

Rinchen, Geshe Sonam. 1994. "Introduction" and commentary to *Yogic Deeds of Bodhisattvas* (*bZhi brgya pa'i rnam bshad legs bhad snying po* by *rGyal tshab dar ma rin chen*). Trans. and ed. by Ruth Sonam. Ithaca, N.Y.: Snow Lion.

Rips, Lance J., Sarah K. Brem, and Jeremy N. Bailenson. 1999. "Reasoning Dialogues." *Current Directions in Psychological Science* 8, no. 6: 172-77.

Risley, Sir Herbert Hope. 1891. *The People of India*. Calcutta: Thacker, Spink & Co.

Ruegg, David Seyfort. 1962. "A Propos of a Recent Contribution to Tibetan and Buddhist Studies." *Journal of the American Oriental Society* 82.

———. 1989. *Buddha Nature, Mind, and the Problem of Gradualism in a Comparative Perspective*. London: University of London School of Oriental and African Studies.

Said, Edward. 1978. *Orientalism*. New York: Random House.

Scanlon, John. 1997. "Psychologism." In Lester Embree et al. 1997. Pages 572-77.

Schieffelin, Buck. 1998. "After Post-modernism." Paper presented at the conference, "After Post-modernism." University of Chicago.

Schrag, Calvin. 1992. *The Resources of Rationality*. Bloomington, Ind.: Indiana University Press.

Schutz, Alfred. 1967. *Phenomenology of the Social World*. Evanston, Ill.: Northwestern University Press.

———. 1971. *Collected Papers, Vol. I*. and *Vol. II*. The Hague: Martinus Nijhoff.

Shakya, Tsering. 1999. *The Dragon in the Land of Snows: a History of Modern Tibet*. London: Penguin Compass.

Sierksma, F. 1964. "*Rtsod-pa*, The Monacal Disputations in Tibet." *Indo-Iranian Journal* 8, no. 2: 130-52.

Smith, Gene. 1969. "Introduction." *Gzhan gyis brstad pa*, Sonam T. Kazi, ed.. New Delhi: Gondals Press.

———. 2002. *Among Tibetan Texts*. Ithaca, N.Y.: Wisdom.

Sopa, Geshe Lhundup. 1996. Interview in *Mandala* (November-December), Page 45.

Spivak, Gayatri Chakravorty. 1988. *Marxism and the Interpretation of Culture*. Urbana, Ill.: University of Illinois Press.

———. 1990. *The Post-colonial Critic*. London: Routledge.

Srinivas, M. N. 1962. "Village Studies and Their Significance." In *Caste in Modern India and Other Essays*. Pages 120-35. Bombay: Asia Publishing House.

Stcherbatsky, Theodore. "Philosophical Doctrine of Buddhism." In *Studies in the History of Indian Philosophy, Vol. III*, D. Chattopadhyaya, ed. Atlantic Highlands, N.J.: Humanities Press.

Sudarsan, P. 1997. "Jurgens Habermas' Rational Theory of Social Action." Ph.D. Dissertation, Pondicherry University.

Sudnow, David. 1979. *Ways of the Hand.* New York: Harper and Row.

Thapar, Romila. 1991. "Wrongs of History Best Left Alone." *Deccan Herald,* Sept. 16.

Tillemans, Tom J. F. 1999. *Scripture, Logic, Language.* Boston: Wisdom Publications.

Trautmann, Thomas R. 1997. *Aryans and British India.* Berkeley: University of California Press.

Tucci, Giuseppe. 1987. *To Lhasa and Beyond.* Ithaca, N.Y.: Snow Lion.

Tuck, Andrew P. 1990. *Comparative Philosophy and the Philosophy of Scholarship.* New York: Oxford University Press.

Venturino, Steven. 1998. "Tibet Studies and Contemporary Culture Theory." Bloomington, Ind.: Eighth Seminar of the International Association for Tibetan Studies.

Visker, Rudy. 1997. "Merleau-Ponty and Nature." Paper presented at the Merleau-Ponty Circle, Seattle University.

Viyagappa, Ignatius. 1983. "G. W. F. Hegel's Critique of Indian Religion and Philosophy." *Journal of Madras University* 55, no. 1: 1-124.

Vostrikov. 1935. "Some Corrections." *Bulletin of the School of Oriental Studies* 8: 151-76.

Waddell, L. Augustine. 1972. *Tibetan Buddhism.* N.Y.: Dover.

Wayman, Alex. 1979. "Introduction." In Tsong-Kha-pa's *Calming the Mind and Discerning the Real.* Delhi: Motilal Banarsidass. (See also Tsong Khapa 1997).

Williams, Robert R. 1992. *Recognition.* Albany, N.Y.: SUNY Press.

Wittgenstein, Ludwig. 1972. *Philosophical Investigations.* Oxford: Blackwell.

Tibetan Texts

Baso Chokyi Gyalsten, et. al. (*Ba so chos kyi rgyal mtshan, Ngag dbang rab brtan, 'Jam dbyangs bzhad pa,* and *Rin chen don grub*). n.d. *Myan med rje btsun tsong kha pa chen pos mdzad pa'i gnad rnams mchan bu bzhi'i sgo nas legs par bshad theg chen lam gyi gsal sgron* (*The Lamp That Clarifies the Mahayana Path of Tsong Khapa's* Great Treatise on the Stages to Enlightenment). China.

Gyalstab Dharma Rinchen (*rGyal tshab dar ma rin chen*). n.d. *bZhi brgya pa'i rnam bshad legs bshad snying po* (*The Ornament of the Essence of Explanation*). Dharamsala: Tibetan Cultural Printing Press.

Jetsun Chogyi Gyaltsen (*rJe btsun chos gyi rgyal mtshan*). 1997. *dBu ma'i spyi don skal bzang ngu'i rgyan* (*Overview of the Middle Way*). Bylakuppe, India: Sera Je Computer Project.

Jnanagarbha. 1987. *Bden gnyis rnam 'byed 'grel pa.* Albany, N.Y.: SUNY Press.

Khedrup Gelek Palsang (*mKhas grub dge legs dpal bzang*). n.d. *sTong thun chen mo* (*Great Digest on Emptiness*). Dharamsala: Tibetan Cultural Printing Press.

Rabten, Geshe. 1989. *Zab mo'i lta ba'i nyams mgur rgyan chags sdang dgra 'joms pa'i spu gri bzhugs so* (*Song of the Profound View*). Trans. by Stephen Batchelor. London: Wisdom Publications.

Sakya Pandita (*Sa skya Pandita*). 1984. *Mkhas pa rnams 'jugs pa'i sgo.* Rajpur, India: Sakya Institute.

Tsong Khapa. 1982. *Brten brel bstod pa* (*In Praise of Interdependent Origination*). Sarnath: Institute of Higher Tibetan Studies.

———. 1985a. *Lam gyi gtso bo rnam gsum gyi rtsa ba.* Dharamsala: Tibetan Cultural Printing Press.

———.1985b. *Dbu ma rtsa ba'i tshig le'ur byas pa shes rab ces bya ba'i rnam bshad rigs pa'i rgya mtsho* (*Ocean of Reasoning*, also known as *Rtsa shes 'tik chen*). Dharamsala: Tibetan Cultural Printing Press.

———. 1988. *Dbu ma dgongs pa rab gsal* (*The Elucidation of the Thought, The Great Commentary on the Middle Way*). Sarnath: Institute of Higher Tibetan Studies.

———. 1997. *Lam rim Chen Mo* (*Great Treatise on the Stages to Enlightenment*). China.

———. n.d a. *Dbu ma gongs pa rab gsal* (*The Elucidation of the Thought, The Great Commentary on the Middle Way*). Mongolian edition.

———. n.d b. (circa 1996). *Drang ba dang nges pa'i don rnam par phye ba'i bstan bcos legs bshad snying po* (*The Essence of Good Explanation Regarding How to Distinguish Between the Meanings of the Middle View and the Extreme Views*). Bylakuppe, India: Sera-Me Computer Project Centre.

Yongdzin (*Yongs 'dzin byams pa tshul khrims rgya mtsho*). 1979. *Tshad ma'i gzhung pa'i bsdus grva'i rnam bzhag rigs blam 'phrul gyi lde mig ces bya ba las rigs lam che ba'i skor gyi rnam par bshad pa zhugs so.* Bylakuppe, India: Sera Monastic University.

Index